JOURNAL FOR THE STUDY OF THE OLD TESTAMENT SUPPLEMENT SERIES

265

Editors
David J.A. Clines
Philip R. Davies

Executive Editor
John Jarick

Editorial Board
Richard J. Coggins, Alan Cooper, J. Cheryl Exum, John Goldingay, Robert P. Gordon, Norman K. Gottwald, Andrew D.H. Mayes, Carol Meyers, Patrick D. Miller

Sheffield Academic Press

Yahweh and the Gods and Goddesses of Canaan

John Day

Journal for the Study of the Old Testament
Supplement Series 265

Published by
Sheffield Academic Press Ltd
Mansion House
19 Kingfield Road
Sheffield S11 9AS
England

http://www.SheffieldAcademicPress.com

Typeset by Sheffield Academic Press
and
Printed on acid-free paper in Great Britain
by Antony Rowe Ltd,
Chippenham, Wiltshire

British Library Cataloguing in Publication Data

A catalogue record for this book is available
from the British Library

ISBN 1-85075-986-3

CONTENTS

Preface 7
Abbreviations 8

Chapter 1
YAHWEH AND EL 13

Chapter 2
YAHWEH AND ASHERAH 42

Chapter 3
YAHWEH VERSUS BAAL 68

Chapter 4
YAHWEH'S APPROPRIATION OF BAAL IMAGERY 91

Chapter 5
YAHWEH AND THE GODDESSES ASTARTE AND ANAT
(AND THE QUEEN OF HEAVEN) 128

Chapter 6
YAHWEH AND THE ASTRAL DEITIES
(SUN, MOON AND LUCIFER) 151

Chapter 7
YAHWEH AND THE UNDERWORLD DEITIES
(MOT, RESHEPH, MOLECH AND THE REPHAIM) 185

Chapter 8
CONCLUSION: THE CANAANITE GODS AND GODDESSES AND THE RISE OF MONOTHEISM 226

Bibliography 234
Index of References 264
Index of Authors 276

PREFACE

Ever since I started doctoral research under Professor John Emerton at Cambridge in 1973 much of my time has been devoted to studying the impact, both positive and negative, of Canaanite mythology and religion on ancient Israel and the Old Testament. Although I have written various books and articles on the subject over the years, I have long harboured the ambition of completing a more thoroughgoing and comprehensive investigation of the relationship between Yahweh and the gods and goddesses of Canaan, and this is what now appears before the reader.

Unfortunately, various other projects have delayed the appearance of this work. I should therefore express my thanks to those who have helped speed the book on its way. First of all I must express my deep gratitude to the British Academy and the Leverhulme Trust for the honour of awarding me a British Academy/Leverhulme Trust Senior Research Fellowship for a year, which enabled me to make considerable progress on the work that would not otherwise have been possible. Next, I am once again greatly indebted to Carol Smith, who over the years and even in the midst of adversity has cheerfully word processed countless drafts of the various chapters which appear in this book. Finally, I am grateful to Sheffield Academic Press for accepting this work into their Old Testament Supplement Series and to all those who work for the Press for the careful attention they have bestowed on the work.

ABBREVIATIONS

AB	Anchor Bible
ABD	David Noel Freedman (ed.), *The Anchor Bible Dictionary* (New York: Doubleday, 1992)
ABRL	Anchor Bible Reference Library
AcOr	*Acta orientalia*
AfO	*Archiv für Orientforschung*
AION	*Annali dell'istituto orientale di Napoli*
AJSL	*American Journal of Semitic Languages and Literatures*
AnBib	Analecta biblica
ANEP	James B. Pritchard (ed.), *Ancient Near East in Pictures Relating to the Old Testament* (Princeton: Princeton University Press, 1954)
ANET	James B. Pritchard (ed.), *Ancient Near Eastern Texts Relating to the Old Testament* (Princeton: Princeton University Press, 1950)
AOAT	Alter Orient und Altes Testament
AOS	American Oriental Series
AP	A. Cowley (ed.), *Aramaic Papyri of the Fifth Century B.C.* (Oxford: Clarendon Press, 1923)
ArOr	*Archiv orientální*
ARW	*Archiv für Religionswissenschaft*
ATANT	Abhandlungen zur Theologie des Alten und Neuen Testaments
ATD	Das Alte Testament Deutsch
AulOr	*Aula Orientalis*
AulOr Sup	Aula Orientalis Supplement
AV	Authorized Version
BA	*Biblical Archaeologist*
BARev	*Biblical Archaeology Review*
BASOR	*Bulletin of the American Schools of Oriental Research*
BBB	Bonner biblische Beiträge
BETL	Bibliotheca ephemeridum theologicarum lovaniensium
BH^3	*Biblia hebraica*, 3rd edition
BHS	*Biblia hebraica stuttgartensia*
BHT	Beiträge zur historischen Theologie
Bib	*Biblica*

BibInt Series	Biblical Interpretation Series
BibOr	Biblica et orientalia
BJRL	*Bulletin of the John Rylands University Library of Manchester*
BKAT	Biblischer Kommentar: Altes Testament
BN	*Biblische Notizen*
BNTC	Black's New Testament Commentaries
BR	*Bible Review*
BSO(A)S	*Bulletin of the School of Oriental (and African) Studies*
BTB	*Biblical Theology Bulletin*
BWANT	Beiträge zur Wissenschaft vom Alten und Neuen Testament
BZ	*Biblische Zeitschrift*
BZAW	Beihefte zur *ZAW*
CAD	Ignace I. Gelb *et al.* (eds.), *The Assyrian Dictionary of the Oriental Institute of the University of Chicago* (Chicago: Oriental Institute, 1964–)
CAT	Commentaire de l'Ancien Testament
CBC	Cambridge Bible Commentary
CBQ	*Catholic Biblical Quarterly*
CBQMS	*Catholic Biblical Quarterly*, Monograph Series
CGTC	Cambridge Greek Testament Commentary
ConBOT	Coniectanea biblica, Old Testament
CT	Cuneiform Texts from Babylonian Tablets, &c in the British Museum
DBSup	*Dictionnaire de la Bible, Supplément*
DDD	K. van der Toorn, B. Becking, P.W. van der Horst, *Dictionary of Deities and Demons* (Leiden: E.J. Brill, 1995; 2nd edn, 1999)
DJD	Discoveries in the Judaean Desert
EPROER	Etudes Préliminaires aux religions orientales dans l'empire romain
EstBíb	*Estudios bíblicos*
ET	English Translation
EvQ	*Evangelical Quarterly*
ExpTim	*Expository Times*
FRLANT	Forschungen zur Religion und Literatur des Alten und Neuen Testaments
HAR	*Hebrew Annual Review*
HAT	Handbuch zum Alten Testament
HCOT	Historical Commentary on the Old Testament
HDR	Harvard Dissertations in Religion
HKAT	Handkommentar zum Alten Testament
HR	*History of Religions*
HSM	Harvard Semitic Monographs
HSS	Harvard Semitic Studies
HTR	*Harvard Theological Review*

HUCA	*Hebrew Union College Annual*
ICC	International Critical Commentary
IDB	George Arthur Buttrick (ed.), *The Interpreter's Dictionary of the Bible* (4 vols.; Nashville: Abingdon Press, 1962)
IDBSup	*IDB*, Supplementary Volume
IEJ	*Israel Exploration Journal*
Int	*Interpretation*
JA	*Journal asiatique*
JANESCU	*Journal of the Ancient Near Eastern Society of Columbia University*
JAOS	*Journal of the American Oriental Society*
JBL	*Journal of Biblical Literature*
JCS	*Journal of Cuneiform Studies*
JEA	*Journal of Egyptian Archaeology*
JJS	*Journal of Jewish Studies*
JNES	*Journal of Near Eastern Studies*
JNSL	*Journal of Northwest Semitic Languages*
JPOS	*Journal of the Palestine Oriental Society*
JQR	*Jewish Quarterly Review*
JSJ	*Journal for the Study of Judaism in the Persian, Hellenistic and Roman Period*
JSOT	*Journal for the Study of the Old Testament*
JSOTSup	*Journal for the Study of the Old Testament*, Supplement Series
JSS	*Journal of Semitic Studies*
JTS	*Journal of Theological Studies*
KAI	H. Donner and W. Röllig, *Kanaanäische und aramäische Inschriften* (3 vols.; Wiesbaden: Otto Harrassowitz, 1962–64)
KAT	Kommentar zum Alten Testament
KTU^2	M. Dietrich, O. Loretz, J. Sanmartín, *The Cuneiform Alphabetic Texts from Ugarit, Ras Ibn Hani and Other Places (KTU: Second Enlarged Edition)* (Münster: Ugarit-Verlag, 1995) (2nd edn of M. Dietrich, O. Loretz, J. Sanmartín, *Die keilalphabetischen Texte aus Ugarit* [Neukirchen–Vluyn: Neukirchener Verlag, 1976])
MIO	*Mitteilungen des Instituts Orientforschung*
MT	Masoretic Text
MVAG	Mitteilungen der vorderasiatisch-ägyptischen Gesellschaft
NAB	*New American Bible*
NCB	New Century Bible
NEB	*New English Bible*
NICOT	New International Commentary on the Old Testament
NRSV	New Revised Standard Version
NS	New Series
OBO	Orbis biblicus et orientalis
OLP	*Orientalia lovaniensia periodica*

Or	*Orientalia*
OrAnt	*Oriens antiquus*
OTG	Old Testament Guides
OTL	Old Testament Library
OTS	*Oudtestamentische Studiën*
PEQ	*Palestine Exploration Quarterly*
PG	J.-P. Migne (ed.), *Patrologia cursus completa… Series graeca* (166 vols.; Paris: Petit-Montrouge, 1857–83)
PJ	*Palästina-Jahrbuch*
PL	J.-P. Migne (ed.), *Patrologia cursus completus… Series prima [latina]* (221 vols.; Paris: J.-P. Migne, 1844–65)
PSBA	*Proceedings of the Society of Biblical Archaeology*
RA	*Revue d'Assyriologie et d'archéologie orientale*
RB	*Revue biblique*
REB	Revised English Bible
RHR	*Revue de l'histoire des religions*
RIH	Ras Ibn Hani
RivBib	*Rivista biblica*
RLA	*Reallexikon der Assyriologie*
RS	Ras Shamra
RSF	*Rivista di Studi Fenici*
RSV	Revised Standard Version
SBLDS	SBL Dissertation Series
SBLMS	SBL Monograph Series
SBS	Stuttgarter Bibelstudien
SBT	Studies in Biblical Theology
SEÅ	*Svensk exegetisk årsbok*
SEL	*Studi epigrafici e linguistici*
Sem	*Semitica*
SJOT	*Scandinavian Journal of the Old Testament*
SJT	*Scottish Journal of Theology*
SKPAW	*Sitzungsberichte der Preußischen Akademie der Wissenschaften, Berlin*
ST	*Studia theologica*
StudOr	Studia orientalia
TDOT	G.J. Botterweck and H. Ringgren (eds.), *Theological Dictionary of the Old Testament*
THAT	Ernst Jenni and Claus Westermann (eds.), *Theologisches Handwörterbuch zum Alten Testament* (Munich: Chr. Kaiser, 1971–76)
ThWAT	*Theologisches Wörterbuch zum Alten Testament* (Stuttgart: W. Kohlhammer, 1970–)
TynBul	*Tyndale Bulletin*
TZ	*Theologische Zeitschrift*
UBL	Ugaritisch–Biblische Literatur

UCOP	University of Cambridge Oriental Publications
UF	*Ugarit-Forschungen*
UUÅ	Uppsala universitetsårsskrift
VD	*Verbum domini*
VT	*Vetus Testamentum*
VTSup	*Vetus Testamentum*, Supplements
WBC	Word Biblical Commentary
WO	*Die Welt des Orients*
WMANT	Wissenschaftliche Monographien zum Alten und Neuen Testament
WUNT	Wissenschaftliche Untersuchungen zum Neuen Testament
WZKM	*Wiener Zeitschrift für die Kunde des Morgenlandes*
ZA	*Zeitschrift für Assyriologie*
ZAH	*Zeitschrift für Althebraistik*
ZAW	*Zeitschrift für die alttestamentliche Wissenschaft*
ZDMG	*Zeitschrift der deutschen morgenländischen Gesellschaft*
ZDPV	*Zeitschrift des deutschen Palästina-Vereins*
ZTK	*Zeitschrift für Theologie und Kirche*

Chapter 1

YAHWEH AND EL

Were Yahweh and El originally the same Deity or not?

What was the relationship between Yahweh and the Canaanite god El? In the Old Testament Yahweh is frequently called El. The question is raised whether Yahweh was a form of the god El from the beginning or whether they were separate deities who only became equated later. The Old Testament itself indicates some sense of discontinuity as well as continuity, in that both the E and P sources imply that the patriarchs did not know the name Yahweh and that this was first revealed to Moses (Exod. 3.13-15, E; 6.2-3, P), in contrast to the J source, where the name Yahweh was already known in primaeval times (Gen. 4.26). The P source specifically states that the patriarchs had previously known God under the name El-Shaddai (Exod. 6.3).

In the nineteenth century J. Wellhausen[1] believed Yahweh to be the same as El, and more recently this has been particularly argued by F.M. Cross and J.C. de Moor.[2] However, the following arguments may be brought against this. First, in the Ugaritic texts the god El is revealed to be wholly benevolent in nature, whereas Yahweh has a fierce as well as a kind side.[3] Secondly, as T.N.D. Mettinger[4] has rightly emphasized,

1. J. Wellhausen, *Prolegomena to the History of Israel* (trans. J.S. Black and A. Menzies; Edinburgh: A. & C. Black, 1885), p. 433 n. 1 (not in German original).

2. F.M. Cross, *Canaanite Myth and Hebrew Epic* (Cambridge, MA: Harvard University Press, 1973), pp. 60-75; J.C. de Moor, *The Rise of Yahwism* (BETL, 91: Leuven: Leuven University Press and Peeters, 1990), pp. 223-60 (2nd edn, 1997, pp. 310-69).

3. This has been especially emphasized by F. Løkkegaard, 'A Plea for El, the Bull, and other Ugaritic Miscellanies', in F.F. Hvidberg (ed.), *Studia Orientalia Ioanni Pedersen septuagenario dicata* (Copenhagen: E. Munskgaard, 1953), pp. 219-35. P.D. Miller, 'El the Warrior', *HTR* 60 (1967), pp. 411-33, tries to find evidence of an earlier concept of El as a warrior in Philo of Byblos. However, though

the earliest evidence, such as that found in Judg. 5.4-5, associates Yahweh with the storm, which was not something with which El was connected at all. Rather, this is reminiscent of Baal. Thirdly, as for F.M. Cross's view[5] that Yahweh was originally a part of El's cultic title, 'El who creates hosts' (*'il ḏū yahwī ṣaba'ōt*), this is pure speculation. The formula in question is nowhere attested, whether inside or outside the Bible. Cross's reasons for thinking that *yhwh ṣb't* cannot simply mean 'Lord of hosts', namely, that a proper name should not appear in the construct, is incorrect.[6] Further, *hyh* (*hwh*) is not attested in Hebrew in the hiphil ('cause to be', 'create'), though this is the case in Aramaic and Syriac. Yahweh in any case more likely means 'he is' (qal) rather than 'he causes to be/creates' (hiphil): to suppose otherwise requires emendation of the Hebrew text in Exod. 3.14 (*'ehyeh*, 'I am'), which explains the name Yahweh. I conclude, therefore, that El and Yahweh were originally distinct deities that became amalgamated. This view was held as long ago as F.K. Movers,[7] and has been argued since by scholars such as O. Eissfeldt and T.N.D. Mettinger.[8]

It is interesting that the Old Testament has no qualms in equating Yahweh with El, something which stands in marked contrast to its vehement opposition to Baal, let alone the equation of Yahweh with Baal (cf. Hos. 2.18 [ET 16]).[9] This must reflect a favourable judgment

the late Philo of Byblos (c. 100 CE) does preserve some genuinely ancient traditions, it would be most surprising for his picture of a warlike El to antedate the second-millennium BCE Ugaritic texts.

4. T.N.D. Mettinger, 'The Elusive Essence: YHWH, El and Baal and the Distinctiveness of Israelite Faith', in E. Blum, C. Macholz and E.W. Stegemann (eds.), *Die Hebräische Bibel und ihre zweifache Nachgeschichte: Festschrift für Rolf Rendtorff zum 65. Geburtstag* (Neukirchen–Vluyn: Neukirchener Verlag, 1990), pp. 393-417 (409-10).

5. Cross, *Canaanite Myth and Hebrew Epic*, pp. 60-75.

6. The closest parallels are the references to 'Yahweh of Teman' (*yhwh tmn*) and 'Yahweh of Samaria' (*yhwh šmrn*) at Kuntillet 'Ajrud, as J.A. Emerton has pointed out, who also notes other instances of proper names in the construct. See J.A. Emerton, 'New Light on Israelite Religion: The Implications of the Inscriptions from Kuntillet 'Ajrud', *ZAW* 94 (1982), pp. 2-20 (3-9).

7. F.K. Movers, *Die Phönizier*, I (2 vols. in 4 parts; Bonn: E. Weber, 1841), pp. 312-16.

8. O. Eissfeldt, 'El and Yahweh', *JSS* (1956), pp. 25-37; reprinted in German as 'El und Jahwe', in O. Eissfeldt, *Kleine Schriften*, III (Tübingen: J.C.B. Mohr [Paul Siebeck], 1966), pp. 386-97; Mettinger, 'The Elusive Essence'.

9. This contrast in attitude was noted by Eissfeldt, 'El and Yahweh'.

on El's characteristic attributes: as supreme deity, creator god and one possessed of wisdom, El was deemed wholly fit to be equated with Yahweh.[10] Baal, on the other hand, was not only subordinate to the chief god El,[11] but was also considered to be dead in the underworld for half the year, something hardly compatible with Yahweh, who 'will neither slumber nor sleep' (Ps. 121.4).

Since Yahweh and El were originally separate deities, the question is raised where Yahweh originated. Yahweh himself does not appear to have been a Canaanite god in origin: for example, he does not appear in the Ugaritic pantheon lists. Most scholars who have written on the subject during recent decades support the idea that Yahweh had his origins outside the land of Israel to the south, in the area of Midian (cf. Judg. 5.4-5; Deut. 33.2; Hab. 3.3, 7)[12] and there has been an increasing tendency to locate Mt Sinai and Kadesh in N.W. Arabia rather than the Sinai peninsula itself.[13] The former view, long held by German scholars,

10. One may compare the fact that the name of an ancient Chinese god, Shang Ti, is used to denote the God of the Bible in one of the translations of the Bible into Chinese, Shang Ti being regarded as a worthy deity.

11. This certainly holds true of the Ugaritic texts. Cf. C. L'Heureux, *Rank among the Canaanite Gods: El, Ba'al, and the Repha'im* (HSM, 21; Missoula, MT: Scholars Press, 1979). H. Niehr, however, in *Der höchte Gott* (BZAW, 190; Berlin: W. de Gruyter, 1990), maintains that, by way of contrast, in first-millennium BCE Syria–Palestine Baal-Shamem had decisively overtaken El as the chief god. Though there is some evidence for this, K. Engelkern, 'Ba'alšamem: Eine Auseinandersetzung mit der Monographie von H. Niehr', *ZAW* 108 (1996), pp. 233-48, 391-407, shows that this was not universally so—cf. Ahiqar, where El is much more prominent than Baal, and the Deir 'Allā text, where El seems to be supreme. More particularly I would note that Niehr's extra-biblical evidence is drawn from Phoenicia and Syria, not Palestine, and I believe that in the latter there was much greater continuity with the older Canaanite mythology from Ugarit. Only thus can we explain the origin of the imagery in Dan. 7, where the Ancient of Days and the one like a son of man reflect the nature and positions of El and Baal in the Ugaritic texts. Moreover, unlike in Phoenicia and Syria, Baal was not worshipped under the specific name Baal-Shamem in Palestine, except when foreign influence intervened (Jezebel, Antiochus IV Epiphanes).

12. Even the arch-'minimalist' N.P. Lemche feels confident about this, in 'The Development of Israelite Religion in the Light of Recent Studies on the Early History of Israel', in J.A. Emerton (ed.), *Congress Volume, Leuven 1989* (VTSup, 43; Leiden: E.J. Brill, 1991), pp. 97-115 (113-15).

13. E.g. F.M Cross, 'Reuben, First-born of Jacob', *ZAW* 100 Supplement (1988), pp. 46-65.

has been supported by evidence of a civilization in the Hejaz area in N. W. Arabia (Midian) in the Late Bronze Age/Early Iron Age, in contrast to the general lack of this in this period in the Sinai peninsula. Also, the epithet 'Yahweh of Teman' in one of the Kuntillet 'Ajrud inscriptions fits in with this. References to the Shasu Yahweh in Egyptian texts alongside the Shasu Seir may also be cited in support. Though M.C. Astour[14] has questioned this, claiming that the reference was not to Seir in Edom but to Šarara in Syria, on balance, however, the Egyptian *Ś*ᶜ*rr* still seems more likely to be a slip for *Ś*'*r* (Seir) than the name Šarara.

As will be seen at various points later on in this chapter, a plausible case can be made that several of the El epithets referred to in Genesis in connection with patriarchal religion do indeed derive from the worship of the Canaanite god El (El-Shaddai, El-Olam, El-Bethel, and possibly El-Elyon). As Eissfeldt and others[15] have also noted, the promises of progeny to the patriarchs bear comparison with the promise of progeny by the god El to Keret and Aqhat in the Ugaritic texts. Although no one can today maintain that the patriarchal narratives are historical accounts, there are grounds for believing that their depiction of an El religion does at least in part reflect something of pre-monarchical religion, however much it has been overlaid by later accretions. In favour of a pre-monarchic El religion amongst the Hebrews one may first of all note the very name Israel, meaning probably 'El will rule', a name already attested in the late thirteenth century BCE on the stele of the Egyptian pharaoh Merneptah. It is surely an indication of El's early importance that the very name of the people incorporates the name of the god El. Secondly, as various scholars have noted,[16] prior to the rise

14. M.C. Astour, 'Yahweh in Egyptian Topographic Texts', in M. Görg and E. Pusch (eds.), *Festschrift Elmar Edel* (Ägypten und Altes Testament, 1; Bamberg: M. Görg, 1979), pp. 17-34.

15. O. Eissfeldt, 'Der kanaanäischer El als Geber der den israelitischen Erzvätern geltenden Nachkommenschaft- und Landbesitzverheissungen', in *Studia Orientalia in memoriam Caroli Brockelmann* (Wissenschaftliche Zeitschrift der Martin-Luther-Universität Halle–Wittenberg, Gesellschafts- und Sprachwissenschaftliche Reihe 17; 1968), vols. 2–3, pp. 45-53; reprinted in O. Eissfeldt, *Kleine Schriften*, V (Tübingen: J.C.B. Mohr [Paul Siebeck], 1973), pp. 50-62; C. Westermann, *Die Verheissungen an die Väter* (FRLANT, 116; Göttingen: Vandenhoeck & Ruprecht, 1976), pp. 151-67; ET *The Promises to the Fathers* (trans. D. Green; Philadelphia: Fortress Press, 1980), pp. 165-84.

16. E.g. M. Noth, *Die israelitischen Personennamen im Rahmen der gemeinsemitischen Namengebung* (BWANT, 3.10; Stuttgart: W. Kohlhammer, 1928),

of the monarchy theophoric personal names including the name *'ēl* are very common, whereas explicitly Yahwistic personal names are very rare (apart from Joshua only five from the Judges period).

El's Influence on Yahweh Accepted by the Old Testament

Granted that El and Yahweh were originally separate deities who became equated, the question now arises what was the nature of El's influence on the depiction of Yahweh. Here several points emerge which will be discussed under the following headings.

Yahweh as an Aged God

One instance where a strong case can be made for the influence of El symbolism on Yahweh concerns those few places where Yahweh is represented as an aged God with many years. In the Ugaritic texts El is frequently given the epithet *'ab šnm*, 'Father of Years'[17] (e.g. *KTU*[2]

pp. 90, 107; Mettinger, 'The Elusive Essence', p. 402.

17. This is now the standard rendering: first suggested by C. Virolleaud, it has been accepted by many scholars, including Cassuto, Emerton, Hvidberg, Cross and Caquot. It fully coheres with the reference to El's grey hair. (The aged El is often thought to be depicted on the Ugaritic stele, *ANEP*, pl. 493.) That *šnm* as well as *šnt* should mean 'years' in Ugaritic agrees with the fact that Hebrew has a plural construct form *š^enôt* (besides *š^enê*) as well as the absolute plural form *šānîm* (cf. variant Ugaritic plural forms *r'ašm*, *r'ašt* and *r'išt*, from *r'iš* 'head'). None of the various alternative proposals is compelling. Thus, O. Eissfeldt, *El im ugaritischen Pantheon* (Berichte über die Verhandlungen der Sächsischen Akademie der Wissenschaften zu Leipzig. Phil. Hist. Klasse, 98.4; Berlin: Akademie Verlag, 1951), p. 30 n. 4, translated *'ab šnm* as 'Father of mortals', connecting *šnm* with Hebrew *šānâ* 'to change', Syriac *š^enâ* 'to depart', but the Ugaritic equivalent has a *ṯ*, not *š*, i.e. *ṯn*(*y*). M.H. Pope, *El in the Ugaritic Texts* (VTSup, 2; Leiden: E.J. Brill, 1955), p. 33, translated 'Father of Exalted Ones', comparing Arabic *snw*, *sny* 'shine, be exalted, eminent' or *sanima* 'be tall, prominent', but it is not certain that this root is otherwise attested in Ugaritic. U. Oldenburg, *The Conflict between El and Ba'al in Canaanite Religion* (Leiden: E.J. Brill, 1969), pp. 17-18, renders 'Father of Luminaries', but this epithet is found elsewhere only in the New Testament (Jas 1.17). J. Aistleitner also appealed to the same basic root in comparing Arabic *sanām* 'elevation' and seeing a reference to El's heavenly abode (*Wörterbuch der ugaritischen Sprache* [ed. O. Eissfeldt; Berichte über die Verhandlungen der Sächsischen Akademie der Wissenschaften zu Leipzig. Philologische–Historische Klasse, 106.3; Berlin: Akademie Verlag, 1965], p. 312, no. 2651). Finally, various scholars have have seen in *šnm* the name of a god. S. and S. Rin, '*^alîlôt hā'ēlîm*

1.4.IV.24), a concept reinforced by the references to his grey hair (e.g. *KTU*² 1.3.V.2, 24-25; 1.4.V.4). In the Old Testament there are just three places where Yahweh's 'years' are alluded to, and it is therefore particularly striking that in two of these he is specifically called by the name El.[18] The first of these is in Job 36.26, where Elihu declares, 'Behold, God (*'ēl*) is great, and we know him not; the number of his years is unsearchable'. Clearly Yahweh is being represented as a supremely aged deity. The second occurrence is in Ps. 102.25 (ET 24), where the Psalmist prays, '"O my God (*'ēlî*)", I say, "take me not hence in the midst of my days, thou whose years endure throughout all generations!"' The fact that Yahweh is here referred to as 'my God' (literally, 'my El') is all the more striking in that it is the one place in the whole Psalm in which God is not addressed as Yahweh (cf. vv. 2, 13, 16, 17, 19, 20, 22, 23 [ET 1, 12, 15, 16, 18, 19, 21, 22]). The only other instance in the Old Testament where Yahweh's 'years' are mentioned is Job 10.5, where Job asks God, 'Are thy days as the days of man, or thy years as man's years?' (This is part of a section in which God is called *'ᵉlôah*, a term related to *'ēl*, e.g. in Job 10.2.)

But these specific references to Yahweh's years are not the only places where he is depicted as an aged God. As J.A. Emerton[19] was the first to note, Dan. 7.9 also has this concept and has appropriated it from El. In Daniel's apocalyptic vision God is there entitled the 'Ancient of

(Jerusalem: Israel Society for Biblical Research and 'Inbal, 1968), p. 39, consider *šnm* as a variant of *šlm* (Shalem), but there is no evidence elsewhere of this variant spelling of that divine name in Ugaritic. A Jirku, 'Šnm (Schunama), der Sohn des Gottes 'Il', *ZAW* 82 (1970), pp. 278-79 and C.H. Gordon, 'El, Father of Šnm', *JNES* 35 (1976), pp. 261-62 (who makes no mention of Jirku), noted that the gods *Ṯkmn* and *Šnm* are represented as carrying El when he is drunk (*KTU*² 1.114.15-19), and elsewhere this is represented as a service that a model son should provide for his father (*KTU*² 1.17.I.30-31, 1.17.II.5-6, 19-20), and therefore proposed that *Šnm* was the son of El. Although this is ingenious, one wonders, if it were correct, why this son of all El's many sons should be singled out for special mention in El's epithet.

18. J.C. Greenfield was the first to note this so far as I am aware, in 'The Hebrew Bible and Canaanite Literature', in R. Alter and F. Kermode (eds.), *The Literary Guide to the Bible* (London: Collins, 1987), pp. 545-60 (555).

19. J.A. Emerton, 'The Origin of the Son of Man Imagery', *JTS* NS 9 (1958), pp. 225-42. See also, J. Day, *God's Conflict with the Dragon and the Sea: Echoes of a Canaanite Myth in the Old Testament* (UCOP, 35; Cambridge: Cambridge University Press, 1985), pp. 151-78.

Days', a term reminiscent of 'Father of Years', and we read that 'the hair of his head was like pure wool', which likewise reminds one of El. In keeping with this, the one like a son of man who comes with the clouds of heaven and reigns for ever after being enthroned by the Ancient of Days (Dan. 7.13-14) derives ultimately from Baal, 'the rider of the clouds', and the beasts of the sea, whose rule is succeeded by that of the one like a son of man, reflect Yam, Leviathan, and others, who were defeated by Baal. (See below, Chapter 4.)

It seems inherently plausible that we have an Old Testament allusion related to El's being an aged deity in Gen. 21.33, where the patriarchal deity at Beer-sheba is called El-Olam, 'El, the Eternal One', which may possibly have meant originally 'El, the Ancient One', as F.M. Cross has noted.[20] However, the proposal of F.M. Cross[21] to find an allusion to 'El (god) of eternity' (*'l ḏ 'lm*) in the Proto-Sinaitic text 358 has proved to be unfounded, since M. Dijkstra,[22] having examined the text at first hand, has shown that this reading is invalid. Probably El-Olam was the local Canaanite god of Beer-sheba, but as we know from archaeology that Beer-sheba was not settled before c. 1200 BCE, the cult there will not antedate that time.

Yahweh as Wise

It was the god El who was especially noted for his wisdom according to the Ugaritic texts (*KTU*[2] 1.4.V.65, etc.). It seems that the author of Ezekiel 28 was familiar with this notion, since the king of Tyre's wisdom is emphasized in vv. 2, 3, 4, 5, and elsewhere in the very same context he claims to be God (*'ēl*). As will be seen below, El traditions lie behind the notion of the garden of Eden, so it is striking that the divine wisdom is connected with the story of the first man in Gen. 3.5, 6, 22; Ezek. 28.12, 17, and Job 15.7-8. In my opinion it is probable that it was from the god El that the notion of Yahweh's wisdom was appropriated. Plausibility is added to this view by the fact that wisdom and old age were traditionally associated, and, as noted already, it was from the god El that the notion of Yahweh as an aged deity with many years was derived.

20. Cross, *Canaanite Myth and Hebrew Epic*, p. 50.

21. F.M. Cross, 'Yahweh and the God of the Patriarchs', *HTR* 55 (1962), pp. 225-59 (238), and *Canaanite Myth and Hebrew Epic*, pp. 19, 50.

22. M. Dijkstra, 'El 'Olam in the Sinai?', *ZAW* 99 (1987), pp. 249-50.

Yahweh as Creator

We do not know whether Yahweh was conceived of as a creator god from the beginning or not. One cannot presuppose this from the name itself, for it is more likely that it means 'he is' rather than 'he causes to be' (i.e. creates); certainly the former sense is how the Old Testament itself understands it (cf. Exod. 3.14). Anyhow, whether Yahweh was conceived to be a creator god from the beginning or not, there is some evidence that there are occasions on which the Old Testament has appropriated El language when it speaks of Yahweh as creator. Thus, it can hardly be a coincidence that Gen. 14. 19, 22 speaks of 'El-Elyon, creator (*qōnēh*) of heaven and earth', and Deut. 32.6 declares, 'Is not he your father, who created you (*qānekā)*'. This is so because not only is it the case that the verb *qnh* is used outside the Bible to speak of El's creative activity,[23] but in both cases cited above we have other evidence supporting El influence: Gen. 14.19 and 22 specifically refer to *El*(-Elyon), and Deut. 32.8 also refers to the 'sons of God' (implicitly seventy, deriving from the seventy sons of El) as well as the name Elyon. (We should also note the personal name Elkanah [*'elqānâ*], 'God [El] has created', 1 Sam. 1.1, etc.) It is therefore possible that it is not merely a coincidence when we find the concept of God as creator and the name El together elsewhere in the Old Testament. Psalm 19.2 (ET 1) proclaims, 'The heavens declare the glory of God (*'ēl*)', and Ps. 102.26-27 (ET 25-26), which speaks of God's work as creator, is not only sandwiched between two verses referring to God's years (cf. El; vv. 25, 28, ET 24, 27), but following the only verse in the Psalm (v. 25, ET 24) to refer to God as *'ēlî*, 'my God (lit. El)', rather than Yahweh.

Reference was made above to Gen. 14.19, 22, 'El-Elyon, creator of heaven and earth', where this deity is depicted as the pre-Israelite, Jebusite god of Jerusalem. Elyon also occurs elsewhere as a divine

23. The words *'l qn 'rṣ*, 'El creator of the earth', occur in the Phoenician inscription of Azitawadda from Karatepe (*KAI* 26.A.III.18) and in a neo-Punic inscription from Leptis Magna in Tripolitania (*KAI* 129.1). Further, the form *'lqwnr'* appears in a bilingual text from Palmyra, where he is equated with Poseidon (J. Cantineau, 'Tadmorea (*suite*)', *Syria* 19 (1938), pp. 72-82 [78-79]). N. Avigad, 'Excavations in the Jewish Quarter of the Old City of Jerusalem, 1971', *IEJ* 22 (1972), pp. 193-200 (195-96), alludes to a seventh-century BCE inscription which he restores as [*'l*] *qn 'rṣ*, but there is no certainty that this reconstruction is correct. However, there is no doubt that this form underlies the name of the god Elkuniršа, whose wife is Ašertu (Asherah) in a Hittite–Canaanite mythological text (*ANET*, p. 519).

name or epithet a number of other times in the Old Testament (e.g. Num. 24.16; Deut. 32.8; Ps. 18.14 [ET 13], 46.5 [ET 4], 78.17, 35, 56, 82.6, 87.5; Isa. 14.14; Dan. 7.22, 25, 27). There is dispute as to whether Elyon was originally the same deity as El or not. Philo of Byblos (c. 100 CE) depicts Elioun, as he calls him, as a separate god from El. Interestingly, he refers to Elioun (Eusebius, *Praeparatio Evangelica* 1.10.15) as the father of Heaven (Ouranos) and Earth (Ge), which is reminiscent of the creator god El, and also strongly supports the idea that the reference to El-Elyon as 'Creator of heaven and earth' in Gen. 14.19. 22 is an authentic reminiscence of the Canaanite deity, and not simply invention.[24] *Prima facie* the eighth-century BCE Aramaic Sefire treaty also represents Elyon as a distinct deity from El, since 'El and Elyon' occur together (*KAI* 222.A.11).[25] This is one of a number of cases of paired deities in the treaty, some of whom are god and consort, whilst some others represent two parts of a whole. It is difficult to see how the pairing of El and Elyon fits into either of these categories. It has sometimes been suggested that 'El and Elyon' here might be a compound divine name, analogous to Kothar-and-Ḫasis, for example, in the Ugaritic texts.[26] Whether or not they are the same deity, since Elyon was apparently the creator, which was also the case with El, it would appear that these two gods were functionally equivalent. Some other language associated with the name Elyon in the Old Testament is also El-like, for example, the association of Elyon with the mount of assembly (Isa. 14.13-14), with the sons of God or Elyon (Deut. 32.8; Ps. 82.6), and with the mythical river and streams (Ps. 46.5 [ET 4]).[27]

24. Philo's evidence also serves to reject the idea that 'El-Elyon, creator of heaven and earth' (Gen. 14.19, 22) involves a conflation of Elyon, lord of heaven, and El, lord of earth, as suggested by G. Levi della Vida, 'El 'Elyon in Genesis 14 18-20', *JBL* 63 (1944), pp. 1-9; R. Lack, 'Les origines de *Elyon*, le très-haut, dans la tradition cultuelle d'Israël', *CBQ* 24 (1962), pp. 44-64; R. Rendtorff, 'El, Ba'al und Jahwe', *ZAW* 78 (1966), pp. 277-92.

25. On the Sefire treaty see further J.A. Fitzmyer, *The Aramaic Inscriptions of Sefîre* (BibOr, 19; Rome: Pontifical Biblical Institute, 1967).

26. E.g. E.E. Elnes and P.D. Miller, 'Elyon', *DDD*, cols. 560-71 (562-63) (2nd edn, pp. 293-99 [294-85]). They hold that *šmš. wnr* in line 9 similarly constitute one deity.

27. However, there are occasions when the name Elyon in the Old Testament is used in association with Baalistic imagery; cf. Ps. 18.14 (ET 13), where Elyon thundered ('uttered his voice') and Isa. 14.13-14, where Elyon's dwelling is on Zaphon. Possibly we are to assume that Elyon had absorbed some Baalistic fea-

The Sons of El (God)

In the Old Testament there appears the concept of Yahweh's having a heavenly court, the sons of God. They are referred to variously as the 'sons of God' (*b^e^nê hā'^e^lōhîm*, Gen. 6.2, 4; Job 1.6, 2.2; or *b^e^nê '^e^lōhîm*, Job 38.7), the 'sons of gods' (*b^e^nê 'ēlîm*, Pss. 29.1, 89.7 [ET 6]), or the 'sons of the Most High' (*b^e^nê 'elyôn*, Ps. 82.6). It is also generally agreed that we should read 'sons of God' (*b^e^nê '^e^lōhîm*) for 'sons of Israel' in Deut. 32.8 (see below).

There are further numerous places where the heavenly court is referred to without specific use of the expressions 'sons of God(s)' or 'sons of the Most High'. Thus, the heavenly court is mentioned in connection with the first human(s) (Gen. 1.26, 3.22; Job 15.7-8) or elsewhere in the primaeval history (Gen. 11.7; cf. Gen. 6.2 above), and in the context of the divine call or commission to prophesy (1 Kgs 22.19-22; Isa. 40.3, 6; Jer. 23.18, 22; cf. Amos 3.7). We also find it referred to in connection with the guardian gods or angels of the nations (Isa. 24.21; Ps. 82.1; Ecclus 17.17; *Jub.* 15.31-32; cf. Deut. 32.8 and Ps. 82.6 above; implied in Dan. 10.13, 20; 12.1). Apart from isolated references to the divine assembly on the sacred mountain in Isa. 14.13 and to personified Wisdom in the divine assembly in Ecclus 24.2, the other references to the heavenly court are more general (Zech. 1.10-11, 3.7, 14.5; Ps. 89.6-8 [ET 5-7]; Dan. 4.14 [ET 17], 7.10, 21, 25, 27, 8.10-13; cf. Job 1.6, 2.2, 38.7 and Pss. 29.1, 89.7 [ET 6] above). Just as an earthly king is supported by a body of courtiers, so Yahweh has a heavenly court. Originally, these were gods, but as monotheism became absolute, so these were demoted to the status of angels.

It was H. Wheeler Robinson[28] who first drew attention to this concept

tures. On Elyon and the Old Testament cf. too J. Day, *God's Conflict with the Dragon and the Sea*, pp. 129-36.

28. H.W. Robinson, 'The Council of Yahweh', *JTS* 45 (1944), pp. 151-57. Subsequent studies of this theme include: F.M. Cross, 'The Council of Yahweh in Second Isaiah', *JNES* 12 (1953), pp. 274-77; G. Cooke, 'The Sons of (the) Gods', *ZAW* 76 (1964), pp. 22-47; H.-W. Jüngling, *Der Tod der Götter: Eine Untersuchung zu Psalm 82* (SBS, 38; Stuttgart: Katholisches Bibelwerk, 1969); J.L. Cunchillos Ylarri, 'Los b^e^ne ha'elohîm en Gen. 6, 1-4', *EstBíb* 28 (1969), pp. 5-31; A. Ohler, *Mythologische Elemente im Alten Testament* (Düsseldorf: Patmos, 1969), esp. pp. 204-12; W. Schlisske, *Gottessöhne und Gottessohn im Alten Testament: Phasen der Entmythisierung im Alten Testament* (BWANT, 97; Stuttgart: W. Kohlhammer, 1973), esp. pp. 15-78; E.T. Mullen, *The Assembly of the Gods: The Divine Council in Canaanite and Early Hebrew Literature* (HSM, 24; Chico, CA;

in the Old Testament, though he cited only Babylonian parallels and so concluded that the origin of the Israelite notion was Babylonian, overlooking the more recently discovered Ugaritic parallels concerning the sons of El. It is in connection with the Canaanite god El and his pantheon of gods, known as 'the sons of El', that a direct relationship with the Old Testament is to be found. That this is certain can be established from the fact that both were seventy in number. At Ugarit we read in the Baal myth of 'the seventy sons of Asherah (Athirat)' (*šb'm. bn. 'aṯrt*, *KTU*[2] 1.4.VI.46). Since Asherah was El's consort, this therefore implies that El's sons were seventy in number. Now Deut. 32.8, which is clearly dependent on this concept,[29] declares, 'When the Most High gave to the nations their inheritance, when he separated the sons of men, he fixed the bounds of the peoples according to the number of the sons of God'. The reading 'sons of God' (*b*ᵉ*nê 'ᵉlōhîm*) has the support of the Qumran fragment, 4QDeut,[30] the LXX, Symmachus, Old Latin and the Syro-Hexaplaric manuscript, Cambr. Or. 929.[31] This is clearly the original reading, to be preferred to the MT's 'sons of Israel' (*b*ᵉ*nê yiśrā'ēl*), which must have arisen as a deliberate alteration on the part of a scribe who did not approve of the polytheistic overtones of the phrase 'sons of God'.[32] Interestingly, it is known that the Jews believed

Scholars Press, 1980); M. Dietrich and O. Loretz, *'Jahwe und seine Aschera'* (UBL, 9; Münster: Ugarit–Verlag, 1992), pp. 134-57.

29. This was first proposed as a possibility by R. Tournay, 'Les Psaumes complexes (*Suite*)', *RB* 56 (1949), pp. 37-60 (53), and then put forward more confidently by W.F. Albright, 'Some remarks on the Song of Moses in Deuteronomy XXXII', *VT* 9 (1959), pp. 339-46 (343-44).

30. See E. Ulrich, F.M. Cross, S.W. Crawford, J.A. Duncan, P.W. Skehan, E. Tov, J. Trebolle Barrera, *Qumran Cave 4*. IX. *Deuteronomy, Joshua, Judges, Kings* (DJD, 14; Oxford: Clarendon Press, 1995), p. 90 (= plate XXIII, col. XII, no. 34).

31. With regard to the Cambr. Or. reading (*ml'kwh d'lh*'), cf. M.H. Gottstein, 'Eine Cambridger Syrohexaplahandschrift', *Le Muséon* 67 (1954), pp. 291-96 (293), and J. Hempel, 'Zu IVQ Deut 32 8', *ZAW* 74 (1962), p. 70.

32. As D. Barthélemy argues, in 'Les tiqquné sopherim et la critique textuelle de l'Ancien Testament', in *Congress Volume, Bonn 1962* (VTSup, 9; Leiden: E.J. Brill, 1963), pp. 285-304 (297 n.1), *b*ᵉ*nê yiśrā'ēl* is not simply a scribal slip. The latter was proposed by J.B. Lightfoot and H.L. Ginsberg. Lightfoot, in *The Apostolic Fathers, Part I. St Clement of Rome*, II (London: Macmillan, 2nd edn, 1890), p. 94, followed by NAB (cf. *BH*[3] and *BHS*) suggested that 'Israel' in Deut. 32.8 accidentally came into the text from the end of the following verse (v. 9), where it is found in the LXX and Samaritan versions. H.L. Ginsberg, 'A Strand in the Cord of Hebraic Hymnody', *Eretz-Israel* 9 (W.F. Albright volume; Jerusalem:

there to be seventy nations on earth, so that the sons of God were accordingly also seventy in number. This emerges from the table of the nations in Genesis 10, where there are seventy nations, and from the later Jewish apocalyptic concept according to which there were seventy guardian angels of the nations (*Targum Pseudo-Jonathan* on Deut. 32.8; *1 En.* 89.59-77, 90.22-27). This view, which I have defended previously,[33] seems eminently reasonable. The criticisms that it has received seem unconvincing. Thus, first, R.N. Whybray[34] claims that it is illegitimate to argue from the number seventy, since this is merely a conventional way of referring to a large, but indeterminate, number. But this does not seem to be the case here, since Genesis 10 lists precisely seventy nations on earth. Secondly, D.I. Block[35] has claimed that the seventy gods of the nations implied in Deut. 32.8 are rather to be seen as a back projection from the notion of seventy nations on earth, such as is found in Genesis 10. Since, however, the idea of seventy sons of God (El) is already attested prior to Deut. 32.8, as the Ugaritic texts prove, Block's theory seems strained.

Finally, it is interesting to note that the Old Testament never refers to the heavenly court as 'the sons of Yahweh'. As we have seen above, apart from one instance of *b^e^nê 'elyôn*, we always find 'sons of God', with words for God containing the letters *'l* (*b^e^nê hā'elōhîm*, *b^e^nê 'elōhîm*, *b^e^nê 'ēlîm*). This finds a ready explanation in their origin in the sons of the Canaanite god El.

'El' in the Old Testament as a Reflection of Canaanite El

Eventually, of course, the name El simply became a general word for 'God' in the Old Testament, and so it is found many times. For example, there is the well-known phrase about Yahweh's being 'a jealous God' (*'ēl qannâ'*), which clearly reflects the unique distinctiveness of Yahwism rather than anything to do with the Canaanite god El. Also, in

Israel Exploration Society, 1969), pp. 45-50 (45 n. 4), supposed that *yiśrā'ēl* in the MT came about through a conflation of *b^e^nê 'ēl* and an explanatory gloss, *śārê*.

33. In several places, but first of all in J. Day, *God's Conflict with the Dragon and the Sea*, pp. 174-75.

34. R.N. Whybray, review of *God's Conflict with the Dragon and the Sea*, by John Day, in *JTS* NS 36 (1985), pp. 402-407 (406).

35. D.I. Block, *The Gods of the Nations: Studies in Ancient Near Eastern National Mythology* (Evangelical Theological Monograph Series, 2; Jackson, MI: Evangelical Theological Society; Winona Lake, IN: Eisenbrauns, 1988), pp. 20-21.

many other instances throughout the Old Testament there is no doubt that *'ēl* is simply a general name for God without any reflection of the Canaanite background. This has rightly been noted by R. Rendtorff.[36] However, there are several instances where the use of the word *'ēl* does seem to reflect the Canaanite background. Where a strong case can be made for this is in those instances in which the Old Testament employs the word *'ēl* in a context that is particularly suggestive of the Canaanite El, especially if such a usage occurs more than once. Thus, for example, just as El was the leader of the divine assembly (the sons of El), so the name *'ēl* is twice found in this context. In Ps. 82.1 we read that 'God has taken his place in the divine council' (*'ᵉlōhîm niṣṣāb ba'ᵃdat-'ēl*; cf. Ugaritic *'dt.'ilm*, 'assembly of the gods', in *KTU*² 1.15.II.7, 11). This divine council consists of the 'sons of the Most High' in v. 6, who are here sentenced to death, having previously had jurisdiction over the nations of the earth (v. 8), and in Jewish thought they were numbered as seventy. There can be detected here a connection with the seventy sons of God in Deut. 32.8, deriving from the seventy sons of El, discussed above.

The divine assembly is also referred to in Isa. 14.13 by means of a word from the same root as in Ps. 82.1, where the Shining One, son of the dawn boasts, 'I will ascend to heaven; above the stars of God (*'ēl*) I will set my throne on high; I will sit on the mount of assembly (*har mô'ēd*)'. It will be recalled that at Ugarit El's assembly of the gods did indeed meet on a mountain. It is also interesting that the name of *'ēl* (God) is mentioned in the phrase 'stars of God', and that the stars and the sons of God are sometimes equated (Job 38.7; cf. *KTU*² 1.10.I.3-4). Ezekiel 28.2, 9 should also be recalled, since God is there three times referred to as *'ēl* (a term used elsewhere in Ezekiel only in Ezek. 10.5), part of a passage that has multiple allusions characteristic of Ugaritic El: the emphasis on the divine wisdom (vv. 2-6), the watery nature of the dwelling (v. 2), and the expression *môšab 'ᵉlōhîm* 'seat of God (or gods)' (v. 2). Another distinctively El characteristic that is twice referred to in the Old Testament in the context of the name *'ēl* is the allusion to Yahweh's years (Ps. 102.25, 28 [ET 24, 27]; Job 36.26). The passage in the psalm also speaks of God as creator, another point characteristic of El (Ps. 102.26-27 [ET 25-26]). It may, therefore also be

36. R. Rendtorff, 'Some Observations on the Use of אל in the Hebrew Bible', in S. Aḥituv and B. Levine (eds.), *Eretz-Israel 24*. (Jerusalem: Abraham Malamat volume; Jerusalem: Israel Exploration Society, 1993), pp. 192*-96*.

significant that the first half of Psalm 19, which highlights God's role as creator, specifically refers to him as *'ēl* (v. 2, ET 1).

Another possible instance of influence from El comes in the references to Yahweh as *'ēl ḥannûn w^{e}raḥûm* (Jon. 4.2; Neh. 9.31), *'ēl raḥûm w^{e}ḥannûn* (Exod. 34.6; Ps. 103.8) or *'ēl raḥûm* (Deut. 4.31), that is, 'a God gracious and merciful', 'a God merciful and gracious', or 'a merciful God'. In Ugaritic El is noted for these qualities and is frequently referred to as *lṭpn 'il dp'id*, 'the kindly one, El, the compassionate', and these precise terms have survived in the epithets used of Allah in Arabic, *laṭīf* 'kind' and *ḏū fu'ād*, 'merciful'. One may also recall the frequent introductory allusions to Allah in the Koran: *bismi llāhi r-raḥmāni r-raḥimi*, 'In the name of Allah, the compassionate and merciful'. It is possible that the Old Testament terminology is derived from El as, for example, H. Spieckermann[37] has argued, though R. Rendtorff[38] doubts it, as the words in the Old Testament, unlike those used in Arabic, are not identical to those in Ugaritic. Since Hebrew lacks forms corresponding precisely to those in Ugaritic, however, Rendtorff's objection is not a decisive argument.[39]

In addition to the above points, it may be noted that throughout this chapter indications are given that various occurrences of the name El in the patriarchal narratives are a reflection of Canaanite El religion.

El's Dwelling Place: The Origin of Paradise

Does Ezekiel 28.2-10 Reflect El Traditions? Ezekiel 28.2-10 is an oracle of judgment against the king of Tyre, Ittobaal II. Because of his hubris in striving to be like God, he is cast down into the underworld. It has been debated whether traditions of the god El are reflected here. Among the points that may be appealed to in support of this view are the following:

37. H. Spieckermann, '"Barmherzig und gnädig ist der Herr..."', *ZAW* 102 (1990), pp. 1-18 (3).

38. Rendtorff, 'Some Observations on the Use of אל', p. 196* n. 9.

39. Cf. Løkkegaard, 'A Plea for El, the Bull', who sees influence from El on Yahweh as having contributed to the latter's kindness. On this theme see too now J.F. Healey, 'The Kindly and Merciful God: On Some Semitic Divine Epithets', in M. Dietrich and I. Kottsieper, with H. Schaudig (eds.), *'Und Mose schrieb dieses Lied auf': Studien zum Alten Testament und zum Alten Orient. Festschrift für Oswald Loretz* (AOAT, 250; Münster: Ugarit–Verlag, 1998), pp. 349-56.

(i) The name used for God in Ezek. 28.2 (x2) and 9 is El (*'ēl*). This is found in only one other place in the book of Ezekiel, in Ezek. 10.5 (El-Shaddai). Compare also Ps. 82.1, Job 36.26 and Ps. 102.25-28 (ET 24-27) for some other places in the Old Testament where the name *'ēl* is used for God in association with ideas that actually pertain to El in the Ugaritic texts (divine assembly, aged deity, and creation).

(ii) In saying, 'I am El (God)', the king of Tyre declares, 'I sit in the seat of God [or gods] (*mōšab 'elōhîm*) in the heart of the seas' (Ezek. 28.2). This is suggestive of El, whose dwelling is said in the Ugaritic texts to be 'at the source of rivers, in the midst of the double deep'. Although the location of Tyre itself was 'in the heart of the seas' (cf. Ezek. 27.4, 32), the association of this with the 'seat of God' clearly reflects El. (*Mṯb 'il* actually occurs in Ugaritic, cf. *KTU*² 1.3.V.38, 1.4.I.12, 1.4.IV.52; *mṯbt. 'ilm* occurs in *KTU*² 1.23.19 and *KTU* 1.53.5.)

(iii) Interestingly, the deity is associated especially with wisdom, as in Ezek. 28.2, 'though you consider yourself as wise as God' and 28.6, 'because you consider yourself as wise as God'. Now El was regarded as particularly wise (cf. *KTU*² 1.4.V.3, etc.).

The combination of these three features creates a good case for seeing El traditions reflected here.[40] Attempts such as those of Zimmerli and Van Dijk[41] to avoid this conclusion are to be rejected. (Canaanite traditions are also present in the reference to Daniel in Ezek. 28.3.)[42]

The scholar who first drew attention to El parallels in Ezekiel 28,

40. See, for example, R.J. Clifford, *The Cosmic Mountain in Canaan and the Old Testament* (HSM, 4; Cambridge, MA; Harvard University Press, 1972), pp. 169-71; H.N. Wallace, *The Eden Narrative* (HSM, 32; Atlanta; Scholars Press, 1985), p. 79, though seeing *'ēl* as generic, 'God', rightly in my view envisages a *double entendre* with regard to the god El.

41. H.J. Van Dijk, *Ezekiel's Prophecy on Tyre (Ez. 26,1–28,19)* (BibOr, 20; Rome: Pontifical Biblical Institute, 1968), pp. 95-96. O. Loretz, 'Der Sturz des Fürsten von Tyrus (Ez 28, 1-19)', *UF* 8 (1976), pp 455-58 (456), accepts that the king of Tyre is here striving after the position of El, but rejects the view that El's watery dwelling has influenced Ezek. 28.2.

42. Cf. J. Day, 'The Daniel of Ugarit and Ezekiel and the Hero of the Book of Daniel', *VT* 30 (1980), pp. 174-84.

M.H. Pope,[43] however, was quite wrong in seeing the picture of the fallen figure in Ezek. 28.2-10 as itself being based on the fate of the god El. It is now widely recognized that there is no real evidence for the notion that El was ejected (by Baal) from his seat of authority.[44] In Ezekiel 28, as elsewhere in the Old Testament, El is equated with Yahweh himself, and it is clear that it is the king of Tyre's striving to be like El that leads to his downfall.

Does Ezekiel 28.12-19 belong to the same Mythic Circle as Ezekiel 28.1-10? Ezekiel 28.1-10 and 28.12-19 represent two separate oracles directed against the king of Tyre. However, there is a similarity of theme: in both the king's conceit of wisdom gets the better of him and he is cast down. I have argued above that El traditions are found in Ezek. 28.1-10. Is this the case also in 28.12-19? It would appear so. First, El in the Ugaritic texts dwells on a mountain at the source of the rivers. There is a reference to the waters in the first oracle, but no mountain; it is the second oracle that refers to the mountain of God (Ezek. 28.14, 16). Secondly, Ezek. 28.12-19 is a variant of the garden of Eden story in Genesis 2–3: note the references to Eden, cherub(im) and the casting out of the man in both instances.[45] In Gen. 2.10-14 the

43. Pope, *El in the Ugaritic Texts*, pp. 97-104.

44. L'Heureux, *Rank among the Canaanite Gods*, pp. 3-108, offers a convincing and thorough refutation of this view.

45. As rightly stressed, for example by J.L. McKenzie, 'Mythological Allusions in Ezek 28 12-18', *JBL* 75 (1956), pp. 322-27. Various attempts to deny this are unsatisfactory. A.J. Williams, 'The Mythological Background of Ezekiel 28:12-19?', *BTB* 6 (1976), pp. 49-61, for example, does not think that Ezek. 28.12-19 refers back to the story of Gen. 2–3 or alludes to the myth of a primaeval man, but rather castigates the Tyrian ruler for his hubris in commercial activities and participation in the local sanctuary rites of sacral kingship. But Williams fails to explain why, on his view, the king is represented as initially dwelling in Eden. R.R. Wilson, 'The Death of the King of Tyre: The Editorial History of Ezekiel 28', in J.H. Marks and R.M. Good (eds.), *Love & Death in the Ancient Near East: Essays in Honor of Marvin H. Pope* (Guilford, CN; Four Quarters, 1987), pp. 211-18, believes that Ezek. 28.11-19 was originally a condemnation of the Israelite high priest in the Jerusalem temple, referred to obliquely under the imagery of the king of Tyre. He notes the parallel between the gem stones in v. 13 and those of the high priest in Exod. 28.17-20, 39.10-13, he connects the cherub and mountain of God (vv. 14, 16) with the cherubim of the Jerusalem temple and Mt Zion, and thinks the reference to profaning sanctuaries (v. 18) is more appropriate of the high priest than a pagan king. Wilson admits that, as it is stands, the oracle is directed at the king of Tyre,

garden of God is at the source of the rivers. No mention is made of this in Ezek. 28.12-14, but there is a reference to the watery nature of the divine dwelling in Ezek. 28.2.

If all this is so, then it would appear that El traditions could lie behind the garden of Eden story. This conclusion is further borne out by the Genesis 2–3 narrative, which, as will be seen below, places the garden of Eden/garden of God precisely where Canaanite myth located El's dwelling.

Where Was the Garden of Eden (Paradise)? Although for modern readers the garden of Eden is not a literal place, for the ancients it surely was, in view of the precise geographical indications given in Gen. 2.10-14. These geographical data are sufficient to refute the thesis of C. Westermann[46] that the Yahwist did not have some particular location in mind. Its location at the source of the Tigris and Euphrates rivers suggests either Armenia (at their western end) or the Persian Gulf (at their eastern end). Although the Sumerians placed their Paradise (Dilmun) in the Persian Gulf (at Bahrein)—and certain scholars such as E.A. Speiser[47] supposed this to be in mind in Gen. 2.10-14—this does not appear to be the case here. Two important considerations suggest that Eden was located rather at the other end, in Armenia. First, as Albright pointed out,[48] the river flowing from Eden became four head

and claims that this is due to a later redactor's misunderstanding of its original purpose. However, Wilson's reconstruction is far too speculative to carry conviction. It is passing strange that the Israelite high priest (whom Ezekiel nowhere else specifically singles out for judgment) should be symbolized by the king of Tyre. Rather than seeing the Israelite high priest as being symbolized by the king of Tyre it is more natural to suppose that the king of Tyre is being spoken of under the imagery of the first man expelled from Eden: the combination of references to the garden of Eden, the casting out of a man for sin, and the association of a cherub with this, is too close to Gen. 2–3 for the parallel to be dismissed.

46. C. Westermann, *Genesis 1–11* (BKAT, 1.1; Neukirchen–Vluyn: Neukirchener Verlag, 1974), p. 294; ET *Genesis 1–11: A Commentary* (trans. J.J. Scullion; London: SPCK, 1984), pp. 215-16.

47. E.A. Speiser, 'The Rivers of Paradise', in R. von Kienle, A. Moortgat, H. Otten, E. von Schuler and W. Zaumseil (eds.), *Festschrift Johannes Friedrich* (Heidelberg: Carl Winter, 1959), pp. 473-85; reprinted in Speiser's collected essays, *Oriental and Biblical Studies* (ed. J.J. Finkelstein and M. Greenberg; Philadelphia: University of Pennsylvania Press, 1967), pp. 23-34.

48. W.F. Albright, 'The Location of the Garden of Eden', *AJSL* 39 (1922), pp. 15-31 (18).

(-waters). He writes, 'Like Assyr. *rêš nâri*, and Eg. *rś*, Heb. *râšîm* refers solely to the headwaters of a river and even the Hebrew scribes never went so far as to picture a river running upstream to its source'. Secondly, in Ezek. 28.14, 16 (cf. v. 13) Eden is set on a mountain. This does not fit the Persian Gulf at all, but coheres with Armenia perfectly, since its mountainous terrain is particularly noteworthy. That Gihon and Pishon are not geographically accurate does not matter: this is archaic geography. Gihon, 'which flows around the whole land of Kush' (Gen. 2.13) denotes the Nile (as in Ecclus 24.27 and LXX of Jer. 2.18); and Kush normally represents Nubia. Pishon is possibly the Indus. Note that Pausanias, *Description of Greece* 2.5.3 reports the 'story that the Nile is the Euphrates, which disappears into a marsh, rises again beyond Ethiopia and becomes the Nile', and Arrian (*Anabasis Alexandria* 6.1.2-6) records that Alexander the Great at first thought that the Indus was the upper course of the Nile (cf. Strabo, *Geography* 15.1.25).

Interestingly, it was on one of the mountains of Armenia (Ararat, i.e. Urartu) that Noah's Ark landed (Gen. 8.4). In the Mesopotamian version of the flood story, which underlies the Genesis account, the flood hero was translated to Paradise following the landing of the Ark (Gilgamesh epic, tablet 11, lines 194-97). In Berossos's version[49] the Ark, as in Gen. 8.4, lands in Armenia (as also in Nicolaus of Damascus, cited by Josephus, *Ant.* 1.3.6), while in the Gilgamesh epic (tablet 11, lines 140-44) it lands in Kurdistan (Mt Nimush, previously read Niṣir[50]), adjacent to Armenia. When the Mesopotamian flood hero Utnapishtim is said to be at *pî nârâti*, 'the mouth of the rivers' (tablet 11, lines 194-97), it is natural to suppose that this is at the Armenian source of the Tigris and Euphrates. This also coheres with the fact that Gilgamesh, in seeking Utnapishtim, the Mesopotamian flood hero, crosses Mt Mashu—that is, Mt Masios in Armenia—and the dark tunnel he goes through fits a tunnel at the end of the river Tigris.

Interestingly, there is evidence that the dwelling place of the supreme Canaanite god El was located at the source of the river Euphrates. In the Hittite–Canaanite Elkuniřša myth,[51] Elkuniřša (= El, creator of the

49. See S.M. Burstein, *The Babyloniaca of Berossus* (Sources and Monographs: Sources from the Ancient Near East, I.5; Malibu: Undena, 1978), p. 20.

50. For the reading Nimush, see W.G. Lambert, 'Niṣir or Nimush?', *RA* 80 (1986), pp. 185-86; it is followed, e.g., by S. Dalley, *Myths from Mesopotamia* (Oxford: Oxford University Press, 1989), p. 114.

earth) lives in a tent at the source of the Mala river (Euphrates). This must also be in Armenia, since El characteristically dwells on a mountain (in the Ugaritic texts).

51. For convenience, see *ANET*, p. 519. This was originally published by H. Otten, 'Ein kanaanäischer Mythus aus Boğazköy', *MIO* 1 (1953), pp. 125-50, and there is a more recent edition by H.A. Hoffner, 'The Elkunirsa Myth Reconsidered', *Revue Hittite et Asianique* 23 (1965), pp. 5-16. The Elkuniřsa text is the only explicit evidence of El's dwelling place that we have, and the argument for El's dwelling in Armenia has been laid out by E. Lipiński in 'El's Abode: Mythological Traditions Related to Mount Hermon and to the Mountains of Armenia', *OLP* 2 (1971), pp. 13-69 (41-58). However, Lipiński (pp. 15-41) also makes a reasonable case that the mount of the gods (and therefore El's) could also be envisaged on Mt Hermon. He appeals especially to the fact that it is implied in an old Babylonian version of the Gilgamesh epic that the dwelling of the Anunnaki was in the cedar forest (cf. rev., lines 13, 20), i.e. the Antilebanon-Hermon, of which Mt Hermon is the highest, the Anunnaki in the Old Babylonian period denoting the great gods in general. He also notes the association of the sons of God with Mt Hermon in *1 En.* 6.6, and I have noted that Bashan is called *har 'elōhîm* in Ps. 68.16 (ET 15), and that this most naturally denotes Mt Hermon (J. Day, *God's Conflict with the Dragon and the Sea*, pp. 115-19).

Other locations have, however, been suggested. Thus, Pope, *El in the Ugaritic Texts*, pp. 72-81, argued that El dwelt at Khirbet Afqa at the source of the Nahr Ibrāhīm. Pope's argument rests on the similarity of the word *'apq* 'spring', used in connection with El's dwelling in the Ugaritic texts (e.g. KTU^2 1.6.1.34) to the name Afqa, but since *'apq* is not a proper name, this is uncompelling. Cross, *Canaanite Myth and Hebrew Epic*, pp. 24-39, believes that El's dwelling was located on Mt Amanus. Cross's case for Mt Amanus largely depends on the view that El was the same as the Punic deity Baal-Ḥammon and that this name means 'lord of Amanus'. However, both suppositions are questionable. Elsewhere in Punic inscriptions Baal Ḥammon is often called simply Baal (e.g. *KAI* 86, 87, 94), suggesting that this was the name of the deity and not simply his epithet. It is also more likely that *ḥammôn* means 'incense burner' rather than Amanus (see J. Day, *Molech: A God of Human Sacrifice in the Old Testament* [UCOP, 41; Cambridge: Cambridge University Press, 1989], pp. 37-40).

Finally, the view has more recently been suggest by A. Naccache, 'El's Abode in his Land', in N. Wyatt, W.G.E. Watson and J.B. Lloyd (eds.), *Ugarit, Religion and Culture: Proceedings of the International Colloquium on Ugarit, Religion and Culture, Edinburgh, July 1994; Essays Presented in Honour of Professor John C.L. Gibson* (UBL, 12; Münster: Ugarit–Verlag, 1996), pp. 249-72, that El's dwelling was on Mt Lebanon. However, none of his reasons is compelling, e.g. the Egyptian references to Lebanon as 'Land of the God' (which god?) and the presence of various Arabic villages in the neighbourhood of Mt Lebanon with *el* in their names (how ancient are these place names?).

The thesis I shall defend, therefore, is that the garden of Eden—or garden of God, as it is sometimes called—derives from the dwelling place of El. Other pointers to the origin of the Eden myth in El's dwelling are as follows. First, in the little known fragment of the Paradise myth in Job 15.7-8 the dwelling place of the first man is located 'in the council of God'. The divine council derives from the assembly of the sons of El, which is located on El's mountain in the Ugaritic texts. Secondly, the emphasis on wisdom in Paradise also suggests El, who was particularly noted for his wisdom (see Gen. 3.6, 22; Job 15.8; Ezek. 28.12, 17). Thirdly, the association of Eden with creation is also consonant with El, the creator god. Finally, one of the rivers of Eden is called Gihon, the same name as the spring in Old Testament Jerusalem, which is associated with El (called Elyon) in Ps. 46.5 (ET 4).

El-Shaddai. The most likely interpretation of the divine name El-Shaddai is 'El, the mountain one', with reference to El's dwelling place on a mountain. This is P's preferred term for God in the period between Abraham and the revelation of the name Yahweh to Moses (cf. Gen. 17.1, 28.3, 35.11; Exod. 6.3). However, the name Shaddai is already present in what appear to be early, perhaps tenth-century, texts such as Gen. 49.25, Num. 24.4, 16, and Ps. 68.15 (ET 14). Traditionally, El-Shaddai has been rendered 'God Almighty', following the LXX's παντοκράτωρ and the Vulgate's *omnipotens*, but it is widely accepted that this is a later misunderstanding, possibly arising through association with Hebrew *šdd* 'to destroy' (cf. Isa. 13.6; Joel 1.15, *k^e^šōd miššadday* 'as destruction from Shaddai'). A rabbinic view understanding the name as meaning 'who suffices' (*še* + *day*) is clearly fanciful and has no support. A standpoint occasionally supported by modern scholars connects it with the Hebrew word *šad* 'breast',[52] but since Shaddai was a masculine deity this is far-fetched.

The two most widely accepted views today render the name El-Shaddai either as 'El, the mountain one', relating it to Akkadian *šadû* 'mountain' (and *šaddā'u*, *šaddû'a*, 'mountain inhabitant'),[53] or as 'El of

52. E.g. D. Biale, 'The God of the Breasts: El Shaddai in the Bible', *HR* 21 (1981–82), pp. 240-56.

53. Cf. W.F. Albright, 'The Names Shaddai and Abram', *JBL* 54 (1935), pp. 180-87; Cross, *Canaanite Myth and Hebrew Epic*, pp. 52-60; T.N.D. Mettinger, *In Search of God: The Meaning and Message of the Everlasting Names* (trans. F.H.

the field', connecting it with Hebrew *śādeh* 'field'.[54] It is a disadvantage to the latter understanding that the Hebrew word for 'field' has *ś*, whereas Shaddai has *š*. Since the meaning 'mountain' is thought to derive from the word for 'breast', the fact that Hebrew here has *š* is also appropriate. Further, Cross observes that in a Hurrian hymn El is described as 'El, the one of the mountain' (*'Il paban-ḫi-wi-ni*).[55] He also notes[56] that an epithet resembling *'ēl-šadday*, namely, *bêl šadê* 'lord of the mountain' is employed of the Amorite deity called Amurru; judging from such facts as that this deity is also called Ilu-Amurru and has a liaison with Ašratum, the counterpart of Athirat (Asherah), El's consort, Cross suggests that Amurru is to be regarded as the Amorite El. Interestingly, in the Deir 'Allā inscription, I.5-6 we read, 'I will tell you what the Shadda[yyin have done]. Now come, see the works of the gods! The gods gathered together; the Shaddayyin took their places as the assembly'. In both sentences it is most natural to take the Shaddayyin (*šdyn*) and the gods (*'lhn*) as parallel terms referring to the same deities, who constituted the divine assembly. Logically, El, the supreme deity, who also features in the text (I.2; II.6) would therefore be Shaddai *par excellence*. Since, moreover, this epithet is here applied to the gods in their role as members of the divine assembly, which characteristically met on a mountain, the meaning 'mountain ones' seems very appropriate, much more so than 'those of the field'.[57]

Altogether, though we cannot be certain, a plausible case can be made that Shaddai means 'the mountain one', and derives from an epithet of El. Certainly, in addition to the epithet El-Shaddai, the name Shaddai is found parallel with El a remarkable number of times,

Cryer; Philadelphia: Fortress Press, 1987), pp. 69-72; de Moor, *The Rise of Yahwism*, p. 125 (2nd edn, p. 179).

54. M. Weippert, 'Erwägungen zur Etymologie des Gottesnamens 'Ēl šaddaj', *ZDMG* 111 (1961), pp. 42-62; W. Wifall, 'El Shaddai or El of the Fields', *ZAW* 92 (1980), pp. 24-34; O. Loretz, 'Der kanaanäische Ursprung des biblischen Gottesnamens *El šaddaj*', *UF* 12 (1980), pp. 420-21.

55. Cf. Cross, *Canaanite Myth and Hebrew Epic*, p. 56.

56. Cross, *Canaanite Myth and Hebrew Epic*, pp. 57-60. Contrast L.R. Bailey, 'Israelite *'Ēl Šadday* and Amorite *Bêl Šadê*', *JBL* 87 (1968), pp. 434-38, who thought that Bêl Šadê referred to Sin, the moon god. See Cross's objections, *Canaanite Myth and Hebrew Epic*, p. 57 n. 52. Cf. too J. Ouellette, 'More on 'Êl Šadday and Bêl Šadê', *JBL* 88 (1969), pp. 470-71.

57. In my general conclusions here I agree with J.A. Hackett, *The Balaam Text from Deir 'Allā* (HSM, 31; Chico, CA: Scholars Press, 1980), pp. 85-87.

especially in Job (Num. 24.4, 16; Job 8.3, 5, 13.3, 15.25, 22.17, 23.16, 27.2, 13, 33.4, 34.10, 12, 35.13). If Shaddai originated as an epithet of some other god than El it is surprising that the term became so much approved and was never rejected.

El Influence on Yahweh Ultimately Rejected by the Old Testament

El the Bull: The Origin of Jeroboam's Golden Calves Cult

I have considered above various aspects of the Canaanite god, El, which were appropriated by Yahweh and which have been taken up into the Old Testament. There were a couple of aspects of the El cult, however, that were accepted by many Israelites, but ultimately came to be rejected by the Old Testament. One was the appropriation by Yahweh of El's wife, Asherah, which will be considered below in Chapter 2. The other concerns the symbolism of the deity by a bull. In the Ugaritic texts El is frequently referred to as the 'Bull El' (*ṯr 'il*), as, for example, in *KTU*[2] 1.2.III.21, 1.4.III.31, and elsewhere. This bull symbolism seems to have been symbolic of El's strength rather than fertility, as El was not particularly associated with fertility. I shall argue below that the golden calves set up by King Jeroboam I at Bethel and Dan (1 Kgs 12.26-30) reflect ancient Yahwistic symbolism deriving from the god El. (That bull symbolism—whether associated with El or some other god[s]—was known in Palestine prior to Jeroboam is attested archaeologically.[58]) But first I need to reject other origins of this symbolism that have been suggested.

58. E.g. a ceramic vessel in the shape of a bull has been found at MB Shiloh, a silver-plated statuette of a calf was discovered at MB II Ashkelon, and, most famously, an image of a bull from the so-called 'Bull Site' was found by A. Mazar near Dothan. See I. Finkelstein, 'Shiloh Yields some, but not all of its Secrets', *BARev* 12.1 (1986), pp. 22-41 (29-34); L.E. Stager, 'When Canaanites and Philistines Ruled Ashkelon', *BARev* 17.2 (1991), pp. 25-29; A. Mazar, 'The "Bull Site": An Iron Age I Open Cult Place', *BASOR* 247 (1982), pp. 27-42; A. Mazar, 'Bronze Bull Found in Israelite "High Place" from the Time of the Judges', *BARev* 9.5 (1983), pp. 34-40. A. Mazar, 'On Cult Places and Early Israelites: A Response to Michael Coogan', *BARev* 15.4 (1988), p. 45; M.D. Coogan, 'Of Cults and Cultures: Reflections on the Interpretation of Archaeological Evidence', *PEQ* 119 (1987), pp. 1-8. For a brief survey of these and other Palestinian bull icons, see W.I. Toews, *Monarchy and Religious Institution in Israel under Jeroboam I* (SBLMS, 47; Atlanta: Scholars Press, 1993), pp. 49-51.

Prior to the nineteenth century it was generally thought that Jeroboam's calves (I Kgs 12.26-30), as well as Aaron's golden calf (Exod. 32) were Egyptian in origin. This view is already found in Philo of Alexandria and was followed by the Church Fathers and others. In the twentieth century it has been accepted by R.H. Pfeiffer, E. Danelius and J. Oswalt.[59] Danelius curiously argued that the deity in question was the cow goddess, Hathor, because the LXX speaks of Jeroboam's heifers (1 Kgs 12.28, 33; contrast 'calf' throughout Exod. 32), but there is no reason to believe that the MT is at fault at this point. Against an Egyptian origin it has been noted that it would be improbable for the Hebrews to attribute their deliverance from Egyptian oppression to an Egyptian deity, that the Egyptians worshipped *living* bulls (such as the Apis bull), and finally, that it is improbable that Jeroboam would have imported such a foreign god.[60]

Surprisingly, another view maintained by J. Lewy and L.R. Bailey[61] has it that the golden calves were symbols of the Mesopotamian moon-god, Sin. There is little to be said for this theory, since there is no clear evidence for Sin worship in the Old Testament and moon worship, though not absent, does not seem to have played a prominent role in ancient Israel. (See below, Chapter 6, for Yahweh and the moon.) Moreover, it was Yahweh who was the God of the Exodus, and we never hear of this being attributed to any other deity.

When the Old Testament speaks of Israel's apostasy to other gods, the most prominent deity in this connection is the Canaanite storm and

59. R.H. Pfeiffer, 'Images of Yahweh', *JBL* 45 (1926), pp. 211-22 (217-18), and *Religion in the Old Testament* (London: A. & C. Black, 1961), p. 75; E. Danelius, 'The Sins of Jeroboam Ben-Nabat [*sic*]' *JQR* 58 (1967), pp. 95-114, 204-23; J. Oswalt, 'The Golden Calves and the Egyptian Concept of Deity', *EvQ 45* (1973), pp. 13-20. For a thorough survey of attempts to see Egyptian influence on the calf cult, see J. Hahn, *Das 'Goldene Kalb': Die Jahwe-Verehrung bei Stierbildern in der Geschichte Israels* (Frankfurt: Peter Lang, 2nd edn, 1987), pp. 314-24.

60. These points were already made by S.R. Driver, *The Book of Exodus* (Cambridge Bible for Schools and Colleges; Cambridge: Cambridge University Press, 1911), p. 348.

61. J. Lewy, 'The Old West Semitic Sun-god Ḥammu', *HUCA* 18 (1943–44), pp. 429-81 (442-43) and 'The Late Assyro-Babylonian Cult of the Moon and its Culmination at the Time of Nabonidus', *HUCA* 19 (1945–46), pp. 405-89 (448); for a posthumous summary of Lewy's ideas, see A.F. Key, 'Traces of the Worship of the Moon God Sîn among the Early Israelites', *JBL* 84 (1965), pp. 20-26; L.R. Bailey, 'The Golden Calf', *HUCA* 42 (1971), pp. 97-115.

fertility god, Baal. Baal is, in fact, sometimes associated with bull symbolism,[62] and the view that Jeroboam's golden calves represented Baal is already attested in the Apocrypha in Tob. 1.5. However, although a few modern scholars have adopted this view,[63] it is now generally rejected. Significantly, Jehu's revolution, which 'wiped out Baal from Israel' (2 Kgs 10.28), did not remove the golden calves (2 Kgs 10.29), clearly indicating that they were not perceived as Baal symbols. Likewise, the prophet Elijah, who was adamant in his opposition to Baal, utters no condemnation of the golden calves, and neither does Elisha.

Although not all agree, most scholars now accept that Jeroboam's calves were associated with Yahweh, the God of Israel, rather than some foreign god. Thus, first, Jeroboam was attempting to secure his throne and stop people from going to worship Yahweh in Jerusalem (1 Kgs 12.26-27), and would therefore have been unwise at that point to have imposed some alien god. Secondly, Jeroboam declares of the calves, 'Behold your gods, O Israel, who brought you up out of the land of Egypt' (cf. Exod. 32.4). It is Yahweh who is elsewhere the god of the Exodus, and there is no evidence that this deliverance was ever attributed to any other god. Thirdly, Exodus 32, which is clearly polemicizing against Jeroboam's calves, goes on to connect them with Yahweh in Exod. 32.5, 'Tomorrow shall be a feast to the Lord' (cf. the reference to the feast in 1 Kgs 12.32). Fourthly, Jeroboam's son, Abijah (1 Kgs 14.1) has a Yahwistic name. Fifthly, the one personal name from Israel referring to a bull is *'glyw*, 'calf of Yahweh' (or possibly 'Yahweh is a calf') on Samaria ostracon 41 (about 100 or 150 years later than Jeroboam I),[64] thus associating the calf with Yahweh rather than any other god. Sixthly, the fact that the golden calves were not removed in Jehu's purge suggests that they were perceived to be Yahwistic.

62. See the evidence collected by A.H.W. Curtis, 'Some Observations on "Bull" Terminology in the Ugaritic Texts and the Old Testament', in A.S. van der Woude (ed.), *In Quest of the Past: Studies on Israelite Religion, Literature and Prophetism* (OTS, 26; Leiden: E.J. Brill, 1990), pp. 17-31 (17-20).

63. Those connecting the golden calves with Baal worship include T.J. Meek, 'Aaronites and Zadokites', *AJSL* 45 (1929), pp. 149-66 (149-50); H.M. Barstad, *The Religious Polemics of Amos: Studies in the Preaching of Am 2, 7B-8; 4, 1-13; 5, 1-27; 6, 4-7; 8, 14* (VTSup, 34; Leiden: E.J. Brill, 1984), p. 189 (referring specifically to the calf at Dan). For a list of others who have taken this view see Hahn, *Das 'Goldene Kalb'*, p. 332 n. 134.

64. For convenience, see J.C.L. Gibson, *Textbook of Syrian Semitic Inscriptions*, I (Oxford: Clarendon Press, 1971), p. 10 (cf. also p. 12).

Granted that the golden calves denoted Yahweh rather than some foreign deity, the question still remains whence this imagery was derived. The most likely explanation is that it was appropriated from the Canaanite god El, known as 'Bull El' in the Ugaritic texts, with whom Yahweh was identified.[65] The following points speak in favour of this. First, in Canaanite religion it is supremely the god El with whom bull symbolism is associated so far as we can tell from the Ugaritic texts. Secondly, it may be significant that one of the two sites at which the golden calves were set up was Bethel, a name that literally means 'house of El'. The god of Bethel is called El-Bethel in Gen. 35.7 (cf. 31.13),[66] and in Jer. 48.13 the god of the northern kingdom seems to be called simply Bethel: 'Then Moab shall be ashamed of Chemosh, as the house of Israel was ashamed of Bethel, their confidence'. From the context, Bethel can be only the name of the deity,[67] not the place.[68]

65. Those seeing El symbolism as lying behind the golden calves include Cross, *Canaanite Myth and Hebrew Epic*, pp. 73-75; Curtis, 'Some Observations on "Bull" Terminology', pp. 25-28; Toews, *Monarchy and Religious Institution*, pp. 41-46; N. Wyatt, 'Calf', *DDD*, cols. 344-48 (346-47) (2nd edn, pp. 180-82 [181-82]). Hahn, *Das 'Goldene Kalb'*, p. 334, leaves open whether Baal or El influence was at work, but seems to incline to El.

66. Gen. 35.7 has, 'and he [Jacob] called the place El-Bethel...'. LXX, Syriac and Vulgate simply read 'Bethel', but this looks like the easier reading, and therefore to be rejected. There is ample precedent for including the divine name in names of places or altars: cf. most immediately Gen. 33.20, where Jacob called the altar at Shechem 'El, the god of Israel', and also note Exod. 17.15, Judg. 6.24, Ezek. 48.35. As for Gen. 31.13, the MT has *'ānōkî hā'ēl bêt-ēl*; as the text goes on to refer to 'where' (*'ašer...šām*), we cannot translate 'I am the god Bethel', and we would naturally expect *'ēl* not to have the definite article if the meaning were 'I am the God/El of Bethel'. Possibly we should understand 'I am the God at Bethel', with ellipse of *b*ᵉ 'at' before 'Bethel', as this happens quite a number of times in the Old Testament with place names, including Bethel (cf. Num. 21.14; 2 Kgs 23.17). Some scholars add the words 'who appeared to you at' (*hannir'eh 'ēlêkā b*ᵉ) between *hā'ēl* and *bêt-'ēl* (cf. LXX and Targum), though this might be an interpretation inspired by the apparent grammatical problem of the MT (the latter being supported by the Samaritan Pentateuch) or by a desire to avoid speaking of a localized God of Bethel.

67. On the god Bethel, see O. Eissfeldt, 'Der Gott Bethel', *ARW* 28 (1930), pp. 1-30; reprinted in O. Eissfeldt, *Kleine Schriften*, I (Tübingen: J.C.B. Mohr [Paul Siebeck], 1962), pp. 206-33; J.P. Hyatt, 'The Deity Bethel in the Old Testament', *JAOS* 59 (1939), pp. 81-98; J.T. Milik, 'Les papyrus araméens d'Hermoupolis et les cultes syro-phéniciens en Egypte perse', *Bib* 48 (1967), pp. 546-622 (565-77); E.R. Dalglish, 'Bethel (Deity)', *ABD*, I, pp. 706-10; W. Röllig, 'Bethel', *DDD*, cols.

Thirdly, it may be noted that the cult at Bethel was especially associated with the patriarch Jacob, and Jacob's god is referred to as *'ᵃbîr ya'ᵃqōb*, 'the Mighty one of Jacob' (Gen. 49.24). However, the word *'ᵃbîr* is very similar to *'abbîr*, which means 'bull', so that Jacob's god may well have been called originally 'the Bull of Jacob', which would be appropriate for the deity El. Probably, therefore, Jeroboam's golden calves derived from the old bull cult associated with El-Bethel at Bethel, which was traced back to Jacob. Unlike other El epithets that have been touched on in this chapter, that of El-Bethel is the only one of which we can detect any sign of growing disapproval in the Old Testament (Jer. 48.13), doubtless because of its association with the bull cult at Bethel. Nevertheless, that some Jews continued to worship Bethel is suggested by the personal name Bethel-sharezer (Zech. 7.2) and by the occurrence of Bethel as a theophorous element in personal names from Elephantine,[69] in addition to the presence of the deities Anat-Bethel (*AP* 22.125), Ḥerem-Bethel (*AP* 7.7) and Eshem-Bethel (*AP* 22.124) there, besides Yahu and Anat-Yahu.

Although it does seem most probable that Jeroboam's calves were old Yahwistic symbols of the deity, ultimately appropriated from El, there are some biblical passages that have unconvincingly been brought in to support this view. The first of these are in the oracles of Balaam, where in Num 23.22 and 24.8 we find virtually identical words: 'God (*'ēl*) brings them [or him] out of Egypt, he has as it were the horns of a wild ox'. Do the horns here belong to God or to Israel? If the horns belong to God, who is interestingly here called El, this, combined with the reference to the Exodus, could provide a parallel to the golden calves incident and support the equation of the deity with El.[70]

331-34 (2nd edn, pp. 173-75). Although extra-biblical texts mostly seem to attest Bethel as a deity within the Aramaean sphere of influence, Philo of Byblos evidently knew of him as a Phoenician god (Baitylos, cf. Eusebius, *Praeparatio Evangelica* 1.10.16) and his consort Anat-Bethel (e.g. *ANET*, p. 534) clearly derives from the well-known Canaanite goddess Anat.

68. Attempts to find references to the deity Bethel also in Amos 3.14, 5.5 and Hos. 4.15, 10.15 are unconvincing. The most that one could envisage is that there could conceivably be a *double entendre* in Amos 5.5, since 'but do not seek Bethel' is preceded by 'Seek me and live' (Amos 5.4).

69. See B. Porten, *Archives from Elephantine* (Berkeley: University of California Press, 1968), pp. 328-31.

70. E.g. H. Motzki, 'Ein Beitrag zum Problem des Stierkultes in der Religionsgeschichte Israels', *VT* 25 (1975), pp. 470-85 (484); Toews, *Monarchy and Reli-*

Unfortunately for this view, it seems more likely that the horns are those of Israel, for the following reasons. First, in the succeeding verse, Num. 24.9, the subject ('he') is certainly Israel ('He crouched, he lay down like a lion, and like a lioness; who will rouse him up?'), as the parallel in Num. 23.24 makes indubitable ('Behold, a people! As a lioness it rises up, and as a lion it lifts itself...'). Accordingly, the 'he' of Num. 24.8 is naturally also Israel rather than God, and the same therefore follows for Num. 23.22. Secondly, there is a rather similar passage in Deut. 33.17, where it is explicitly said of Joseph (that is, the Joseph tribes), 'His firstling bull has majesty *and his horns are the horns of a wild ox*; with them he shall push the peoples, all of them to the ends of the earth'. A further text that has been invalidly appealed to is Hos. 8.6. This is part of one of Hosea's oracles condemning the golden calf, and N.H. Tur-Sinai[71] was the first to propose that the words *kî miyyiśrāʼēl* should be redivided to read *kî mî šōr ʼēl*, 'For who is the bull El?', a viewpoint followed by Motzki[72] and NEB (the latter translating, 'For what sort of a god is this bull?'). This conjecture, which is lacking all versional support, has generally failed to carry conviction and appears more ingenious than correct.

The Golden Calves: Pedestals or Images?

On the face of it the golden calves were images. There is little to be said for the view of O. Eissfeldt[73] that they were on the end of a pole or standard: Eissfeldt could cite only one example of a calf in such a role, namely from Mari,[74] though J. Debus[75] notes that such standards were common among the Hittites. As no parallels have been found within the

gious Institution, pp. 67-68, 145-46; Wyatt, 'Calf', col. 346.

71. N.H. Tur-Sinai, 'אֲבִיר, אַבִּיר', *Encyclopaedia Biblica*, I (Hebrew; Jerusalem: Bialik, 1965), cols. 31-33 (31).

72. Motzki, 'Ein Beitrag zum Problem', p. 471.

73. O. Eissfeldt, 'Lade und Stierbild', *ZAW* 58 (1940–41), pp. 190-215; reprinted in O. Eissfeldt, *Kleine Schriften*, II (Tübingen: J.C.B. Mohr [Paul Siebeck], 1963), II, pp. 282-305. Eissfeldt has been followed by J. Debus, *Die Sünde Jerobeams* (FRLANT, 95; Göttingen: Vandenhoeck & Ruprecht, 1967), p. 39 n. 25, and K. Jaroš, *Die Stellung der Elohisten zur kanaanäischen Religion* (OBO, 4; Freiburg: Unversitätsverlag; Göttingen: Vandenhoeck & Ruprecht, 1982), p. 223.

74. Eissfeldt, 'Lade und Stierbild', p. 209 (see also depiction on p. 210); reprinted in *idem*, *Kleine Schriften*, II, p. 299 (see depiction on p. 300).

75. Debus, *Die Sünde Jerobeams*, p. 39 n. 25, citing E. Akurgal and M. Hirmer, *Die Kunst der Hethiter* (Munich: Hirmer Verlag, 1961), plates 3-6.

Canaanite cultural sphere, this view does not appear likely. More frequently it has been supposed, following the suggestion of H.T. Obbink,[76] that the golden calves were pedestals on which the deity was believed to be invisibly enthroned. Yahweh's presence on the cherubim in the Jerusalem temple, and Syrian and Anatolian depictions of the god Hadad standing on a bull, are cited as analogies.[77]

There are, however, good reasons for believing that this view is mistaken and for supposing instead that the golden calves were intended to be images of the deity.[78] First, the Old Testament itself consistently represents them as such. Thus, in 1 Kgs 12.28 we read that Jeroboam 'took counsel, and made two calves of gold. And he said to the people, "You have gone up to Jerusalem long enough. Behold your gods, O Israel, who brought you up out of the land of Egypt."' Then, a few verses later, we read that Jeroboam was 'sacrificing to the calves that he had made'. This also seems to be the implication of Exod. 32.5, which states that Aaron 'made a molten calf; and they said, "These are your gods, O Israel, who brought you out of the land of Egypt!"' (The plural 'gods' is doubtless a projection back from Jeroboam's two calves at Bethel and Dan.) Finally, in Hos. 8.6 we read of the calf of Samaria that 'A workman made it; it is not God', which is a pointless statement unless there were those who did consider the calf to be a god. The words of Hosea show that this idea cannot be dismissed simply as anti-northern polemic from the Southern Kingdom.[79] Secondly, I have argued above that the bull imagery appropriated by Yahweh derives from El, not Hadad (Baal). Now, El in the Ugaritic texts is called 'Bull El' (*ṯr 'il*): significantly, the epithet 'Bull' is applied to El himself and not to his pedestal. Thirdly, it is to be noted that one of Jeroboam's two calves was set up at Bethel, a site with which the patriarch Jacob was

76. H.T. Obbink, 'Jahwebilder', *ZAW* 47 (1929), pp. 264-74; W.F. Albright, *From the Stone Age to Christianity* (Garden City, NY: Doubleday, 1957), pp. 299-301; J. Gray, *I and II Kings* (OTL; London: SCM Press, 3rd edn, 1977), p. 315; E. Würthwein, *Das erste Buch der Könige* (ATD, 11.1; Göttingen: Vandenhoeck & Ruprecht, 1977), p. 165. For a long list of those who have followed the pedestal view, see Hahn, *'Das Goldene Kalb'*, p. 333 n. 140, who also notes the little known fact that Obbink was anticipated by W. Caspari and F.M.T. Böhl.

77. Cf. *ANEP*, plates 500, 501, 531.

78. M. Weippert, 'Gott und Stier', *ZDPV* 77 (1961), pp. 93-117; Curtis, 'Some Observations on "Bull" Terminology', pp. 22-25.

79. See also the admittedly much later 2 Chron. 13.8, where Jeroboam is said to have made the calves for gods.

closely associated. As noted earlier, it so happens that Jacob's god is known as *'ªbîr ya'ªqōb*, 'the Mighty One of Jacob' (Gen. 49.24), and the word *'ªbîr* is closely connected with *'abbîr*, 'bull'. If this is correct, one might suppose that Jeroboam took up the old bull symbolism connected with the god of Jacob at Bethel (El-Bethel), and again the epithet would suggest that the bull was more than a mere pedestal.

Chapter 2

YAHWEH AND ASHERAH

Asherah as a Goddess in the Old Testament

In the previous chapter I considered the impact of the supreme Canaanite god El on Yahweh, with whom he became equated. For the most part the Old Testament was happy to appropriate elements of El religion to Yahwism, though it rejected the symbolism of El as a bull, which some Israelites associated with Yahweh. Another aspect of El religion which the Old Testament rejected was his wife. The Ugaritic texts reveal that El's consort was a goddess named Athirat. In equating Yahweh with El it would not be surprising if some Israelites appropriated El's wife to Yahweh. As we shall see, this seems to have taken place, and the name Athirat occurs as Asherah in the Old Testament, but understandably the Yahweh-alone party which compiled the Old Testament rejected the notion that Yahweh had a wife Asherah.

The word 'Asherah' occurs forty times in the Old Testament, sometimes in the singular and sometimes in the plural.[1] As I shall argue below, although most of these refer to a wooden cult object symbolizing the goddess Asherah, there are several passages where Asherah refers directly to the goddess herself: Judg. 3.7; 1 Kgs 14.13, 18.19; 2 Kgs 21.7, 23.4. Prior to the discovery of the Ugaritic texts in 1929 onwards, however, it was common for scholars to deny that Asherah was ever the name of a goddess in the Old Testament,[2] or when this was conceded it was often thought that she was the same as Astarte.[3]

1. The name occurs in Exod. 34.13; Deut. 7.5, 12.3, 16.21; Judg. 3.7, 6.25, 26, 28, 30; 1 Kgs 14.15, 23, 15.13, 16.33, 18.19; 2 Kgs 13.6, 17.10, 16, 18.4, 21.3, 7, 23.4, 6, 7, 14, 15; 2 Chron. 14.2 (ET 3), 15.16, 17.6, 19.3, 24.18, 31.1, 33.3, 19, 34.3, 4, 7; Isa. 17.8, 27.9; Jer. 17.2; Mic. 5. 13 (ET 14).

2. E.g. W. Robertson Smith, *Lectures on the Religion of the Semites* (1st series; London: A. & C. Black, 2nd edn, 1894), p. 188.

3. E.g. W.W. von Baudissin, *Studien zur semitischen Religionsgeschichte*, II (Leipzig: Georg Reimer, 1878), pp. 218-19; P. Torge, *Aschera und Astarte: Ein*

The view generally held today that Asherah in the Old Testament occurs both as the name of an independent goddess and as the name of her wooden cult symbol had already been put forward by A. Kuenen[4] in the nineteenth century, but this remained a minority view and did not become widely accepted till the discovery of the Ugaritic texts, which refer to the goddess Athirat (Asherah) as the consort of El.

As I mentioned earlier, one can make a good case that Asherah is the goddess and not merely her cult symbol, in Judg. 3.7; 1 Kgs 15.13, 18.19; 2 Kgs 21.7, 23.4. The fact that Asherah frequently has the definite article in Hebrew (*hā'ᵃšērâ*) does not matter, since we likewise find Baal referred to regularly as 'the Baal' (*habba'al*) in the Old Testament, and similarly even 'the Tammuz' (*hattammûz*) for Tammuz (Ezek. 8.14).

The first passage to be considered is 2 Kgs 23.4. Here, as part of the account of Josiah's reform, we read that 'the king commanded...to bring out of the temple of the Lord all the vessels made for Baal, for Asherah, and for all the host of heaven'. Since Asherah is referred to in between allusions to Baal and the host of heaven, both of which were worshipped as divinities (cf. v. 5, for example), it would be extremely forced not to understand Asherah here as the name of a deity likewise.[5] The fact that 2 Kgs 23.6 refers to 'the Asherah' cult object does not detract from this, since the latter was clearly a symbol of the former, as the fact that they both occur in comparable contexts in the Old Testament indicates.

Josiah's reform measures very much stand in contrast to the religious policies adopted a little earlier by King Manasseh. Interestingly, Asherah features there too. 2 Kgs 21.7 condemns Manasseh's putting in the Temple 'the graven image of Asherah that he had made'. Here it makes excellent sense to understand *pesel hā'ᵃšērâ* as 'the graven image of [the goddess] Asherah'. Although it would be theoretically possible to

Beitrag zur semitschen Religonsgeschichte (Leipzig: J.C. Hinrichs, 1902); W.F. Albright, 'The Evolution of the West-Semitic Divinity 'An-'Anat-'Attâ', *AJSL* 41 (1925), pp. 73-101 (100).

4. A. Kuenen, *The Religion of Israel*, I (trans. A.H. May; London: Williams & Norgate, 1874), pp. 88-93.

5. *Contra* Mark S. Smith, *The Early History of God* (San Francisco: Harper & Row, 1990), p. 91; J.M. Hadley, *The Cult of Asherah in Ancient Israel and Judah: Evidence for a Hebrew Goddess* (UCOP, 57; Cambridge: Cambridge University Press, 2000), pp. 71-72.

render the phrase as 'the image of the Asherah [cult object]',[6] this would be highly odd, since we would then have a reference to the image of a symbol, namely an image of what was in effect already a kind of image, though also clearly distinguished from a *pesel* elsewhere.

A further passage where the only natural interpretation is to take Asherah as the name of a goddess is 1 Kgs 15.13 (cf. parallel in 2 Chron. 15.16), where we read that King Asa 'removed Maacah his mother from being queen mother because she had a horrid thing (*mipleṣet*) made for Asherah; and Asa cut down her horrid thing and burned it at the brook Kidron'. Although we cannot be sure exactly what the 'horrid thing' was, it must have been some kind of idolatrous object dedicated to the goddess Asherah,[7] for the only alternative would be to suppose that the text was referring to an idolatrous object made for the Asherah [cult object], which would imply an idolatrous object made for another idolatrous object, which does not seem very plausible.[8]

Yet another verse where it is indubitable that Asherah is the name of a goddess, not merely a cult object, is 1 Kgs 18.19, where Elijah is said to have commanded 'the four hundred and fifty prophets of Baal and the four hundred prophets of Asherah' to come to the contest on Mt Carmel. The parallelism of Asherah with Baal can mean only that a divine name is intended. It is true that the reference to the prophets of Asherah is probably an addition to the original text, as many scholars believe, for they play no role in the subsequent account of the ordeal on Mt Carmel, and the words are marked with an asterisk in the Hexapla, implying that they were not an original part of the Septuagint text.[9] It is

6. So Mark S. Smith, *The Early History of God*, p. 90.

7. Most likely an anthropomorphic image of the goddess, as in 2 Kgs 21.7. Curiously, the Vulgate says here that Asa removed his mother *ne esset princeps in sacris Priapi, et in luco eius quem consecraverat*, implying that a phallic symbol is being referred to, and this understanding has been followed by E. Lipiński, 'The Goddess Aṯirat in ancient Arabia, in Babylon, and in Ugarit', *OLP* 3 (1972), pp. 101-19 (113). But there is no evidence for this view, and in any case, it would be odd for a female deity to be symbolized by a male sexual organ.

8. Mark S. Smith does not consider this passage in *The Early History of God*, pp. 88-94, when rejecting the idea that Asherah can be a goddess in the Old Testament.

9. R. Patai, *The Hebrew Goddess* (Detroit: Wayne State University Press, 3rd edn, 1990), p. 43, supposes that the prophets of Asherah are not subsequently mentioned because Elijah had no quarrel with them, unlike with the prophets of Baal, but this seems unlikely in the current context.

also true, as Mark Smith notes,[10] that we would expect the Tyrian Baal to be paired with Astarte rather than Asherah, for the allusion to be historically accurate. However, having said that, it is clear that whoever added the reference to the prophets of Asherah to the text, presumably in the postexilic period, must have understood Asherah to be a divine name, which implies continued awareness of this goddess amongst the Jews at this relatively late date. This does not make sense unless Asherah had been worshipped as a goddess in ancient Israel.

A further place where Asherah appears as a divine name in the Old Testament is Judg. 3.7, where it occurs in the plural form 'Asheroth': 'And the people of Israel did what was evil in the sight of the Lord, forgetting the Lord their God, and serving the Baals and the Asheroth'. The parallelism with 'the Baals' makes it undeniable that a divine reference was intended by 'the Asheroth'. Some scholars prefer to read 'the Ashtaroth' rather than 'the Asheroth' here,[11] which is found parallel with 'the Baals' in Judg. 2.13, 10.6; 1 Sam. 7. 3, 4, and 12.10. Both the Peshiṭta and the Vulgate, as well as two Hebrew manuscripts, actually presuppose 'the Ashtaroth' in Judg. 3.7. However, the fact that 'the Asheroth' is the *lectio difficilior* makes it more likely that this was the original reading. That is to say, the presence of 'the Ashtaroth' parallel with 'the Baals' elsewhere makes it easier to understand how 'the Asheroth' could have become corrupted here to 'the Ashtaroth' than the other way round. The fact that it is the latest of the versions, the Peshiṭta and the Vulgate, which presuppose 'the Ashtaroth', whereas the earlier Septuagint (and Targum) presuppose 'the Asheroth' only serves to support the point being made here. Although the name Asherah here appears in the plural—whether denoting various local manifestations of Asherah or Canaanite goddesses generally is not clear—the parallelism with 'the Baals' (likewise denoting either local manifestations of Baal or Canaanite gods generally) clearly implies that Asherah was understood as a divine name. Even if those are right who see 'the Ashtaroth' as the original reading, which does not seem likely, this still implies that whoever altered the text in the postexilic period understood Asherah to be a divine name, thus attesting continuing awareness of Asherah as a goddess at a relatively late date.[12]

10. Mark S. Smith, *The Early History of God*, pp. 89-90.

11. E.g. S.A. Wiggins, *A Reassessment of 'Asherah'* (AOAT, 235; Kevelaer: Verlag Butzon & Bercker; Neukirchen–Vluyn: Neukirchener Verlag, 1993), p. 102.

12. Mark S. Smith, *The Early History of God*, pp. 91-92, does not emend the

There can therefore be no doubt that there are several places in the Old Testament where the word 'Asherah' denotes the goddess herself, and not simply the cult symbol of Asherah. Nor does there seem to be support from any of the deuteronomistic passages for the view of Judith Hadley that '*perhaps by the time of dtr*, and certainly the Chronicler, the term had ceased to be used with any knowledge of the goddess whom it had originally represented' (my italics).[13] However, with regard to the Chronicler, Hadley is probably correct. On the other hand, C. Frevel[14] is probably wrong in thinking that the Chronicler elsewhere *deliberately* eliminated references to the goddess Asherah in his work. It seems more likely that by the time when the Chronicler was writing, c. 300 BCE, awareness of a goddess Asherah had simply faded away from the Jewish consciousness. The Chronicler has eight allusions to the Asherim (2 Chron. 14.2 [ET 3], 17.6, 24.18, 31.1, 33.19, 34.3, 4, 7) and two to the Asheroth (2 Chron. 19.3, 33.3), both referring to idolatrous cult objects, with seemingly no difference in meaning between the masculine and feminine forms (cf. 2 Chron. 33.3 and 19). In only one instance does the Chronicler use the singular form 'Asherah', in connection with Asa's mother (2 Chron. 15.16). In this instance, the Masoretic pointing (*la'ᵃšērâ*) indicates a goddess ('for Asherah'), but of course, we cannot be certain that the pointing is correct, and with a slight emendation of the pointing we could read *lā'ᵃšērâ* 'for the Asherah', which is probably what the Chronicler intended, as it would bring it into line with the ten other instances in the Chronicler, where the Asherim or Asheroth are cult objects. If Frevel is correct and the Chronicler was deliberately omitting all references to the goddess Asherah, one would have expected him not to retain the ambiguous singular form 'Asherah' in 2 Chron. 15.16. The other instances where the goddess Asherah appears in the Chronicler's *Vorlage* in the book of Kings but does not appear as such in Chronicles (2 Kgs 21.7, 23.4, and

Asheroth to Ashtaroth, but thinks that the term 'Asheroth' (which he understands to denote goddesses generally) may reflect a telescoping of the second-millennium goddess Asherah and the first-millennium goddess Astarte. However, as I show in this chapter, the goddess Asherah was not unknown in the first millennium BCE too, and Smith's explanation surely still implies an awareness of the goddess Asherah in Israel.

13. Hadley, *The Cult of Asherah*, pp. 62-63.

14. C. Frevel, 'Die Elimination der Göttin aus dem Weltbild des Chronisten', *ZAW* 103 (1991), pp. 263-71.

possibly 7) are probably therefore not the object of deliberate suppression. Manasseh's *pesel hā'ašērâ* 'image of Asherah' of 2 Kgs 21.7 has become *pesel hassemel* 'the image of the idol' in 2 Chron. 33.7 (cf. *hassemel* again in v. 15), which certainly does suggest that the Chronicler was unaware of the goddess Asherah. As for the Chronicler's omission of the references to the goddess Asherah in 2 Kgs 23.4, and possibly 7, this need hardly be deliberate suppression, since Chronicles' account of Josiah's reform is in any case greatly abbreviated when compared to Kings.

The general consensus is that the goddess Asherah in the Old Testament is to be equated with the goddess Athirat known from the second-millennium Ugaritic texts. This is indeed the natural assumption. The phonetic equivalence of the names is clear enough, and the word *'šrt* perhaps used of the goddess in the inscriptions from Philistine Ekron (Tel Miqne)[15] and presumably lying behind *'šrth* 'his Asherah' in the Hebrew inscriptions from Kuntillet 'Ajrud and Khirbet el-Qom (see below), is the expected intermediate form. It would be very odd if these equivalent forms did not denote the same deity, because we would then have a prominent Canaanite deity in the Ugaritic texts with no equivalent in the Old Testament, when the other major Canaanite deities are so attested, and a different Canaanite deity in the Old Testament not attested in the Ugaritic texts, when the other ones found there are! Further, Athirat was El's wife in the Ugaritic texts, and we know that Yahweh was equated with El, so it would be entirely expected for Yahweh to have appropriated El's wife. Thirdly, Athirat was the mother of the gods at Ugarit, and on four occasions Asherah is mentioned alongside 'the host of heaven' in the Old Testament (2 Kgs 17.16, 21.31 [= 2 Chron. 33.3], 23.4, 6-7), who, we know, corresponded to the sons of God (originally sons of El); compare Job 38.7, where 'the morning stars' stand parallel to 'all the sons of God' (cf. *KTU*[2] 1.10.I.3-4). Fourthly, as we shall see below, we have evidence that both Athirat and Asherah were symbolized by a stylized tree.

15. See the preliminary reports of S. Gitin, 'Ekron of the Philistines. II. Olive-Oil Suppliers to the World', *BARev* 16.2 (1990), pp. 33-42, 59 (59 n. 18), and 'Seventh Century B.C.E. Cultic Elements at Ekron', in J. Aviram (ed.), *Biblical Archaeology Today, 1990* (Jerusalem: Israel Exploration Society, 1993), pp. 248-58. Two inscriptions possibly mention Asherah, one having *qdš l'šrt* 'dedicated to Asherah' and the other *l'šrt* 'for Asherah'. Hadley, *The Cult of Asherah*, pp. 179-84, however, notes the possibility that *'šrt* here might mean 'shrine'.

It is therefore hypercritical of A. Caquot[16] to claim that Athirat and Asherah have nothing in common but their names, or for T. Binger[17] to feel that we have insufficient evidence to support their being the same goddess. The most detailed critique of the equation of Athirat and Asherah, however, comes from K.-H. Bernhardt.[18] First, he notes that at Ugarit Athirat's role is essentially that of mother of the gods, whereas in the Old Testament Asherah is a fertility goddess. However, we have already noted that the mention of 'the host of heaven' alongside Asherah in several Old Testament references may imply her position as mother of the gods; further, with regard to her fertility aspect, it may be noted that Athirat is sometimes called Qudshu in the Ugaritic texts (*qdš*, cf. *KTU*^{2} 1.16.I.11, 22), and second-millennium BCE representations of Qudshu (roughly contemporary with the Ugaritic texts) have been found in Egypt that show her to have been a fertility goddess of erotic character;[19] comparable representations of Qudshu from the second millennium have also been found in Syria and Palestine.[20] All this shows that Athirat was a fertility goddess, even though this is not emphasized in the Ugaritic texts. Secondly, Bernhardt notes that in the Ugaritic texts Athirat is the consort of El, whereas in the Old Testament Asherah is several times mentioned alongside Baal. However, as we shall see later, the Old Testament's association of Asherah with Baal is probably a polemical move to discredit her—it implies guilt by association—whereas in fact other evidence suggests she was regarded as Yahweh's consort by many Israelites, and this was probably an appropriation from El. Finally, Bernhardt points out that Athirat is referred to as 'Lady Athirat of the sea' at Ugarit, whereas there is no allusion to Asherah having any connection with the sea in the Old Testament. However, this is a rather weak argument from silence, bearing in mind how little the Old Testament tells us about Asherah anyway.

16. A. Caquot, in A. Caquot, M. Sznycer and A. Herdner, *Textes Ougaritiques*, I (Paris: Cerf, 1974), p. 71, though he concedes that there may ultimately have been some connection.

17. T. Binger, *Asherah: Goddesses in Ugarit, Israel and the Old Testament* (JSOTSup, 232; Sheffield: Sheffield Academic Press, 1997), pp. 147-48.

18. K. Bernhardt, 'Aschera in Ugarit und im Alten Testament', *MIO* 13 (1967), pp. 163-74.

19. Cf. *ANEP*, plates 470-74.

20. Cf. J.B. Pritchard, *Palestinian Figurines in Relation to Certain Goddesses Known through Literature* (New Haven: American Oriental Society, 1943), pp. 33-42.

Yahweh and his Asherah in the Kuntillet 'Ajrud and Khirbet el-Qom Texts

What has most contributed to the revival of interest in Asherah and inspired the great flurry of publications on the subject in recent years has been the discovery of inscriptions from both Kuntillet 'Ajrud and Khirbet el-Qom referring to 'Yahweh and his Asherah'. Debate has particularly centred on the question whether Asherah in these texts refers to the goddess or her wooden cult symbol, the Asherah, and whether or not they imply that Asherah functioned as Yahweh's consort.

First, I shall discuss the inscriptions from Kuntillet 'Ajrud, whose name means 'the solitary hill of the water-wells', and which is located in north-east Sinai about fifty miles south of 'Ain el-Qudeirat (sometimes identified with Kadesh-Barnea). On one of the pithoi found there, pithos A, are the words *brkt. 'tkm. lyhwh. šmrn. wl'šrth*, 'I have blessed you by Yahweh of Samaria and his Asherah'. It was originally proposed by the excavator Z. Meshel[21] that *šmrn* be rendered 'our guardian', but it has now become generally accepted[22] that this is rather the place name 'Samaria'. What has led to this preference is the fact that another of the pithoi from Kuntillet 'Ajrud, pithos B, refers to *yhwh tmn w'šrth* 'Yahweh of Teman and his Asherah', Teman being a region in Edom (cf. Hab. 3.3), suggesting that *šmrn* is another place name.

It is generally agreed that Yahweh's Asherah is also mentioned in inscription 3 from grave II at Khirbet el-Qom, which is situated about 12 km. West of Hebron. It has been dated to about 750 BCE by Dever and Lemaire[23] and to about 700 BCE by Cross.[24] There has been some disagreement as to the precise reading of the inscription,[25] but I here

21. Z. Meshel, *Kuntillet 'Ajrud: A Religious Centre from the Time of the Judaean Monarchy on the Border of Sinai* (Catalogue no. 175; Jerusalem: Israel Museum, 1978). There are no page numbers!

22. Following M. Gilula, 'To Yahweh Shomron and his Asherah', *Shnaton* 3 (1978–79), pp. 129-37 (Hebrew); Emerton, 'New Light on Israelite Religion', pp. 2-3. Meshel now accepts this rendering, cf. M. Weinfeld, 'Discussion of Z. Meshel's two Publications of 1978 and 1979', *Shnaton* 4 (1980), pp. 280-84 (284) (Hebrew).

23. W.G. Dever, 'Iron Age Epigraphic Material from the Area of Khirbet el-Kôm', *HUCA* 40–41 (1969–70), pp. 139-204 (165-67); A. Lemaire, 'Les inscriptions de Khirbet el-Qôm et l'Ashérah de Yhwh', *RB* 84 (1977), pp. 595-608 (602-603).

24. According to Dever, 'Iron Age Epigraphic Material', p. 165 n. 53.

25. In addition to the articles by Dever and Lemaire cited in n. 23, and to

follow the transcription of Judith Hadley, who has examined the inscription at first hand.[26]

1 *’ryhw. h‘šr. ktbh*
2 *brk. ’rhw. lyhwh*
3 *wmṣryh l’šrth hwš‘lh*
4 *l’nyhw*
5 *l’šrth*
6 *wl’??rth*

This should probably be translated as follows:

1 Uriah the rich wrote it.
2 Blessed be Uriah by Yahweh,
3 yea from his enemies by his Asherah he has saved him
4 by Oniah
5 by his Asherah
6 and by his A[she]rah.

Some such rendering would now be widely agreed. There is no necessity to emend the text, as Lemaire did, in order to obtain the reference to Yahweh's Asherah.[27]

Debate has centred on whether we should understand Yahweh's Asherah to refer to the goddess Asherah or her wooden cult symbol, the Asherah. Especially in the early days after the Kuntillet ‘Ajrud discoveries it was supposed that the drawings on pithos A underneath the inscription actually depict the deities Yahweh and Asherah. There we find pictured on the far right a lyre player and to the left two other figures resembling each other; the latter were first identified by M. Gilula[28] as respectively Yahweh and the goddess Asherah. However, this view is now widely rejected, especially following the careful study

Hadley's work, cited in n. 26, see e.g. P.D. Miller, ‘Psalms and Inscriptions’, in J.A. Emerton (ed.), *Congress Volume, Vienna 1980* (VTSup, 32; Leiden: E.J. Brill, 1981), pp. 311-32 (315-20); S. Mittmann, ‘Die Grabinschrift des Sängers Uriahu’, *ZDPV* 97 (1981), pp. 139-52; Z. Zevit, ‘The Khirbet el-Qôm Inscription Mentioning a Goddess’, BASOR 255 (1984), pp. 39-47; Wiggins, *A Reassessment of ‘Asherah’*, pp. 106-71.

26. See Hadley, *The Cult of Asherah*, pp. 84-105 (see esp. 86).

27. See n. 23. Lemaire transposed *l’šrth* from after *wmṣryh* to before it, thus arriving at the translation, ‘...Blessed be Uriah by Yahweh and by his Asherah; from his enemies he has saved him...’

28. Gilula, ‘To Yahweh Shomron and his Asherah’, pp. 129-37.

of P. Beck,[29] who showed that the two similar figures are very likely to be equated with the god Bes, in which case they have nothing to do with the inscription. In any case, as Emerton[30] notes, it would be odd for there to be three figures depicted when only two are mentioned.[31]

Granted that the deities Yahweh and Asherah are not depicted on pithos A from Kuntillet ʻAjrud, a number of scholars have still supposed that ʻYahweh and his Asherah' refers to Yahweh and the goddess Asherah. The big obstacle that this view has to overcome is that in ancient Hebrew idiom personal names do not take pronominal suffixes; accordingly, Asherah could appropriately be ʻthe Asherah' but not simply the goddess ʻAsherah'. Attempts to circumvent this argument have been made in various ways. For instance, it has been noted that some other Semitic languages allow a personal name to take a pronominal suffix.[32] But the fact remains that this is nowhere clearly attested in Hebrew itself, so it is more natural to see a reference to the Asherah cult object.[33] It has occasionally been suggested that we can

29. P. Beck, ʻThe Drawings from Ḥorvat Teiman (Kuntillet ʻAjrud)', *Tel Aviv* 9 (1982), pp. 3-68 (27-31).

30. Emerton, ʻNew Light on Israelite Religion', p. 10.

31. W.G. Dever, ʻAsherah, Consort of Yahweh? New Evidence from Kuntillet ʻAjrud', *BASOR* 255 (1984), pp. 21-27, proposed that Asherah was symbolized by the lyre player. However, since Bes was associated with music we have a more immediate explanation of the lyre player, and since Dever accepts that the two figures to the left depict Bes, there seems no reason to think that the lyre player denotes Asherah.

32. E.g. M.D. Coogan, ʻCanaanite Origins and Lineage: Reflections on the Religion of Ancient Israel', in P.D. Miller, P.D. Hanson, S. Dean McBride (eds.), *Ancient Israelite Religion: Essays in Honor of Frank Moore Cross* (Philadelphia: Fortress Press, 1987), pp. 115-24 (118-19); Dietrich and Loretz, *ʻJahwe und seine Aschera'*, pp. 98-10; P. Xella, ʻLe dieu et "sa" déesse: L'utilisation des suffixes pronominaux avec des théonymes d'Ebla à Ugarit et à Kuntillet ʻAjrud', *UF* 27 (1995), pp. 599-610.

33. The arguments have been spelled out particularly thoroughly by Emerton, ʻNew Light on Israelite Religion', and more recently in ʻ"Yahweh and his Asherah": The Goddess or her Symbol?', *VT* 49 (1999), pp. 315-37. In addition, the view that the Asherah cult object is in mind has been followed by such scholars as Lemaire, ʻLes inscriptions', p. 607; J. Day, ʻAsherah in the Hebrew Bible and Northwest Semitic Literature', *JBL* 105 (1986), pp. 385-408 (392); J.H. Tigay, *You Shall Have no other Gods: Israelite Religion in the Light of Hebrew Inscriptions* (HSS, 31; Atlanta: Scholars Press, 1986), pp. 26-30; S.M. Olyan, *Asherah and the Cult of Yahweh in Israel* (SBLMS, 34; Atlanta: Scholars Press, 1988), pp. 25-34;

retain a reference to the goddess by reading 'Yahweh and Ashirta' as in the name of the king Abdi-Ashirta known from the el-Amarna tablets, or as 'Yahweh and Asherata',[34] implying a double feminine ending. However, both of these minority suggestions are improbable, as they are never attested in the Hebrew Bible.

We must therefore accept the translation 'Yahweh and his Asherah' and favour the view that the Asherah cult symbol rather than the goddess Asherah directly is the source of blessing alongside Yahweh. That this is a feasible concept is suggested by various analogies that have been brought forward. For example, in Neo-Assyrian letters we sometimes find the salutation 'May (the city) Uruk and (the temple) Eanna bless my lord', and in an inscription from Byblos, possibly from the first century CE (*KAI* 12.3-4), something is dedicated 'To our Lord and the image of Baal', and it goes on, 'May they bless and keep him [the donor] alive'. Similarly, at Elephantine we read of a Jew swearing 'by the temple and by Anat-Yahu' (*AP* 44.3), and swearing by the temple and by the altar is attested in rabbinic sources (*m. Ket.* 2.9; *m. Ned.* 1.3; *m. Ker.* 1.7; *b. Qidd.* 71A), as well as by the New Testament in Mt. 23.16-22, which also speaks of swearing by the gold of the temple.

Interestingly, as will be seen in the next section, there is considerable cumulative evidence that the Asherah had the nature of a stylized tree, and pithos A from Kuntillet 'Ajrud actually depicts a stylized tree flanked by two ibexes, and this probably illustrates the Asherah alluded to in the inscription.

What Was the Asherah?

At some point, perhaps about the time of the exile, the cult of Asherah disappeared among the Jews as absolute monotheism became solidified.

Mark S. Smith, *The Early History of God*, pp. 85-88; O. Keel and C. Uehlinger, *Göttinnen, Götter und Gottessymbole* (Freiburg: Herder, 1992), pp. 259-63; ET *Gods, Goddesses, and Images of God* (trans. T.H. Trapp; Minneapolis: Fortress Press, 1998), pp. 28-32; Wiggins, *A Reassessment of 'Asherah'*, pp. 170-81; Hadley, *The Cult of Asherah*, pp. 104-105, 124-25.

34. The former suggestion was made by A. Angerstorfer, 'Ašerah als "Consort of Jahwe" oder Aširtah?', *BN* 17 (1982), pp. 7-16, and the latter by Zevit, 'The Khirbet el-Qôm Inscription', pp. 45-46; R.S. Hess, 'Yahweh and his Asherah? Epigraphic Evidence for Religious Pluralism in Old Testament Times', in A.D. Clarke and B.W. Winter (eds.), *One God, One Lord in a World of Religious Pluralism* (Cambridge: Tyndale House, 1991), pp. 5-33 (15-16).

Eventually the Jews seem to have forgotten what exactly the Asherah was. The view that we find in the Septuagint and the Mishnah is that the Asherim were living trees. Thus, the Septuagint generally translated 'Asherah' as 'grove' (ἄλσος), and this was followed by the Vulgate (*nemus*), and hence the well-known rendering of the Authorized Version, 'grove'. For the Mishnah the Asherim were likewise living trees which were worshipped, for example, grapevines, pomegranates, walnuts, myrtle, and willows (cf. *m. 'Or.* 1.7; *m. Suk.* 3. 1-3; *m. 'Abod. Zar.* 3.7, 9, 10; *m. Me'il* 3.8). However, various Old Testament allusions argue against this and suggest that the Asherim were rather man-made cultic objects. Thus, the Old Testament often speaks of the making (*'āśâ*) of Asherim (1 Kgs 14.15, 16.33; 2 Kgs 17.16, 21.3, 7; 2 Chron. 33.3), as well as the building (*bānâ*, 1 Kgs 14.23) and erection (*nāṣab*, 2 Kgs 17.10) of them. Further, Jer. 17.2 makes mention of 'their Asherim, beside every luxuriant[35] tree' and 1 Kgs 14.23 and 2 Kgs 17.10 speak of the Asherim as 'under every luxuriant tree', which is odd if the Asherim were themselves living trees.

As a result of the above points, the view that the Asherim were living trees is not much held at the present time. Nevertheless, A. Lemaire[36] still maintains this view. He argues[37] that the verb *'āśâ* was very broad in usage and was able to be used of a feast, the golden calves and the high places in 1 Kgs 12.32. However, one may reply that to speak of making a tree would be something more difficult to conceive than any of the above. J.E. Taylor[38] has recently argued that the Asherim were pruned living trees, and thinks that the verb *'āśâ* is not incompatible with such, which is more conceivable. Again, both Lemaire and Taylor argue[39] that the verbs *bānâ* and *nāṣab* were only really appropriately used in connection with the high places and sacred pillars, but if this were so one would have expected a different verb to be used with the

35. Not 'green'. See D.W. Thomas, 'Some Observations on the Hebrew Word רַעֲנָן', in B. Hartmann et al. (eds.), *Hebräische Wortforschung: Festschrift zum 80. Geburtstag von Walter Baumgartner* (VTSup, 16; Leiden: E.J. Brill, 1967), pp. 387-97.

36. Lemaire, 'Les inscriptions', pp. 603-608.

37. Lemaire, 'Les inscriptions', p. 606.

38. J.E. Taylor, 'The Asherah, the Menorah and the Sacred Tree', *JSOT* 66 (1995), pp. 29-54.

39. Lemaire, 'Les inscriptions', p. 606; J.E. Taylor, 'The Asherah, the Menorah and the Sacred Tree', pp. 35-36.

Asherim. It is therefore more natural to suppose that the Asherim were objects which could rightly be spoken of as being built or erected, which would not be true of a living tree, whether pruned or otherwise.

One text that might appear to support the view that the Asherah was or could sometimes be an actual living tree is Deut. 16.21, 'You shall not plant any kind of tree [or wood] as an Asherah beside the altar of the Lord your God which you shall make'. However, the verb *nṭ'* 'to plant' is not confined to living trees, but is used also of nails in Eccles. 12.11, a tent in Dan. 11. 45, and people in Jer. 24.6, 32.31; Ps. 44.3 (ET 2). Further, the word *'ēṣ* can mean 'wood' as well as 'tree'. Nevertheless, the combination of 'plant' and *'ēṣ* is suggestive of a tree. I shall be arguing below that the Asherim were stylized trees, and there seems no reason why the language of Deut. 16.21 should not be as applicable to such objects as to living trees.

An unusual position has been put forward by Lipiński.[40] He believes that the Asherah is sometimes a grove and sometimes a shrine. However, this is extremely forced, since examples of what Lipiński believes to represent each of the two meanings are found in comparable contexts, for example, 2 Kgs 18.4, 23.14, 15, where Asherah is alleged to mean 'grove' and 1 Kgs 14.23, 2 Kgs 17.10, where Asherah is claimed to mean 'shrine'. This indicates that Asherah has only one meaning in these passages. Since the former group of passages alludes to the cutting down of the Asherah, a shrine cannot be meant (and Lipiński does not deny this), while the latter group of passages mention Asherim as being under every luxuriant tree, which suggests that the Asherim there are not trees. Since, as we have noted, the Asherah must refer to the same entity in both sets of passages, it follows that the Asherah can be neither a grove nor a shrine.

A further suggestion as to the nature of the Asherim was put forward by W.L. Reed in 1949.[41] He proposed that they are to be understood simply as images of the goddess Asherah. However, though the evidence suggests that they symbolized the goddess Asherah in some way, they do not appear to have been simply images of her, since the Asherim are mentioned several times alongside *p^esîlîm* 'graven images' (which include images of wood) in the Old Testament as distinct objects (cf. Deut. 7.5, 12.3; Mic. 5.12-13 [ET 13-14]; 2 Chron. 33.7, 19, 34.3, 4, 7).

40. Lipiński, 'The Goddess Aṯirat', pp. 112-14.

41. W.L. Reed, *The Asherah in the Old Testament* (Fort Worth: Texas Christian University Press, 1949).

This is not to deny that there were anthropomorphic images of the goddess Asherah. This is the most natural meaning of *pesel hā'ᵃšērâ* 'image of Asherah' in 2 Kgs 21.7 (cf. 2 Chron. 33.15). Further, Asherah is attested iconographically in anthropomorphic form in various plaque and pendant images[42] and it is now widely thought that she is depicted on the so-called pillar figurines.[43] The latter, mostly discovered in Judah, and especially common in the eighth and seventh centuries BCE, have a pillar base, with the female figure grasping her prominent breasts, suggestive of a fertility goddess. J.R. Engle[44] believes that these pillar figurines are what is meant when the Old Testament speaks of Asherim in the plural, especially in Chronicles, and the Asherah in the singular denotes a larger statue of the goddess. However, this theory is certainly to be rejected. It is arbitrary to distinguish between the singular and plural forms of the word Asherah in this way, the verbs used in connection with the destruction of the Asherim indicate a wooden, not a pottery object, and the Asherim are represented as part of the syncretistic public worship in the Old Testament, whereas the pillar figurines are mostly found in private houses. Further, there is the point noted above that on several occasions the Asherim are clearly distinguished from images *per se*.[45]

Often throughout the last century or so the Asherah has been spoken of as some kind of pole.[46] One might perhaps compare Philo of Byblos, who mentions that the Phoenicians 'consecrated pillars and staves (ῥάβδους) after their names [i.e. of the gods]' (Eusebius, *Praeparatio Evangelica* 1.9.29; cf. 1.10.10). However, there has been growing evidence in recent years that enables us to be more precise and specify that the Asherah was not simply a bare pole but more specifically a stylized tree. Several depictions of stylized trees have been plausibly equated

42. See, for example, the depictions on gold and electrum pendants from Ugarit and Minet el-Beida in R. Hestrin, 'The Lachish Ewer and the 'Asherah', *IEJ* 37 (1987), pp. 212-23 (217).

43. See most recently the detailed and thorough study of R. Kletter, *The Judean Pillar-Figurines and the Archaeology of Asherah* (British Archaeological Reports, International Series, 636; Oxford: Tempus Reparatum, 1996).

44. J.R. Engle, 'Pillar Figurines of Iron Age Asherah/Asherim' (PhD dissertation, University of Pittsburgh, 1979).

45. There is a good critique of Engle's thesis in Hadley, *The Cult of Asherah*, pp. 196-205, some of whose criticisms I have taken up above.

46. E.g. W. Robertson Smith, *The Religion of the Semites*, p. 188; Patai, *The Hebrew Goddess*, p. 39.

with the Asherah. On pithos A from Kuntillet ʿAjrud containing a reference to a blessing by Yahweh of Samaria and his Asherah we have a depiction of a stylized tree flanked by two ibexes—the scenes being placed above a standing lion—and R. Hestrin and J.M. Hadley have plausibly argued that this denotes the Asherah.[47]

Again, a ewer from Lachish dating from the late thirteenth century BCE contains a picture consisting of a row of animals and trees. The best preserved tree is one on the right flanked by two ibexes, and this motif is found elsewhere on the ewer. (The first of the animals is a lion, known elsewhere as a symbol of Asherah.) Above and between the picture is a Canaanite alphabetic inscription *mtn. šy l[rb]ty ʾlt*, 'Mattan. An offering to my Lady Elat'. Note that the word *ʾlt* (Elat) = Asherah appears directly above the drawing of the tree, thus strengthening the view that this is her symbol.[48] R. Hestrin[49] has also drawn attention to a decorated goblet from Lachish which four times depicts two ibexes flanking a pubic triangle instead of a tree, thus further strengthening the view that the tree symbolizes a fertility goddess. Hestrin also mentions some Late Bronze Age pendants from Syria and Palestine depicting a naked female with a tree or branch above the pubic triangle. Sometimes the female has a Hathor headdress characteristic of Qudshu = Asherah.

A tenth-century BCE cult stand from Taanach also has good reason to be thought to show a depiction of the Asherah.[50] The stand consists of four tiers, those appearing to relate to Asherah being the second and the fourth. The fourth tier shows a naked female, with lions standing each side of her. The second tier similarly has two flanking lions, but instead

47. Cf. Hestrin, 'The Lachish Ewer', p. 221; J.M. Hadley, 'Yahweh and "his Asherah": Archaeological and Textual Evidence for the Cult of the Goddess', in W. Dietrich and M.A. Klopfenstein (eds.), *Ein Gott allein?* (OBO, 139; Freiburg: Universitätsverlag, 1994), pp. 235-68 (248); Hadley, *The Cult of Asherah*, pp. 152-54 (with fig. 5, p. 117).

48. Hestrin, 'The Lachish Ewer', pp. 212-23, esp. pp. 212-14, with fig. 1 on p. 213.

49. Hestrin, 'The Lachish Ewer', p. 215, with fig. 2.

50. Cf. R. Hestrin, 'The Cult Stand from Taʿanach and its Religious Background', in E. Lipiński (ed.), *Phoenicia and the East Mediterranean in the First Millennium B.C.* (Phoenicia, 5; Leuven: Peeters, 1987), pp. 61-77, with fig. 1 on p. 62; J.G. Taylor, 'The Two Earliest Known Representations of Yahweh', in L. Eslinger and J.G. Taylor (eds.), *Ascribe to the Lord: Biblical and Other Studies in Memory of Peter C. Craigie* (JSOTSup, 67; Sheffield: JSOT Press, 1988), pp. 557-66; Hadley, *The Cult of Asherah*, pp. 169-76.

of the naked female there is a sacred tree between two ibexes. The connection of Asherah with the lion makes it natural to suppose that the naked female is the goddess Asherah. Since the second tier has very similar flanking lions it is natural to suppose that this relates to the same deity, and as it has a sacred tree in the place corresponding to Asherah in the fourth tier, it is natural to suppose that this is her symbol.

Further evidence which might support the equation of the Asherim with stylized trees comes from Pella in Transjordan. Here, two cult stands were fairly recently discovered, dated to about the tenth century BCE. One has depictions of two nude goddesses standing on a lion's head (cf. the lion as a symbol of Qudshu = Asherah, noted above), and the other has stylized trees on its sides.[51] Cumulatively, therefore, there is a considerable amount of evidence to suggest that the goddess Asherah could be symbolized by a stylized tree.

In this context attention should be drawn to Hos. 14.9 (ET 8), 'Ephraim, what has he[52] still to do with idols? It is I who answer and look after him. I am like a luxurious cypress, from me comes your fruit'. Yahweh is here unusually and uniquely in the Old Testament compared with a tree, and it is striking that this comes in the same context as the prophet's condemnation of idols. This combination of ideas has suggested to a number of scholars that Hosea is polemicizing against Canaanite idolatry associated with tree symbolism.[53] This at

51. Cf. T.F. Potts, in T.F. Potts, S.M. Colledge, and P.C. Edwards, 'Preliminary Report on a Sixth Season of Excavations by the University of Sydney at Pella in Jordan (1983/84)', in *Annual of the Department of Antiquities of Jordan* 29 (1985), pp. 181-210 (204), and pls. XLI-XLII on pp. 339-40. On p. 204 Potts speaks of Astarte, whilst in R.H. Smith and T.F. Potts, 'The Iron Age', in A.W. McNicoll *et al.*, *Pella in Jordan*, II (Mediterranean Archaeology Supplement, 2; Sydney: Meditarch, 1992), pp. 83-101 (99-100) (see pl. 70), he speaks of Astarte–Asherah. J.M. Hadley, whose attention I had drawn to this cult stand when it was temporarily on show in Oxford's Ashmolean Museum, discusses them in *The Cult of Asherah*, pp. 165-69, with figs. 10-12.

52. Emending *lî* to *lô* with LXX. It was Ephraim, not Yahweh, that was 'joined to idols' (Hos. 4.17).

53. E.g. H.W. Wolff, *Dodekapropheton*. I. *Hosea* (BKAT, 144.1; Neukirchen–Vluyn: Neukirchener Verlag, 2nd edn, 1965 [1961]), p. 307; ET *Hosea* (trans. G. Stansell; Hermeneia; Philadelphia: Fortress Press, 1974), p. 237, and the scholars listed in the following three footnotes.

once makes us think of the Asherah.[54] What adds strength to this idea is the presence in this context of the words 'It is I who answer and look after him', in Hebrew *'ᵃnî 'ānîtî wa'ᵃšûrennû*, which could well be a play on the names of the goddesses Anat and Asherah. J. Wellhausen[55] actually suggested that we should emend the text here to read *'ᵃnî 'ᵃnātô wa'ᵃšērātô*, 'I am his Anat and his Asherah', and a few have followed this subsequently,[56] but this is generally and rightly felt to be an overadventurous emendation lacking sufficient supporting evidence.[57] However, that there is a word play on the names of these deities is plausible enough. Hosea elsewhere has a tendency to engage in word play and interestingly the very same root *šûr* which occurs here appears also in a hostile sense in Hos. 13.7, 'like a leopard I will lurk (*'āšûr*) beside the way', and in view of the point of the allusion it is natural to see here a word play on the name of Assyria (*'aššûr*), the agent of divine judgment. In addition to Hosea's liking for word play, this understanding fits well with Hosea's tendency not simply to polemicize against Canaanitizing religion, but to appropriate its imagery for his own purposes, for example, his reuse of Baalistic death and resurrection imagery (see below, Chapter 4) and his insistence that Yahweh, not Baal, is the true fertility god (cf. Hos. 2). That Hosea should claim for Yahweh the role that the syncretists attributed to Asherah and Anat by symbolizing Yahweh as a life-giving tree in Hos. 14.9 (ET 8) would be consistent with this. This view has been criticized by S.M. Olyan[58] on the basis that a stylized tree is not the same as a living tree like the cypress, but it is possible that by comparing Yahweh to a cypress Hosea was intending to depict him as more effective than the Asherah.[59]

As I have pointed out elsewhere,[60] Hosea 13–14 was taken up by the

54. E.g. J. Day, 'Asherah', pp. 404-406, and the scholars listed in the following two footnotes.

55. J. Wellhausen, *Die kleinen Propheten übersetzt und erklärt* (Berlin: Georg Reimer, 3rd edn, 1898), p. 134.

56. E.g. G. Fohrer, 'Umkehr und Erlösung beim Propheten Hosea', *TZ* 11 (1955), pp. 161-85 (171, with n. 18); E. Jacob, in E. Jacob, C.-A. Keller, and S. Amsler, *Osée, Joël, Abdias, Amos* (CAT, 11a; Neuchâtel: Delachaux & Niestlé, 1965) pp. 95, 97.

57. See most Hosea commentaries on this passage.

58. Olyan, *Asherah and the Cult of Yahweh*, p. 21.

59. Cf. Hadley, *The Cult of Asherah*, p. 76.

60. J. Day, 'A Case of Inner Scriptural Interpretation: The Dependence of Isaiah

writer of Isaiah 26–27, which contains eight parallels, all of which except one appear in the same order.

1. Israel knows no lords/gods but Yahweh. Hos. 13.4. Cf. Isa. 26.13 (LXX).
2. Imagery of birthpangs, but child refuses to be born. Hos. 13.13. Cf. Isa. 26.17-18.
3. Deliverance from Sheol. Hos. 13.14 (LXX, etc.). Cf. Isa. 26.19.
4. Imagery of destructive east wind symbolic of exile. Hos. 13.15. Cf. Isa. 27.8.
5. Imagery of life-giving dew. Hos. 14.6 (ET 5). Cf. Isa. 26.19.
6. Israel blossoming and like a vineyard. Hos. 14.6-8 (ET 5-7). Cf. Isa. 27.2-6.
7. Condemnation of idolatry, including the Asherim. Hos. 14.9 (ET 8). Cf. Isa. 27.9.
8. The importance of discernment: judgment for the wicked. Hos. 14.10 (ET 9). Cf. Isa. 27.11.

Interestingly, the writer of the so-called Isaiah apocalypse detected a reference to the Asherah in Hos. 14.9 (ET 8), as his negative judgment in Isa. 27.9 indicates. One may grant the point made by S.M. Olyan and C. Frevel[61] that the dependence of Isa. 27.9 on Hos. 14.9 (ET 8) does not prove that the writer of Isa. 27.9 was correct to detect an allusion to Asherah in the Hoseanic passage, but in the light of the arguments which I have put forward above I believe that he was.

Did Asherah Function as Yahweh's Consort?

A question which has much exercised the minds of scholars, especially since the discovery of the texts at Kuntillet 'Ajrud and Khirbet el-Qom, is whether the goddess Asherah functioned as Yahweh's consort in the syncretistic Israelite circles which worshipped her. Opinion has been

xxvi.13–xxvii.11 on Hosea xiii.4–xiv.10 (ET 9) and its Relevance to some Theories of the Redaction of the "Isaiah Apocalypse"', *JTS* NS 31 (1980), pp. 309-19; reprinted (with minor revisions) in C.C. Broyles and C.A. Evans (eds.), *Writing and Reading the Scroll of Isaiah: Studies of an Interpretive Tradition*, I (VTSup, 70.1; Leiden: E.J. Brill, 1997), pp. 357-68; J. Day, 'Asherah', pp. 404-406.

61. Olyan, *Asherah and the Cult of Yahweh*, p. 21; C. Frevel, *Aschera und der Ausschließlichkeitsanspruch YHWHs* (BBB, 94.1; 2 vols.; Weinheim: Beltz Athenäum Verlag, 1995), I, p. 342.

divided on this matter, but the majority view seems to regard this as probable, and this is indeed the conclusion to which I believe the evidence points.

First of all, it is unquestionable that the Asherah cult object stood in a special relationship with Yahweh. This is clear both from the texts from Kuntillet 'Ajrud and Khirbet el-Qom referring to 'Yahweh and his Asherah', and also from the Old Testament, which attests the presence of the Asherah in Yahweh's sanctuary. For example, Deut. 16.21 declares 'You shall not plant any tree as an Asherah beside the altar of the Lord your God which you shall make'. The next verse condemns the *maṣṣēbâ*, the symbol of the male deity (here Yahweh), 'You shall not set up a pillar (*maṣṣēbâ*), which the Lord your God hates'.

Secondly, as we have seen, the Asherah cult object was clearly regarded as a symbol of the goddess Asherah. Not only the identical name, but the fact that 'Asherah' and 'the Asherah' occur in the same cultic contexts in the Old Testament (e.g. 2 Kgs 21.3, 23.4) indicates the close relationship between them. Accordingly, we may clearly speak of a close relationship not only between Yahweh and the Asherah cult object but between Yahweh and the goddess Asherah.

What was this relationship? The obvious conclusion that comes to mind is one of a god and his consort. This becomes a near certainty when we recall that in Canaanite religion Asherah was the consort of El and that the Old Testament equates Yahweh and El. As we have seen in the previous chapter, this equation led to Yahweh's appropriation of the sons of God (El), the notion of Yahweh as an aged and wise god, and also—though the Old Testament itself rejects this—the association of Yahweh with bull symbolism. Yahweh's appropriation of El's consort, Asherah, fits naturally into this schema, and like the bull symbolism, this was something which the Old Testament rejected.

If Asherah was Yahweh's consort, how then are we to explain the fact that Baal and Asherah are paired together several times in the Old Testament (e.g. Judg. 6.35, 28, 30; 1 Kgs 18.19)? It has sometimes been thought that Baal might have appropriated El's wife. However, this is never attested even once in any known extra-biblical text, and is thus to be deemed unlikely. It has sometimes been thought that the Hittite–Canaanite myth of Elkuniřsa (El) provides evidence that Asherah (Ašertu) was going awhoring after Baal (the storm god),[62] but in fact

62. E.g. Pope, *El in the Ugaritic Texts*, pp. 37, 42. I formerly took this view in 'Asherah', p. 391, but I have since changed my mind.

the storm god's sleeping with Ašertu is at Elkuniřša's (El's) command, and at the end Elkuniřša and Ašertu are clearly united, and it is Ishtar (presumably Astarte) who appears to be the storm god's wife there.[63] A more likely explanation has been offered by S.M. Olyan,[64] who argues that the pairing of Baal and Asherah was a polemical move by the Deuteronomists to discredit Asherah, associating her with the abominated deity Baal, and thus implying guilt by association.

The Etymology of Asherah

There is no complete agreement with regard to the etymology of the name Asherah, though as will be seen, one proposal does have the merit of a certain plausibility. A view that may definitely be excluded, however, is the later opinion of W.F. Albright, which has been followed widely subsequently,[65] that the common Ugaritic epithet *rbt. 'ṯrt. ym*, generally rendered 'Lady Athirat of the sea', etymologically means 'the Lady who traverses the sea', or 'the Lady who treads on the sea (dragon)'. The problem with this understanding is that it presupposes that the longer version is the original form of her name and that Athirat is a later abbreviation of it. Against this, however, stands the fact that this goddess is already known by the name Ašratum as early as the First Dynasty of Babylon (c. 1830–1531 BCE),[66] which strongly supports the originality of the short form. A more plausible explanation, which was Albright's earlier view,[67] connects the name with the Semitic root *'ṯr*

63. Cf. Olyan, *Asherah and the Cult of Yahweh*, pp. 44-45, who rightly objects to the interpretation put on the Elkuniřša by scholars such as Pope, *El in the Ugaritic Texts*, p. 37. For the Elkuniřša myth, see Otten, 'Ein Kanaanäischer Mythus', pp. 125-50 or the translation by A. Goetze in *ANET*, p. 519.

64. Cf. Olyan, *Asherah and the Cult of Yahweh*, p. 74.

65. W.F. Albright, *Yahweh and the Gods of Canaan* (London: Athlone Press, 1968), pp. 105-106; *idem*, *Archaeology and the Religion of Israel* (Garden City, NY: Doubleday, 5th edn, 1969), pp. 77-78; Cross, *Canaanite Myth and Hebrew Epic*, p. 31; M.H. Pope, 'Athirat', in H.W. Haussig (ed.), *Götter und Mythen in vorderen Orient* (Wörterbuch der Mythologie, 1.1; Stuttgart: E. Klett, 1965), pp. 246-49 (247); W.A. Maier, *'Ašerah: Extrabiblical Evidence* (HSM, 37; Atlanta: Scholars Press, 1986), pp. 194-95; N. Wyatt, 'Who Killed the Dragon?', *AulOr* 5 (1987), pp. 185-98 (185); Olyan, *Asherah and the Cult of Yahweh*, pp. 70-71.

66. Cf. E. Ebeling, 'Ašratu', *RLA*, I, p. 169.

67. Albright, 'The Evolution of the West-Semitic Divinity 'An-'Anat-'Attâ', pp. 99-100; H. Gese, in M. Gese, M. Höfner, K. Rudolph, *Die Religionen Altsyriens,*

'place', which came to denote 'holy place, sanctuary', and in this meaning is attested for Akkadian *aširtu, ešertu, iširtu, išertum, ašru* and *ašratu*, Phoenician *'šrt*, Aramaic *'tr* and *'trt'*, and Ugaritc *'aṯr*. In support it may be noted that in Ugaritic Athirat is several times referred to under the name of Qudshu (*qdš*, cf. *KTU*² 1.16.I.11, 22), which similarly means 'holiness' or 'sanctuary'. Sanctuaries are elsewhere personified as deities amongst the Semites, as in the case of the god Bethel, whose name means 'house of El'. There is much less to be said for the view of B. Margalit,[68] according to which Athirat means 'wife, consort', literally, 'she-who-follows-in-the footsteps (of her husband)', for unlike the previously mentioned suggestion, there is no clear evidence for this meaning in any Semitic language.

EXCURSUS:
UNCERTAIN AND DUBIOUS REFERENCES TO (THE) ASHERAH

Uncertain References to Asherah

Ezekiel 8.3, 5

In Ezek. 8. 3, 5 the first of the 'abominations' which Ezekiel sees in the Jerusalem temple is the 'image of jealousy' (*semel haqqin'â*). It has sometimes been hypothesized that this might be a reference to an image of the goddess Asherah,[69] especially as her image is later referred to as a *semel* in 2 Chron. 33.7, 15. This is a possibility but it must remain speculative, since we simply have no information on the identity of the deity in question.

Even if this were correct, we should certainly reject the theory of H.C. Lutzky,[70] that *semel haqqin'â* should be emended to *semel haqqōnâ* 'the image of the Creatress'. There are no adequate grounds for rejecting

Altarabiens und der Mandäer (Stuttgart: W. Kohlhammer, 1970), p. 150; J.C. de Moor, 'אֲשֵׁרָה', *ThWAT*, I, pp. 473-74 (ET *TDOT*, I, p. 438); J. Day, 'Asherah', pp. 388-89; Wiggins, *A Reassessment of 'Asherah'*, pp. 192-93.

68. B. Margalit [Margulis], 'The Meaning and Significance of Asherah', *VT* 40 (1990), pp. 264-97.

69. E.g. M. Greenberg, *Ezekiel 1–20* (AB, 22; Garden City, NY: Doubleday, 1983), p. 168.

70. H.C. Lutzky, 'On the "Image of Jealousy" (Ezekiel VIII 3, 5)', *VT* 46 (1996), pp. 121-25.

the MT, and although Asherah is called *qnyt 'ilm*, 'Creatress of the gods' in Ugaritic, it would be extraordinary for Ezekiel to refer to what was for him an abomination by such a positive sounding epithet as 'the Creatress'.

Hosea 4.12

Another possible but very uncertain allusion to the Asherah is in Hos. 4.12, where we read, 'My people inquire of a thing of wood, and their staff gives them oracles. For a spirit of harlotry has led them astray, and they have left their God to play the harlot.' It has been proposed that the parallel expressions 'a thing of wood' (*'ēṣô*) and 'their staff (*maqlô*) refer to the wooden Asherah cult object.[71] One can see the attraction of this view, since the context in Hos. 4.12-14 is clearly the Canaanitizing fertility cult and the form of the Asherah as a kind of pole might appropriately be described as 'a thing of wood' or a 'staff'. Interestingly, the LXX renders *maqlô* by ἐν ῥάβδοις αὐτοῦ, just as Philo of Byblos uses the word ῥάβδους to describe the Phoenician staves named after gods, which were noted as a possible analogy for the Asherah earlier. However, it cannot be claimed as certain that Hos. 4. 12 is referring to the Asherah.[72] It is possible that the verse is rather referring to the wooden image of a god, or, less likely, to rhabdomancy.[73]

Dubious References to Asherah

Genesis 30.13

An allusion to Asherah has occasionally been found in Gen. 30.13. The verse is generally rendered, 'And Leah said, "Happy am I (*b^e'ošrî*)! For the women will call me happy"; so she called his name Asher.' C.J. Ball,[74] however, thought that the word *b^e'ošrî* 'happy am I!' was an attempt by a later scribe to eliminate a reference to the goddess Asherah, and in this he has been followed by W.L. Reed.[75] Since this

71. This view was favoured by W. Robertson Smith, *The Religion of the Semites*, p. 196.

72. W. Rudolph, *Hosea* (KAT, 13.1; Gütersloh: Gerd Mohn, 1966), pp. 110-11 and Wolff, *Hosea*, p. 105 (ET *Hosea*, p. 84), both emphasize the wide varieties of possibilities here. Cf. J.L. Mays, *Hosea* (OTL; London: SCM Press 1969), p. 73.

73. This possibility is favoured by F.I. Andersen and D.N. Freedman, *Hosea* (AB, 24; Garden City, NY: Doubleday, 1980), p. 366.

74. C.J. Ball, 'Israel and Babylon', *PSBA* 16 (1894), pp. 188-200 (189-90).

75. Reed, *The Asherah in the Old Testament*, p. 81.

involves conjectural emendation when the text makes excellent sense as it stands (cf. too the verb *'šr* 'to call happy' later in the verse, which coheres with the traditional rendering of *b^{e}'ošrî*), the onus of proof is surely on those who wish to translate 'By Asherah's help!'

Isaiah 6.13

W.F. Albright,[76] S. Iwry,[77] T. Binger,[78] and the NEB have sought to find a reference to Asherah in Isa. 6.13. This involves changing the relative particle *'^{a}šer* to *'^{a}šērâ*, which is certainly conjectural. Both Iwry and Albright thought that the relative particle *'^{a}šer* was strange in poetry, but it is found in v. 11 and, as W.H. Brownlee pointed out, in a number of other poetic passages in Isaiah.[79]

Jeremiah 2.27

Another passage which a number of scholars have thought was referring to the Asherah is Jer. 2.27, where the prophet declares with regard to the people of Judah that they 'say to a wooden thing, "You are my father", and to a stone, "You gave me birth". For they have turned their back to me and not their face.' The proposal has been made that the wooden thing (*'ēṣ*) is a reference to the Asherah and the stone (*'eben*) alludes to the sacred pillar (*maṣṣēbâ*).[80] If this interpretation is correct

76. W.F. Albright, 'The High Place in Ancient Palestine', in *Volume du Congrès, Strasbourg 1956* (VTSup, 4; Leiden: E.J. Brill, 1957), pp. 242-58 (254-55).

77. S. Iwry, '*Maṣṣēbāh* and *bāmāh* in IQ Isaiah ^{A} 6 13', *JBL* 76 (1957), pp. 225-32.

78. Binger, *Asherah*, p. 136.

79. W.H. Brownlee, *The Meaning of the Qumrân Scrolls for the Bible with Special Attention to the Book of Isaiah* (New York: Oxford University Press, 1964), p. 238. Cf. too J.A. Emerton, 'The Translation and Interpretation of Isaiah vi. 13', in J.A. Emerton and S.C. Reif (eds.), *Interpreting the Hebrew Bible: Essays in Honour of E.I.J. Rosenthal* (UCOP, 32; Cambridge: Cambridge University Press, 1982), pp. 85-118, which offers an exhaustive survey of the interpretation of this verse, and offers further criticisms of attempts to find allusions to Asherah in this passage on pp. 102-103.

80. Cf. E. Nielsen, 'The Righteous and the Wicked in Habaqquq', *ST* 6 (1952), pp. 54-78 (63); K. Jeppesen, 'Myth in the Prophetic Literature', in B. Otzen, H. Gottlieb and K. Jeppesen, *Myths in the Old Testament* (trans. F.H. Cryer; London: SCM Press, 1980), pp. 94-123, 134-38 (137 n. 37); J.A. Thompson, *The Book of Jeremiah* (NICOT; Grand Rapids: Eerdmans, 1980), p. 180. S.M. Olyan, 'The Cultic Confession of Jer 2, 27a', *ZAW* 99 (1987), pp. 254-59, sees the masculine deity as Yahweh.

Jeremiah must have been either confused or ironical, since the Asherah was the female symbol and the *maṣṣēbâ* was the masculine symbol (whether for Baal or Yahweh). However, quite apart from the unlikelihood that Jeremiah would have been ignorant of such an elementary point, there is no reason to believe that the Asherah and *maṣṣēbâ* are being referred to here. We need only compare Hab. 2.19, 'Woe to him who says to a wooden thing, Awake; to a dumb stone, Arise! Can this give revelation? Behold it is overlaid with gold and silver, and there is no breath in it at all.' This verse is clearly speaking of images of wood and stone rather than the Asherah and *maṣṣēbâ*. (Similarly Deut. 4.28; Isa. 37.19; Ezek. 20.32.) It is likely that Jeremiah is similarly speaking of wood and stone idols rather than of the Asherah and *maṣṣēbâ* and that we are not to suppose that Jeremiah has got their genders mixed up, either due to ignorance or irony. The fact that *'ēṣ* is masculine and *'eben* is generally feminine readily accounts for the respective forms of address in Jer. 2.27.

Hosea 2.4-7, 12-14 (ET 2.2-5, 10-12)

W.D. Whitt[81] has recently put forward a new idea, according to which Hos. 2.4-7, 12-14 (ET 2.2-5, 10-12) originally referred to Yahweh's divorce[82] of the goddess Asherah. He admits that in the final form of the text as we now have it the passage refers to Yahweh's relationship with Israel rather than Asherah (e.g. Hos. 2. 16-17, 18-19, 21-22, ET 14-15, 16-17, 19-20), but claims that this is the work of later redactors. This, however, is highly speculative and without compelling evidence. As C. Frevel[83] has pointed out, Whitt's isolation of Hos. 2.4-7, 12-14 (ET 2.2-5, 10-12) as the original text is arbitrary, and too obviously depends on expunging those verses which do not fit his theory, for example, 2.15 (ET 2.13), where the woman offers incense to the Baals, which is not suggestive of a goddess. In any case, as John J. Schmitt[84] has rightly pointed out, it is most unlikely that such a fanatical mono-

81. W.D. Whitt, 'The Divorce of Yahweh and Asherah in Hos 2, 4-7. 12ff', *SJOT* 6 (1992), pp. 31-67.

82. Actually, it is doubtful whether divorce is spoken of in Hos. 2, since the whole point of Yahweh's deliberations is to win back his faithless spouse.

83. Frevel, *Aschera und der Ausschließlichkeitsanspruch YHWHs*, I, pp. 263-65. On pp. 260-72 Frevel offers many other detailed criticisms of Whitt's arguments.

84. J.J. Schmitt, 'Yahweh's Divorce in Hosea 2: Who is that Woman?' *SJOT* 9 (1995), pp. 119-32.

latrist as Hosea would have represented Asherah as being previously married to Yahweh, and as Israel's mother (v. 4, ET 2), even for the sake of an *ad hominem* argument with his opponents, for elsewhere the Old Testament simply regards her as a pagan abomination and nothing more. Indeed, as we have seen earlier, this is probably why the Deuteronomists connect her with Baal rather than Yahweh when condemning syncretism. However, Schmitt's own suggestion that the woman in Hosea 2 denotes the city of Samaria is also unlikely, for the chapter reads more naturally as referring to the people as a whole rather than simply the capital city (contrast Ezek. 16, 23, where Jerusalem and Samaria are explicitly depicted as Yahweh's wives).

Amos 8. 14

Another verse where it has been proposed that Asherah is mentioned is Amos 8.14. F. Neuberg[85] claimed that MT *b'šmt* should be emended to *b'šrt*, so that we would have to read 'Those who swear by Asherah of Samaria...' rather than 'Those who swear by the guilt of Samaria...' Neuberg supposed that *'ašmat* 'guilt' was deliberately substituted for the name of the hated goddess Asherah. However, as A. Cooper[86] has rightly said, 'Neuberg's emendation of Amos 8.14 seems gratuitous'. Further I would add that there are no known instances in the Old Testament where the name of the goddess Asherah has been deliberately altered (contrast Baal and Astarte), which tells against Neuberg's emendation here. Moreover, without intending to discuss all the problems of this notorious crux, I may point out that the deities of Dan and Beer-Sheba seem to be mentioned allusively rather than by name in this verse, so it appears more appropriate for this to be the case with regard to Samaria too.

The Personification of Wisdom in Proverbs 1–9

The final example which I shall discuss concerns not a dubious reference to Asherah as such, but rather a dubious example of alleged Asherah influence on an Old Testament figure. Mark Smith[87] has

85. F. Neuberg, 'An Unrecognized Meaning of Hebrew *dôr*', *JNES* 9 (1950), pp. 215-17 (215).

86. A. Cooper, 'Divine Names and Epithets in the Ugaritic Texts', in S. Rummel (ed.), *Ras Shamra Parallels*, III (Rome: Pontifical Biblical Institute, 1981), pp. 333-469 (347).

87. Mark S. Smith, *The Early History of God*, pp. 94-95.

recently proposed that the figure of the goddess Asherah lies behind the personification of Wisdom in Jewish thought. Both are feminine divine figures, Wisdom is connected several times in Proverbs with the tree of life (cf. Prov. 3.18, 11.30, 15.4), which one might compare with the stylized tree symbols of Asherah, and the word *'ašrê* 'blessed' appears in Prov. 3.13 and 18, one of the passages concerned with the personification of Wisdom. However, though ingenious, this proposal does not seem very convincing. Nowhere in the Ugaritic texts, Old Testament or elsewhere is the goddess Asherah associated with wisdom (unlike her Canaanite consort, the god El), the relation of Wisdom to Yahweh is more akin to that of a daughter than a wife (cf. Prov. 8.22), the tree of life seems to have been more than a stylized tree, and there is no special significance in the occurrence of the word *'ašrê* 'blessed' in Prov. 3. 13, 18, since this word is quite frequent in Proverbs and related Wisdom literature (cf. Prov. 8.32, 34, 13.21, 16.20, 20.7, 28.14, 29.18; Ps. 127.5, 128.1). The origin of the personification of Wisdom is clearly to be sought elsewhere. Since Wisdom appears to be already personified outside Israel in the Wisdom of Ahiqar, lines 94b-95, one may perhaps envisage it as an appropriation and development of the West Semitic Wisdom tradition.[88] Judith Hadley,[89] however, more modestly claims that, though not derived from Asherah, the personification of Wisdom filled the slot that had been left vacant in Jewish thought through the elimination of the goddess Asherah. If by this is meant that the female personification of Wisdom unconsciously fulfils the psychological desire for a feminine element in the deity, this might be true; if what is envisaged is a more deliberate replacement of Asherah by Wisdom, then this seems unlikely.

88. J. Day, 'Foreign Semitic Influence on the Wisdom of Israel and its Appropriation in the Book of Proverbs', in J. Day, R.P. Gordon and H.G.M. Williamson (eds.), *Wisdom in Ancient Israel: Essays in Honour of J.A. Emerton* (Cambridge: Cambridge University Press, 1995), pp. 55-70 (68-70).

89. J.M. Hadley, 'Wisdom and the Goddess', in Day, Gordon and Williamson (eds.), *Wisdom in Ancient Israel*, pp. 234-43.

Chapter 3

YAHWEH VERSUS BAAL

The Various Manifestations of Baal

Curiously, whilst in the Old Testament the name Baal occurs 58 times in the singular (always with the article), it also appears 19 times in the plural, 'the Baals' (*habbe'ālîm*). This latter form is to be found in Judg. 2.11, 13, 3.7, 8.33, 10.6, 10; 1 Sam. 7.4, 12.10; 1 Kgs 18.18; Jer. 2.23, 9.13 (ET 14); Hos. 2.15, 19 (ET 13, 17), 11.2; 2 Chron. 17.3, 24.7, 28.2, 33.3 and 34.4. Prior to the discovery of the Ugaritic texts, as for example in the work of the great nineteenth-century scholar, W. Robertson Smith,[1] it was sometimes supposed that 'the Baals' referred to quite distinct Canaanite deities, each Baal having its separate local identity. The Ugaritic texts revealed, however, that Baal, 'the Lord', was the epithet (though becoming a personal name) of one great cosmic deity, Hadad, so that the local Baals were, in fact, simply local manifestations of this particular deity, analogous to the local manifestations of the Virgin Mary in the Roman Catholic Church.

Although on occasion the phrase 'the Baals' might be a way of referring to Canaanite gods generally (cf. Jer. 2.23, where it is likely that the cult of Molech is specifically in mind), it seems that more usually it is indeed a way of referring to different manifestations of the one god, Baal. Interestingly, in the Ugaritic pantheon list (*KTU*^{2} 1.47.5-11) the name Baal is repeated seven times, suggesting that for the Ugaritians he could appear in various manifestations. In the Old Testament some of these manifestations are in a particular geographical location. Thus there is Baal-Gad (Josh. 11.17, 12.7, 13.5), Baal-Hamon (Cant. 8.11), Baal-Hazor (2 Sam. 13.23), Baal-Hermon (Judg. 3.3; 1 Chron. 5.23), Baale-Judah (2 Sam. 6.2), also known as Kiriath-Baal (Josh. 15.60, 18.14) or Baalah (Josh. 15.9; 1 Chron. 13.6), that is Kiriath-jearim,

1. Cf. W. Robertson Smith, *The Religion of the Semites*, pp. 93-113.

Baal-Meon (Num. 32.34; 1 Chron. 5.8) or Beth-Baal-Meon (Josh. 13.17), Baal-Peor (Deut. 4.3; Hos. 9.10; Ps. 106.28; cf. Num. 25.1-5, 31.16; Josh. 22.17), Baal-Perazim (2 Sam. 5.20; 1 Chron. 14.11), Baal-Shalisha (2 Kgs 4.42), Baal-Tamar (Judg. 20.22), Baalah (Josh. 15.11, 29), Baalath (Josh. 19.44), Baalath-Beer (Josh. 19.8), Bamoth-Baal (Josh. 13.17), Bealoth (Josh. 15.24), and in Egypt, Baal-Zephon (Exod. 14.2, 9; Num. 33.7). Interestingly, local manifestations of Baal are also mentioned outside the Bible. For example, Baal-Zaphon, the god of Mt Zaphon in Syria, is frequently mentioned at Ugarit (see Chapter 4 on Zaphon). Baal of Lebanon (*KAI* 31.1, 2) and the place Baal-Meon are also attested, the latter on the Moabite stone (lines 9, 30). Recent studies of Palestinian place names with a Baal component suggest that they arose at about the time of the emergence of the Israelites in Canaan.[2]

In addition to the above local manifestations, there are also a number of Baal epithets which are not in themselves limited to a particular sanctuary. Thus, for example, Baal was sometimes worshipped under the title Baal-Shamem, 'Baal of the heavens', and it will be seen below that the Phoenician form of Baal, promoted by Jezebel and opposed by Elijah, was this deity rather than Melqart, contrary to what is often asserted. Again, as will also be seen below, the name Baal-zebub (2 Kgs 1.2, 3, 6, 16) represents a distortion of the name Baal-zebul, a variant of the name *zbl b'l*, 'Prince Baal', attested of the universal Baal in the Ugaritic texts, even though in 2 Kings 1 he is specifically associated with the sanctuary at Ekron.

A Canaanite god with a temple at Shechem is called Baal-Berith 'Baal of the Covenant' (Judg. 9.4), and the Deuteronomist also represents him as being worshipped more widely by the Israelites in Judg. 8.33. Curiously, we also find a reference to a temple of El-Berith 'El/God of the Covenant' in Shechem in Judg. 9.46. Sometimes these have been seen as separate deities,[3] but it seems more natural to regard them as variants of the same name. Granted this, it is debated whether we have to do with a form of El or Baal. F.M. Cross[4] suggests El-Berith, regarding Baal 'lord' as an epithet, pointing to a deity named *'ilbrt* in a Hurrian text from Ugarit (*Ugaritica* V, RS 24.278 [= *KTU*²

2. See B. Rosen, 'Early Israelite Cultic Centres in the Hill Country', *VT* 38 (1988), pp. 114-17.

3. E.g. M.J. Mulder, 'Baal-Berith', *DDD*, cols. 266-72 (269) (2nd edn, 141-44 [142]).

4. Cross, *Canaanite Myth and Hebrew Epic*, pp. 39, 49 n. 23.

1.128]), though it has been queried whether Hurrian *'ilbrt* should not rather be understood as referring to the god Ilabrat, not to El-Berith.[5] Significantly, however, the association of the Shechem deity with a wine festival in Judg. 9.27 suggests the agricultural god Baal rather than El, and Judg. 8.33 implies that the worship of this deity was a form of apostasy associated with the Baals, so if only one deity is spoken of it is surely Baal-Berith, not El-Berith. The reference to El-Berith in Judg. 9.46 might then be attributed to 'scribal orthodoxy',[6] or alternatively El is simply being used in an appellative sense.[7] One can only speculate about the nature of the Covenant referred to in the name, and attempts to trace influence on Israel's own notion of divine Covenant are probably over bold.[8]

Baal Worship in Ancient Israel

When reading the Old Testament it becomes clear that it was the Baal cult that provided the greatest and most enduring threat to the development of exclusive Yahweh worship within ancient Israel. The fact that the Israelites were settled among the Canaanites, for whom the worship of Baal was so important, and that Palestine is a land utterly dependent for its fertility upon the rain, which was held to be Baal's special realm of influence, accounts for the tempting nature of this cult as well as the strength of the Old Testament polemic against it.

At the time of entry into the promised land there appears the temptation to participate in the cult of Baal-Peor at Mt Peor in the land of Moab (Num. 25.1-9; Deut. 4.3; Ps. 106.28; Hos. 9.10). Subsequently, during the period of the judges, Israel worshipped the Baals (Judg. 2.11, 13; 3.7; 10.6; 1 Sam. 7.4; 12.10). The text recounts that Gideon pulled down an altar of Baal and cut down an Asherah (Judg. 6.25-32). During the divided monarchy Ahab married Jezebel, daughter of Ittobaal (Ethbaal), king of the Sidonians, and worshipped Baal. He erected an altar for Baal in the house of Baal, which he built in Samaria, and made an Asherah (1 Kgs 16.31-33). Ahab's promulgation of the Baal cult

5. M. Dietrich and W. Mayer, 'Hurritische Weihrauch–Beschwörungen in ugaritischer Alphabetschrift', *UF* 26 (1994), pp. 73-112 (92).

6. J. Gray, 'Baal-Berith', *IDB*, I, p. 331.

7. Cf. R.E. Clements, 'Baal-Berith of Shechem', *JSS* 13 (1968), pp. 21-32 (26 n. 3).

8. Cf. Clements, 'Baal-Berith of Shechem', pp. 31-32.

provides the background for the famous confrontation between Elijah and the prophets of Baal on Mt Carmel in 1 Kings 18. Unlike Elijah, Ahab clearly did not see his promulgation of Baal as being incompatible with Yahweh worship; in fact, Ahab's sons Ahaziah and Jehoram bear Yahwistic names. (On the identification of Ahab's Baal, see below.) Ahaziah is said to have worshipped Baal (1 Kgs 22.53)—indeed, he consulted Baal-zebub, the god of Ekron, when he was ill (2 Kgs 1.2-16), a name (literally, 'Lord of the fly') that looks as though it is a distortion of Baal-zebul ('Baal the Prince', cf. Ugaritic *zbl b'l* and New Testament Beelzebul; see below). Ahab's other son, Jehoram, is said to have put away the pillar of Baal that his father had made (2 Kgs 3.2), though he is still regarded by the Deuteronomist as an evil king (2 Kgs 3.2-3). It is clear, however, that Baal worship persisted, for Jehu was later ruthlessly to massacre the Baal priests, prophets and worshippers in the temple of Baal as well as destroy the temple itself and the pillar of Baal within it (2 Kgs 10.18-27). This act was later to receive the condemnation of the prophet Hosea (cf. Hos. 1.4). In addition to the Northern Kingdom (2 Kgs 17.16), Manasseh is singled out as worshipping Baal (2 Kgs 21.3), but Josiah, in his great reformation, put an end to his cult (2 Kgs 23.4-5). Among the canonical prophets it is Hosea and Jeremiah who seem most exercised by the Baal cult (e.g. Hos. 2.19 [ET 2.17]; 13.1; Jer. 2.8, 23.13). It is surprising that the other canonical prophets do not mention the name of Baal, even when they condemn syncretism, for example, Ezekiel. Perhaps some prophets were reluctant to mention the names of detested deities (the only one explicitly mentioned by Ezekiel is Tammuz, Ezek. 8.14).

In the postexilic period Baal is not heard of, apart from a reference in Zech. 12.11 to the Aramaean cult of Hadad-rimmon in the plain of Megiddo. Also, it needs to be remembered that Antiochus IV Epiphanes rededicated the temple in Jerusalem in 168 BCE to Zeus Olympios,who was a Hellenistic form of Baal-Shamem. 'The abomination of desolation' (*šiqqûṣ šōmēm* or *šiqqûṣ m*[e]*šōmēm*) in Dan. 9.27, 11.31 and 12.11 is a play on the name of the god Baal-Shamem (see below).

In the early period the Old Testament mentions a number of Israelites whose personal names include the theophorous element *ba'al*. These include Jerubbaal, an alternative name of the judge Gideon (Judg. 6.32, 7.1, etc.).[9] Although the Old Testament interprets the name as meaning

9. See J.A. Emerton, 'Gideon and Jerubbaal', *JTS* NS 27 (1976), pp. 289-312,

'Let Baal contend against him' (Judg. 6.32), this is generally agreed not to be the original meaning, since it would be extraordinary for a man to bear a name containing a statement directed against himself. More likely suggestions as to the original meaning include 'May Baal show himself great' or 'May Baal give increase'.[10] Other early names with *ba'al* include Saul's son Eshbaal (1 Chron. 8.33, 9.39; distorted to Ish-bosheth in 2 Sam. 2.10, etc.), and the son of Saul's son Jonathan, Meribbal or Meribaal (1 Chron. 8.34, 9.40, distorted to Mephibosheth in 2 Sam. 4.4, 9.6, 19.25, etc.; there is another Mephibosheth in 2 Sam. 21.8). Further, David had a son called Beeliada, that is, Baaliada (1 Chron. 14.6; named Eliada in 2 Sam 5.16; 1 Chron. 3.8). Other Baal names are found outside the Old Testament, for example, in the ninth-century Samaria ostraca, where five individuals have Baal names, in contrast to nine who have Yahwistic names.[11] So far as the above biblical names are concerned, we cannot be certain whether they simply allude to the Canaanite god Baal, or refer to Yahweh as being equated with Baal, or are simply an epithet 'Lord' for Yahweh without actual identification with the god Baal. Whatever the case with the above names (and the same explanation need not apply to Jerubbaal and the others), we have definite evidence that Yahweh could be referred to as Baal from the personal names Bealiah (2 Chron. 12.6 [ET 5]), one of David's warriors, and Yehobaal, a name found on a seal,[12] which seem to mean respectively 'Baal is Yahweh' and 'Yahweh is Baal'. That Yahweh could actually be equated with Baal is clearly indicated by Hosea 2.

In v. 18 (ET 16) Hosea declares, 'And in that day, says the Lord, you

for a defence of the view that Gideon and Jerubbaal probably are two names of the same individual, contrary to the supposition of some modern scholars.

10. These are the views of Noth, *Die israelitischen Personennamen*, pp. 206-207, and Albright, *Archaeology and the Religion of Israel*, pp. 109, 205 n. 57, respectively, both proposing the verb is *rbb*, which is suggest by the daghesh forte in the beth. J.J. Stamm, *Beiträge zur hebräischen und altorientalischen Namenskunde* (ed. E. Jenni and M.A. Klopfenstein; OBO, 30; Freiburg/Göttingen: Universitätsverlag/Vandenhoeck & Ruprecht, 1980), pp. 145-46, prefers, however, to translate 'Baal hat Recht geschafft'/'Baal ist eingetreten', seeing the verb as *rîb*/*rûb*.

11. The five Baal names and literature on the Samaria ostraca are cited by Mark S. Smith, *The Early History of God*, p. 65 n. 3.

12. See, for example, N. Avigad, 'Hebrew Seals and Sealings and their Significance for Biblical Research', in J.A. Emerton (ed.), *Congress Volume, Jerusalem 1986* (VTSup, 40; Leiden: E.J. Brill, 1988), pp. 7-16 (8-9).

will call me "My husband", and no longer will you call me "My Baal"'. The following verse goes on to say, 'For I will remove the names of the Baals from your mouth, and they shall be mentioned by name no more'. Now 'the Baals' were mentioned earlier in this chapter in v. 15 (ET 13), and these clearly refer to the fertility deity, Baal, whom the people regarded as being responsible for the grain, wine, oil and so on in v. 10 (ET 8), and also the 'lovers' of v. 7 (ET 5). From all this it can hardly be doubted that Hosea was not simply objecting to the epithet 'Lord' (*ba'al*) being applied to Yahweh, but was countering a tendency of the people to conflate Yahweh and Baal to such an extent that the essential identity and uniqueness of the former was compromised.

Further evidence in support of the view there were some who equated Yahweh with Baal derives from the fact that such a hypothesis has explanatory power in accounting for the rise of the Son of Man imagery in Daniel 7.[13]

Jezebel's Baal

It would appear that Yahwistic hostility to Baal greatly intensified from the time of Elijah and Jezebel in the ninth century BCE. What was the identity of the Baal whose worship Jezebel promoted in Israel (cf. 1 Kgs 18.19, 'the 450 prophets of Baal and the 400 prophets of Asherah,[14] who eat at Jezebel's table') and against whom the prophet Elijah struggled, made famous in the contest between Elijah and the prophets of Baal in 1 Kings 18?

The god is simply called Baal in 1 Kings 18. However, a majority of scholars tend to suppose that this is not the familiar Baal known from elsewhere in the Old Testament, but rather Melqart, spoken of by modern scholars as the Baal of Tyre and the chief god of Tyre.[15]

13. Cf. Emerton, 'The Origin of the Son of Man Imagery', pp. 225-42; J. Day, *God's Conflict with the Dragon and the Sea*, pp. 151-77.

14. It is widely agreed that the reference to the 400 prophets of Asherah is a later gloss, since they play no role in the subsequent story in 1 Kgs 18 and the words are marked with an asterisk in the Hexapla.

15. This is the view found in many standard works on this narrative. The argument has been most strongly presented by R. de Vaux, 'Les Prophètes de Baal sur le Mont Carmel', *Bulletin du Musée de Beyrouth* 5 (1941), pp. 7-20; reprinted in the collected essays of de Vaux, *Bible et Orient* (Paris: Cerf, 1967), pp. 485-97; ET 'The Prophets of Baal on Mount Carmel', in *The Bible and the Ancient Near East* (trans. D. McHugh; London: Darton, Longman & Todd, 1972), pp. 238-51. More

What evidence is adduced to support this view? Basically, three main points of comparison have been made. First, Elijah's allusion to the possibility that Baal is musing (1 Kgs. 18.27) has been compared to the description of Herakles (with whom Melqart was equated) as a philosopher (e.g. *Chronicon Pascale* 43, in *PG* XCII, col. 161). The suggestion that Baal might be on a journey (1 Kgs 18.27) has been compared with the fact that the Tyrian Herakles is alleged to have made a journey to Libya (Eudoxus of Cnidus, in Athenaeus 9.392). Thirdly, the possibility that Baal 'is asleep and must be awakened' (1 Kgs 18.27) has been compared with the fact that there was a ceremony of waking Melqart from his winter sleep (Menander of Ephesus, in Josephus, *Ant.* 8.5.3).

However, none of these points is compelling. For a start, it should be noted that the sources in question are late, and there is no certainty that they reflect traditions going back to the ninth century BCE. Moreover, a much better case can be made that Jezebel's Baal was Baal-Shamem, another important god worshipped at Tyre, whose role as a storm god suggests that he was essentially the same as the Ugaritic Baal and the Baal known elsewhere in the Old Testament.[16] For instance, with regard to the third point above, bearing in mind that death could be spoken of as sleep (cf. Isa. 26.19; Dan. 12.2, etc.), it may be argued that the death and resurrection of the Ugaritic Baal is a more appropriate parallel to 1 Kings 18 than is Melqart, since the celebration of Melqart's awakening from sleep in the month of Peritios, that is, February/March (Josephus, *Ant.* 8.5.3), does not cohere with a storm god, whereas the Ugaritic Baal's summer sojourn in the underworld corresponds to his role as a storm god who brought the lightning and the rain, the point at issue between Elijah and the prophets of Baal in 1 Kings 18.

An important indicator is that it was not Melqart, but rather Baal-Shamem who was endowed with the attributes of the weather god at

recently this view has been followed by, for example, C. Bonnet, *Melqart: Cultes et mythes de l'Héraclès tyrien en Méditerranée* (Studia Phoenicia, 8; Leuven: Peeters and Presses Universitaires de Namur, 1988), pp. 136-44.

16. This has been proposed by O. Eissfeldt, 'Ba'alšamēm und Jahwe', *ZAW* 57 (1939), pp. 1-31 (18-23); reprinted in Eissfeldt, *Kleine Schriften*, II, pp. 170-98 (186-91). It has been ably defended by M.J. Mulder, *De naam van de afwezige god op de Karmel: Onderzoek naar de naam van de Baäl van de Karmel in 1 Koningen 18* (Leiden: Universitaire Pers, 1979). Others who have taken this line include Mark S. Smith, *The Early History of God*, p. 44; B. Mazar, *Biblical Israel: State and People* (Jerusalem: Magnes Press and Israel Exploration Society, 1992), pp. 118, 128; and the present writer, in earlier publications.

Tyre in the seventh century BCE—only two centuries after the incident at 1 Kings 18—as is illustrated by the treaty between Esar-haddon and Baal, king of Tyre. There, in the list of Tyrian deities, we read, 'May Baal-sameme, Baal-malage and Baal-saphon raise an evil wind against your ships, to undo their moorings, tear out their mooring pole, may a strong wave sink them in the sea, a violent tide [...] against you. May Melqart and Eshmun deliver your land to destruction, your people to be deported; from your land [...]'[17] Moreover, this passage, which clearly distinguishes Melqart from various Baal deities, makes it very dubious whether at this early period it is even correct to speak of Melqart as a Baal deity at all, as scholars frequently imagine when they refer to him as Baal-Melqart or the Baal of Tyre. The title 'Baal of Tyre' is, in fact, only attested of Melqart much later, in a second-century BCE Phoenician inscription from Malta ('Our Lord Melqart, Lord of Tyre [*b'l ṣr*]' [*KAI* 47.1]). Classical sources regularly equate Melqart with Herakles, not Zeus, who was the equivalent of Baal. Nor, it will be noted, does the Esar-haddon treaty associate Melqart with the storm, unlike the varioius manifestations of Baal.

If Melqart was really the most important god of Tyre, it is surprising that the element 'Melqart' does not occur in any of the names of the kings of Tyre. On the other hand, a large number of them contain the theophoric element, Baal, which most naturally refers to Baal-Shamem. That Baal-Shamem was, indeed, the most important Tyrian god at this period is also indicated by the above-mentioned treaty between Esar-haddon and Baal, king of Tyre, since Baal-Shamem (Baal-sameme) is, in fact, the Tyrian deity mentioned first.

Yet a further piece of information supports the view that it was Baal-Shamem who was the deity promoted by Jezebel. In 1 Kings 18 the contest between Elijah and the prophets of Baal takes place on Mt Carmel. The god of Carmel was always equated with Zeus, and it was Baal-Shamem who was identified with Zeus, Melqart being rather equated with Herakles. This is most interestingly reflected in an inscription discovered on part of a marble foot on Mt Carmel itself, in which

17. See *ANET*, p. 534. Even earlier, the eighth-century BCE inscription from Karatepe's reference to Baal-Shamem in the Phoenician version is rendered in the hieroglyphic Hittite version by a sign for the Hittite storm and thunder god, Tarḫunt. The view of R.A. Oden, 'Ba'al Šāmēm and 'Ēl', *CBQ* 39 (1977), pp. 457-73, that Baal Shamem is to be equated with El rather than Baal thus seems far-fetched.

the dedication is made 'to Heliopolitan Zeus [god of] Carmel',[18] and in the fourth-century BCE Pseudo-Scylax's *Periplus* 104 attests Mt Carmel as the 'holy mountain of Zeus'. This is presumably the 'Mount Ba'li-ra'-si [Baal of the Headland] which is (over against) the sea and by (over against) the land of Tyre' referred to in the annals of Shalmaneser III in 841 BCE.[19] Since the local Baal would have been simply a local form of the universal Baal, there is no need to follow A. Alt and K. Galling in seeing the Baal of 1 Kings 18 as simply the local Baal of Mt Carmel and nothing more.[20]

Since the Baal promoted by Jezebel was the same Baal who had been worshipped by the Canaanite population of Israel and syncretistic Israelites, it can readily be understood how he gained such a large following. This would not be the case with Melqart, the city god of Tyre, and, as M.J. Mulder has emphasized, Ahab would have committed political suicide had he attempted to promote such a foreign god.

Strong polemic against Baal is clearly to be seen in 1 Kings 18, where Yahweh defeats Baal in the contest on Mt Carmel by making fire come down from heaven. Since this is immediately followed by the return of the rain after the long drought (1 Kgs 18.41-45) we must understand the fire from heaven as lightning. Accordingly, the polemic is especially marked, as Yahweh is shown as the God who can bring

18. Cf. M. Avi-Yonah, 'Mount Carmel and the God of Baalbek', *IEJ* 2 (1952), pp. 118-24.

19. See Y. Aharoni, *The Land of the Bible: A Historical Geography* (trans. and ed. A.F. Rainey; Philadelphia: Westminster Press, 1979), p. 341. The sacredness of Mt Carmel may be attested already in the annals of the fifteenth-century BCE Pharaoh Thutmose III as 'Rosh-Kadesh', i.e. 'Holy Head' (*ANET*, p. 243), but this identification is uncertain.

20. A. Alt, 'Das Gottesurteil auf dem Karmel', in A. Weiser (ed.), *Festschrift G. Beer zum 60. Geburtstage dargebracht* (Stuttgart: W. Kohlhammer, 1935), pp. 1-18; reprinted in A. Alt, *Kleine Schriften*, II (Munich: C.H. Beck, 1953), pp. 135-49; K. Galling, 'Der Gott Karmel und die Ächtung der fremden Götter', in G. Ebeling (ed.), *Geschichte und Altes Testament: Festschrift A. Alt zum 70. Geburstag* (BHT, 16; Tübingen: J.C.B. Mohr [Paul Siebeck], 1953), pp. 105-25. On the subject of the god of Carmel, see also O. Eissfeldt, *Der Gott Karmel* (Sitzungsberichte der deutschen Akademie der Wissenschaften zu Berlin. Klasse für Sprachen, Literatur und Kunst, Jahrgang 1953, 1; Berlin: Akademie Verlag, 1953), who rightly emphasizes that we should not make too great a distinction between the Tyrian Baal and the local Baal of Carmel (cf. pp. 5-6).

lightning and the rain, which were regarded as Baal's particular sphere of influence.

A few scholars[21] have attempted greatly to increase the number of passages in the Elijah and Elisha stories which are to be envisaged as displaying polemic against the Baal cult, more or less seeing any healing or nature miracle on the part of these prophets as an implicit sign of the superiority of Yahweh to Baal, but this is not clearly indicated in the text and seems to go beyond the evidence.

Polemical Distortions of the Name of Baal

a. *Baal-zebub (Baal-zebul, Beelzebul)*

In 2 Kings 1 we read that after Ahaziah had fallen through the lattice in his upper chamber in Samaria and lay sick, he sent messengers to enquire of Baal-zebub, the god of Ekron, whether he would recover from his sickness.

How is the name Baal-zebub to be explained? Since *z^e^bûb* is the Hebrew word for 'fly', the name, on the face of it, seems to mean, 'Baal/Lord of the fly/flies'. This was the traditional understanding in the past, prior to the discovery of the Ugaritic texts. Some scholars still accept this as the real name of the deity, but those who do are not united in the explanation they give for it.

(i) First, there are those who believe that Baal-zebub was a god who gave oracles through the buzzing of flies.[22] This phenomenon is, however, unattested in the Semitic world.

21. Cf. L. Bronner, *The Stories of Elijah and Elisha as Polemics against Baal Worship* (Pretoria Oriental Studies, 6; Leiden: E.J. Brill, 1968); J.K. Battenfield, 'YHWH's Refutation of the Baal Myth through the Actions of Elijah and Elisha', in A. Gileadi (ed.), *Israel's Apostasy and Restoration: Essays in Honor of Roland K. Harrison* (Grand Rapids, MI: Baker Book House, 1988), pp. 19-37; F.E. Woods, *Water and Storm Polemics against Baalism in the Deuteronomistic History* (American University Studies, Series 7, Theology and Religion, 150; New York: Peter Lang, 1994), pp. 95-121. The study of F.C. Fensham, 'A Few Observations on the Polarisation Between Yahweh and Baal in 1 Kings 17–19', *ZAW* 92 (1980), pp. 227-36, does not go as far as this, but he does see the miracles of Elijah associated with the widow of Zarephath in 1 Kgs 17 as emphasizing the power of Yahweh over Baal.

22. R.A.S. Macalister, *The Philistines: Their History and Civilization* (Schweich Lectures; London: Oxford University Press, 1913), pp. 91-93.

(ii) M. Riemschneider and T.H. Gaster[23] think that the name may originally have been a Philistine one, which was then reinterpreted by the Hebrews as 'fly', and Gaster maintains that 'fly' may have been a symbol of death and disease. However, with regard to the first point, although this was a deity worshipped by the Philistines, the name is probably Semitic in origin: the first element, 'Baal', is certainly Semitic, and it is known that the Philistines, like the Israelites, appropriated other Canaanite deities: Dagon (Judg. 16.23; 1 Sam. 5.2-5, 7; 1 Chron. 10.10), Ashtaroth (1 Sam. 31.10), and, as is now known from discoveries at Ekron, possibly Asherah.[24] With regard to the second point, while Gaster cites a number of examples from various parts of the world where the fly is a symbol of death and disease, none of them pertains to the Semitic world.

(iii) F. Saracino[25] has appealed to a Ugaritic text found at Ras Ibn Hani (*KTU*^{2} 1.169.1 = RIH 78/20, line 1), where he renders *ydy.dbbm.dġzr* as 'May he [i.e. Baal] drive away the flies of the Hero'. He cites this as evidence that Baal drove away flies and thinks it explains the name Baal-zebub. However, most other scholars translate *dbbm* otherwise.[26]

(iv) Another recent suggestion is that of A. Tångberg,[27] who thinks that Baal-zebub means 'Baal (statue) with flies (ornament)'; he compares a description of the mother goddess, Nintu, of whom it is stated that 'she wears a fly'. But Baal-zebub sounds very much like a title of a god, rather than a description of this kind. Moreover, against this and all the above views it may be

23. M. Riemschneider, 'Die Herkunft der Philister', *Acta Antiqua Academiae Scientiarum Hungaricae* 4 (1956), pp. 17-29 (25); T.H. Gaster, 'Baalzebub', *IDB*, I, p. 332, and in *Myth, Legend, and Custom in the Old Testament* (London: Gerald Duckworth, 1969), p. 515.

24. On the last, see above, Chapter 2, n. 15.

25. F. Saracino, 'Ras Ibn Hani 78/20 and Some Old Testament Connections', *VT* 32 (1982), pp. 338-43.

26. For instance, Y. Avishur, 'The Ghost-expelling Incantation from Ugarit (Ras Ibn Hani 78/20)', *UF* 13 (1981), pp. 13-25 (15, 17), renders 'enemies'; K. Aartun, 'Neue Beiträge zum ugaritischen Lexikon I', *UF* 16 (1984), pp. 1-52 (10-11), translates 'hinterhältige Unternehmungen'; and A. Caquot and J. de Tarragon, in *Textes Ougaritiques*, II (Paris: Cerf, 1989), p. 54, see the meaning as 'les paroles'.

27. A. Tångberg, 'A Note on Ba'al Zĕbūb in 2 Kgs 1,2.3.6.16', *SJOT* 6 (1992), pp. 293-96.

stated that nowhere else is the epithet 'Baal of flies' attested. I shall therefore reject the understanding that 2 Kings 1 refers to a 'Baal of flies'.

Another view, one which accepts the spelling Baal-zebub, though rejecting any allusion to flies, is that of F.C. Fensham,[28] who suggests as a possibility that the name means 'Baal of the flame', which links up with references to fire coming down from heaven in 2 Kgs 1.10, 12, 14. He compares *z*^{e}*bûb* with the word *ḏbb*, 'flame', the name of a deity mentioned in the Ugaritic texts, which appears to be cognate with Aramaic *š*^{e}*bîbâ*, 'flame', the name of a monster defeated by Baal's consort, Anat. In *KTU*^{2} 1.3.III.45-46, she declares, *mḫšt. k{.}lbt. 'ilm. 'išt klt. bt. 'il. ḏbb*, 'I destroyed the bitch of the gods, Fire, I made an end of the daughter of El, Flame'. However, no such epithet, 'Baal of the flame', is ever attested and the vocalization *z*^{e}*bûb* also seems inappropriate on this view in the light of Aramaic *š*^{e}*bîbâ*.

None of the attempts to justify the Masoretic reading Baal-zebub in 2 Kings 1 is therefore convincing. I come now to consider the view that the original reading was rather Baal-zebul. Interestingly, Symmachus presupposes Baal-zebul in 2 Kgs 1.2, according to the manuscripts j and z.

M.J. Mulder[29] has proposed that *b'l zbl* was the original form of the name and thinks it means 'Baal of illness' (cf. Ugaritic *zbln*, 'illness'). However, since *zbl b'l* and *b'l zbl* are attested as epithets of Baal in the Canaanite world (see below), Mulder's understanding of *zbl* as 'illness' here seems uncalled for.

The most probable explanation of the name Baal-zebub is that which sees the name as a deliberate distortion of Baal-zebul, 'Baal the Prince'. That Baal-zebub was a distortion of Baal-zebul was already suggested by the scholar T.K. Cheyne,[30] but he thought the meaning was 'lord of the high house'.[31] With the discovery of the Ugaritic texts and the

28. F.C. Fensham, 'A Possible Explanation of the Name Baal-zebub of Ekron', *ZAW* 79 (1967), pp. 361-64.

29. M.J. Mulder, *Kanaänitische Goden in het Oude Testament* (Exegetica, fourth series, 4 and 5; The Hague: N.V. Van Keulen Periodieken, 1965), p. 35.

30. T.K. Cheyne, 'Baalzebub', in T.K. Cheyne and J.S. Black (eds.), *Encyclopaedia Biblica* (one vol. edn; London: A. & C. Black, 1904), cols. 407-408.

31. W. Herrmann, 'Baal Zebub', *DDD*, cols. 293-96 (294) (2nd edn, pp. 154-56 [154-55]), mistakenly states that already Movers, *Die Phönizier*, I, p. 260 and S. Guyard, 'Remarques sur le mot assyrien *zabal* et sur l'expression biblique *bet*

finding there of Baal's frequent epithet, *zbl b'l*, 'Prince Baal', the view has gained support that Baal-zebub is a deliberate distortion of this.[32]

Less well known is the occurrence of the same epithet in reverse order, such as is postulated as lying behind Baal-zebub, in a second-century BCE Punic personal name from Tharros, in Sardinia, *b'l 'zbl* (*KAI* 67.1-2). The distortion of this name to Baal-zebub is in keeping with other examples of the distortion of the names of Canaanite deities in the Old Testament, such as *bōšet*, 'shame', for Baal and Ashtoreth (with the vowels of *bōšet*) for Ashtart.

That the name Baal-zebul was known to the Jews is attested in the New Testament, where Beelzebul has become the name of the Prince of the Demons, Satan (Mt. 10.25, 12.24, 27; Mk 3.22; Lk. 11.15, 18-19). The reading Beelzebul in the New Testament is certainly original: almost all the Greek manuscripts read Βεελζεβούλ. Only Vaticanus (B) and, in every case except one, Sinaiticus (א) read Βεεζεβούλ. The reading Beelzebub is found later in the Vulgate and Peshiṭta, and is clearly inferior, making the New Testament demonic name agree with the god of Ekron in 2 Kings 1. It is all the more remarkable that the form Beelzebul is attested in the New Testament when we reflect that it is not found in the Old Testament, and it testifies to the continuation of a Canaanite numen in transformed demonized form in popular Jewish religion at a late date.

It is not surprising that the name became a term for the 'Prince of the Demons' (cf. *zbl*, 'prince'): the name of the leading god, when abominated, naturally became transformed into that of the leading demon. The idea that pagan gods are demons is found in Deut. 32.17; Ps. 105.37; Bar. 4.7 and Ps. 95.5 (LXX); also in 1 Cor. 10.20 and Rev. 9.20. However, although ultimately deriving from the name Baal-zebul, 'Baal the Prince', it should not be supposed that this is how the term was understood in the New Testament. *Z^e^bûl* was probably then understood in its meaning 'dwelling', so that Beelzebul now meant 'lord of

zeboul', *JA* 12 (7th series, 1878), pp. 220-25, understood Baal-zebul to be the original form of Baal-zebub in 2 Kings 1.

32. So far as I am aware, the connection with *zbl b'l* was first suggested by W.F. Albright, 'The North-Canaanite Epic of 'Al'êyân Ba'al and Mot', *JPOS* 12 (1932), pp. 185-208 (191), though he took the meaning to be 'Lord of the Abode [i.e. Shrine]'. But in 'Zabûl Yam and Thâpiṭ Nahar in the Combat between Baal and the Sea', *JPOS* 16 (1936), pp. 17-20 (17), Albright accepted the meaning 'exalted Baal'.

the dwelling'. This is supported by the apparent word play on the name in Mt. 10.25, 'If they have called *the master of the house* Beelzebul, how much less will they malign those of his household' (cf. also Mk 3. 25, 27).[33]

Other explanations of the New Testament demonic term are unconvincing. Thus, an older explanation supposed that Beelzebul represents Aramaic *b*ᵉ*'ēl-z*ᵉ*bûl*, 'lord of dung',[34] or *b*ᵉ*'ēl-zîbbûl*, 'lord of dung',[35] but *z*ᵉ*bûl* and *zîbbûl* 'dung' are not known in the Aramaic of New Testament times.

It has sometimes been claimed[36] that the New Testament demonic term derives from Aramaic *b*ᵉ*'ēl d*ᵉ*bābâ* 'enemy' (which in Syriac became a name for Satan). P.L. Day,[37] though admitting that Baal-zebul ultimately derives from Ugaritic *zbl b'l*, believes that the Aramaic expression contributed to its becoming a term for Satan. However, this is most unlikely, granted that Beelzebul, not Beelzebub, is the original form and that the Aramaic demonic name (as shown by the New Testament transliteration) had a *z* and not a *d*.

b. *Bosheth, 'shame'*

Another example of Hebrew scribal distortion of the name of Baal for polemical purposes occurs in the use of the expression *bōšet*, 'shame', to denote Baal.[38] This is explicitly the case in Hos. 9.10, 'But they came

33. New Testament scholars often show awareness of this later understanding, but fail to note the origin in the Canaanite god Baal-zebul, e.g. C.E.B. Cranfield, *The Gospel according to Saint Mark* (CGTC; Cambridge: Cambridge University Press, 1963), p. 136; J.C. Fenton, *Saint Matthew* (Pelican Gospel Commentaries; Harmondsworth: Penguin Books, 1963), p. 162; D.E. Nineham, *Saint Mark* (Pelican Gospel Commentaries; Harmondsworth: Penguin Books, 1963), p. 124; H. Anderson, *The Gospel of Mark* (NCB; London: Oliphants, 1976), p. 121; M.D. Hooker, *The Gospel according to St Mark* (BNTC; London: A. & C. Black, 1991), p. 115.

34. First suggested by J.B. Lightfoot, in 1658; see his *Horae Hebraicae et Talmudicae*, II (new edn by R. Gandell; 4 vols.; Oxford: Oxford University Press, 1859), pp. 203-204.

35. H.L. Strack and P. Billerbeck, *Kommentar zum Neuen Testament aus Talmud und Midrasch*, I (4 vols.; Munich: Beck, 1922), p. 632.

36. A. Schlatter, *Der Evangelist Matthäus* (Stuttgart: Calwer, 1929), p. 343.

37. P.L. Day, *An Adversary in Heaven:* śāṭān *in the Hebrew Bible* (HSM, 43; Atlanta: Scholars Press, 1988), pp. 157-59.

38. This was first argued by O. Thenius, *Die Bücher Samuels* (Kurzgefasstes exegetisches Handbuch zum Alten Testament; Leipzig: Weidmann'sche Buchhand-

to Baal-Peor, and consecrated themselves to the shameful thing (*bōšet*), and became detestable like the thing they loved', and in Jer. 11. 13, 'For your gods have become as many as your cities, O Judah; and as many as the streets of Jerusalem are the altars you have set up to the shameful thing (*bōšet*), altars to burn incense to Baal'. In the light of these examples, Baal must also be intended in Jer. 3. 24, 'But from our youth the shameful thing (*bōšet*) has devoured all for which our fathers laboured, their flocks and their herds, their sons and their daughters'.

It is generally accepted that *bōšet*, 'shame', has also been substituted for *ba'al*, 'Baal', by later scribes in the personal names Ish-bosheth (2 Sam. 2.10, etc.) for Eshbaal (1 Chron. 8.33, 9.39), Mephibosheth (2 Sam. 4.4, 9.6, 19.25, etc.; there is another Mephibosheth in 2 Sam. 21.8) for Meribaal or Meribbaal (1 Chron. 8.34, 9.40), and also Jerubbesheth (2 Sam. 11.21) for Jerubbaal (Judg. 6.32). This view has, however, been questioned by M. Tsevat,[39] who proposes that in these names *bōšet* is rather equivalent to the Akkadian *bāštu*, 'dignity, pride, vigour', and is to be understood as a divine epithet, original to the Hebrew text at these points. The individuals in question are thus understood to have had two names. However, Tsevat's arguments are unconvincing, for two fundamental reasons. First, he fails to explain why, on his view, it should be precisely certain individuals with *ba'al* in their name who also have a name including the element *bōšet*, and no others. Secondly, it is curious that Tsevat makes no reference whatsoever to the passages listed above (Hos. 9.10; Jer. 3.24, 11.13) where *bōšet*, 'shame', is clearly used to denote Baal outside of personal names. (The context in all three passages is condemnatory, making the meaning 'dignity, pride, vigour' quite inappropriate.)

Similar arguments to Tsevat's have recently been put forward by G.J. Hamilton,[40] and similar objections apply. Hamilton agrees with

lung, 1842), pp. 142, 175. Cf. also A. Geiger, 'Der Baal in den hebräischen Eigennamen', *ZDMG* 16 (1862), pp. 728-32.

39. M. Tsevat, 'Ishbosheth and Congeners: The Names and their Study', *HUCA* 46 (1975), pp. 71-87.

40. G.J. Hamilton, 'New Evidence for the Authenticity of *bšt* in Hebrew Personal Names and for its Use as a Divine Epithet in Biblical Texts', *CBQ* 60 (1998), pp. 228-50. On p. 229, n. 7, Hamilton states that in my article on 'Baal' in *ABD*, I, pp. 545-49 (548), I simply assume without argument that *bōšet* is a scribal substitution for Baal. However, he overlooks the fact that I had already defended it and raised objections to Tsevat's view in my book, *Molech*, pp. 56-58.

Tsevat in rejecting the understanding that *bōšet* in the above mentioned contexts means 'shame' and connecting it rather with Akkadian *bāštu*. Hamilton suggests that *bōšet* be translated 'protective spirit'; since, however, the meaning of *bāštu* is 'dignity, pride, vigour', such an understanding seems forced.

The word *bōšet* having become a term for Baal, its vowels were also used by Hebrew scribes to distort the name of the goddess Astarte, so that Ashtart became Ashtoreth. It also seems likely that the vowels of the divine name, Molech (*mōlek*), are also a polemical distortion, whether from *mōlēk* or *melek*.[41]

c. *The Abomination of Desolation (*šiqqûṣ šōmēm*) as a Word Play on Baal-Shamem*

In Dan. 9.27, 11.31 and 12.11 there occurs the expression 'abomination of desolation' used in three slightly different Hebrew forms to denote a hated cult object set up in the Jerusalem temple from 168–165 (or 167–164) BCE by Antiochus IV Epiphanes to the god Zeus Olympios. We know from 1 Macc. 1.54, 59 that the cult object denoted by the term 'abomination of desolation' was not an image but an altar set up on the altar of burnt offerings that was in the temple courtyard.[42] Dan. 12.11 has *šiqqûṣ šōmēm,* while Dan. 11. 31 has the variant form, *haššiqqûṣ mᵉšōmēm*, and the *šiqqûṣîm mᵉšōmēm* of Dan. 9.27 should, on the basis of grammar, similarly be corrected to *šiqqûṣ mᵉšōmēm.* A related expression, *happeša' šōmēm*, 'the transgression that makes desolate', appears in Dan. 8.13.

It was E. Nestle,[43] in 1884, who first recognized that *šiqqûṣ (mᵉ)šōmēm* is a word play on the name of the god Baal-Shamem (*Ba'al šāmēm*), literally 'lord of the heavens'. That Baal-Shamem was indeed the Semitic equivalent of the god Zeus Olympios, to whom Antiochus IV Epiphanes dedicated to the temple, is supported by the Peshiṭta

41. See J. Day, *Molech*, pp. 57-58.

42. The earliest sources speak only of an altar, not an image to Zeus Olympios in the Jerusalem temple. The view of H.H. Rowley, 'Menelaus and the Abomination of Desolation', in F.F. Hvidberg (ed.), *Studia Orientalia Ioanni Pedersen septuagenario dicata* (Copenhagen: E. Munksgaard, 1953), pp. 303-15, esp. pp. 309-15, that there was both an altar and an image is now generally rejected. The first explicit reference to an image is in Jerome's Commentary on Dan. 11.31, in *PL*, XXV, col. 569, and *m. Ta'an*. 4.6.

43. E. Nestle, 'Zu Daniel. 2. Der Greuel der Verwüstung', *ZAW* 4 (1884), p. 248.

version of 2 Macc. 6.2, which refers to the deity in question as *b'lšmyn* here. On this understanding, *šiqqûṣ* 'abomination' would have been substituted for the name Baal, just as it is used to denote other detested pagan gods in the Old Testament (cf. 1 Kgs 11.5, 7), and *šōmēm*, 'desolation' (literally 'desolating') would have replaced *šāmēm*, 'heavens'. Such a distortion of the name of Baal-Shamem is in keeping with other deliberate malformations of divine names, such as Baal-zebub for Baal-zebul, noted earlier. Nestle's widely accepted understanding of the expression 'abomination of desolation' has been disputed by O. Keel.[44] He claims that there is no real evidence that Zeus Olympios was equated with Baal-Shamem, and sees him as rather an *interpretatio Graeca* of Yahweh, maintaining that the expression 'abomination of desolation' simply refers to the abominable swine offered on the altar, not the altar itself. However, 1 Macc. 1.54, 59 clearly indicates that the term refers to the altar, as noted above; moreover, we have abundant evidence elsewhere that Antiochus IV was particularly dedicated to the god Zeus Olympios, and for a Hellenized Syrian, as opposed to one who was simply a Greek, this must have constituted some form of the Syrian god Baal, for Baal and Zeus were commonly equated in the ancient world. Since, moreover, Mt Olympus was frequently equated with heaven,[45] it would be natural for Zeus Olympios to be equated with Baal-Shamem ('Baal of the heavens'). It is therefore entirely plausible that *šiqqûṣ šōmēm* and the like are a play on his name.

E. Bickerman(n)[46] has claimed that the cult of Zeus Olympios/Baal-Shamem was merely an extreme form of syncretistic Yahwism, and that Yahweh was actually equated with Zeus Olympios/Baal-Shamem by the Hellenizing Jewish party under Menelaus. Bickerman(n)'s view has subsequently been accepted by M. Hengel.[47] It is more likely, however,

44. O. Keel, 'Die kultischen Massnahmen Antiochus' IV. in Jerusalem: Religionsverfolgung und/oder Reformversuch? Eine Skizze', in J. Krašovec (ed.), *The Interpretation of the Bible: The International Symposium in Slovenia* (JSOTSup, 289; Sheffield: Sheffield Academic Press, 1999), pp. 217-42.

45. Cf. R. Mackrodt, 'Olympos', in W. Roscher (ed.), *Ausführliches Lexikon der griechischen und römischen Mythologie*, III (6 vols.; Leipzig: B.G. Teubner, 1897–1909), cols. 847-58 (851-57).

46. E. Bickerman(n), *Der Gott der Makkabäer* (Berlin: Schocken Verlag and Jüdischer Buchverlag, 1937), pp. 90-116; ET *The God of the Maccabees* (trans. H.R. Moehring; SJLA, 32; Leiden: E.J. Brill, 1979), pp. 61-75.

47. M. Hengel, *Judentum und Hellenismus* (WUNT, 10; 2 vols.; Tübingen: J.C.B. Mohr [Paul Siebeck], 2nd edn, 1973), II, pp. 515-54; ET *Judaism and*

that Antiochus' cult should rather be envisaged as pure paganism. This is the viewpoint found in both the earliest Jewish and gentile sources. 2 Macc. 6.7 (cf. 14.33) speaks also of the worship of Dionysus being enforced on the Jews, which suggests that this is not simply a form of monotheism.[48] Although Antiochus did see himself as a god (*theos epiphanes*), the idea that he equated himself with Zeus Olympios is now universally rejected. Antiochus' god, Zeus Olympios (Baal-Shamem), is also referred to as 'the god of fortresses' (Dan. 11. 38),[49] suggesting that he was the god worshipped by the Syrian occupying forces in the fortress known as Acra on Jerusalem's south-eastern hill.

Dagon

Another Canaanite deity who appears in the Old Testament and about whom something needs to be said is Dagon. There is no totally satisfactory place to deal with him but here seems best, as he is sometimes described as the father of Baal in the Ugaritic texts and, as we shall see, he seems to have had something of the nature of a weather and fertility god, like Baal.

As a specifically Canaanite god Dagon appears in the Old Testament only in two place names in Palestine known as Beth-Dagon, one in Judah (Josh. 15.41) and the other in Asher (Josh. 19.27), both names testifying to the presence of temples to this god there.[50] Otherwise, Dagon occurs in the Old Testament only as a god worshipped by the Philistines. Although the Philistines were a non-Semitic people, they were quick to adopt the Canaanite deities, as the Israelites were, and elsewhere we also learn of their worship of Baal-zebul (or Baal-zebub, 2 Kgs 1.2, 3, 6, 16), Astarte (1 Sam. 31.10) and possibly Asherah (in texts from Ekron/Tel Miqne). The impression is given, however, that Dagon was the chief god of the Philistines. We read of sacrifice being made to Dagon at Gaza in the Samson story (Judg. 16.23), implying a

Hellenism (trans. J.S. Bowden; 2 vols.; London: SCM Press, 1974), I, pp. 283-303.

48. So F.G.B. Millar, 'The Background to the Maccabean Revolution: Reflections on Martin Hengel's *Judaism and Hellenism*', *JJS* 29 (1978), pp. 1-21.

49. See J.G. Bunge, 'Der "Gott der Festungen" und der "Liebling der Frauen"', *JSJ* 4 (1973), pp. 169-82.

50. The Beth-Dagon in Judah has sometimes been equated with Beit Dajan, 9 km. south-east of Jaffa, but the latter seems to be far too much to the north-west. The precise location of the Beth-Dagon in Asher is also unknown.

temple there. More particularly we hear of a temple of Dagon at the Philistine city of Ashdod: the image of Dagon fell down there before the Ark of the Covenant after the Philistines had taken it there (1 Sam. 5.1-7), a story which illustrates the superiority of Yahweh to Dagon.[51] Interestingly we know that there was still a temple of Dagon at Ashdod (Azotus) in the middle of the second century BCE, when it was burnt down by Jonathan Maccabaeus (1 Macc. 10.83-84, 11.4). We also hear of a temple of Dagon to which the Philistines are alleged to have fastened Saul's head, presumably at Beth-Shan (1 Chron. 10.10), but this can hardly be an early tradition (cf. 1 Sam. 31.10).

There have been three main views as to the meaning of the name Dagon. The first connects it with the word *dāg* 'fish' and supposes that Dagon was some kind of fish god. This idea is already presupposed in Jerome, who analyses the name Dagon as 'piscis tristitiae', and the concept of Dagon as a fish god is attested in the mediaeval Jewish commentators Rashi and Kimchi, but is now widely rejected as lacking evidence of any antiquity.[52] In 1 Sam. 5.1-7 we read the story of how, when the Philistines had captured the Ark at the battle of Ebenezer/Aphek, the image of Dagon twice fell down before the Ark, and on the second occasion 'behold, Dagon had fallen downward on the ground before the Ark of the Lord, and the head of Dagon and both his hands were lying cut off upon the threshold, and only Dagon was left upon him' (1 Sam. 5.4). The words 'only Dagon was left upon him' (*raq dāgon niš'ar 'ālāyw*) do not make sense. In the nineteenth century, when the fish god view of Dagon still had some credence, J. Wellhausen[53] suggested that the text originally read *dāgô* 'his fishy part', not *dāgôn*, so that we would then read, 'only his fishy part was left on him'. However, for all its ingenuity, this view has been widely rejected, since

51. This is especially emphasized by P.D. Miller and J.J.M. Roberts, *The Hand of the Lord: A Reassessment of the 'Ark Narrative' of 1 Samuel* (Baltimore: The Johns Hopkins University Press, 1977). Cf. M. Delcor, 'Jahwe et Dagon ou le Jahwisme face à la religion des Philistins, d'après 1 Sam. V', *VT* 14 (1964), pp. 136-54; reprinted in M. Delcor, *Etudes bibliques et orientales de religions comparées* (Leiden: E.J. Brill, 1979), pp. 30-48.

52. K. Holter, 'Was Philistine Dagon a Fish-God? Some New Questions and Old Answers', *SJOT* 1 (1989), pp. 142-47, still wants to keep open the possibility that Philistine Dagon might have been regarded as a fish god, but there is no evidence for this.

53. J. Wellhausen, *Der Text der Bücher Samuelis* (Göttingen: Vandenhoeck & Ruprecht, 1871), p. 59.

there is no convincing evidence of sufficient antiquity to suggest that Dagon was of fishy form. From the context and because of its graphical resemblance to *dāgôn*, it has been generally conjectured that the Hebrew text originally read either *gēwô* 'his back' [i.e. trunk], or *gēw dāgôn* 'the back [i.e. trunk] of Dagon'.[54]

A second explanation of the meaning of the name Dagon supposes that it means 'corn' or 'grain'. Unlike the fish explanation, this view can at least claim some ancient support, including some from the Canaanite world. Thus, Philo of Byblos, c. 100 CE, refers to 'Dagon, who is Grain' (Δαγών ὅς ἐστι Σίτων), and states that 'Dagon, since he discovered grain and plough, was called Zeus Ploughman' (Eusebius, *Praeparatio Evangelica* 1.10.16, 1.10.25). Again, Dagon is represented at Palmyra alongside stalks of grain.[55] This coheres with the Hebrew word *dāgān*—a word reflecting the original pronunciation of the divine name as Dagan—which means 'grain, corn', suggesting that the Israelites may well have associated the name of the god with this meaning. The Philistine plain where Dagon was especially worshipped in Palestine was a particularly corn-rich area.[56] That the people at Ugarit much earlier also associated Dagon with the corn is supported by the fact that there is one occasion in the Ugaritic Keret epic where the word *dgn* clearly means 'corn' rather than being the name of the god: 'The ploughmen did lift up their heads, they that prepared the corn[57] [did lift up their heads] on high' (*nš'u. r'iš. ḥrṯm lẓr. 'bd. dgn, KTU*^{2} 1.16.III.13-14).

Although there is thus evidence that the name Dagon was understood already in ancient Canaanite times to mean 'grain' or 'corn', suggesting that Dagon had the nature of a fertility god, it is quite likely that this

54. An alternative conjecture, followed by F.M. Cross and P. Skehan in the *NAB*, is to read *giz'ô* 'his trunk'. Cf. LXX ἡ ῥάχις Δαγὼν 'the spine of Dagon' and Targum *gwpyh* 'his body'. Wellhausen (*Der Text der Bücher Samuelis*, p. 59) thought that LXX's ῥάχις simply reflected MT's *raq* 'only', but this is unlikely as it is already translated by LXX as πλὴν 'only' just prior to this.

55. So H.W. Attridge and R.A. Oden, *Philo of Bybos: The Phoenician History* (CBQMS, 9; Washington DC: Catholic Biblical Association of America, 1981), p. 87.

56. The northern part of this area is referred to in the Phoenician Eshmunazar inscription, which alludes to 'Dor and Joppa, the rich corn lands (or lands of Dagon, *'rṣt dgn*) which are in the plain of Sharon' (*KAI* 14.19).

57. Cf. Isa. 19.9 for a comparable expression, *'ōbᵉdê pištîm* 'the workers in flax'.

was not the original meaning of the name, and that the meaning 'grain' or 'corn' was derivative from the name of the god rather than *vice versa*, just as the word 'cereal' derives from the name of the Roman god Ceres, or, to revert to the Canaanite world, 'the young of your flock' (*'aštᵉrôt ṣō'nekā*), literally 'the Astartes of your sheep', is an expression derived from the name of the fertility goddess Astarte. What supports this understanding is the fact that the earliest sources do not particularly connect Dagon with the grain, though they do suggest that Dagon was a storm god,[58] and of course a storm god is implicitly a fertility god, whence the corn would derive. There is considerable evidence in Mesopotamian sources that Dagon, or Dagan as he originally was, was equated with Enlil (cf. CT 24, 6.22 = 22.120), who was both a high god and one associated with the storm. Further, Dagan at Mari has the goddess Šalaš as a wife, a name which closely resembles that of Šala, wife of the Assyrian storm god Adad (= Hadad). On this understanding, the name Dagon is plausibly connected with the verbs *dagana*, *dagga* and *dagâ* 'to be cloudy, rainy', a view originally suggested by Albright and quite widely followed since.[59] However, although plausible, complete certainty is not possible, as this root is not attested in any other Semitic language apart from vocabulary-rich Arabic.

It has been further claimed, especially by J.J.M. Roberts,[60] that Dagon was also an underworld god, but the evidence for this is not particularly compelling.[61] The earliest firmly dated mention of Dagon, or Dagan as he was originally called, is on an inscription of Sargon of Akkad, about 2350 BCE,[62] who recounts his worship of Dagan at Tutul, a god who gave to Sargon Mari, Iarmuti and Ebla as far as the Cedar Forest and the Silver Mountain. This indicates that the Upper Euphrates

58. Cf. H. Schmökel, 'Dagan', *RLA*, II, pp. 99-101 (100); F.J. Montalbano, 'Canaanite Dagon: Origin, Nature', *CBQ* 13 (1951), pp. 381-97 (396); J.J.M. Roberts, *The Earliest Semitic Pantheon: A Study of the Semitic Deities Attested in Mesopotamia before Ur III* (Baltimore: The John Hopkins University Press, 1972), pp. 18-19.

59. Cf. W.F. Albright, 'Gilgames and Erigidu: Mesopotamian Genii of Fecundity', *JAOS* 40 (1920), pp. 306-35 (319 n. 27); Montalbano, 'Canaanite Dagon', p. 344; Roberts, *The Earliest Semitic Pantheon*, pp. 18-19; N. Wyatt, 'The Relationship of the Deities Dagan and Hadad', *UF* 12 (1980), pp. 375-79 (377).

60. Roberts, *The Earliest Semitic Pantheon*, p. 19.

61. Cf. J.F. Healey, 'The Underworld Character of the God Dagan', *JNSL* 5 (1977), pp. 43-51.

62. Cf. *ANET*, p. 268.

and parts of Syria were particularly Dagon's territory, and this is further confirmed by such texts as those from Ebla and Mari, where Dagon appears as the chief deity.

However, in spite of the early prominence of the god Dagon or Dagan in the Upper Euphrates and in Syria, at Ugarit he underwent such a severe decline that he became virtually redundant. Although Baal is repeatedly called *bn dgn* 'son of Dagon' (cf. KTU^2 1.2.I.18-19; 1.5.VI.23-24), Dagon plays no role in the Ugaritic mythological texts, and is mentioned otherwise only in offering lists (KTU^2 1.46.3; 1.48.5), the pantheon list (KTU^2 1.47.4), in another list (KTU^2 1.123.4), in dedicatory stelae (KTU^2 6.13.2; 6.14.2, whence the assumption that the temple by them was Dagon's, though it could plausibly be El's), and in references to him in connection with a dwelling place at Tutul (KTU^2 1.24.14; 1.100.15). Most likely Dagon's decline at Ugarit is accounted for because his role as storm and fertility god was usurped by Baal, and his position as supreme deity was assumed by El.

A further problem is posed by the fact that in addition to being referred to as the son of Dagon, as noted above, Baal is also represented in the Ugaritic texts as having El as his father (KTU^2 1.3.V.35; 1.4.IV.47). One theory put forward to explain this by J. Fontenrose[63] is certainly to be rejected, namely the idea that Dagon and El are the same deity. If this were the case, it becomes impossible to explain why the names of Dagon and El never occur together in poetic parallelism in the manner of other deities who have various names and titles. Furthermore, Dagon and El appear to be clearly distinguished from one another in offering lists, which makes Fontenrose's supposition that these are different names for the same deity implausible. A further attempt to explain Baal's apparent dual paternity has been proposed by N. Wyatt,[64] who claims that *bn dgn* with regard to Baal is not to be taken literally of his parentage, but rather like Hebrew expressions such as *ben ḥayil*, literally 'son of valour', that is, 'strong/brave man', he believes it means 'son of rain', that is, 'Rainy One'. However, there are various reason why this seems unlikely. First, although 'to be cloudy/rainy' may well be the ultimate etymological meaning of the name Dagon, there is no other evidence for *dgn* 'rain' in Ugaritic; apart from the divine name it means 'grain', as noted above. Secondly, a literal

63. J. Fontenrose, 'Dagon and El', *Oriens* 10 (1957), pp. 277-79.

64. Wyatt, 'Relationship', pp. 375-79. Wyatt curiously thinks that Dagon and Baal are hypostases of the same deity.

meaning of *bn* 'son' is the normal usage of the word, and Wyatt cites no other instances of its metaphorical usage in Ugaritic, as opposed to Hebrew. Thirdly, as Wyatt notes, Baal is also referred to as *ḥtk dgn* (*KTU*^{2} 1.10.III.34), generally rendered 'scion of Dagon', which can claim support from the fact that a related form *ḥtk* means 'parent', being found parallel with *'ab* 'father' (cf. *KTU*^{2} 1.6.IV.34-35). When taken alongside the examples of *bn dgn* in Ugaritic it seems forced for Wyatt to have to explain *ḥtk dgn* as meaning rather 'Lord/Ruler of rain' or possibly 'Lord/Ruler of grain'.[65] It therefore appears that Baal is represented as the son of Dagon as well as being a son of El. This might be viewed as the result of divergent mythological traditions. However, the fact that both notions are found in the same cycle of Baal myths makes this unlikely. The most plausible view is that Baal was literally regarded as the son of Dagon, but that he was also understood as the son of El in the sense that all the Ugaritic gods were, that is, they were his descendants, members of the pantheon which had its origin in El.[66] One may compare the New Testament's references to Jesus Christ as 'son of David'.

65. A further unlikely identification of Dagon is that of F. Løkkegaard, 'Some Comments on the Sanchuniathon Tradtition', *ST* 8 (1954), pp. 68-73, who believes that Dagon is to be equated with Mot. But there is no evidence for this, and the names of Mot and Dagon do not appear together in poetic parallelism. In any case, since Baal was the son of Dagon and Mot was Baal's arch-enemy, it hardly seems likely that Mot is the same deity as Dagon.

66. Perhaps he was son of Dagon and grandson of El (a private communication from D. Pardee).

Chapter 4

YAHWEH'S APPROPRIATION OF BAAL IMAGERY

In the Ugaritic Baal cycle (*KTU*^{2} 1.1-6) there are three main sections. The first is concerned with the conflict between Baal and Yam, the god of the sea, in which Baal is victorious and exalted as king. The second, following on from this, results in the building of a house (palace/ temple) for Baal on Mt Zaphon. The third and final section concerns Baal's conflict with the god of the underworld, Mot, in which Baal is first swallowed up by Mot, which results in the cessation of rain, and this is followed by Baal's resurrection, which presages the return of the rain and guarantees fertility. Each of these three main sections has left echoes in the pages of the Old Testament. These I will consider in turn below. But first I shall consider ways in which the Old Testament has appropriated storm theophany language from Baal.

Yahweh's Appropriation of Baalistic Storm Theophany Language[*]

In Ps. 104.3 Yahweh rides a cloud chariot. This imagery ultimately derives from Baal, whose stock epithet, *rkb 'rpt* (e.g. *KTU*^{2} 1.2.IV.8, 29), may be accepted with the majority of scholars to mean 'rider of the clouds'. Ullendorff, followed by Brock,[1] however, comparing the

* With some additional material and stylistic alterations, this section and the following section on Ps. 29 (pp. 91-98) are taken from my book, *God's Conflict with the Dragon and the Sea*, pp. 30-33, 57-60 and are reprinted here by kind permission of Cambridge University Press.

1. E. Ullendorff, 'Ugaritic Studies within their Semitic and Eastern Mediterranean Setting', *BJRL* 46 (1963–1964), pp. 236-49 (243-44); S.P. Brock, 'Νεφεληγερέτα = *rkb 'rpt*', *VT* 18 (1968), pp. 395-97. For a study of both these expressions, 'rider of the clouds' and 'gatherer of the clouds', see M. Weinfeld, '"Rider of the Clouds" and "Gatherer of the Clouds"', *JANESCU* 5 (Festschrift T.H. Gaster, 1973), pp. 421-26. Weinfeld shows that both concepts are found in Greek mythology and Near Eastern mythology, in which latter, he claims, they both had their origin.

epithet of Zeus, νεφεληγερέτης, or νεφεληγερέτα, holds that Baal's epithet should rather be translated 'gatherer of the clouds', but against this the following points may be made. First, as de Moor has pointed out,[2] the name *Be-'-li-ra-kab-bi* 'Baal of the chariot', is known from Sam'al, and the Egyptian King Rameses III compared himself with Baal when he drove out in his chariot. Secondly, the rare occasions when *rkb* is found in Ugaritic apart from the expression *rkb 'rpt* show that 'ride' or 'mount' is the meaning, not 'gather'. Thus, in *KTU*[2] 1.14.IV.2-4 there appears, *w'ly lẓr. mgdl. rkb ṯkmm. ḥmt.* 'he went up to the top of the tower, mounted the shoulder of the wall', and there are almost identical words in *KTU*[2] 1.14.II.21-22. Thirdly, it is significant that in various Old Testament texts, including the one currently under consideration, the verb *rkb* 'to ride', or related nouns meaning 'chariot', are associated with the clouds, whether explicitly or implicitly (Deut. 33.26; Ps. 18.11 [ET 10] = 2 Sam. 22.11 [emended], 68.34 [ET 33] 104.3; Isa. 19.11, 66.16). Since the Israelites were far more intimately related to the Canaanites than the Greeks, the Old Testament parallels involving *rkb* are far more relevant in elucidating the meaning of Ugaritic *rkb 'rpt* than an epithet of the Greek god Zeus. (Interestingly, where Canaanite and other Near Eastern traditions are appropriated to Zeus, in conflict with the dragon Typhon, he is represented as *mounting* a winged horse.)

However, I do not think that the Ugaritic *rkb 'rpt* 'rider of the clouds' has its exact equivalent in the expression *rōkēb bā'ᵃrābôt*, used of Yahweh in Ps. 68.5 (ET 4), contrary to what is now a widely held opinion.[3] It is a sound principle that if a Hebrew word makes good

2. J.C. de Moor, *The Seasonal Pattern in the Ugaritic Myth of Ba'lu* (AOAT, 16; Neukirchen–Vluyn: Neukirchener Verlag, 1971), p. 98.

3. Earliest of all in perceiving a reference to the clouds in this expression, even before the discovery of the Ugaritic texts, was apparently Bishop J.W. Colenso, *The Pentateuch and Book of Joshua Critically Examined* (7 parts; London: Longmans, Green & Co., 1879), VII, appendix 150, pp. 114-15, who compared Ps. 68.34 (ET 33) and wondered whether *bā'ᵃrābôt* should be emended to *bā'ābôt*. Similarly, S. Mowinckel, *Det Gamle Testamentes Salmebok. Første del: Salmene i oversettelse* (Kristiania: H. Aschehoug, 1923), p. 94, rendered 'clouds', 'vielleicht in Anlehnung an Grätz's Vorschlag 'ꜥaḇoṯ' (S. Mowinckel, *Der achtundsechzigste Psalm* [Avhandlinger utg. av det Norske videnskaps-akademii Oslo. II. Historisk-filosofisk Klasse, 1953, 1; Oslo: J. Dybwad, 1953], p. 27 n. 1). Since the discovery of the Ugaritic texts it has become very common to equate *rōkēb bā'ᵃrābôt* with *rkb 'rpt*. Some even emend the Hebrew text to *rōkēb* (*bā*)*'ᵃrāpôt* in order to bring it even

sense in its normally attested meaning, it should be accepted, rather than creating an unnecessary *hapax legomenon*. Therefore, since *'ᵃrābâ* in Hebrew means 'desert', it would seem wiser to translate *rōkēb bā'ᵃrābôt* as 'rider through the deserts', rather than 'rider of the clouds'. Moreover, as A.R. Johnson rightly points out,[4] this rendering makes excellent sense in the context, which clearly reflects the Hebrew traditions of the Wandering and the Settlement. Thus, for example, vv. 8-9 (ET 7-8), like Judg. 5.4-5, recall Yahweh's marching through the wilderness from Sinai, and v. 7 (ET 6) refers to 'the wilderness' (*ṣᵉḥîḥâ*). The full phrase in Ps. 68.5 (ET 4) is *sōllû lārōkēb bā'ᵃrābôt*, the verb *sll* that is used here being found elsewhere in the Old Testament with the meaning 'to cast up a way (or highway)', and never with the meaning 'lift up a song', which is sometimes understood here. Now, in Isa. 40.3 there appears *bā'ᵃrābâ mᵉsillâ* 'a highway in the desert'. The fact that here, *'ᵃrābâ*, 'desert', is used in connection with a noun from the root *sll* adds support to the view that *rōkēb ba'ᵃābôt* should be rendered 'rider through the deserts'.[5] Deutero-Isaiah may have been dependent on this very psalm for the expression; if so, this would be in keeping with his dependence on other psalms concerned with Yahweh's kingship, which is generally conceded. Nevertheless, in spite of all that has been said, it is still likely that Yahweh is here conceived as riding *on* a cloud (cf. Ps. 68.34 [ET 33]), though it perceives him as riding on a cloud *through* the deserts. It is also possible, perhaps even probable, that the expression *rōkēb bā'ᵃrābôt* is a deliberate distortion of the epithet *rkb 'rpt*.[6]

Returning to Ps. 104.3, we read that Yahweh 'rides on the wings of

closer to the Ugaritic, such as H.L. Ginsberg, 'The Ugaritic Texts and Textual Criticism', *JBL* 62 (1943), pp. 109-15 (112-13), and W.F. Albright, 'A Catalogue of Early Hebrew Lyric Poems (Psalm LXVIII)', *HUCA* 23 (1950–51), pp. 1-39 (12, 18). Others, such as G.R. Driver, *Canaanite Myths and Legends* (Edinburgh: T. & T. Clark, 1956), p. 128, noting the interchange of Ugaritic *p* and Hebrew *b*, maintain that no emendation is necessary. The emendation of *'ᵃrābôt* to *'ᵃrāpôt* was made even before the discovery of the Ugaritic texts by F.X. Wutz, *Die Psalmen, textkritisch untersucht* (Munich: Kösel & Pustet, 1925), p. 171, referring to Akkadian *eriptu*, *urpatu*, 'clouds', with the secondary form, *irbitu*.

4. A.R. Johnson, *Sacral Kingship in Ancient Israel* (Cardiff: University of Wales Press, 2nd edn, 1967), p. 78 n. 6.

5. This point has also been made by Ohler, *Mythologische Elemente*, p. 63.

6. This is noted as a possiblity by J.C. de Moor, 'Cloud', *IDBSup*, pp. 168-69 (169), but the same idea occurred to me independently.

the wind', which implies that his cloud chariot is drawn by winged horses symbolizing the wind. This concept is found in the context of the *Chaoskampf*, not only in the almost identical phrase in Ps. 18.11 (ET 10) alluded to above, but also in Hab. 3.8, which reads: 'Was your wrath against the rivers, O Lord? Was your anger against the rivers, or your indignation against the sea, when you rode your horses, upon your chariot of victory?' (Admittedly, no wings are mentioned here.) Very striking also is the fact that Zeus is represented as mounting a winged horse in his conflict with the dragon Typhon (Apollodorus, *The Library* 1.6.3), a conflict that certainly reflects Baal's struggle with the dragon, since part of it takes place at Mt Casius, that is, Mt Zaphon, the mountain where Baal was in conflict with the dragon (Apollodorus, *The Library* 1.6.3; cf. *KTU*^{2} 1.3.III.37-1.3.IV.1). It may therefore be plausibly argued that this motif is ultimately derived from Baal mythology.[7] The very fact that Baal had a cloud chariot implies that it was drawn by horses, and I have elsewhere argued that the Ugaritic texts may actually allude to them (in the word *mdl*).[8] Thus, *KTU*^{2}

7. That Mt Casius (Zaphon) was the location of the struggle between Zeus and Typhon is also supported by the evidence of Strabo (16.2.7), who reports the local tradition thtat the struggle between Zeus and Typhon took place near the river Orontes—a river, it should be noted, that flows into the Mediterranean just a little north of Mt Casius—and that this was carved out by Typhon, who disappeared in the earth at its source, whence the Orontes was originally called Typhon. Also, it may be noted that Herodotus (3.5) reports that Typhon was buried by the Sirbonian Sea, which in its turn was adjacent to the Egyptian Mt Casius (Baal-Zaphon). Although the location of the struggle between Zeus and Typhon at Mt Casius clearly goes back ultimately to the Canaanite myth of Baal and the dragon, it seems that this motif was mediated not directly from Canaan, but through the Hurrian–Hittite myth of Ullikummi, as this is now generally held to be behind the Typhon myth. Cf. H.G. Güterbock, *Kumarbi* (Zürich and New York: Europaverlag, 1946), pp. 100-15, and in S.N. Kramer (ed.), *Mythologies of the Ancient World* (Garden City, NY: Doubleday, 1961), p. 172. In the Ullikummi myth it is at Mt Ḫazzi (i.e. Casius) that the monster Ullikummi is seen rising out of the sea. For the text of Ullikummi, see H.G. Güterbock, 'The Song of Ullikummi: Revised Text of the Hittite Version of a Hurrian Myth', *JCS* 5 (1951), pp. 135-61, and *JCS* 6 (1952), pp. 8-42. There is also a translation by A. Goetze in *ANET*, pp. 121-25.

8. J. Day, 'Echoes of Baal's Seven Thunders and Lightnings in Psalm xxix and Habakkkuk iii 9 and the Identity of the Seraphim in Isaiah vi', *VT* 29 (1979), pp. 143-51 (147 n.18). The meaning of *mdl* is, however, disputed. J.C. de Moor, 'Der *mdl* Baals im Ugaritischen', ZAW 78 (1966), pp. 69-71, suggests the translation 'thunderbolt', comparing Akkadian *mudulu*, 'pole', but the fact that the Hebrew and

1.5.V.6b-11 states that the god Mot commanded Baal to descend into the underworld with his meteorological phenomena: *w'at. qḥ 'rptk. rḥk. mdlk mṭrk. 'mk. šb't ġlmk. ṯmn. ḫnzrk 'mk. pdry. bt. 'ar 'mk. {t}ṭly. bt. rb.*, 'And you take your clouds, your wind, your chariot team, your rain, take with you your seven servitors and your eight boars, take Pidriya daughter of dew with you, and Ṭaliya daughter of showers with you.'

The Seven Thunders of Psalm 29 as an Appropriation from Baal

Psalm 29

1 Give to the Lord, O gods,[9]
Give to the Lord glory and strength.
2 Give to the Lord the glory of his name,
worship the Lord in the beauty of holiness.
3 The voice of the Lord is upon the waters,
the God of glory thunders,
the Lord, upon many waters.
4 The voice of the Lord is powerful,
the voice of the Lord is majestic.
5 The voice of the Lord breaks the cedars,
the Lord breaks the cedars of Lebanon.
6 He makes Lebanon skip like a calf,
and Sirion like a young wild ox.
7 The voice of the Lord flashes forth flames of fire.
8 The voice of the Lord shakes the wilderness,
the Lord shakes the wilderness of Kadesh.

Aramaic cognates have *ṭ* rather than *d* renders this improbable. Driver, *Canaanite Myths and Legends*, p. 161, holds the word to mean 'bucket' (cf. Hebrew, *d[e]lî*, Akkadian, *madlû*). The translation 'chariot team' is admittedly uncertain, but rests on a comparison with the Ugaritic verb *mdl*, meaning 'to harness' (cf. *KTU*[2] 1.4.IV.9 and 1.19.II.3. 8). Baal's *mdl* would then be 'that which is harnessed', that is, his 'chariot team', drawing the clouds (cf. Hab. 3.8). Cf. Aistleitner's translation, 'Gespann', *Wörterbuch*, no. 744a. Note that Hebrew and Ugaritic *ṣmd* are similarly employed, both as a verb meaning 'to harness' and as a noun denoting the animals thus yoked together. One may compare the fact that in a hymn to Ishkur, Ishkur, who 'rides the storm' like Baal, is commissioned by Enlil: 'Let the seven winds be harnessed before you like a team, harness the winds before you' (*ANET*, p. 578). According to J.C. Greenfield, 'Ugaritic *mdl* and its Cognates', *Bib* 45 (1964), pp. 527-34, the verbal form *mdl* is to be understood as a metathesis of the *lmd*, 'to bind, tie', which is attested in Mishnaic Hebrew and Syriac.

9. Literally, 'sons of gods' (*b[e]nê 'ēlîm*). Compare the expression 'sons of the prophets'.

9 The voice of the Lord makes the oaks whirl,
and strips the forests bare,[10]
and in his temple all say, 'Glory!'
10 The Lord sits enthroned over the flood,
the Lord sits enthroned as king for ever.
11 May the Lord give strength to his people,
may the Lord bless his people with peace.

This is a psalm connected with the theme of Yahweh's kingship (cf. v. 10) and surely had its *Sitz im Leben* at the Feast of Tabernacles, a fact still attested by the superscription to the psalm in the LXX. Yahweh's lordship over the cosmic waters is alluded to in v. 3, and it is most natural to suppose that this is also being referred to in v. 10, rather than an allusion to Noah's flood.[11]

Yahweh's kingship in this psalm is manifested in the thunder, just like that of Baal, and the thunder is represented as his voice, as was also the case with Baal (cf. *KTU*² 1.4.VII.29-31). Yahweh's lordship over the cosmic waters (vv. 3, 10) and exaltation over the other gods of the divine assembly (v. 1) is also ultimately derived from Baal mythology. In addition, I have pointed out[12] a further striking parallel with Baal mythology that was previously unnoted. This is the sevenfold manifestation of the deity in the thunder, the *qôl yahweh* (vv. 3a, 4a, 4b, 5, 7, 8, 9). In *KTU*² 1.101.3b-4 (*Ugaritica*, V, 3.3b-4), it is said of Baal:

3b *šbʿt. brqm.* [[.ṯ]]	Seven lightnings...
4 *ṯmnt. ʾiṣr rʿt. ʿṣ. brq. y*[ ]	Eight storehouses of thunder. The shaft of lightning...

Now, the numerical sequence 7/8 is capable of meaning simply seven in Ugaritic, the second number having the nature of what has been called

10. Reading *ʾêlôt* 'oaks' for MT *ʾayyālôt* 'hinds', since this provides a more appropriate parallel to the following line's reference to forests (*yᵉʿārôt*). Moreover, if the MT were to be retained and we read 'The voice of the Lord makes the hinds to calve', this would be unique in the Old Testament theophany depictions. On the other hand, references to Yahweh's theophanic manifestations against oaks, alongside cedars of Lebanon (cf. Ps. 29.5-6) are well attested (cf. Isa. 2.13; Zech. 11.1-2). This also makes one sceptical of G.R. Driver's proposal ('Studies in the Vocabulary of the Old Testament, II', *JTS* 32 [1930–31], pp. 250-57 (255-56) to read the second half of the verse as 'and he causes the premature birth of kids', reading *wayyaḥśēp* for MT, *wayyeḥᵉśōp*.

11. *Contra* A. Weiser, *Die Psalmen* (ATD, 14/15; Göttingen: Vandenhoeck & Ruprecht, 5th edn, 1959), p. 178; ET *The Psalms* (OTL; London: SCM Press, 1962), p. 265.

12. J. Day, 'Echoes', pp. 143-45.

'automatic parallelism'[13] (cf. *KTU*² 1.6.V.8-9 and *KTU*² 1.19.I.42-44). It therefore seems that this is a reference to Baal's seven thunders as well as lightnings (cf. Hab. 3.9), the parallel to Psalm 29 being even closer when it is noted that in *KTU*² 1.101.1-3a, immediately before the reference to Baal's seven thunders and lightnings, we read of Baal's enthronement like the flood: *b'l. yṯb. kṯbt. ġr. hd. r*[ ] *kmdb. btk. ġrh. 'il ṣpn. b*[*tk*] *ġr. tl'iyt*, 'Baal sits enthroned, like the sitting of a mountain, Hadad [ ] like the flood, in the midst of his mountain, the god of Zaphon in the [midst of] the mountain of victory', just as Ps. 29.10 states, 'The Lord sits enthroned over the flood, the Lord sits enthroned as king for ever'. The fact that the seven thunders of Psalm 29 go back to Baal mythology means that they are an integral part of the original psalm, a fact that serves to rebut the article of S. Mittmann,[14] who holds that the original psalm consisted of only vv. 1bc (ET 1), 2, 3, 4, 5, 8, 9bc and 10, which leaves him with only a fivefold *qôl yahweh* in the thunder. O. Loretz[15] sees only six thunders as original here, v. 7 being understood as secondary, but this is highly speculative.

There can thus be no doubt that Psalm 29 stands remarkably close to the circle of mythological ideas surrounding Baal as they are attested in the Ugaritic texts. A number of scholars, in particular H.L. Ginsberg, T.H. Gaster, F.M. Cross and A. Fitzgerald,[16] go so far as to maintain that Psalm 29 is a Canaanite psalm taken over wholesale, with the simple substitution of the name of Yahweh instead of Baal for the deity concerned (Ginsberg and Cross also maintaining that v. 11 is a Yahwistic addition). This is possible, but cannot claim to be proven. Verse 8 refers to Yahweh's shaking the wilderness of Kadesh in connection with his theophany. If this alludes to Yahweh's theophany at Sinai (cf. Deut. 33.2, which seems to refer to Meribath-Kadesh, cf. LXX; Exod. 19.16-19; Judg. 5.4-5; Ps. 68.8-9 [ET 7-8] etc.), widely attested else-

13. Cf. M. Haran, 'The Graded Numerical Sequence and the Phenomenon of "Automatism" in Biblical Poetry', *Congress Volume, Uppsala 1971* (VTSup, 22; Leiden: E.J. Brill, 1972), pp. 238-67.

14. S. Mittmann, 'Komposition und Redaktion von Psalm XXIX', *VT* 28 (1978), pp. 172-94.

15. O. Loretz, *Psalm 29: Kanaanäische El- und Baaltraditionen in jüdischer Sicht* (UBL, 2; Altenberge: CIS–Verlag, 1984), pp. 42-46, 114-16.

16. H.L. Ginsberg, *Kitᵉbê 'ûgārît* (Jerusalem: Bialik Foundation, 1936), pp. 129-31; T.H. Gaster, 'Psalm 29', *JQR* 37 (1946–47), pp. 55-65; F.M. Cross, 'Notes on a Canaanite Psalm in the Old Testament', *BASOR* 117 (1950), pp. 19-21; A. Fitzgerald, 'A Note on Psalm 29', *BASOR* 215 (1974), pp. 61-63.

where in the Old Testament, this would appear to militate against the view that Psalm 29 is nothing more than a Canaanite psalm with the simple substitution of Yahweh for Baal. It is probably safer to suppose that Psalm 29 is an Israelite composition largely modelled on the language used by the Canaanites about Baal, rather than to suppose that it is a Baal psalm *pure simple* with the substitution of the name Yahweh for Baal. O. Loretz's view[17] that Psalm 29 combines three originally separate compositions, vv. 1-2 and 9c based on El traditions and vv. 3-9b and 10-11 based on two separate Baal traditions, seems overly speculative. The mere fact that Ps. 29.1 refers to the 'sons of gods', reminiscent of the Ugaritic sons of El, does not prove that this section is indebted to El rather than Baal traditions. One may compare *KTU*² 1.4.VI.44-59, where Baal entertains the sons of El in his palace, the symbol of his victory.

Yahweh's Conflict with the Dragon and the Sea: The Appropriation of a Baal Motif[*]

The Divine Conflict with the Dragon and the Sea at the Time of Creation

The Old Testament contains a number of allusions to Yahweh's battle with a dragon and the sea. Sometimes this is associated with the time of the creation of the world, at other times the dragon or sea is historicized, alluding to a hostile nation or nations, and occasionally the imagery is eschatologized, referring to some hostile power at the end time. At the end of the nineteenth century H. Gunkel[18] claimed that this was a Yahwistic version of the Babylonian myth of the god Marduk's conflict with the female sea monster Tiamat, narrated in Enuma elish, which preceded Marduk's creation of the world. This view to some extent persisted into the twentieth century, especially with regard to the Priestly creation account in Genesis 1, where it has often been thought that *t*ᵉ*hōm* 'deep' in Gen. 1.2 is a reminiscence of the name of Tiamat (but see below). However, in general, since the discovery of the Ugaritic texts from 1929 onwards, it has become generally accepted that the Old

17. Loretz, *Psalm 29*, *passim*.

* For a much more detailed consideration of all the topics considered in this section, with thorough documentation, see J. Day, *God's Conflict with the Dragon and the Sea*, *passim*.

18. H. Gunkel, *Schöpfung und Chaos in Urzeit und Endzeit* (Göttingen: Vandenhoeck & Ruprecht, 1895).

Testament's references to a divine conflict with a dragon and the sea are an echo of Canaanite rather than Babylonian mythology.

In the Old Testament the dragon is sometimes called Leviathan, and he is said to have had more than one head (Ps. 74.14) and is referred to as a *tannîn* 'dragon' and is described as a 'twisting serpent' (Isa. 27.1). In the Ugaritic texts we similarly read of a seven-headed dragon (*tnn*) called *ltn*, frequently vocalized by modern scholars as Lotan, but more probably Litan,[19] and he is referred to as having been defeated by the god Baal (KTU^2 1.5.I.1-3) as well as by the goddess Anat (KTU^2 1.3.III.40-42). Elsewhere in the Old Testament we find the dragon called Rahab (e.g. Ps. 89.11 [ET 10]): this name is not attested in any extra-biblical text, though as he is called 'the twisting serpent' (Job 26.12-13) this is presumably an alternative name for Leviathan.

The Ugaritic texts only give brief allusions to the victory of Baal and Anat over Leviathan. On the other hand, we have a detailed account of the victory of Baal over Yam. The latter does not appear to be a creation account and one can but speculate that the former may have been associated with the creation of the world, as is the case with some of the Old Testament's allusions to God's conflict with the dragon and the sea. How exactly the Canaanite myth of Baal's conflict with the dragon and the sea relates to the Babylonian conflict of Marduk with Tiamat is also unclear. Conceivably some connection might be indicated by a Mari text from the reign of King Zimri-Lim, which states, quoting the storm god Adad, 'When you [Zimri-Lim] sat on the throne of your father, I gave you the weapons with which I fought against sea (*tâmtum*)'.[20]

Quite a number of the references to God's conflict with the dragon and the sea at the time of creation occur in the Psalms. Both Psalms 74 (cf. vv. 12-17) and 89 (cf. vv. 10-15 [ET 9-14]) cite Yahweh's defeat of the dragon (Leviathan or Rahab) and the sea as grounds of hope in Yahweh's power in the exile when the temple and Davidic monarchy had come to an end and the powers of chaos appeared to have triumphed. Such use of the *Chaoskampf* motif implies that it was already well known in the pre-exilic period. Psalms which have this theme that are probably pre-exilic include Pss. 93.3-4, 65.7-8 (ET 6-7), 104.6-9, which

19. See J.A. Emerton, 'Leviathan and *ltn*: The Vocalization of the Ugaritic Word for the Dragon', *VT* 32 (1982), pp. 327-31.

20. See D. Charpin and J.-M. Durand, '"Fils de Sim'al": Les origines tribales des rois de Mari', *RA* 80 (1986), pp. 141-83 (174).

set the conflict with the waters in the time of the creation of the world, and Ps. 29.3, 10, which associate it with Yahweh's continuing lordship over creation. As I have argued in detail elsewhere,[21] there are good grounds for continuing to accept S. Mowinckel's thesis[22] that the theme of Yahweh's kingship, with which the divine victory over the dragon and the sea was closely associated, had its cultic setting in ancient Israel in the feast of Tabernacles.

In addition to the Psalms another book which has a considerable number of references to God's conflict with the dragon and the sea is Job (Job 3.8, 7.12, 9.8, 13, 26.12-13, 38.8-11, 40.15–41.26 [ET 34]). In some of these passages the context of the conflict is clearly implied to be the creation of the world (Job 9.8, 13, 26.12-13, 38.8-11), and this is probably the case with the others too. Why should the dragon and the sea conflict be prominent in the book of Job? First, belief in God as creator is the fundamental presupposition of the Wisdom literature, including the book of Job, and as has just been noted, the dragon and sea imagery in Job is very much bound up with the time of creation. Although the *Chaoskampf* imagery is remarkably absent in the other Wisdom books (though cf. Prov. 8.24, 27-29), the writer of the book of Job appears to have been dependent on cultic psalms of praise in which the conflict had a place (cf. Job 9.8, 13). A second reason for the prominence of the *Chaoskampf* theme in Job is that the writer clearly saw a parallel between Job' argument with God and the conflict between the dragon/sea and God (cf. Job 7.12, 9.13-14, 40.15–41.26 [ET 34]). (See below on Job 40.15–41.26 [ET 34].) Just to quote one example, one may note Job 7.12, where Job complains, 'Am I the sea, or a sea monster, that you set a guard over me?'

There are several passages in the Old Testament where Yahweh does not have a battle with the waters at the time of creation but simply controls them. Especially noteworthy here is the P account of creation in Gen. 1.2, 6-10, but other passages include Ps. 33.7-8, Prov. 8.24, 27-29, Jer. 5.22 and 31.35. There are good grounds for thinking that this represents a demythologization of the divine conflict with the dragon and the

21. See J. Day, *Psalms* (OTG; Sheffield: Sheffield Academic Press, 1990), pp. 67-87. A.R. Petersen, *The Royal God: Enthronement Festivals in Ancient Israel and Ugarit?* (JSOTSup, 259; Sheffield: Sheffield Academic Press, 1998), fails to take account of my arguments when questioning Mowinckel's theory of an Enthronement festival in ancient Israel.

22. S. Mowinckel, *Psalmenstudien*, II (6 vols.; Kristiania: J. Dybwad, 1922).

sea, so that the battle has become simply a job of work. In the case of Genesis 1 it seems possible to prove this. The order of creation in Genesis 1 as a whole is the same as in Psalm 104, in which a battle with the waters occurs, and there is clearly a literary relationship between them.

Psalm 104		*Genesis 1*
1-4	Creation of heaven and earth	Cf. 1-5
5-9	Waters pushed back	Cf. 6-10
10-13	Waters put to beneficial use	Implicit in 6-10
14-18	Creation of vegetation	Cf. 11-12
19-23	Creation of luminaries	Cf. 14-18
24-26	Creation of sea creatures	Cf. 20-22
27-30	Creation of living creatures	Cf. 24-31

That it is Genesis 1 which is dependent on Psalm 104 rather than the reverse is suggested by the following points. First, Psalm 104 is more mythological, speaking as it does of a battle with the waters (vv. 6-9) and referring to Leviathan (v. 26), whereas Genesis 1 simply has God's control of the waters (vv. 6-10) and speaks of great sea monsters (v. 26), and it seems more natural to suppose that Genesis 1 has demythologized Psalm 104 than that Psalm 104 has remythologized Genesis 1. The fact that Psalm 104 also displays remarkable parallels with the fourteenth-century BCE Egyptian Pharaoh Akhenaten's Hymn to the Sun further suggests that this is Psalm 104's basic source, not Genesis 1. Secondly, the form of the word for 'beasts' in Gen. 1.24, *ḥay*ᵉ*tô*, occurs elsewhere only in poetry, including Ps. 104.11, 20, suggesting that a poetic source, indeed Psalm 104, underlies Genesis 1.

Interestingly, Gen. 1.2's use of the word *t*ᵉ*hōm* to denote the primaeval waters appears also in Ps. 104.6. This, together with the fact that the form of the word *t*ᵉ*hōm* lacks the feminine ending, suggests that it is not directly taken over from the Mesopotamian sea monster Tiamat. Since the word *thm* occurs in Ugaritic it is more natural to assume a Canaanite prototype for the *t*ᵉ*hōm* here.

As D.T. Tsumura and T. Fenton have shown,[23] *tōhû wābōhû* in Gen. 1.2 strictly denotes nothingness rather than chaos. Nevertheless, this

23. D.T. Tsumura, *The Earth and the Waters in Genesis 1 and 2: A Linguistic Investigation* (JSOTSup, 83; Sheffield: JSOT Press, 1989); T. Fenton, 'Chaos in the Bible? Tohu vabohu', in G. Abramson and T. Parfitt (eds.), *Jewish Education and Learning: Published in Honour of Dr David Patterson on the Occasion of his Seventieth Birthday* (London: Harwood Academic Publishers, 1993), pp. 203-20.

does not mean that we should cease to speak of chaos in connection with the Old Testament's myth of the dragon and the sea, since watery chaos does seem a fair description of the uncontrolled raging waters that the Old Testament depicts as the primaeval state of affairs in various poetic passages. As J.D. Levenson[24] has emphasized, though provisionally tamed at creation, the powers of chaos are able to reassert themselves in threatening ways.

The Alleged Naturalization of the Chaos Monsters

Job 40.15–41.26 (ET 34) contains a description of two beasts, Behemoth and Leviathan. It has often been claimed that these are the names of two actually existing creatures rather than mythical beasts. The most commonly held view, following S. Bochart in his *Hierozoicon* of 1663,[25] is that Behemoth is the hippopotamus and Leviathan the crocodile. Such views are, however, seriously open to question. It is clearly implied that Job and, by implication, humans generally, are unable to overcome these creatures and that only Yahweh has control over them. This alone tends to rule out the various natural creatures suggested for Behemoth and Leviathan such as the hippopotamus and crocodile, since these were certainly captured in the ancient Near East. Moreover, the particular details given in the descriptions do not fit actual known creatures. Thus, Leviathan is said to breathe out fire and smoke (Job 40.10-13, ET 1-21), a clear indication that a dragon is in mind. Leviathan is elsewhere in the Old Testament (including Job, cf. 3.8) as well as in Ugaritic no natural creature but a mythical sea serpent or dragon, and it is most natural to suppose that this is also the case here, though from the description it appears that he now has only one head rather than seven.

There are good grounds for seeing Behemoth too as a mythical monster. Certainly the description of its tail as high and lifted up like a cedar (Job 40.19) is odd if the allusion is to the hippopotamus or other natural creatures that have been suggested. As with Leviathan, it is implied that it cannot be captured and that God alone can master it (Job 40.9-14, 24). The name Behemoth means 'great ox', and interestingly the Ugaritic texts twice mention a mythical ox-like creature alongside

24. J.D. Levenson, *Creation and the Persistence of Evil: The Jewish Drama of Divine Omnipotence* (San Francisco: Harper & Row, 1988).

25. S. Bochart, *Hierozoicon* (2 vols.; London, 1663), II, cols. 769-96. Many commentators have followed this view since then.

Leviathan known as Arsh or El's calf Atik (*KTU*[2] 1.3.III.40-44; 1.6.VI.51-53), and this must surely be the ultimate source of the figure of Behemoth. Moreover, in the second Ugaritic allusion Arsh is represented as being in the sea, just as Behemoth is depicted as dwelling in a river in Job 40.23.

Granted that Leviathan and Behemoth are mythical creatures, it seems natural to suppose that the presupposition is that Yahweh had overcome them in connection with the creation of the world. Leviathan's defeat by Yahweh is clearly associated with the time of creation in Ps. 74.14. Nothing in the text suggests that Leviathan and Behemoth are here symbolic of foreign nations. Rather the implication seems to be that, just as Job cannot overcome the chaos monsters Behemoth and Leviathan, which Yahweh defeated at creation, how much less can he (Job) overcome the God who vanquished them. His only appropriate response is therefore humble submission to God (Job 42.1-6). The point being made here is very similar to that found in Job 9.13-14.

The Historicization of the Divine Conflict with the Dragon and the Sea

One interesting phenomenon which we find in the Old Testament is that the dragon and the sea are sometimes historicized to denote a particular nation or nations which are deemed to be God's enemies. Thus, Rahab, which we have seen is an alternative name for Leviathan, is used to denote Egypt in Isa. 30.7, 'For Egypt's help is worthless and empty, therefore I have called her "the silenced Rahab"' (reading *rahab hammošbāt* for the meaningless MT *rahab hēm šābet*, which can hardly be rendered 'Rahab who sits still' [RSV]). Again, Rahab clearly appears as the name of a country in Ps. 87.4, 'I reckon Rahab and Babylon as those that know me; behold Philistia and Tyre with Ethiopia...', and from the context Rahab here must surely be Egypt: its mention in the first place suggests an important country, and it would be odd for Egypt not to be mentioned when Ethiopia is.

Further, the Egyptian Pharaoh is referred to as the dragon in Ezek. 29.3-5, 32.2-8, reading *tannîn* 'dragon' for the MT's *tannîm* 'jackals' (Ezek. 29.3, 32.2), which does not make sense, as is generally agreed. There are no grounds for supposing that a crocodile is thereby denoted, as some imagine.

The *Chaoskampf* imagery seems to be applied to Egypt at the time of the Exodus in Isa. 51.9 (cf. v. 10) and Ps. 77. 17-21 (ET 16-20). Related to this but somewhat different is the Song of Moses in Exod. 15.1-18, where the divine battle is no longer with the sea but rather at the sea, as F.M. Cross[26] has emphasized. The influence of Baal's conflict with Yam on the depiction is supported by the association of the divine conflict at the sea with the kingship of God (Exod. 15.18) and the construction of the deity's mountain sanctuary, described in language reminiscent of that of Baal on Zaphon (see below). However, it seems to be going too far to claim with C. Kloos[27] that the Reed Sea miracle is nothing more than a Yahwistic historicization of Baal's victory over Yam.

The chaos waters appear to be taken up to denote the Assyrians who attack Zion in Isa. 17.12-14 (cf. 8.5-8), and both the waters and the dragon symbolize the Babylonians in the time of the conquering King Nebuchadrezzar in Hab. 3.8-10, 15 and Jer. 51.34 respectively. Jeremiah 51.34 says of Judah, 'Nebuchadrezzar the king of Babylon has devoured me, he has crushed me; he has made me an empty vessel, he has swallowed me like a monster (*tannîn*); he has filled his belly with my delicacies, he has rinsed me out'. Because of a certain similarity to the imagery of the great fish swallowing up Jonah in the book of Jonah, it has sometimes been thought that the latter is an allegory for the exile and is dependent on Jer. 51.34. Both ideas are to be rejected, however. Elsewhere in the Old Testament allegories are clearly indicated as such (cf. Ezek. 17, 19), and if Jonah in the fish symbolizes Israel in exile, it is odd that the Assyrian empire is still in power after the 'exile' as well as before it. Further, the verbal parallels are not such as to suggest Jonah's direct dependence on Jer. 51.34. Nevertheless, it is quite likely that the Canaanite chaos dragon ultimately lies behind the great fish: this is suggested by the fact that Joppa, Jonah's place of embarkation, is also strongly associated with the story of Perseus' deliverance of Andromeda from a mythical sea monster, a tradition already attested by Pseudo-Scylax in the fourth century BCE, the probable date of the book of Jonah.

It has sometimes been supposed that Bashan in Ps. 68.23 (ET 22) is a name for the dragon and is cognate with Ugaritic *bṯn* 'serpent', employed of Leviathan in *KTU*^{2} 1.5.I.1. However, Hebrew already has *peten* 'snake' cognate with Ugaritic *bṯn*, so it is not likely to have also had *bāšān*; moreover, Bashan has just occurred in Ps. 68.16-17 (ET 15-16) as the name of a mountain (probably Mt Hermon), so this is doubt-

26. Cross, *Canaanite Myth and Hebrew Epic*, pp. 131-32.

27. See C. Kloos, *Yhwh's Combat with the Sea: A Canaanite Tradition in the Religion of Ancient Israel* (Leiden: E.J. Brill, 1986), pp. 127-212.

less the case in v. 23 (ET 22) too, now mentioned as a high place in antithetic parallelism with the sea. The reference to 'the beasts of the reeds', the herd of bulls with the calves of the people' a few verses later in Ps. 68.30 (ET 29) is also unlikely to denote a chaos monster (cf. Behemoth), since Behemoth was a single monster, but this verse refers to a multiplicity of bulls and calves, making it more likely that this is an example of animal terms being used to denote leaders and warriors, as in 1 Sam. 21.8, Job 24.22, 34.20, and Lam. 1.5.

There are occasions where the chaos waters seem to represent hostile nations generally rather than simply a specific nation. This is the case, for example, in Psalm 46, one of the Zion Psalms depicting nations coming up to attack Jerusalem, who are then miraculously defeated by Yahweh, a motif found also in Psalms 48 and 76, taken up by the prophet Isaiah to refer to the invading Assyrians (cf. Isa. 17.12-14, 29.1-8, 31.1-9), and eschatologized in Joel 4 (ET 3), Zechariah 12 and 14. Probably those scholars are right who have seen this motif as an embodiment of the theme of Yahweh's conflict with the chaos waters. In keeping with their view it may be noted that not only does Ps. 46.3, 7 (ET 2, 6) employ the same verbs in connection with the waters and the nations, but Ps. 48.3 (ET 2) applies the name Zaphon to Yahweh's dwelling place on Zion (see below, section on Zaphon), a term originally denoting Baal's dwelling place, which the chaos waters attacked (cf. *KTU*^{2} 1.3.III.47–IV.1). Again, Ps. 48.8 (ET 7) speaks of Yahweh's shattering of the ships of Tarshish, a motif which seems originally more at home by the coastal site of Mt Zaphon than in the landlocked Jerusalem (Baal-Zaphon was noted for his shattering of ships with his wind, cf. *ANET*, p. 534).

The Eschatologization of the Dragon Conflict

In accordance with the *Urzeit wird Endzeit* principle, the divine conflict with the dragon and the sea becomes projected into the future in connection with the Eschaton. The earliest known example of this is in Isa. 27.1, where we read that 'On that day the Lord with his hard and great and strong sword will punish Leviathan the twisting serpent, Leviathan the crooked serpent, and he will slay the dragon that is in the sea'. The language used of Leviathan here is remarkably similar to that employed almost a thousand years earlier in the Ugaritic Baal epic, where Mot says to Baal that 'you smote Leviathan the twisting serpent and made an end of the crooked serpent' (*KTU*^{2} 1.5.I.1-2), and elsewhere in the Ugaritic Baal epic Leviathan is called a dragon (*tnn*, *KTU*^{2} 1.3.III.40), just as in Isa. 27.1 (*tannîn*). The Ugaritic parallel makes it clear that simply one dragon, not three, is being referred to in Isa. 27.1. Leviathan here presumably symbolizes some political power that is to be overcome at the end time, but it is not certain what that is, whether the world power of the time of composition (something which is itself disputed, though the Persian period seems most likely), or conceivably Egypt, which is singled out at the end of other proto-apocalyptic works (Joel 4.19 [ET 3.19]; Zech. 14.18-19).

The first full-blown apocalyptic work in the Old Testament, the book of Daniel, has a most interesting reinterpretation of the Canaanite myth in Daniel 7. Although apocalyptic is a complicated phenomenon with a multifaceted background, a good case can be made, as was first argued by J.A. Emerton,[28] that the Canaanite dragon conflict myth is the single most important contributor to the background of Daniel 7, since it can explain well the combination of the following three factors: (i) Daniel 7 is one of the few places in the Old Testament where Yahweh is depicted as an aged god: he is named 'the Ancient of Days' and he has white hair. As has been noted in Chapter 1, this is reminiscent of the supreme Canaanite god El, who was called 'the Father of Years' and has grey hair (cf. *KTU*^{2} 1.4.IV.24; 1.4.V.4). (ii) Just as Baal's kingship was ultimately dependent on and subordinate to that of El, so the one like a son of man in Daniel 7 owes his rule to the Ancient of Days. Moreover, the one like a son of man comes with the clouds of heaven, just as Baal's stock epithet was 'rider of the clouds' (*rkb 'rpt*) by virtue of his role as a storm god. (iii) Baal's kingship was dependent on his victory over Yam, the god of the sea, just as the one like a son of man's rule takes the place of that of the beasts of the sea, especially the fourth one.

Probably the one like a son of man in Daniel 7 is to be equated with the angel Michael. Similar terms are used elsewhere for angels (Dan. 8.15, 10.16, 18), and the angel Michael is explicitly mentioned in Dan. 12.1 in a role comparable to that of the one like a son of man in Daniel 7. Implicitly we are to understand that this figure overcomes the fourth beast in Daniel 7.

Even in the New Testament, the dragon conflict has clearly exercised

28. Emerton, 'The Origin of the Son of Man Imagery'. See too J. Day, *God's Conflict with the Dragon and the Sea*, pp. 151-78.

its influence on the book of Revelation.[29] In Revelation 12 the angel Michael defeats a dragon, symbolizing Satan, with seven heads and ten horns. The seven heads clearly derive from the seven-headed Leviathan, whilst the ten horns identify the figure with the fourth beast of Daniel 7, whose implicit vanquisher there, as has been noted, was Michael (the one like a son of man). The fact that it is Michael, not Christ, who defeats the dragon in Revelation 12, suggests that a Jewish source equating the one like a son of man with Michael underlies the passage. A seven-headed beast symbolizing Rome appears in Rev. 13.1-10, and this figure likewise derives from Leviathan, just as another beast, symbolizing the false prophet, probably derives from Behemoth (Rev. 13.11-18).

Zaphon as the Divine Dwelling Place

The Ugaritic texts frequently make mention of *ṣpn* (Zaphon[30]), the name of Baal's mountain (e.g. *KTU*² 1.5.I.11; 1.6.I.57-59, etc.), and since Eissfeldt[31] persuasively argued the case in 1932, this has generally been accepted as referring to Jebel el-Aqra', known as Mt Casius (the seat of the god Zeus Casius) in classical times, the highest mountain in Syria, some 1770 metres high and 25-30 miles north of Ugarit. This identification has been proved by administrative tablets from

29. On this see A. Yarbro Collins, *The Combat Myth in the Book of Revelation* (HDR, 9; Missoula, MT: Scholars Press, 1976).

30. On Zaphon, note the following: O. Eissfeldt, *Baal Zaphon, Zeus Kasios und der Durchzug der Israeliten durchs Meer* (Beiträge zur Religionsgeschichte des Altertums; Halle: Niemeyer, 1932); W.F. Albright, 'Baal-Zephon', in W. Baumgartner, O. Eissfeldt, K. Elliger and L. Rost (eds.), *Festschrift Alfred Bertholet* (Tübingen: J.C.B. Mohr [Paul Siebeck], 1950), pp. 1-14; R. de Langhe, *Les Textes de Ras Shamra–Ugarit et leurs Rapports avec le Milieu Biblique de l'Ancien Testament* (2 vols.; Gembloux: Duculot, 1945), II, pp. 217-44; A. Lauha, *Zaphon: Der Norden und die Nordvölker im Alten Testament* (Annales Academiae scientiarum Fennicae, 49.2; Helsinki: Druckerei-A.G. der finnischen Literaturgesellschaft, 1943), esp. pp. 36-52; J. Morgenstern, 'Psalm 48', *HUCA* 16 (1941), pp. 47-87; B. Alfrink, 'Der Versammlungsberg im äussersten Norden', *Bib* 14 (1933), pp. 41-67; R.E. Clements, *God and Temple* (Oxford: Basil Blackwell, 1965), pp. 4-9; A. Robinson, 'Zion and Ṣāphôn in Psalm XLVIII 3', *VT* 24 (1974), pp. 118-23; Clifford, *The Cosmic Mountain*; J.J.M. Roberts, 'ṢĀPÔN in Job 26, 7', *Bib* 56 (1975), pp. 554-57.

31. Eissfeldt, *Baal Zaphon*, esp. pp. 1-48.

Ugarit in Akkadian and Ugaritic which make certain the identification of Mt Ḫazi (Casius) and Mt *ṣpn* (Zaphon).[32]

It is probable that it was this Syrian Mt Zaphon that gave its name to the word *ṣāpôn* in Hebrew, meaning 'north' (literally, 'watch-out place' from *ṣph*), Mt Zaphon in Syria being to the north of Israel. This is supported by the fact that only in Hebrew, Phoenician and Aramaic, of all the Semitic languages, is this the word for 'north'. One may compare the fact that other geographical designations, such as *yām*, 'sea', and *negeb* (the Negeb desert in the south of Israel, literally, 'dry place') also came to denote cardinal points, namely, 'west' and 'south'.[33]

The name of the mountain was clearly transferable to other sites (as also was Tabor),[34] since a place name, Baal-Zaphon, is attested also in Egypt (cf. Exod. 14.1). Likewise, Ps. 48.3 (ET 2) applies the name Zaphon to Jerusalem, where it is under attack from the forces of chaos, just as in the Ugaritic texts Baal's dwelling, Zaphon, has to be defended against enemies (cf. *KTU*² 1.3.III.47-IV.1). Prior to the discovery of the Ugaritic texts it was impossible to make proper sense of Ps. 48.3 (ET 2), where we apparently read that Jerusalem is 'beautiful in elevation, is

32. Albright, 'Baal-Zephon', p. 2.

33. As it appears that *ṣāpôn* was originally the name of a high mountain, the meaning 'look-out point', from *ṣph* 'look out', seems most likely, as originally suggested by Eissfeldt, *Baal Zaphon*, pp. 17-18, and frequently followed. Further in support of this it may be noted that the equivalent Hurrian name for Mt Zaphon, namely, Ḫazi, could be explained from the root *ḥzh*, 'to see', particularly frequent in Aramaic, which is very comparable in meaning to *ṣph*. Various other minority suggestions of the etymology of the name of Mt Zaphon are less likely. Thus, E. Lipiński connects *ṣpn* with *ṣûp*, 'to swim, float', and thinks that this name was used of Baal's mountain because he was 'Lord of the float/sea travel', but this seems fanciful. (See Lipiński, 'El's Abode', pp. 61-64, and 'צְפוֹנִי צָפוֹן', in *ThWAT*, VI, cols. 1093-1102 [1095-96].) C. Grave, 'The Etymology of Northwest Semitic *ṣapānu*', *UF* 12 (1980), pp. 221-29, thinks that *ṣpn* originally referred to the north wind. While discussing etymological questions, it may be noted that it has been repeatedly claimed that the name Zaphon lies behind that of the dragon Typhon, defeated by Zeus in Greek mythology. However, although the Typhon myth has an oriental origin—it derives from the Hurrian myth of Teshub's defeat of Ullikummi—and although part of the conflict was at Mt Casius (Ḫazi in the Hurrian version), it does seem unlikely that the name of the sacred mountain has been appropriated by that of the dragon defeated there. A more plausible etymology of Typhon is from the Greek verb, τύφω 'to smoke'.

34. Cf. O. Eissfeldt, 'Der Gott des Tabor und seine Verbreitung', *ARW* 31 (1934), pp. 14-41, reprinted in O. Eissfeldt, *Kleine Schriften*, II, pp. 29-54.

the joy of all the earth, Mount Zion, *in the far north*, is the city of the great king'. The description of Jerusalem as being in the far north simply did not make sense, although this has not presented some modern translations, such as the NRSV, from following this rendering.[35] However, if *yark^{e}tē ṣāpôn* is taken to be 'the heights of Zaphon' it could be made sense of as the appropriation of the name of Baal's mountain dwelling place to Jerusalem.[36]

Interestingly, in the Demotic/Aramaic Papyrus Amherst 63, which contains a paganized version of Psalm 20, Zion has been replaced by Zaphon.[37] (Lines 11-19 of the former are dependent on the Psalm.)

Papyrus Amherst Egyptian 63, Lines 13-14

> 13 Send your emissary from the temple of Arash, and from Zaphon
> 14 may Horus sustain us.

Psalm 20.3 (ET 2)

> May he send you(r) help from the sanctuary
> and from Zion may he sustain you.

I shall now consider various other Old Testament texts which refer, or have been alleged to refer, to a Mt Zaphon. The first text with which I shall deal is Isa. 14.12-15. There, the goal of the Shining One, son of the dawn, is to ascend above the clouds and stars and sit on the Mount of Assembly, on *yark^{e}tê ṣāpôn*, and so be like the Most High (Elyon), but he is cast down because of his hubris into the depths of the Pit (*yark^{e}tê bôr*), that is, Sheol. *Yark^{e}tayim* in the Old Testament usually means 'remote parts'. In the light of the fact that *yark^{e}tê ṣāpôn* is clearly set in opposition to *yark^{e}tê bôr*, and the Shining One's goal is to ascend into the heavens, it seems most natural, as Eissfeldt[38] first

35. M.D. Goulder, *The Psalms of the Sons of Korah* (JSOTSup, 20; Sheffield: JSOT Press, 1982), pp. 162-63, who reads *yark^{e}tê ṣāpôn* as 'the frontiers of the north', explains this on the basis of his hypothesis that originally the text referred to Mt Hermon, not Mt Zion. But there was never a 'city' on Mt Hermon. (Dan, with which Goulder associates the liturgy of the Korahite psalms, was not actually on Mt Hermon). For other objections to Goulder's Danite interpretation of the Korahite psalms, see J. Day, *Psalms*, pp. 115-17.

36. Following, Eissfeldt, *Baal Zaphon*, and frequently since then.

37. C.F. Nims and R.C. Steiner, 'A Paganized Version of Psalm 20:2-6 from the Aramaic Text in Demotic Script', *JAOS* 103 (1983), pp. 261-74 (264).

38. Eissfeldt, *Baal Zaphon*, pp. 14-15.

argued, that the *yark^{e}tê ṣāpôn* are to be understood in a vertical rather than a horizontal sense, that is, 'the heights of Zaphon'. That such a meaning is feasible is also suggested by Isa. 37.24, where *yark^{e}tê l^{e}bānôn* is parallel to *m^{e}rôm hārîm* (*'^{a}nî 'ālîtî m^{e}rôm hārîm yark^{e}tê l^{e}bānôn*). That Zaphon is here a mountain is implied by its description as 'the mount of assembly', and it clearly relates to the firmament, understood as a cosmic mountain. The reader is directed below to Chapter 6 for a full and detailed discussion of the mythological background and meaning of Isa. 14.12-15, including the reference to Zaphon in v. 13. I shall there argue that behind the attack on the heavenly Mt Zaphon by the Shining One, son of the dawn, (which is a variant of the myth of the attempt of Athtar, the morning star, Venus, to usurp Baal's dwelling on Mt Zaphon), there lies Nebuchadrezzar's attack on Jerusalem in 586 BCE. The myth may have been mediated by the Jebusites, as the reference to the Most High (Elyon) in v. 14 suggests.

That Zaphon was a name applicable to the firmament of heaven is suggested further by Job 26.7, 'He stretches out Zaphon over the void, and hangs the earth upon nothing'. Some have seen Zaphon, or the north, as the northern[39] and heaviest[40] part of the earth. Since the discovery of the Ugaritic texts, some scholars such as Eissfeldt, Pope, Dahood and Roberts,[41] have seen here a direct reference to the Syrian Mt Zaphon. However, against all these views the significant fact must be set that elsewhere the verb *nṭh* is used of the stretching out of the heavens, often in parallelism with the earth.[42] In view of the fact that Zaphon seems to be equated with the vault of heaven in Isa. 14.13 there seems every probability that this is the case here too. Presumably, we are to think of the firmament of heaven as the cosmic mountain on

39. S.R. Driver and G.B. Gray, *A Critical and Exegetical Commentary on the Book of Job* (ICC; Edinburgh: T. & T. Clark, 1921), p. 221, note this as one possibility, though they prefer the view that it refers to heaven.

40. Cf. K. Budde, *Das Buch Hiob* (HAT, 2.1; Göttingen: Vandenhoeck & Ruprecht, 1896), p. 145.

41. Eissfeldt, *Baal Zaphon*, pp. 13-14; M.H. Pope, *Job* (AB, 15; Garden City, NY: Doubleday, 3rd edn, 1973), p. 183; M.J. Dahood, *Psalms* (AB, 16, 17, and 17A; 3 vols.; Garden City, NY: Doubleday, 1966–70), I, p. 290; Roberts, 'ṢĀPÔN', p. 557.

42. The verb *nṭh* is used of heavens in parallelism with the earth in Isa. 40.22, 42.5, 44.24, 45.12, 51.13; Jer. 10.12, 51.15; Zech. 12.1; and without parallelism with the earth in Ps. 104.2; Job 9.8.

which Yahweh dwells.[43] As further examples, Ezek. 1.4 and Job 37.22 may be cited. In the former passage we read, 'As I looked, behold, a stormy wind came out of Zaphon, and a great cloud, with brightness round about it, and fire flashing continually, and in the midst of the fire, as it were gleaming bronze'. The storm theophany comes from Zaphon. In view of the fact that in v. 1 Ezekiel refers to the same event by saying that 'the heavens were opened, and I saw visions of God', one may agree with Zimmerli[44] that Yahweh's coming form 'the north' is but another way of referring to the self-opening of heaven. (That Ezekiel was quite familiar with the concept of Yahweh's heavenly mountain is clear from Ezekiel 28.) This is more natural than to suppose that Yahweh came north from Jerusalem to north Syria, then over the Euphrates south to Ezekiel.[45]

A number of scholars, beginning with Eissfeldt, think that the Syrian Mt Zaphon is referred to in Ps. 89.13 (ET 12). The MT reads as follows: *ṣāpôn w*^{e}*yāmîn 'attâ b*^{e}*rā'tām tābôr w*^{e}*ḥermôn b*^{e}*šim*^{e}*kā y*^{e}*rannēnû.* This is customarily translated, 'You have created the north and the south, Tabor and Hermon joyously praise your name'. Eissfeldt and others,[46]

43. Those seeing a reference to the heavens here with a mythological background to the term *ṣāpôn*, include G. Fohrer, *Das Buch Hiob* (KAT, 16; Gütersloh: Gerd Mohn, 1963), pp. 382, 384; Clifford, *The Cosmic Mountain*, p. 162 n. 85; M. Greenberg, J.C. Greenfield, and N.M. Sarna (eds.), *The Book of Job* (Philadelphia: Jewish Publication Society of America, 1980), p. 37; J.E. Hartley, *The Book of Job* (NICOT; Grand Rapids: Eerdmans, 1988), pp. 365-66; Niehr, *Der höchste Gott*, pp. 105-106. Others have envisaged a reference to the heavens here, without any background in a mythical divine dwelling place or mountain, for example, Driver and Gray, *The Book of Job*, pp. 220-21; H.H. Rowley, *Job* (NCB; London: Oliphants, 1976), pp. 172-73; W.H. Schmidt, 'צָפוֹן ṣāfōn Norden', *THAT*, II, cols. 575-82 (579).

44. W. Zimmerli, *Ezechiel*, I (BKAT, 13.1; Neukirchen–Vluyn: Neukirchener Verlag, 1969), p. 52; ET *Ezekiel*, I (trans. R.E. Clements; Hermeneia; Philadelphia: Fortress Press, 1979), p. 120.

45. A. Bertholet, *Hesekiel* (HAT, 13; Tübingen: J.C.B. Mohr [Paul Siebeck], 1936), p. 5.

46. Eissfeldt, *Baal Zaphon*, pp. 12-13; O. Mowan, 'Quatuor Montes Sacri in Ps. 89, 13?', *VD* 41 (1963), pp. 11-20; M.H. Pope, 'Baal-Hadad', in Haussig (ed.), *Götter und Mythen*, pp. 253-64 (258); R. de Vaux, 'Jérusalem et les prophètes', *RB* 73 (1966), pp. 481-509 (506); Cross, *Canaanite Myth and Hebrew Epic*, p. 135 n. 79; C. Bonnet, 'Typhon et Baal Saphon', in E. Lipiński (ed.), *Phoenicia and the East Mediterranean in the First Millennium B.C.* (Studia Phoenicia, 5; Leuven:

however, argue that since the second half of the verse mentions mountain names, mountains, moreover, which had been the seats of pagan cults, it is natural to expect that the first half should also mention sacred mountains, and on this basis it is natural to understand *ṣāpôn* as Mt Zaphon in Syria, not a vague reference to the north. As for *yāmîn*, Eissfeldt says that this could allude to Sinai, Strabo's Antikasion (which was south of Mt Zaphon), or it could be a corruption of Amanus or Amana. Proponents of this theory now generally hold the word to be a corruption of Amanus or Amana, and emend *yāmîn* to *'amn*, *ḥmn*, or *'amnh*.[47] O. Mowan[48] has written a detailed study of the question of whether the first half of this verse does, in fact, name two mountains, and he gives his answer strongly in the affirmative. He holds that *yāmîn* is nowhere else found parallel to *ṣāpôn* in the Old Testament and that this supports the view that the word *yāmîn* is corrupt and does not refer to the south. However, this is to ignore the evidence of Ps. 107.3. Here, the MT reads: *ûmē'ᵃrāṣôt qibbᵉṣām mimmizrāḥ ûmimma ʿᵃrāb miṣṣāpôn ûmiyyām*. Since the verse clearly refers to east, west and north, it is only natural to expect that the final word should refer to the south, and *yām* is unsatisfactory here, since when used as a geographical term in Hebrew it means 'west'. The text, as is generally done, should therefore be emended to 'south'. There is therefore no reason why Ps. 89.13 (ET 12) should not similarly refer to the north and the south. This has the advantage that there is no need to emend *yāmîn* to create the name of a mountain elsewhere unattested in biblical Hebrew. Tabor and Hermon might then represent the centre of the known world, set over against the extremities of north and south. For the latter, we may compare Deutero-Isaiah, who has a considerable number of parallels with Psalm 89, and who refers to Yahweh as 'the creator of the ends of the earth' (*bōrē' qᵉṣôt hā'āreṣ*). It is also possible that though the reference is to the north and south, the thought of the mountainous in them is not excluded, since in the archaic world-view reflected in the Old Testament, at the extremities of the earth there were the 'pillars of heaven' (cf. Job 26.11). These last two points do not seem to have been noted by other scholars.

Peeters, 1987), pp. 101-43 (115-16); Lipiński, 'צְפוֹנִי צָפוֹן', col. 1097. This view is also followed by NEB.

47. Dahood, *Psalms*, II, pp. 308, 314, does not emend, but regards *yāmîn* as an unparalleled alternative spelling of *'amn*.

48. Mowan, 'Quatuor Montes Sacri'.

Eissfeldt[49] also seeks a reference to Mt Zaphon, or, rather, the land of Zaphon, in Ezek. 32.30. As usually rendered, the verse reads: 'The princes of the north are there, all of them, and all the Sidonians...' The fact that the most northerly nations have already been referred to leads Eissfeldt to think that *ṣāpôn* must here refer to (the land of) Zaphon. However, this is not necessary. Perhaps the areas immediately to the north of Israel could be simply referred to as 'the north' without indicating that the most northern point of the earth was meant, somewhat comparable to the way we can speak of 'the north' when we mean the north of England, without implying that this is the earth's most northern area.

In Joel 2.20 we read, 'I will remove the northerner far from you, and drive him into a parched and desolate land...' Kapelrud[50] holds that primarily this term is related to Baal's mountain, Zaphon: the north is therefore the region from which the mythical forces of chaos come. However, this view is surely to be rejected, since in the Old Testament (Ps. 48.3 [ET 2]; Isa. 14.13), as in Ugaritic (*KTU*[2] 1.3.III.47-IV.1), Zaphon is the place that the mythical forces attack, not the place whence they come. Rather, the term 'the northerner' here must be related in some way to the concept of 'the foe from the north', such as is found in Jeremiah (Jer. 1.13-15, 4.6, 6.1, 22; cf. Ezek. 38.6, 15, 39.2), and which does not derive from Baal mythology. Rather, it derives from the simple fact of experience that the enemies of Israel and Judah tended to come from the north.[51] However, the context requires that in Joel 2.20 'the northerner' refers to the locusts;[52] this is in keeping with the fact that elsewhere Joel describes the locusts in military terms (cf. 2.1-11, 25) and associates them with the Day of the Lord (1.15, 2.1, 11).

49. Eissfeldt, *Baal Zaphon*, pp. 11-12.

50. A.S. Kapelrud, *Joel Studies* (UUÅ, 4; Uppsala: Lundeqvist, 1948), pp. 93-108.

51. There is therefore no need to follow the compromise position of those like J.L. Crenshaw, *Joel* (AB, 24C; Garden City, NY: Doubleday, 1995), p. 151, who see Joel as indebted to both the foe from the north and the mythical Mt Zaphon concept here.

52. This is generally accepted by the commentators. To see the reference to 'the northerner' as alluding to a political invasion, as, for example, does D. Stuart, in *Hosea–Joel* (WBC, 31; Waco, TX: Word Books, 1987), p. 258, is unsatisfactory in the context. Throughout the work Stuart believes the Babylonian or Assyrian invasion is spoken of metaphorically as locusts (pp. 232-34), whereas it is more natural to suppose that the locusts are metaphorically understood as an army.

Although in Palestine locusts tend to come from the south or east, they can come from the north, as in the plague that afflicted Jerusalem in 1915.[53] This could therefore have been the case in Joel's time.[54] There is no justification for the emendation of 'the northerner' (*haṣṣ^{e}pônî*) to 'the chirper' (*haṣṣapṣ^{e}pônî*), a *hapax legomenon* proposed by E. Sellin,[55] since the three other cardinal points of the zodiac are alluded to in this verse as the places whither the locusts are driven.[56]

An example of *implicit* 'Zaphonic' language is to be found in Exod. 15.17. This verse reads: 'You will bring them in, and plant them on the mountain of your inheritance, the place for your dwelling which you have made, O Lord, the sanctuary, O Lord, which your hands have established'. The expressions 'mountain of your inheritance' (*har naḥ^{a}lāt^{e}kā*) and 'the place for your dwelling' (*mākôn l^{e}šibt^{e}kā*) most naturally refer to the temple in Jerusalem, especially since the latter expression is so used in 1 Kgs 8.13.[57] These terms appear to be derived from similar terms used in the Ugaritic texts of Baal's Mt Zaphon and the dwellings of other gods (cf. e.g. *KTU*^{2} 1.3.III.29-30; 1.3.VI.15-16), and has led such scholars as Albright and Cross and Freedman[58] to hold a quite early date (pre-monarchic) for the song of Moses in Exodus 15, so that these references would not allude to Jerusalem. However, one can maintain that Canaanite language, probably deriving ultimately from descriptions of Baal's dwelling on Mt Zaphon (perhaps mediated

53. J.D. Whiting, 'Jerusalem's Locust Plague', *National Geographic Magazine* 28 (1915), pp. 511-50 (513).

54. So L.C. Allen, *The Books of Joel, Obadiah, Jonah and Micah* (NICOT; London: Hodder & Stoughton, 1976), p. 88.

55. E. Sellin, *Das Zwölfprophetenbuch*. I. *Hosea–Micha* (KAT, 12; Leipzig: A. Deichertsche Verlagsbuchhandlung, 3rd edn, 1929), p. 165.

56. Here 'the eastern sea' is the Dead Sea, 'the western sea' is the Mediterranean, and 'a parched and desolate land' is the Negeb to the south.

57. Clements, *God and Temple*, pp. 53-55; B.S. Childs, *The Book of Exodus* (OTL; London: SCM Press, 1974), p. 252; Jörg Jeremias, *Das Königtum Gottes in den Psalmen: Israels Begegnung mit dem kanaanäischen Mythos in den Jahwe-König-Psalmen* (FRLANT, 141; Göttingen: Vandenhoeck & Ruprecht, 1987), p. 103; T.N.D. Mettinger, *The Dethronement of Sabaoth: Studies in the Shem and Kabod Theologies* (ConBOT, 18; Lund: C.W.K. Gleerup, 1982), p. 27; C. Houtman, *Exodus*, II (HCOT; Kampen: Kok, 1996), pp. 291-92.

58. W.F. Albright, *The Archaeology of Palestine* (Harmondsworth: Penguin Books, rev. edn, 1960), p. 233; F.M. Cross and D.N. Freedman, 'The Song of Miriam', *JNES* 14 (1955), pp. 237-50.

through the cult of El-Elyon) has here been used, but this by no means requires that the passage be pre-monarchic, since Canaanite imagery is found in the Old Testament even in very late passages (such as Isa. 27.1). Nothing, therefore, prevents Exod. 15.17 from alluding to Jerusalem. Such an understanding is further supported by the fact that it is stated that Yahweh himself established the sanctuary, something which is paralleled of the Zion temple in Ps. 78.69. Furthermore, we know of no other sanctuary in the Old Testament apart from Jerusalem (cf. Ps. 48.3 [ET 2]) to which 'Zaphonic' language is applied.

Alternative explanations are less plausible. The view that Mt Sinai is in mind as the final destination is unlikely in view of the fearful reaction of Philistines, Edomites, Moabites and Canaanites (Exod. 15.14-16), as Mark Smith rightly notes,[59] and the same objection holds for S. Norin's view that Mt Zaphon on Lake Sirbonis in the north of the Sinai peninsula is intended.[60] Another view sometimes held is that the reference is to the land of Canaan,[61] but against this it may be noted that Canaan is never elsewhere spoken of as a 'sanctuary' (*miqdāš*). The view that originally the sanctuary at Gilgal was meant[62] or that at Shiloh was intended[63] have no particularly strong claim, since unlike Zion these are never called mountains in the Old Testament, and the phrase *mākôn l*^{e}*šibt*^{e}*ka* is never elsewhere applied to them. We have no evidence in the Old Testament that Zaphon language was applied to

59. Mark S. Smith, *The Pilgrimage Pattern in Exodus* (JSOTSup, 239; Sheffield: Sheffield Academic Press, 1997), p. 223, *contra* e.g. D.N. Freedman, 'A Letter to the Readers', *BA* 40 (1977), pp. 46-48. (Contrast the work cited in n. 61 for Freedman's earlier view.)

60. S. Norin, *Er spaltete das Meer: Die Auszugsüberlieferungen in Psalmen und Kult des alten Israels* (ConBOT, 9; Lund: C.W.K. Gleerup, 1977), pp. 85-91.

61. M. Noth, *Das zweite Buch Mose, Exodus* (ATD, 5; Göttingen: Vandhoeck & Ruprecht, 1959), p. 100; ET *Exodus* (trans. J.S. Bowden; OTL; London: SCM Press, 1962), pp. 125-26; D.N. Freedman, 'Strophe and Meter in Exodus 15', in H.N. Bream, R.D. Heim and C.A. Moore (eds.), *A Light unto my Path: Old Testament Studies in Honor of Jacob M. Myers* (Philadelphia: Temple University Press, 1974), pp. 163-203 (190-91); reprinted in D.N. Freedman, *Pottery, Poetry and Prophecy: Studies in Early Hebrew Poetry* (Winona Lake, IN: Eisenbrauns, 1980), pp. 187-227 (214-15). Freedman also believes that Exod. 15.17 refers to heaven in addition to the land of Canaan.

62. Cross, *Canaanite Myth and Hebrew Epic*, pp. 142-43.

63. E.g. J. Goldin, *The Song at the Sea: Being a Commentary on a Commentary in Two Parts* (New Haven: Yale University Press, 1971), pp. 34-58.

any other site in Palestine apart from Jerusalem.

I conclude that there are therefore a number of places in the Old Testament where the firmament of heaven is called Zaphon and that similarly this term could be applied to Jerusalem. In view of the connection between Zaphon and Elyon in Isa. 14.13-14 and the fact that Ps. 48.3 (ET 2) refers to Jerusalem as Zaphon, while the closely related Ps. 46.5 (ET 4) refers to Jerusalem as 'the holy habitation of the Most High (Elyon)', it is probable that the concept of Zaphon as applied to Yahweh was mediated through the Jebusite cult of El-Elyon, rather than being directly taken over from Baal.

Finally, it has been suggested by C. Bonnet and E. Lipiński[64] that there is a further instance of the influence of the Canaanite sacred mountain, Zaphon, on ancient Israel in the personal name Zephaniah (*ṣ^{e}panyāh*[*û*]). Bonnet compares the Punic personal name Sophonibaal, and Lipiński the Ugaritic personal name *ṣpnb'l*, both allegedly meaning 'Zaphon is Baal', so that Zephaniah would then mean 'Zaphon is Yahweh'. However, Zephaniah more naturally means 'Yahweh protects' and M.H. Pope[65] claims that *ṣpnb'l* likewise probably means, 'Baal protects'. So far as we know, neither Baal nor Yahweh were actually equated with their sacred mountain so that the view of C. Bonnet and E. Lipiński should probably be rejected.

Resurrection Imagery from Baal to the Book of Daniel[*]

A more precise and fuller title for this section would be 'Death and Resurrection Imagery from Baal to the book of Daniel via Hosea and the so-called "Isaiah Apocalypse"'. I hope to demonstrate that the first clear reference to the literal resurrection of the dead in the Old Testament in Dan. 12.2 is a reinterpretation of the verse in Isa. 26.19 about resurrection, which, I shall argue, refers to restoration after exile, rather than literal life after death. Isaiah 26.19 in turn, I shall argue, is dependent on the death and resurrection imagery in the book of Hosea,

64. Bonnet, 'Typhon et Baal Ṣaphon', p. 113; Lipiński, 'צָפוֹן', col. 1097.

65. Pope, 'Baal-Hadad', p. 256.

* With some additions and stylistic alterations this section is taken from my article 'Resurrection Imagery from Baal to the Book of Daniel', in J.A. Emerton (ed.), *Congress Volume, Cambridge 1995* (VTSup, 66; Leiden: E.J. Brill, 1997), pp. 125-33, and is reprinted here by kind permission of the publisher.

especially on a reinterpretation of Hos. 13.14. Finally, the imagery of death and resurrection in Hosea (both in chs. 5–6 and 13–14), which likewise refers to Israel's exile and restoration, is directly taken over by the prophet from the imagery of the dying and rising fertility god, Baal.

That Baal was regarded as a dying and rising god cannot seriously be disputed. In the Ugaritic Baal myth we read of his being swallowed by Mot, the god of death, and it is declared several times that 'Mightiest Baal is dead, the prince, Lord of the earth has perished'. He is buried by Anat and lamented in the customary way by her and El. The land becomes hot, dry and parched, for Baal has taken the rain, wind and most of the dew with him into the underworld. Then El has a vision in which the heavens rain oil and the ravines run with honey. El rejoices and declares, 'mightiest Baal is alive, for the prince, Lord of the earth exists'. Baal then resumes his throne. (See *KTU*^{2} 1.4.VIII-1.6.VI for all of the above.)

There have been attempts to deny that Baal was a dying and rising god, but these have failed in my view. Mark Smith[66] claims that Baal is a disappearing and returning god like the Hittite weather god Telepinus. However, the two myths use clearly distinct language: Telepinus vanishes, is sought for and eventually found,[67] whereas, as noted above, in the Baal myth there are repeated references to his death, after which he is spoken of as alive. Both H.M. Barstad and Mark Smith claim that the words 'mightiest Baal is alive' (*ḥy 'al'iyn b'l*) do not have to imply resurrection.[68] However, their context in the text, which has previously spoken of Baal's death, requires such an interpretation. I agree with T.N.D. Mettinger when he states that 'The contrast between life and death is basic to the myth'.[69] Occasionally it has been supposed, as by

66. Mark S. Smith, *The Ugaritic Baal Cycle*. I. *Introduction with Text, Translation and Commentary of KTU 1.1–1.2* (VTSup, 55; Leiden: E.J. Brill, 1994), pp. 72-73.

67. *ANET*, pp. 126-28; H.A. Hoffner, *Hittite Myths* (SBL Writings from the Ancient World, 2; Atlanta: Scholars Press, 1990), pp. 14-20.

68. Barstad, *Religious Polemics*, pp. 150-54; Mark S. Smith, *The Ugaritic Baal Cycle*, I, p. 71.

69. Mettinger, *In Search of God*, p. 214 n. 6. Mettinger is currently writing a book on dying and rising gods, and amongst other things he will defend that notion that Baal was such a god. For a preliminary survey, see Mettinger, 'The "Dying and Rising God": A Survey of Research from Frazer to the Present Day', *SEÅ* 63 (1998), pp. 111-23.

J.C. de Moor and J.C.L. Gibson,[70] that it is not Baal himself who dies, but a substitute born of the union between Baal and a heifer. But as A. Waterston says,[71] there is no indication of this in the text. Further evidence that Baal was a dying god is revealed by the reference in Zech. 12.11 to 'the mourning for Hadad-rimmon in the valley of Megiddo', Hadad being another name for Baal. Mark Smith[72] thinks that there may have been influence from Adonis and/or Tammuz here, but there is no evidence of this, and the concept seems rather to show continuity with Baal as known from the Ugaritic texts.

Hosea, of course, was highly polemical against the cult of Baal. But polemic can sometimes involve taking up one's enemies' imagery and reutilizing it for one's own purposes. It was W.W. Graf Baudissin in his book, *Adonis und Esmun*,[73] who first argued that Hosea took up the imagery of death and resurrection from a fertility deity. But strange to say, he does not mention Baal in this connection, but rather speaks of Adonis and Eshmun, since, prior to the discovery of the Ugaritic texts, he had to depend on late classical sources, which curiously do not mention the death and resurrection of Baal. (Not even Philo of Byblos refers to them.) Subsequently, a number of scholars[74] have argued that it was from Baal that Hosea drew his imagery. But some other scholars[75] have questioned this.

One point that has frequently been claimed is that Hosea is referring not to death and resurrection but rather to illness and healing.[76] The fol-

70. De Moor, *Seasonal Pattern*, p. 188; J.C.L. Gibson, 'The Last Enemy', *SJT* 32 (1979), pp. 151-69 (159-60).

71. A. Waterston, 'Death and Resurrection in the A.B. Cycle', *UF* 21 (1989), pp. 425-34.

72. Mark S. Smith, *The Ugaritic Baal Cycle*, I, p. 73.

73. W.W. von Baudissin, *Adonis und Esmun* (Leipzig: J.C. Hinrichs, 1911), pp. 404-16; cf. H.G. May, 'The Fertility Cult in Hosea', *AJSL* 48 (1932), pp. 74-98 (74-78).

74. E.g. R. Martin-Achard, *From Death to Life* (trans. John Penney Smith; Edinburgh: Oliver & Boyd, 1960), pp. 81-86; F.F. Hvidberg, *Graad og Latter i Det gamle Testamente* (Copenhagen: G.E.C. Gad, 1938), pp. 109-13; ET *Weeping and Laughter in the Old Testament* (trans. N. Haislund; Leiden: E.J. Brill; Copenhagen: Nyt Nordisk Forlag, 1962), pp. 126-31.

75. Cf. Rudolph, *Hosea*, pp. 136-37; D.N. Freedman and F.I. Andersen, *Hosea* (AB, 24; Garden City, NY: Doubleday, 1980), p. 420. See below, n. 66 for the more nuanced position of G.I. Davies.

76. E.g. Mays, *Hosea*, p. 95; Wolff, *Hosea*, p. 149, ET *Hosea*, p. 117; Rudolph,

lowing points, however, may be made in favour of seeing death and resurrection imagery in Hosea 5–6.[77] First, in support of the resurrection understanding of Hos. 6.2 it may be noted that the verbs employed are the hiphil of *qûm*, 'raise up', and the piel of *ḥāyâ*, 'revive': 'After two days he will revive us (*y^eḥayyēnû*); on the third day he will raise us up (*y^eqîmēnû*), that we may live before him'. All the other places in the Old Testament where these two verbs (*ḥyh*, *qwm*) appear as word pairs the meaning clearly relates to resurrection from death, not simply healing. This is the case in Isa. 26.14, 19 and Job 14.12, 14. Secondly, three verses later, in Hos. 6.5, the prophet implies that the people are dead: 'Therefore I have hewn them by the prophets, I have slain them by the words of my mouth...' Thirdly, in Hos. 5.14 Hosea uses the image of a lion carrying off its prey and says 'and none shall rescue'. Elsewhere in the Old Testament the image of the lion carrying off its prey implies certain death (cf. Amos 3.12; Jer. 2.30; Mic. 5.7 [ET 8]). This is clear elsewhere in the book of Hosea itself, as we see from Hos. 13.7, 9, where Yahweh's devouring Israel like a lion is explicitly said to be equivalent to destruction.

The last observation brings me to my fourth and most decisive argument, which has been strangely neglected by scholars writing on this subject. This is the fact that there are a whole series of parallel images between Hosea 5–6 and 13–14, and in the latter it is made abundantly clear that the image is that of death and resurrection, not merely illness and healing. That death is envisaged in Hosea 13 is shown by v. 1, 'he [i.e. Ephraim] incurred guilt through Baal and died', v. 9, where Yahweh states, 'I will destroy you, O Israel', and v. 14, which speaks of Israel as being in the grip of Death and Sheol. Now the parallels between Hosea 5–6 and 13–14 are as follows. Hosea 5.14 says, 'For I will be like a lion to Ephraim, and like a young lion to the house of Judah. I even I, will rend and go away, I will carry off, and none shall rescue.' We may compare Hos. 13.7-8, 'So I will be to them like a lion, like a leopard I will lurk beside the way. I will fall upon them like a

Hosea, p. 135; G.I. Davies, *Hosea* (NCB; London: Marshall Pickering; Grand Rapids: Eerdmans, 1992), p. 161.

77. Those supporting the view that death and resurrection are envisaged here include Baudissin, *Adonis und Esmun*, pp. 404-407; Martin-Achard, *From Death to Life*, pp. 80-86; Freedman and Andersen, *Hosea*, pp. 418-20; B.C. Pryce, 'The Resurrection Motif in Hosea 5:8–6:6: An Exegetical Study' (PhD dissertation, Andrews University, Ann Arbor, 1989), *passim*.

bear robbed of her cubs, and I will tear open their breast, and there I will devour them like a lion, as a wild beast would rend them.' Hosea 6.1 states, 'Come let us return to the Lord; for he has torn, that he may heal us; he has stricken, and he will bind us up'; compare Hos. 14.2 (ET 1), 'Return, O Israel to the Lord your God...', and 14.5 (ET 4), 'I will heal their faithlessness...' Hosea 6.3 reads, 'he will come to us as the showers, as the spring rains that water the earth', which may be compared with Hos. 14.5 (ET 4), 'I will be as the dew to Israel'. Since, as we have seen, Hosea 13–14 clearly imply death and resurrection, this must likewise be the case in Hosea 5–6, where the identical imagery is used. Interestingly, Hos. 14.5 (ET 4) speaks of Yahweh's healing Israel's faithlessness: the use of the verb 'heal' in Hos. 6.1 therefore does not require something less than death in Hosea 5–6, as has sometimes been claimed.[78]

Granted that Hosea 5–6 and 13–14 allude to Israel's death and resurrection, are we to suppose that this imagery derives from Baal? One strong argument in favour of this that has not previously been noted by other scholars[79] is to be found in Hos. 13.1, where we read that 'Ephraim...incurred guilt through Baal and died'. This must surely be deliberately ironical. For Hosea it is not Baal who dies and rises but Israel who dies through worshipping Baal, followed, if repentant, by resurrection. In keeping with this Hos. 6.3 associates Israel's resurrection with the rain ('he will come to us as the showers, as the spring rains that water the earth'), and Hos. 14.6 (ET 5) likewise mentions the dew as bringing about renewed fertility in Israel ('I will be as the dew to Israel...'). This is striking, since in the Ugaritic Baal myth we read that Baal took the rain and two of the dew goddesses with him when he went into the underworld, and it is implied that they reappeared when he rose again.

A further striking parallel with Baal mythology occurs in Hos. 13.14-15. In v. 14 Israel is said to be in the grip of Death (*māwet*) and Sheol, and in the following verse we read that Israel's 'fountain will dry up,

78. Cf. scholars cited above in n. 76.

79. I have myself noted this earlier in passing in 'Baal', *ABD*, I, pp. 545-49 (549), and in 'Ugarit and the Bible: Do they Presuppose the Same Canaanite Mythology and Religion?', in G.J. Brooke, A.H.W. Curtis and J.F. Healey (eds.), *Ugarit and the Bible: Proceedings of the International Symposium on Ugarit and the Bible, Manchester, September 1992* (UBL, 11; Münster: Ugarit-Verlag, 1994), pp. 35-52 (42).

his spring will be parched'. Similarly, in the Ugaritic Baal myth, when Baal goes down into the realm of Mot (Death) we read that the land becomes dry and parched.[80] Again, the resurrection of Israel in Hosea 14 is symbolized by fertility in nature, just as Baal's resurrection ensured the fertility of the land in Canaanite mythology.

One final possible parallel occurs in both Hos. 5.14 and 13.7-8. Yahweh is depicted as destroying Israel like a ravenous beast. Similarly, in the so-called Hadad text (*KTU*² 1.12), which provides a variant on the main Baal myth, Baal appears to owe his death to ravenous beasts, which is followed by dryness, though the text is not wholly clear. It is perhaps also relevant to note that Mot's appetite is compared to that of a lion in *KTU*² 1.5.I.14.

However, in arguing that Hosea takes over the image of Baal's death and resurrection and applies it to Israel, I would not appeal, as some have done, to the reference in Hos. 6.2 to Israel's resurrection on the third day. Some scholars have claimed that this was derived from a fertility god.[81] Thus, we have evidence of the celebration of the resurrection of the Egyptian god Osiris on the 19th Athyr, two days after his death on 17th Athyr (cf. Plutarch, *De Iside et Osiride* 13.356 C; 19.366 F), and the resurrection of the Phrygian god, Attis, took place on 25th March, three days after his death (22nd March), according to Firmicus Maternus, writing of fourth-century Rome. But these are both very late, and influence from Osiris or Attis on Hosea is most unlikely. Also very late, but nearer geographically and culturally, is Lucian, *De Syria Dea* 6, who states that at Byblos the faithful expected the resurrection of Adonis 'on another day', though this is very vague. However, nowhere do we hear of a third-day resurrection of Baal—the god whose imagery influenced Hosea—and it is far more likely that 'on the third day' is a poetic way of saying 'after a short while'. We may recall that Hebrew *'etmôl* or *t*ᵉ*mûl šilšōm*, literally 'yesterday, the third day', means 'formerly', and in Lk. 13.32 Jesus says, 'Behold I cast out demons and perform cures today and tomorrow and the third day I finish my course' (cf. v. 33). Jesus' prediction of his resurrection 'after

80. Davies, *Hosea*, p. 297, finds it attractive to see influence from the myth of Baal's swallowing by Mot here, even though he rejects this in the case of Hos. 5–6 (p. 61).

81. E.g. Baudissin, *Adonis und Esmun*, pp. 408-10; Martin-Achard, *From Death to Life*, pp. 82-83.

three days' (Mk 8.31, 9.31, 10.34) also probably originally meant 'after a short while'.[82]

Just as imagery from Baal's death and resurrection has influenced the book of Hosea, so the next stage of my argument is that the book of Hosea has influenced the references to resurrection in Isa. 26.19: 'Your dead shall live, their bodies[83] shall rise, the dwellers in the dust shall awake and sing for joy,[84] for your dew is a dew of light, and the earth shall give birth to the shades'.

In support of this claim I would first point out that there is a whole series of parallels between Hosea 13–14 and Isaiah 26–27—eight in number—all occurring in the same order, with one minor exception. As I have already pointed out in an earlier article,[85] as well as above in Chapter 2, these parallels are as follows:

1. Israel knows no lords/gods but Yahweh. Hos. 13.4. Cf. Isa. 26.13 (LXX).
2. Imagery of birthpangs, but child refuses to be born. Hos. 13.13. Cf. Isa. 26.17-18.
3. Deliverance from Sheol. Hos. 13.14 (LXX, etc.). Cf. Isa. 26.19.
4. Imagery of destructive east wind symbolic of exile. Hos. 13.15. Cf. Isa. 27.8.
5. Imagery of life-giving dew. Hos. 14.6 (ET 5). Cf. Isa. 26.19.
6. Israel blossoming and like a vineyard. Hos. 14.6-8 (ET 5-7). Cf. Isa. 27.2-6.
7. Condemnation of idolatry, including the Asherim. Hos. 14.9 (ET 8). Cf. Isa. 27.9.
8. The importance of discernment; judgment for the wicked. Hos. 14.10 (ET 9). Cf. Isa. 27.11.

One of the verses in Hosea that corresponds to the resurrection verse, Isa. 26.19, it will be noted, is Hos. 13.14, 'Shall I ransom them from the power of Sheol? Shall I redeem them from Death? O Death where are

82. Cf. B. (F.C.) Lindars, *New Testament Apologetic* (London: SCM Press, 1961), p. 61.

83. Following Targum and Peshiṭta I read 'their bodies' (*niblōtām*) for MT's 'my body' (*nᵉbēlātî*), which does not seem appropriate here.

84. Instead of MT's imperatives, *hāqîṣû* and *wᵉrannᵉnû*, I read the imperfects *yāqîṣû* and *wîrannᵉnû*, with the support of 1QIsa[a], LXX, Aquila, Symmachus and Theodotion.

85. See J. Day, 'A Case of Inner Scriptural Interpretation', pp. 309-19.

your plagues? O Sheol, where is your destruction? Compassion is hid from my eyes.' This, of course, is saying the opposite of Isa. 26. 19. However, we know from the LXX and the other ancient versions (similarly, 1 Cor. 15.55) that Hos. 13.14 was widely interpreted in a positive sense in the ancient world, 'I shall ransom them from the power of Sheol, I shall redeem them from Death...', and this was clearly how the author of Isa. 26.19 interpreted it. What is most striking and adds considerably to the evidence for the dependence of Isa. 26.19 on Hos. 13.14 at this point, is the fact that the immediately preceding verses in both Hosea and Isaiah have the imagery of a woman in labour pains but the child not presenting itself (Hos. 13.13; cf. Isa. 26.17-18), something too remarkable to be ascribed to mere coincidence. It is further possible that Isa. 26.19 shows dependence on the other resurrection passage, Hos. 6.2-3, since both passages employ the verbs *ḥyh* and *qwm* to describe the resurrection, as well as the imagery of light: compare 'his going forth is sure as the *dawn*' in Hos. 6.3 with 'your dew is a dew of *light*' in Isa. 26.19.

Granted that we have found the sources of the imagery in Isa. 26.19, the further question arises as to its meaning. Is there here a literal belief in life after death (as in the book of Daniel) or is the resurrection symbolism simply an image for national restoration (as in Hos. 6.1-3 and Ezekiel 37)? Scholarly opinion is quite divided on this question.[86] In favour of the literal life after death view it is sometimes argued that the contrast with the wicked rulers in Isa. 26.14 is with those who are literally dead, 'They are dead, they shall not live; they are shades, they will not arise; to that end you have visited them with destruction and wiped out all remembrance of them. However, since the imagery of Isa. 26.14 could similarly be taken either metaphorically or literally, this verse does not provide a decisive argument. What does provide a strong, if not decisive, argument in favour of the metaphorical interpre-

86. For example, literal resurrection here is supported by G.F. Hasel, 'Resurrection in the Theology of Old Testament Apocalyptic', *ZAW* 92 (1980), pp. 267-84 (272-75), and E. Puech, *La Croyance des Esséniens en la Vie Future: Immortalité, Résurrection, Vie Éternelle?* (2 vols.; Paris: J. Gabalda, 1993), I, p. 71, whereas communal restoration is maintained by H. Wildberger, *Jesaja* (BKAT, 10.1-3; 3 vols.; Neukirchen–Vluyn: Neukirchener Verlag, 1972–82), II, p. 995; ET *Isaiah 13–27* (trans. T.H. Trapp; Minneapolis: Fortress Press, 1997), pp. 567-60, and R.E. Clements, *Isaiah 1–39* (Grand Rapids: Eerdmans; London: Morgan, Marshall & Scott, 1980), p. 16.

tation of the resurrection as national restoration, comparable to Ezekiel 37, is the fact that the very next chapter, in Isa. 27.8, actually speaks of the exile: 'By expelling her,[87] by exiling her, you did contend with her; he removed them with his fierce blast in the day of the east wind'. Isa. 27.8 most naturally refers back to the distress referred to in Isaiah 26, including 26.19. Moreover, as I have noted above, Isa. 26.19 and 27.8 have their sources in two adjacent verses in Hosea 13, namely vv. 14 and 15, which further supports reading Isa. 26.19 in the light of 27.8.

I now come to the final stage of literary dependence in my argument, namely the claim that Isa. 26.19 has in turn influenced Dan. 12.2. This seems in every way likely. The language of the two verses is very similar, both of them referring to awaking (hiphil of *qîṣ)* from the dust (*'āpār*) in connection with resurrection. As I have already noted, Isa. 26.19 declares, 'Your dead shall live, their bodies shall rise, the dwellers in the dust shall awake and sing for joy'; with this may be compared Dan. 12.2, which predicts, 'And many of those who sleep in the *dust* of the earth shall *awake*'. Now at last the language of resurrection has been 'remythologized', speaking as it does of a literal renewal of life in an afterlife, and no longer simply of national restoration.

The view that Dan. 12.2 was dependent on Isa. 26.19 at this point is made all the more credible by the fact that Daniel 12 shows other evidence of dependence on the book of Isaiah. The last but one word of Dan. 12.2, *dērā'ôn*, 'abhorrence', used of the destiny of the wicked in the phrase 'everlasting abhorrence' (*l^{e}dir^{e}'ôn 'ôlām*), occurs only once elsewhere in the Old Testament, namely in Isa. 66.24, where it is likewise used of the eschatological judgment of the wicked: 'And they shall go forth and look on the dead bodies of the men that have rebelled against me, for their worm shall not die, their fire shall not be quenched, and they shall be an *abhorrence* (*dērā'ôn*) to all flesh'.

Interestingly, there is clear evidence that Daniel was also dependent on another passage containing death and resurrection imagery,[88] namely

87. Reading *b^{e}sa's^{e}āh* for *b^{e}sa'ss^{e}â*, as the following word, *b^{e}šal^{e}ḥāh*, which is probably an explanatory gloss, suggests that there is here *b^{e}* + infinitive construct + 3rd p.s. feminine suffix. The verb is a *hapax legomenon* and is probably a pilpel form, and likely to be cognate with Arabic *sa'sa'a*, 'to shoo away'. Cf. G.R. Driver, 'Some Hebrew Verbs, Nouns, and Pronouns', *JTS* 30 (1929), pp. 371-78 (371-72).

88. R.N. Whybray, *Thanksgiving for a Liberated Prophet* (JSOTSup, 4; Sheffield: JSOT Press, 1978), pp. 79-106 has argued that Isa. 53 does not allude to death and resurrection, but rather to imprisonment and release, but the piling up of so

the fourth Servant song in Isa. 52.13–53.12.[89] The very next verse, Dan. 12.3, speaks of the resurrected righteous as 'those who turn many to righteousness (*maṣdîqê hārabbîm*), language that clearly echoes Isa. 53.11, where the suffering and resurrected Servant is described as one 'who makes many to be accounted righteous (*yaṣdîq…lārabbîm*)'. The next verse (Dan. 12.4) then speaks of these martyrs as 'the wise' (*hammaśkîlîm*), which seems to take up the verb *yaśkîl* used of the suffering Servant in Isa. 52.13, where the original meaning was probably '[he] will prosper', rather than '[he] will be wise'. However, since a modern scholar of the stature of C.C. Torrey[90] was of the opinion that it was the root *śkl*, 'to be wise' in Isa. 52.13, there is no reason why an ancient writer like the author of Daniel 12 should not have thought the same. The idea in Isaiah 53 of the vicarious death of the Servant[91] has also probably influenced the imagery in Dan. 11.35, 'and some of those who are wise shall fall, to refine and to cleanse among them and to make them white'. This interpretation of Isaiah 53 is clearly the source of the idea that the Maccabaean martyrs' deaths were atoning in their effect, which is found in 2 Macc. 7.37-38, *4 Macc.* 6.27-29, 17.22 and 18.4.

If the thesis I have put forward is correct, we must assume that the resurrection imagery had its ultimate origin in Canaanite Baal mythology, that it was 'demythologized' in prophets such as Hosea and in the 'Isaiah apocalypse' as a way of referring to Israel's restoration after exile, and then 'remythologized' in the book of Daniel, where it again refers to literal life after death.

Assuming this thesis to be correct, we cannot claim that the Jewish belief in resurrection was derived from the Zoroastrians, as has sometimes been supposed.[92] One can, of course, see the attractions of such a

much language to do with death cannot be so easily explained away. In any case, the writer of Dan. 12 clearly interpreted Isa. 53 in this way.

89. Cf. H.L. Ginsberg, 'The Oldest Interpretation of the Suffering Servant', *VT* 3 (1953), pp. 400-404.

90. C.C. Torrey, *The Second Isaiah* (Edinburgh: T. & T. Clark, 1928), pp. 252, 415.

91. Whybray, *Thanksgiving*, pp. 29-76, has attempted to deny that there is vicarious suffering in Isa. 53, but this seems a *tour de force*. He has no explanation of the use of the word *'āšām*, 'guilt offering', used of the Servant in Isa. 53.11, other than to suggest that the text is corrupt (pp. 63-66).

92. Cf. W. Bousset, *Die Religion des Judentums im späthellenistischen Zeitalter* (Tübingen: J.C.B. Mohr [Paul Siebeck], 3rd edn, 1906), pp. 506-20; M. Boyce, *A*

standpoint: the belief in individual resurrection emerged in Israel only after the period when the Jews had been subject to the rule of the Persians, contacts with whom they were friendlier than with the previous harsher Assyrian and Babylonian imperial powers. Moreover, although the problem of dating Zoroastrian sources is notoriously difficult, we do have indisputable evidence that the Zoroastrians already believed in resurrection by c. 350 BCE from the writer Theopompus,[93] who lived about that time. However, when we come to examine the Zoroastrian belief carefully, we find that it differs considerably from the Jewish notion. As has been pointed out by others, the Jewish sources repeatedly speak of death as a sleep, and resurrection as an awakening from it (e.g. Isa. 26.19; Dan. 12.2; *4 Ezra* 7.32), whereas such a concept is completely alien to the Zoroastrians. However, in keeping with the ultimately Canaanite origin which I have postulated, it is interesting to note that we do have some evidence that the Canaanites conceived resurrection as an awakening from sleep. Thus, Menander of Ephesus, as reported by Josephus (*Ant.* 8.5.3), refers to the festival of the resurrection of the Tyrian god Herakles (i.e. Melqart) as his *egersis*—an awakening from a condition similar to sleep. Also, we may note, much earlier, in the Ugaritic texts (*KTU*[2] 1.19.III.45), Aqhat's death is referred to as 'sleep' (*šnt*; cf. *qbr* 'grave', in the previous line).

The re-emergence of resurrection imagery in a literal sense in the book of Daniel and later Jewish apocalyptic may therefore be seen as yet a further example of the recrudescence of myth that has been detected in other aspects of apocalyptic symbolism.

Interestingly, the original connection of resurrection imagery with the cycle of nature, observable in Hos. 6.2-3, 13-14, and Isa. 26.19, was never totally forgotten, and traces of it may be found in the New Testament and rabbinic literature.[94] Speaking of the resurrection of the dead, St Paul states, 'What you sow does not come to life unless it dies. And what you sow is not the body which is to be, but a base kernel,

History of Zoroastrianism, II (Leiden: E.J. Brill, 1982), p. 193, and III (Leiden: E.J. Brill, 1991), p. 408; B. Lang, 'Street Theater, Raising the Dead, and the Zoroastrian Connection in Ezekiel's Preaching', in J. Lust (ed.), *Ezekiel and his Book* (BETL, 74; Leuven: Leuven University Press and Peeters, 1986), pp. 297-316.

93. As reported by Plutarch, *De Iside et Osiride* 46; Diogenes Laertius *Proemium* 9, and Aeneas of Gaza, *De Animali Immortalitate* 77.

94. Cf. G. Stemberger, 'Zur Auferstehungslehre in der rabbinischen Literatur', *Kairos* NS 15 (1973), pp. 239-47.

perhaps of wheat, or of some other grain (1 Cor. 15.36-37). Again, in Jn 12.24, speaking of the resurrection, John has Jesus declare, 'Truly, truly I say to you, unless a grain of wheat falls in to the earth and dies, it remains alone; but if it dies, it bears much fruit'. There are also various rabbinic allusions comparing the resurrection body to corn.

Chapter 5

YAHWEH AND THE GODDESSES ASTARTE AND ANAT (AND THE QUEEN OF HEAVEN)

Astarte

Ashtoreth and Ashtaroth in the Old Testament

It is generally accepted that the vocalization of the name of the goddess *'aštōret* in the Old Testament is a deliberate scribal distortion of an original *'aštart*, which is the form we should naturally expect in the light of the extra-biblical parallels (cf. Greek Astarte, Akkadian Ishtar, etc.).[1] It is virtually certain that the distorted vocalization reflects the vowels of the Hebrew word, *bōšet*, 'shame',[2] a term employed in place of the divine name Baal in such references as Hos. 9.10 and Jer. 11.13, as well as in some personal names (for example, the Eshbaal in 1 Chron. 8.33 and 9.39 is called Ish-bosheth in 2 Sam. 2.10, 12, and elsewhere). The name of the Canaanite god, Molech (*mōlek*), is probably likewise distorted: in Hebrew the vocalization should more naturally be expected to be *mōlēk* or *melek*. A. Cooper,[3] however, has recently argued that *'aštōret* is not a scribal distortion but represents the actual vocalization of the name in Hebrew, with the original *a* vowel having become *ō*, as in the change from *dāgān* to *dāgôn*. Quite apart from the inherent

1. There is is no evidence that the name was originally vocalized Athtarat (for Ugaritic) or Ashtarat (for Hebrew), *contra* Gray, *I and II Kings*, p. 275; G.H. Jones, *1 and 2 Kings* (NCB; London: Marshall, Morgan & Scott; Grand Rapids: Eerdmans, 1984), I, p. 234; and N. Wyatt, 'Astarte', *DDD*, cols. 203-13 (209-10) (2nd edn, pp. 109-14 [112]).

2. The view that the vowels of *'aštōret* were deliberately distorted appears to have been first suggested by T. Nöldeke, review of *Grammatik des Biblisch-Aramäischen*, by E. Kautzsch, in *Göttingische gelehrte Anzeigen* (1884), p. 1022, though he does not explicitly mention *bōšet*.

3. A. Cooper, 'A Note on the Vocalization of עַשְׁתֹּרֶת', *ZAW* 102 (1990), pp. 98-100.

plausibility of the *bōšet* explanation, however, the following two objections to Cooper's view may be made. First, we should expect *'aštōrt* rather than *'aštōret*, if it was simply a case of *a* becoming *ō*; none of the extra-biblical renderings has a vowel between the 'r' and the 't'. Secondly, if the pronunciation had really developed into Ashtoreth, it is surprising that this is nowhere reflected in the later extra-biblical sources. The Greek rendering is regularly Astarte, with an *a* not an *o*, and with no *e* between the *r* and the *t*. Cooper says that it must be assumed that the Greek form of the name originated before the *a* to *ō* vowel change had occurred, but this would be surprising, since the Greek sources are all relatively late, dating from after the time when the alleged *a* to *ō* change had occurred. Moreover, the Syrian goddess Atargatis, known from later times, is a conflation of the names Astarte and Anat,[4] and this name also attests an *a* vowel. In the Old Testament we find the singular form, Ashtoreth, only in 1 Kgs 11.5, 33 and 2 Kgs 23.13. In 1 Kgs 11.5, 33 she is referred to as 'the goddess of the Sidonians', and 2 Kgs 23.13 speaks of her as 'the abomination of the Sidonians'. 1 Kings 11 refers to her cult as one of a number of idolatrous practices pursued by Solomon as a result of the influence of his foreign wives. 2 Kings 23.13 mentions that Josiah defiled the high place that Solomon had set up for Ashtoreth, and this is stated to have been east of Jerusalem, to the south of the Mount of Corruption. The reference to Ashtoreth as 'the goddess/abomination' of the Sidonians is entirely understandable, since we know from extra-biblical sources that Astarte was the leading goddess of Sidon. Astarte's cult is also attested elsewhere in Phoenicia, for example in Tyre, and her cult spread throughout the Mediterranean (Carthage and North Africa, Cyprus, Italy, Malta, Spain, Greece) as a result of Phoenician colonization and other contacts.[5]

4. The most common spelling of the name in Aramaic is *'tr'th*, though variants such as *'tr't'* are also attested. *'tr* represents Astarte and *'th* (*'atta*) is an Aramaizing form of the name Anat. This deity was popular in Syria during the Hellenistic and Roman periods. The second-century CE writer Lucian of Samosata in *De Syria Dea* describes her cult at the important Syrian site of Hierapolis (Bambyke), referring to her as Hera and her consort (Hadad) as Zeus. There is no compelling evidence to support the theory of R.A. Oden, *Studies in Lucian's* De Syria Dea (HSM, 15; Missoula, MT: Scholars Press, 1977), pp. 58-107, that Atargatis combined not only Astarte and Anat but also Asherah.

5. For a detailed survey of the cult of Astarte in its various geographical locations in the Mediterranean and ancient Near East, see C. Bonnet, *Astarté: Dossier documentaire et perspectives historiques* (Collezione di Studi Fenici, 37;

All the other allusions in the Old Testament are to the plural form, Ashtaroth. N. Wyatt,[6] however, has recently conjectured that *'aštārôt* was originally not the plural form of the name (as it came to be understood in the MT), but the singular form of the deity's name in Hebrew. But this is pure speculation, and against it stands the fact that all the extra-biblical forms of the name presuppose the vocalization was *'aštart*, not *'aštārôt*.

It has often been supposed that Ashtaroth should be emended to Ashtoreth[7] in 1 Sam. 31.10,[8] where we read that the Philistines 'put Saul's armour in the temple of Ashtaroth and fastened his body to the wall of Beth-shan', a passage which may imply that the temple itself was in Beth-shan. The emendation is attractive and it is worthy of note that Astarte was, amongst other things, a goddess of war, as various Egyptian references make clear,[9] which makes the placing of armour in her temple not inappropriate. However, it should be pointed out that the parallel in 1 Chron. 10.10 says that Saul's armour was placed 'in the temple of their gods', which may presuppose that the plural reading, Ashtaroth, was already in the Chronicler's *Vorlage*. As will be seen below, however, it may be that the temple was actually that of Anat.

All the other references to the Ashtaroth are alongside allusions to Baal (Judg. 2.13), or the Baals (Judg. 10.6; 1 Sam. 7.4, 12.10), or simply 'the foreign gods' (1 Sam. 7.3) and are mentioned in connection

Rome: Consiglio Nazionale delle Ricerche, 1996). See also J. Day, 'Ashtoreth', *ABD*, I, pp. 491-94 (492-94), for a wider consideration of Astarte outside the Old Testament than is possible here.

6. Wyatt, 'Astarte', cols. 209-10.

7. Those emending to Ashtoreth include S.R. Driver, *Notes on the Hebrew Text of the Books of Samuel* (Oxford: Clarendon Press, 1890), p. 178; H.P. Smith, *A Critical and Exegetical Commentary on the Books of Samuel* (ICC; Edinburgh: T. & T. Clark, 1899), p. 235; E.(P.) Dhorme, *Les Livres de Samuel* (Paris: V. Lecoffre & J. Gabalda, 1910), p. 260; J. Mauchline, *1 and 2 Samuel* (NCB; London: Oliphants, 1971), p. 192.

8. See below, in section on Anat, for more on this verse.

9. Astarte's cult was particularly prominent in Egypt during the New Kingdom. She is sometimes depicted riding a horse, holding either a bow and arrow or a spear and shield (cf. J. Leclant, 'Astarté à cheval', *Syria* 37 [1960], pp. 1-67). She is also represented as a military patron of Pharaohs Amenhotep II (c. 1427–1396 BCE), Thutmose IV (c. 1396–1386 BCE) and Rameses III (c. 1185–1154 BCE), and was protector of the city of Pi-Ramesse in Lower Egypt built by Rameses II (c. 1279–1213 BCE).

with the apostate worship of the Israelites during the period of the Judges. It may be that when we read of 'the Baals and the Ashtaroth' this is simply a way of speaking about Canaanite gods and goddesses generally, just as in Akkadian *ilāni u ištarāti* means simply 'gods and goddesses'. On the other hand, it is not impossible that various local manifestations of Baal and Astarte are intended. It has sometimes been supposed that 'the Baals and the Asheroth' in Judg. 3.7 should be emended to 'the Baals and the Ashtaroth', a proposal supported by the Vulgate and the Syriac version, as well as two Hebrew manuscripts, but 'the Asheroth' should perhaps be preferred as the *lectio difficilior* (that is, 'the more difficult reading', and therefore unlikely to have been corrupted from 'the Ashtaroth'), as has already been noted in Chapter 2.

The pairing of the Ashtaroth with the Baals is appropriate, since it is clear from the Ugaritic texts and elsewhere that Astarte was a consort of Baal, as also was Anat. However, whereas Astarte was apparently more prominent as Baal's consort in the world reflected in the Old Testament (as is certainly the case in first-millennium Phoenician inscriptions), it is Anat who plays the preponderant role as Baal's consort in the Ugaritic texts. Astarte does appear as Baal's spouse in the Ugaritic mythological texts, but she is less dominant. These differences may reflect regional or temporal variations. Awareness of Astarte as the consort of Baal clearly lived on late, since in Philo of Byblos (c. 100 CE) we read that 'Greatest Astarte and Zeus, called both Demarous and Adodos, king of gods, were ruling over the land with the consent of Kronos' (*Praeparatio Evangelica* 1.10.31).

Astarte may be the 'Queen of Heaven' mentioned in Jer. 7.18 and 44.17-19, 25 to whom the women made cakes of bread, burned incense and poured out drink offerings. See the separate discussion of this question towards the end of this chapter.

The name of the goddess Astarte occurs in the place name Ashtaroth or Ashteroth-Karnaim, 'Ashtaroth of the two horns', which may be compared with the statement in Philo of Byblos that 'Astarte placed upon her own head a bull's head as an emblem of kingship'. The name of the goddess also lingers on in an interesting expression found in the book of Deuteronomy. This is the phrase '*ašt*^{e}*rôt ṣō'nekā* (Deut. 7.13; 28.4, 18, 51),[10] commonly rendered as 'the young of your flock', and in

10. On this phrase, see especially, M. Delcor, 'Astarté et la fécondité des troupeaux en Deut. 7,13 et parallèles', *UF* 6 (1974), pp. 7-14; reprinted in M. Delcor, *Religion d'Israël et Proche Orient Ancien* (Leiden: E.J. Brill, 1976),

each case mentioned alongside *šᵉgar ʾᵃlāpêkā*, 'the offspring of your cattle'. This expression is clearly a hangover from an earlier stage of belief in which the goddess Astarte was thought to be responsible for the fertility of the flocks of sheep. We may compare the fact that concern for livestock is explicitly attested of Astarte's Mesopotamian equivalent, Ishtar, and the Ugaritic phrase, *ʿṯtrt šd* 'Astarte of the field' (*KTU*² 1.148.18), presumably alludes to her concern for the fertility of the field and what was in it. The older view, found in the work of such scholars as W.Robertson Smith and S.R. Driver,[11] that Astarte could actually be represented in sheep form, is without supporting evidence.

Interestingly, there is evidence that *šgr* was also regarded as a deity by the Canaanites and he is mentioned alongside Asherah as receiving a sheep by way of offering in *KTU*² 1.148.31.[12] (This is the same text as that containing the phrase, 'Astarte of the field' noted above.) Note also the Balaam text from Deir ʿAllā, I.16, where mention is made of *šgr.wʿštr* '*šgr* and Ashtar'.

What relation, if any, did Astarte have to Yahweh? If, as has been seen, Astarte was the consort of Baal, and if, as I have noted in Chapter 3, Yahweh and Baal were sometimes equated, then it follows that Astarte could sometimes function as Yahweh's consort. However, unlike in the case of Anat (who is attested in the form of Anat-Yahu at Elephantine), there is no explicit evidence of this.

Anat

Probable or Possible Allusions to Anat in the Old Testament

The goddess Anat is never directly mentioned by name in the Old Testament, in contrast to the goddesses Asherah and Astarte. Nevertheless, there are indirect allusions. The most obvious occurrences are in place names, where her name forms a part—Beth-Anat (*bêt-ʿᵃnāt*) in Naphtali

pp. 86-93. Also, J.M. Hadley, 'The Fertility of the Flock? The De-personalization of Astarte in the Old Testament', in B. Becking and M. Dijkstra (eds.), *On Reading Prophetic Texts: Gender-specific and Related Studies in Memory of Fokkelien van Dijk-Hemmes* (BibInt Series, 18; Leiden: E.J. Brill, 1996), pp. 115-33.

11. W.Robertson Smith, *The Religion of the Semites*, pp. 310-11; S.R. Driver, *A Critical and Exegetical Commentary on Deuteronomy* (ICC; Edinburgh: T. & T. Clark, 1895), p. 103. This view had already been rejected by G.A. Barton, 'Ashtoreth and her Influence in the Old Testament', *JBL* 10 (1891), pp. 73-91 (75).

12. *Ugaritica*, V.9, rev. 9 restored [*ʿṯt*]*rt* 'Astarte' here, but *KTU*² 1.148.31 simply reads *ʾaṯrt* 'Asherah'.

(Josh. 19.38; Judg. 1.33); Beth-Anot (*bêt-ʿ^{a}nôt*) in Judah (Josh. 15.59), and Anathoth in Benjamin (*ʿ^{a}nātôt*, in Josh. 21.18; 1 Kgs 2.26 and *ʿ^{a}nātōt* in 1 Kgs 2.26; Isa. 10.30; Jer. 1.1, 11.21, 23, 32.7, 8, 9; 1 Chron. 6.45; Ezra 2.23; Neh. 7.27; cf. also the adjective 'the Anathothite', *hāʿann^{e}tōtî* in 2 Sam. 23.27, 1 Chron. 12.3 and Jer. 29.27; and *hāʿann^{e}tôtî* in 1 Chron. 11.28, 27.12), most famous as the birthplace of Jeremiah, but also as the place to which the priest Abiathar was exiled by Solomon (1 Kgs. 2.26). The place names Beth-Anat and Beth-Anot indicate the presence of a temple to the goddess Anat there.[13]

Shamgar ben Anat. In the book of Judges there twice appears Shamgar ben Anat (Judg. 3.31 and 5.6), and it is said of him that he killed six hundred of the Philistines with an ox-goad and delivered Israel (Judg. 3.31). The name Shamgar is often thought to be Hurrian (cf. Šimigari in the Nuzi texts[14]), though it could conceivably be Canaanite (understood as a shaphel formation).[15]

As for the expression 'ben Anat', with which I am concerned here, it has quite frequently been thought to be a shortened form of *ben bêt-ʿ^{a}nāt*, literally, 'a son of Beth-Anat', thus indicating him to have been a resident of Beth-Anat in Galilee.[16] However, this view is not particularly likely. First, as will be seen below, *bn ʿnt* is found elsewhere in the Canaanite world in a number of cases where a place name is not

13. The latter (Josh. 15.59) has been questioned by A.G. Auld, 'A Judean Sanctuary of 'Anat (Josh. 15:59)?', *Tel Aviv* 4 (1977), pp. 85-86; reprinted in A.G. Auld, *Joshua Retold* (Old Testament Studies; Edinburgh: T. & T. Clark, 1998), pp. 61-62, who prefers either of the LXX's readings, βαιτανων (LXX A) or βαιταναμ (LXX B), i.e. *byt ʿn*(*w*)*n* or *byt ʿnm*, rather than MT's *byt ʿnwt*. However, scrutiny of the LXX's many inaccuracies in rendering place names in Joshua does not convey confidence that it is to be preferred here to the MT.

14. First noted by B. Mazar [Maisler], 'Shamgar ben 'Anat', *PEQ* 66 (1934), pp. 192-94 (193). See E. Chiera and E.A. Speiser, 'Selected "Kirkuk" Documents', *JAOS* 47 (1927), pp. 36-60 (49, no. 15) for this name.

15. As suggested by A. Van Selms, 'Judge Shamgar', *VT* 14 (1964), pp. 294-309 (299-301). Cf. the personal name *šʿtqt* in the Keret epic (*KTU*^{2} 1.16.VI. 1, 2, 13).

16. E.g. W.F. Albright, 'A Revision of Early Hebrew Chronology', *JPOS* 1 (1921), pp. 49-79 (55 n.1); A. Alt, 'Institut im Jahre 1925', *PJ* 22 (1926), pp. 5-80 (55-59); Noth, *Die israelitischen Personennamen*, p. 123 n. 1; Mazar [Maisler] 'Shamgar ben Anat', pp. 192-94 (194); A. Alt, 'Megiddo im Übergang vom kanaanäischen zum israelitischen Zeitalter', *ZAW* 60 (1944), pp. 67-85 (73 n. 4).

credible. Secondly, it is much more usual for a person's ancestry than his or her place of origin to be cited in the Old Testament. Thirdly, on the analogy of persons coming from Bethel, Bethlehem and Beth-Shemesh, we should expect *bêt-hā'ᵃnātî* rather than *ben bêt-'ᵃnāt* or *ben-'ᵃnāt*.[17]

Another geographical explanation of the expression *ben-'ᵃnāt* has been proposed by F.C. Fensham,[18] who suggests that it may denote Shamgar as a Ḫanaean, a nomadic group known from the Mari texts and other sources. However, the references to the Ḫanaeans are about five hundred years prior to the time of Shamgar ben Anat and this explanation must remain unlikely. Fensham himself concedes its hypothetical nature.

Much more relevant to the explanation of Shamgar as son of Anat is the fact that there are various individuals in the Canaanite world who are also described as *bn 'nt*, 'son of Anat'. This is unlikely to be simply a literal patronymic, since *'nt* is a feminine personal name, and it is customary for the father's, not the mother's name, to be cited, if only one is given. If we do not have here the name of the literal father or mother, the explanation that suggests itself is that the persons in question are each metaphorically described as 'son of (the goddess) Anat'. What makes this explanation plausible is the fact that Anat was a warrior goddess and that, not only Shamgar ben Anat, but some of the other Canaanites described as *bn 'nt*, are also known to have been warriors. The term would thus function as an honorific military title. Although the occurrences in Ugaritic (*KTU*² 4.307.6; 4.320.4) do not enable the drawing of any conclusions about the significance of *bn 'nt*,[19] it is noteworthy that the owners of two inscribed arrowheads from elsewhere are described as *bn 'nt*, 'son of Anat', which fits the honorific military explanation. The first, an arrowhead from El-Khaḍr, is inscribed

17. Cf. Van Selms, 'Judge Shamgar', p. 301, for objections to the view that *ben-'ᵃnāt* indicates a person from Beth-Anat. Van Selms criticizes the claim that the reference to Hadadezer, king of Zobah, the 'son of Rehob' in 2 Sam. 8.3, 12, means that he is from Beth-rehob, since 2 Sam. 10.6 distinguishes the Syrians of Zobah and Beth-rehob.

18. F.C. Fensham, 'Shamgar ben 'Anat', *JNES* 20 (1961), pp. 197-98.

19. Contrast F.M. Cross, 'Newly Found Inscriptions in Old Canaanite and Early Phoenician', *BASOR* 238 (1980), pp. 1-20 (7), who believes that Anat in all these instances is simply a human personal name.

with the personal name *'bdlb't bn 'nt*,[20] 'Abdlabit, son of Anat', while another, from the Beqa' valley, has *ḥṣ zkrb*['*l*] *bn bn 'n*[*t*], 'arrow of Zakarba[al], son of the son of Ana[t]'.[21] This explanation of 'son of Anat' as an honorofic military title in the name of Shamgar ben Anat has been followed by such scholars as R. Kittel, C.H. Gordon, A. Van Selms, O. Eissfeldt, P.C. Craigie, and N. Shupak.[22]

1 Samuel 31.10. In 1 Sam. 31.10 Saul's armour is said to have been taken to the temple of Ashtaroth at Beth-Shan after his death. A temple of Anat has been discovered at Beth-Shan and A. Rowe[23] has suggested that this was the temple in question. Rowe was of the mistaken view that Anat and Ashtoreth were the same deity. Nevertheless, although it cannot be certain, it is still possible that this Anat temple was the temple in question. Both Anat and Ashtoreth (Astarte) were similar goddesses of warfare, amongst other things, so that a temple of either of them would be a suitable receptacle for Saul's armour. P.L. Day[24] also thinks that the temple of Anat may be the one in question, and claims that the plural, Ashtaroth, in 1 Sam. 31.10 means 'goddesses' (like Akkadian *ištarātu*) and so does not explicitly name any particular goddess.

Hosea 14.9 (ET 8). I refer the reader to my discussion of this passage in Chapter 2 on Asherah, where, though rejecting Wellhausen's ingenious

20. See Cross, 'Newly Found Inscriptions', pp. 6-7.

21. J.T. Milik, 'An Unpublished Arrowhead with Phoenician Inscription of the 11th–10th Century B.C.', *BASOR* 143 (1956), pp. 3-6. For the reconstruction of '*n*[*t*] see J.T. Milik, 'Note sur une Pointe de Flèche inscrite provenant de la Beqaa (Liban)', *RB* 65 (1958), pp. 585-89.

22. R. Kittel, 'Das Buch der Richter', in E. Kautzsch and A. Bertholet (eds.), *Die heilige Schrift des Alten Testaments* (Tübingen: J.C.B. Mohr [Paul Siebeck], 4th edn, 1922), pp. 367-407 (375); C.H. Gordon, *Before the Bible* (London: Collins, 1962), pp. 61-62; A. Van Selms, 'Judge Shamgar', p. 303; O. Eissfeldt, 'Gottesnamen in Personennamen als Symbole menschlicher Qualitäten', in K. Rudolph, R. Heller and E. Walter (eds.), *Festschrift Walter Baetke* (Weimar: Hermann Böhlaus Nachfolger, 1966), pp. 110-17; reprinted in Eissfeldt, *Kleine Schriften*, IV (Tübingen: J.C.B. Mohr [Paul Siebeck], 1968), pp. 276-84; P.C. Craigie, 'A Reconsideration of Shamgar ben Anath (Judg 3:31 and 5:6)', *JBL* 91 (1972), pp. 239-40; N. Shupak, 'New Light on Shamgar ben 'Anath', *Bib* 70 (1989), pp. 517-25.

23. A. Rowe, *The Four Canaanite Temples of Beth-Shan* (Philadelphia: University of Pennsylvania Press, 1940), p. 31.

24. P.L. Day, 'Anat', in *DDD*, cols. 62-77 (75) (2nd edn, pp. 36-43 [42]).

emendation of the Hebrew text to read 'I am his Anat and his Asherah', I nevertheless concluded that it is probable that there is a deliberate word play on the names of these two goddesses.

Dubious Allusions to Anat in the Old Testament

Exodus 32.18. This verse has traditionally been rendered in some way such as the following: 'But he said, "It is not the sound of shouting (*'ᵃnôt*) for victory, or the sound of the cry (*'ᵃnôt*) of defeat, but the sound of the singing (*'annôt*) that I hear"'. The words are those of Moses subsequent to the making of the golden calf. However, the suggestion was first made by R. Edelmann[25] and supported by R.N. Whybray[26] and advocated in greatest detail by M. Delcor[27] that *'annôt* refers to the goddess Anat rather than 'singing' or the like. R.M. Good[28] has subsequently proposed to render 'the sound of reverse', but to see a *double entendre* with reference to Anat. This view seems extremely dubious, however. Quite apart from the uncertainty over whether the goddess's name could be spelt *'annôt*, it should be noted that the golden calf is clearly represented not as a goddess, but as a god, in that it is called by the masculine term for 'calf', *'ēgel*, not the feminine, *'eglâ*, 'heifer', and it is clearly symbolic of the god Yahweh (cf. Exod. 32.5). Although in Hos. 10.5 there is the feminine plural form, *'eglôt*, used of the golden calf of the Northern Kingdom, this is clearly an error, since the same verse uses masculine suffixes of it, and the LXX, Peshiṭta and Theodotion similarly presuppose *'ēgel* here; compare also Hos. 8.5, where the same object is spoken of as *'eglēk*, 'your calf' (masc.).

Coming back to Exod. 32.18, it may further be noted that the context clearly implies that the sound is made by the people. Thus, v. 17 states, 'When Joshua heard the voice of the people as they shouted, he said to Moses, "There is a sound of war in the camp"'. Verse 19 further goes on to speak of Moses' seeing 'the calf and the dancing', making it natural to suppose that *'annôt* refers in some way to the revelry of the people. This problem is avoided in Delcor's rendering of Exod. 32.18,

25. R. Edelmann, 'Exodus 32:18', *JTS* 1 (1950), p. 56; *idem*, 'To עַנּוֹת Exodus XXXII 18', *VT* 16 (1966), p. 355.

26. R.N. Whybray, '*'annôt* in Exodus XXXII 18', *VT* 17 (1967), p. 122.

27. M. Delcor, 'Une allusion à 'Anath, déesse guerrière', *JJS* 32 (1982), pp. 145-60.

28. R.M. Good, 'Exodus 32:18', in Marks and Good (eds.), *Love & Death in the Ancient Near East*, pp. 137-42.

in which the text is emended by the addition of the words *t^e^rû'at l^e^* before *'annôt*, thus achieving the translation, 'I hear the sound of a hurrah in honour of Anat'.[29] But this is totally speculative and without any supporting evidence. It is far more natural to render *'annôt* as 'singing', a meaning well attested elsewhere in the Old Testament.[30]

Judges 5. P.C. Craigie[31] has argued that the description of Deborah in Judges 5 has been influenced by imagery associated with the goddess Anat found in the Ugaritic texts. He seeks to find five parallels. (i) Deborah has a male warrior assistant, Barak, just as Anat has a male warrior assistant, Yaṭpan, in the Aqhat epic. (ii) Deborah is a leader of warriors, just as Anat is. (iii) Anat is called *b'lt drkt*, 'Mistress of Dominion', in *KTU*² 1.108, lines 6-7. Similarly, in Judg. 5.21, Craigie thinks that Deborah's words, *tidr^e^kî napšî 'ōz*, should be rendered as 'You shall dominate, O my soul, mightily'. (iv) Anat is sometimes called *rḥm 'nt*, 'the maiden Anat'. In Judg. 5.30 Sisera's mother's wisest ladies suppose that Sisera is late in returning home because he is dividing the spoil, with a maiden or two (*raḥam raḥ^a^mātayim*) for every man. Craigie believes that there is a deliberate irony here: it is rather the maiden Deborah, in addition to Jael, who is dividing the spoil! Hence, implicitly, Deborah is called *raḥam*, 'maiden'. (v) Craigie thinks that Anat is 'the Mistress of the stars'.[32] He admits that the Ugaritic evidence is somewhat ambiguous, but endeavours to find it in

29. Delcor, 'Une allusion à 'Anath', p. 160.

30. For discussions of the precise meaning of *'annôt*, see F.I. Andersen, 'A Lexicographical Note on Exodus XXXII 18', *VT* 16 (1966), pp. 108-12, and J.M. Sasson, 'The Worship of the Golden Calf', in H.A. Hoffner (ed.), *Orient and Occident: Essays Presented to Cyrus H. Gordon on the Occasion of his Sixty-fifth Birthday* (AOAT, 22; Kevelaer: Butzon & Bercker; Neukirchen–Vluyn: Neukirchener Verlag, 1973), pp. 151-59, esp. p. 157, in addition to the Hebrew lexicons. A. Deem, 'The Goddess Anath and some Biblical Cruces', *JSS* 23 (1978), pp. 25-30 (29), renders 'the sound of an orgy'. She supposes that the text originally had the qal *'^a^nôt* rather than the piel *'annôt*, and that since the piel can mean 'to rape', the qal could mean 'to make love'. However, there is no clear instance of this meaning in biblical Hebrew, and where the qal occurs corresponding to the piel 'to humiliate' (including rape) the meaning rather appears to be 'to be afflicted' (Ps. 116.10; Isa. 31.4).

31. P.C. Craigie, 'Deborah and Anat: A Study of Poetic Imagery (Judges 5)', *ZAW* 90 (1978), pp. 374-81.

32. Cf. Craigie's earlier article, 'Three Ugaritic Notes on the Song of Deborah', *JSOT* 2 (1976), pp. 33-49.

*KTU*² 1.13.13, [*k*]*bkbm.ṯm.tpl. klbnt*, which H. Cazelles had earlier rendered, 'les étoiles tomberont là comme une vieille'.[33] Craigie then compares Judg. 5.20, 'from heaven fought the stars, from their courses they fought against Sisera', which he believes is a poetic description of Deborah's warriors.

What is to be said about this bold and original theory? With regard to points (i) and (ii), the parallels are not sufficiently striking to require that Deborah is here modelled on Anat. Further, points (iii), (iv) and (v) are dubious. Thus, with respect to (iii), it is very doubtful whether cognates of the Ugaritic word *drkt*, 'dominion', are found anywhere in the Old Testament. In the present case, there is no good reason to question the common rendering, 'March on, my soul, with might!' With regard to (iv), it must be noted that Deborah is not actually called *rḥm*, 'maiden'. Craigie has to suppose that it is implied in a rather convoluted way. It is doubtful whether it would have occurred to anyone who did not already have Craigie's thesis in mind. Finally, as for (v), not only is the Ugaritic evidence very uncertain, but it is very doubtful whether the host of the stars is a poetic description of Deborah's warriors. It is far more natural to suppose that the stars here form Yahweh's heavenly host. All in all, therefore, Craigie's thesis must be rejected as unconvincing.

Susan Ackerman[34] has also recently argued that the depiction of Deborah in Judges 5 has been influenced by the image of the Canaanite warrior goddess Anat. However, her positive reasoning is very thin, for she rejects all or most of Craigie's detailed points of comparison between Anat and Deborah listed above.[35] She also notes that Deborah is not Anat *pure simple*: 'Deborah wears no necklace of skulls or girdle of hands; she does not eat flesh; she does not drink blood'.[36] All that seems to be left by way of comparison is that Deborah was a female military leader. But granted that Deborah was a genuine historical figure, one wonders what in her depiction requires specific influence from the mythological figure of Anat. It should be added that Ackerman[37] also

33. H. Cazelles, 'L'hymne ugaritique à Anat', *Syria* 33 (Hommage à M. Charles Virolleaud, 1956), pp. 48-57 (56).

34. S. Ackerman, *Warrior, Dancer, Seductress, Queen: Women in Judges and Biblical Israel* (ABRL; New York: Doubleday, 1998), pp. 56-72.

35. Ackerman, *Warrior, Dancer, Seductress, Queen*, pp. 84-85 n. 92.

36. Ackerman, *Warrior, Dancer, Seductress, Queen*, p. 58.

37. Ackerman, *Warrior, Dancer, Seductress, Queen*, pp. 59-72.

sees influence from Anat on the depictions of Jael in Judges 5 and even on that of Judith in her striking down of Holofernes, as well as in the woman of Thebez in Judges 9, but the connections are tenuous and highly speculative.

Job 31.1. 'I have made a covenant with my eyes; how then could I look upon a virgin?'

On the face of it this verse is simply referring to lust. However, a number of scholars have thought that this is rather an allusion to the Virgin Anat. Thus, A.R. Ceresko and W. Michel have found here a reference to this goddess, and this view has been followed by D.N. Freedman, E.M. Good and D. Wolfers.[38] Earlier, in 1928, G. Jeshurun[39] was the first to see a reference to a goddess here, but he envisaged Ishtar–Astarte–Venus, the Regent of the constellation of Virgo (*b^e^tûlâ*). Contrary to what is implied by some scholars,[40] Jeshurun did not find here an allusion to Anat.

The arguments adduced in favour of seeing a reference to Anat are that looking on a virgin was a mere peccadillo, and that something more serious must be meant, namely, idolatry, and that sexual sin does not occur until later in the chapter (31.9-12), so it is not to be expected here. Some have accordingly emended *b^e^tûlâ*, 'virgin', to *n^e^bālâ*, 'folly',[41] or *b^e^hālâ*, 'calamity',[42] or have removed the verse to later in the chapter (e.g. NAB, NEB, REB). But there is no versional evidence for any other reading or positioning. Furthermore, Ecclus 9.5 clearly attests

38. A. Ceresko, *Job 29–31 in the Light of Northwest Semitic* (BibOr, 36; Rome: Biblical Institute Press, 1980), pp. 100, 103, 106-107; W.L. Michel, 'BTWLH, "Virgin" or "Virgin (Anat)" in Job 31:1?', *Hebrew Studies* 23 (1982), pp 59-66; D.N. Freedman, review of *Job 29–31 in the Light of Northwest Semitic*, by A. Ceresko, in *JBL* 102 (1983), pp. 138-44 (143); E.M. Good, *In Turns of Tempest: A Reading of Job with a Translation* (Stanford, CA: Stanford University Press, 1990), p. 130; D. Wolfers, *Deep Things out of Darkness* (Grand Rapids: Eerdmans; Kampen: Kok, 1995), pp. 355, 437.

39. G. Jeshurun, 'A Note on Job XXX [*sic*]: 1', *Journal of the Society of Oriental Research* 12 (1928), pp. 153-54.

40. Cf. Good, *In Turns of Tempest*, p. 130; Wolfers, *Deep Things out of Darkness*, p. 437.

41. So A.S. Peake, *Job* (Century Bible; Edinburgh: T.C. & E.C. Jack, 1905), p. 267.

42. So E.J. Kissane, *The Book of Job* (Dublin: Browne and Nolan, the Richview Press, 1939), pp. 200, 203, 205.

knowledge of this verse c. 200 BCE in the form in which we have it. Thus, Ecclus 9.5 reads, 'Do not look intently at a virgin' (*bib*ᵉ*tûlâ 'al-titbônēn*), while Job 31.1 declares, 'how then could I look upon a virgin?' (*ûmāh 'etbônēn 'al-b*ᵉ*tûlâ*). This is one of a number of instances in which Ecclesiasticus displays dependence on Job.[43]

Anat in the Song of Songs? One feature of M.H. Pope's bold and learned commentary on the Song of Songs[44] is his claim that the setting of this work was in the *marzēaḥ* ceremony, in which aspects of both a love feast and funerary lamentations were allegedly combined. This view has gained little following. Quite apart from uncertainties over the precise function of the *marzēaḥ* ceremony, the absence of any obvious funerary motifs in the Song of Songs is a strong objection to this interpretation, a problem not offset by the famous declaration in Cant. 8.6 that 'love is strong as death'.

Another bold feature of Pope's commentary, perhaps not so well known, is his view that the woman in the poem is the goddess Anat. This is also a dubious claim. One cannot but be impressed by the thoroughgoing peaceful nature of the Song of Songs—as is appropriate for a love poem—in contrast to much of the Old Testament. The goddess Anat, however, was a violent goddess of battle as well as one of love, but the former aspect is not reflected in the Song. Pope's attempt to find it in the Song is based on dubious philology, as in his view that the woman's epithet, 'the Shulammite' (Cant. 7.1 [ET 6.13]), means 'the pacified one', with reference to Anat's pacification after the scene of her bloody carnage in the Ugaritic texts (*KTU*² 1.3.II.3-41).[45] Rather, a female equivalent of the name Solomon seems more appropriate.[46] Again, the alleged description of the woman as 'awesome with trophies' (Cant. 6.4, 10), which Pope connects with 'the grisly trophies of

43. F.V. Reiterer, 'Das Verhältnis Ijobs und Ben Siras', in W. Beuken (ed.), *The Book of Job* (BETL, 114; Leuven: Leuven University Press and Peeters, 1994), pp. 405-29.

44. M.H. Pope, *Song of Songs* (AB, 7C; Garden City, NY: Doubleday, 1977).

45. Pope, *Song of Songs*, p. 600. Cf. Pope, *Song of Songs*, pp. 606-607, where he likewise implausibly connects *maḥ*ᵃ*nayim* (Cant. 7.1 [ET 6.13]) with this Ugaritic scene, translating it as 'two camps'.

46. Cf. H.H. Rowley, 'The Meaning of "the Shulammite"', *AJSL* 56 (1939), pp. 84-91.

the violent virgin goddess of Love and War',[47] is based on a mistranslation; *nidgālôt* does not mean 'trophies', but 'these great sights' (cf. Akkadian *dagālu*, 'to see'), as R. Gordis has made probable.[48] Pope compares Anat's seeking for Baal with the woman's seeking her beloved in Song of Songs 3,[49] but the context is quite different, since Baal is dead in the underworld, whereas the beloved in the Song is merely absent. Again, with regard to the statement in Cant. 4.4 that 'your neck is like the tower of David', Pope declares that 'If the lady is divine, her proportions would not be abnormal'.[50] But this is surely reading too much into poetic language, and the closest parallels to the extravagant language of the Song that are found in ancient Egyptian love poetry[51] clearly envisage human lovers. Such is the dubious character of the argumentation by which Pope endeavours to persuade us that the lady of the Song is the goddess Anat![52]

Anat and Bloodshed Imagery in the Old Testament

There is a noteworthy passage in the Ugaritic Baal myth (*KTU*[2] 1.3.II.3-30) in which the goddess Anat wreaks havoc on her enemies in battle in a most ruthless and bloody manner. We read such things as 'Heads were like balls beneath her, palms above her like locusts... She plunged her knees in the blood of the guards, her skirts in the gore of the warriors...' A few scholars[53] have compared this language with that

47. Pope, *Song of Songs*, p. 561.

48. R. Gordis, 'The Root דגל in the Song of Songs', *JBL* 88 (1969), pp. 203-204; reprinted in R. Gordis, *The Word and the Book: Studies in Biblical Language and Literature* (New York: Ktav, 1976), pp. 311-12.

49. Pope, *Song of Songs*, pp. 419-20.

50. Pope, *Song of Songs*, p. 465.

51. Cf. J.B. White, *A Study of the Language of Love in the Song of Songs and Ancient Egyptian Poetry* (SBLDS, 36; Missoula, MT: Scholars Press, 1978); M.V. Fox, *The Song of Songs and Ancient Egyptian Love Songs* (Wisconsin: University of Wisconsin Press, 1985).

52. Ackerman, *Warrior, Dancer, Seductress, Queen*, p. 72 does not refer to Pope, nor does she equate the woman of the Song with Anat, but she does think the Song has radically reinterpreted earlier Anat traditions. She appeals to some of the same verses that Pope did, 4.4 and 6.4, 10, but also to 8.9-10, where the woman is compared to a wall and her breasts are its towers; since, however, this particular imagery is never attested of Anat, there are no good grounds for seeing influence from this goddess on the imagery.

53. J. Gray, 'The Wrath of God in Canaanite and Hebrew Literature', *Journal of the Manchester University Egyptian and Oriental Society* 25 (1947–53), pp. 9-19;

used of Yahweh on a number of occasions in the Old Testament where he ruthlessly wreaks vengeance on his enemies, in Zeph. 1.7-18, Isa. 34.6-10, 63.1-6, Ezek. 39.17-20, Zech. 9.15, and think there might be some connection. However, in view of the unfortunate prevalence of ruthless and bloody warfare in the ancient world, one may wonder whether it is necessary to posit any real dependence of the biblical imagery on that applied to Anat in the Ugaritic texts. Even less does it seem necessary to follow W.F. Albright,[54] who actually imports the name of Anat into the biblical text in Ps. 68.24 (ET 23), reading 'Why, O Anath(?) dost thou wash thy feet in blood, the tongues of thy dogs in the blood of the foes?', by emending *l^ema'an* 'in order that' to *lāmmāh 'ᵃnāt* 'Why, O Anath'. (The emendation of *timḥaṣ* 'you shall smite' to *tirḥaṣ* 'you shall wash' is generally accepted.) Albright supposes that Anat is here the representative of an enemy nation, but quite apart from the gratuitous introduction of Anat into the text, it seems more natural to see v. 24 (ET 23) as continuing the imagery of Yahweh's vengeance in vv. 22-23 (ET 21-22).

Did Anat Function as Yahweh's Consort?

If Anat was Baal's consort, and if Yahweh could be equated with Baal, it would seem natural to assume that Anat could serve as Yahweh's consort. This last point, in turn, would appear to be confirmed by a reference to the deity Anat-Yahu in the fifth-century BCE Elephantine texts (*AP* 44.3). However, each of the points in the chain of argument has, on occasion, been questioned.

Thus, in recent years, even the common assumption that Anat was one of Baal's consorts has been challenged by P.L. Day and N. Walls.[55] They claim that the heifer with whom Baal copulates and who bears him offspring (*KTU*² 1.5.V.18-22, 1.10.II.26-III.25) is not Anat, and they further query whether *KTU*² 1.11.1 and 1.13 refer to sexual intercourse between Baal and Anat. Whatever the case about these instances, other evidence seems to make a good, cumulative case for concluding

P.D. Hanson, 'Zechariah 9 and the Recapitulation of an Ancient Ritual Pattern', *JBL* 92 (1973), pp. 37-59 (46-47 n. 25); Mark S. Smith, *The Early History of God*, pp. 61-64.

54. Albright, 'Catalogue', pp. 15, 28-29, 38.

55. P.L. Day, 'Anat, Mistress of Animals', *JNES* 51 (1992), pp. 181-90; N. Walls, *The Goddess Anat in Ugaritic Myth* (SBLDS, 135; Atlanta: Scholars Press, 1992).

that Anat is Baal's consort (similarly Astarte—also widely accepted to be Baal's consort). Baal is constantly paired with Anat and Astarte in the Ugaritic texts, and in the Egyptian text on the contest of Horus and Seth for the rule, Anat and Astarte are both explicitly stated to be Seth's (i.e. Baal's) wives.[56] Walls, following H. Te Velde,[57] tries to negate the evidence of the text by arguing that Anat is nowhere else called the consort of Seth. However, as A.H. Gardiner has noted,[58] it is implied on the Tanis obelisk that Anat is Seth's wife. Moreover, much later, the wife of Hadad is called Atargatis, a name which is generally accepted to reflect a combination of Astarte and Anat (Aramaic *'tr'th*).[59]

Consequently, if Anat was Baal's consort, and Baal could be equated with Yahweh, as we have seen from Chapter 3, it is plausible that Yahweh could appropriate Anat as his wife. The idea that Anat could serve as Yahweh's consort has often been thought to be confirmed by a reference to the goddess Anat-Yahu in the fifth-century BCE Jewish Aramaic papyri from Elephantine in Egypt (*AP* 44.3). Yahu (Yahweh) was very much the main deity worshipped there, and Anat-Yahu, literally, 'Anat of Yahu' would seem to be his consort; the Jews of Elephantine also worshipped Anat-Bethel, Ḥerem-Bethel and Eshem Bethel. An attempt to deny the presence of a goddess Anat-Yahu, as well as of Anat-Bethel, was made by W.F. Albright, who at one point claimed that *'nt* in *'ntyhw* and *'ntbyt'l* means 'providence',[60] whilst later he suggested 'sign'.[61] However, these conjectures were disproved by the fact that a deity Anat-Bethel is attested c. 675 BCE in the treaty between Esar-haddon of Assyria and Baal, king of Tyre.[62] If Anat-Bethel is the name of a deity, then so must be Anat-Yahu. It therefore

56. See conveniently *ANET*, p. 15.

57. Walls, *The Goddess Anat*, pp. 145-46; H. Te Velde, *Seth: God of Confusion* (Leiden: E.J. Brill, 2nd edn, 1977), pp. 29-30.

58. A.H. Gardiner, *Hieratic Papyri in the British Museum, Third Series*, I (London: British Museum, 1935), p. 62.

59. See too Mark S. Smith, 'The God Athtar in the Ancient Near East and his Place in KTU 1.6 I', in Z. Zevit, S. Gitin and M. Sokoloff (eds.), *Solving Riddles and Untying Knots: Biblical, Epigraphic, and Semitic Studies in Honor of Jonas C. Greenfield* (Winona Lake: Eisenbrauns, 1995), pp. 627-40 (631 n. 28).

60. Albright, 'The Evolution of the West-Semitic Divinity 'An-'Anat-'Attâ', pp. 92-97.

61. Albright, *Archaeology and the Religion of Israel*, pp. 168, 192 n. 14.

62. Cf. R. Borger, 'Anath-Bethel', *VT* 7 (1957), pp. 102-104. (The text is in *ANET*, p. 534.)

seems indubitable that the goddess Anat, in the form of Anat-Yahu, did function as Yahweh's wife amongst the Jews at Elephantine in the fifth century BCE. A further problem arises, however, when we try to determine the origin and antiquity of the concept of Anat as Yahweh's wife attested at Elephantine:

(i) It could reflect pre-722 BCE syncretism in the Northern Kingdom of Israel.
(ii) It could reflect pre-586 BCE syncretism in the Southern Kingdom of Judah.
(iii) It could reflect syncretism arising in Egypt itself.
(iv) It could reflect syncretism after 722 BCE in the area of the former Northern Kingdom following the exile of Syrians (amongst other people) to that region (2 Kgs 17.24-28).

We can probably eliminate (ii), since the divine name Bethel occurs as an element in several of the deities also worshipped at Elephantine, and Bethel is unknown in Judah. (iii) and (iv) have recently been suggested by Mark Smith and K. van der Toorn respectively.[63] Both, in fact, reject the notion that Anat was actually known at all in pre-exilic Israel. However, they exaggerate the extent to which Anat was absent in the first-millennium BCE Mediterranean world,[64] and, as I have argued earlier, Hos. 14.9 (ET 8) probably contains a word play on her name as well as that of Asherah from the eighth-century Israelite prophet, implying that she had been a consort of Yahweh then. It is also of note that Bethel is attested in Jer. 48.13 as the name of the detested Northern Kingdom's deity (paralleling Kemosh in Moab), so Anat-Bethel could have had a role there too. In the light of all this I prefer to see the notion of Anat as Yahweh's wife as going back to pre-exilic Israel, rather than as a later accretion.

The Queen of Heaven

The 'Queen of Heaven' is the title of a goddess referred to in the Old Testament in Jer. 7.18 and 44.17-19, 25. Thus, in Jeremiah's deuteronomistically edited Temple sermon in Jer. 7.18, the prophet complains,

63. Mark S. Smith, *The Early History of God*, p. 61; K. van der Toorn, 'Anat-Yahu, some other Deities, and the Jews of Elephantine', *Numen* 39 (1992), pp. 80-101.

64. Cf. P.L. Day, 'Anat', *DDD*, cols. 62-77 (68-70) (2nd edn, pp. 36-43 [39-40]).

'The children gather wood, the fathers kindle fire, and the women knead dough, to make cakes for the Queen of Heaven; and they pour out drink offerings to other gods, to provoke me to anger'. Then, in Jeremiah 44 we read that the Jews who dwelt in Pathros in the land of Egypt said to Jeremiah,

> 'But we will do everything that we have vowed, burn incense to the Queen of Heaven and pour out libations to her as we did, both we and our fathers, our kings and our princes in the cities of Judah and in the streets of Jerusalem; for then we had plenty of food, and prospered, and saw no evil. But since we left off burning incense to the Queen of Heaven and pouring out libations to her, we have lacked everything and have been consumed by the sword and by famine.' And the women said,[65] 'When we burned incense to the Queen of Heaven and poured out libations to her, was it without our husbands' approval that we made cakes for her bearing her image and poured out libations to her?'

Jeremiah goes on to condemn the people for their worship of other gods:

> Thus says the Lord of hosts, the God of Israel: You and your wives have declared with your mouths, and have fulfilled it with your hands, saying, 'We will surely perform our vows that we have made, to burn incense to the Queen of Heaven and to pour out libations to her.' Then confirm your vows and perform your vows! (vv. 17-19, 25)

It is generally accepted that the word for 'Queen of' (*malkat*) has been deliberately distorted by a scribe to *m*^{e}*leket*, which is found in the MT in every instance of the word here (Jer. 7.18; 44. 17, 18, 19, 25). A number of Hebrew manuscripts, in fact, actually read *m*^{e}*le'ket* 'host' in each instance, and it is widely agreed that this was an apologetic alteration to avoid the suggestion that the people of Judah worshipped the Queen of Heaven.[66]

We shall now consider in turn the various suggestions as to the identity of the Queen of Heaven that have been put forward.

Shapash

An eccentric view that has gained no support apart from its proposer, M. J. Dahood,[67] holds that Jeremiah's 'Queen of Heaven' is to be

65. Cf. Syriac. Hebrew lacks 'And the women said'.

66. Cf. R.P. Gordon, 'Aleph Apologeticum', *JQR* 69 (1978–79), pp. 112-16, who finds another possible example of this phenomenon in 2 Sam. 11.1.

67. M.J. Dahood, 'La Regina del Cielo in Geremia', *RivB* 8 (1960), pp. 166-68.

identified with the Canaanite sun-goddess Shapash. This view has nothing to commend it, and is simply based on Dahood's rendering of a Ugaritic text involving Shapash, *KTU*² 1.23.54, *'db. lšpš. rbt. wlkkbm. knm*, as 'prepare cakes for lady Shapash and the stars'. Dahood's translation of *knm* as 'cakes' and connecting it with *kawwānîm* have gained no support.

Asherah

The view that the Queen of Heaven was the goddess Asherah has not been widely followed. However, it has gained a little support in recent years.[68] Its strongest point is the prominence given to Asherah in the Deuteronomist's account of Manasseh's apostasy and Josiah's reformation in 2 Kings 21 and 23, and the recent archaeological discoveries suggesting that Asherah was indeed understood to be Yahweh's consort by some pre-exilic Israelites. Qudshu (Asherah), like Anat, Astarte and Ishtar is called the 'Lady of Heaven' (*nb.t p.t*) in New Kingdom Egyptian texts.

However, there is nothing in first-millennium BCE texts that singles out Asherah as 'Queen of Heaven' or associates her particularly with the heavens at all. Asherah was not the only consort Yahweh was capable of appropriating, since his equation with Baal by some meant that he was capable of appropriating Astarte and Anat too (cf. Anat-Yahu at Elephantine), both of which have first-millennium attestation connecting them with the heavens (similarly Ishtar). Koch, Keel and Uehlinger believe that Asherah was syncretistically equated with Ishtar, but this is unlikely, since the West Semitic equivalent of Ishtar was not Asherah but Astarte.

Anat

Another goddess who has been proposed to be equated with Jeremiah's 'Queen of Heaven' is the Canaanite goddess Anat.[69] In favour of this

68. K. Koch, 'Aschera als Himmelskönigin in Jerusalem', *UF* 20 (1988), pp. 97-120; Keel and Uehlinger, *Göttinnen, Götter und Gottessymbole*, pp. 386-90, ET *Gods, Goddesses and Images of God*, pp. 338-41.

69. Anat has been favoured by A. Vincent, *La Religion des Judéo-Araméens d'Eléphantine* (Paris: P. Geuthner, 1937), pp. 635, 649-51; Albright, *Yahweh and the Gods of Canaan*, p. 113; Porten, *Archives from Elephantine*, pp. 176-77; M.D. Cogan, *Imperialism and Religion* (SBLMS, 19; Missoula, MT: SBL and Scholars

suggestion it may be noted that the term 'Lady of Heaven' (*nb.t p.t*) is employed of Anat in New Kingdom Egypt (as also of Astarte, Ishtar and Qudshu [Asherah]) and that the title 'Lady of Exalted Heaven' (*b'lt. šmm. rmm*) is given to Anat in a Ugaritic text (KTU^2 1.108.7). More strikingly, it has been pointed out that the precise term 'Queen of Heaven' probably refers to Anat in the fourth of the Aramaic letters from Hermopolis in Egypt, dating from the fifth century BCE, about a century after the date of the deuteronomistically edited passages in Jeremiah. Line 1 of the letter sends 'Greetings to the temple of Bethel and the temple of the Queen of Heaven'[70] at Syene. Syene was next to Elephantine, where the fifth-century BCE syncretistic Jews worshipped Anat-Bethel and Anat-Yahu alongside Yahu and other deities. Further, in the treaty between Esarhaddon of Assyria and Baal king of Tyre (c. 675 BCE), the deities Bethel and Anat-Bethel are cited together. This suggests that Bethel's consort was Anat-Bethel and that she is the deity intended as the 'Queen of Heaven' alongside Bethel in the Hermopolis letter. However, although this is probably the case, it does not follow that Anat was the goddess referred to as the 'Queen of Heaven' in Jeremiah. As has been pointed out earlier, Anat does not seem to have been as prominent as Astarte in first-millennium Palestine. The Deuteronomist (to whose work Jer. 7 and 44 are to be attributed) never once polemicizes against her cult elsewhere; rather Asherah and Astarte appear to have been the dominant goddesses in first-millennium Palestine and are consequently the ones against whom the Deuteronomist polemicizes. Moreover, if the Elephantine cult of Anat-Bethel (and Anat-Yahu) reflects pre-exilic Israelite syncretism rather than approriation from the Aramaeans in Egypt, it will doubtless go back to the Northern Kingdom of Israel, as the name Bethel suggests (cf. Jer. 48.13); there is no evidence of the worship of Bethel in Judah.

Press, 1974), pp. 85-86; F.O. Hvidberg-Hansen, *La déesse TNT: Une étude sur la religion canaanéo-punique* (2 vols.; Copenhagen: G.E.C. Gad, 1979), I, p. 96; P.C. Schmitz, 'Queen of Heaven', *ABD*, I, pp. 586-88.

70. *Šlm byt bt'l wbyt mlkt šmyn.* See E. Bresciani and M. Kamil, *Le lettere aramaiche di Hermopoli* (Atti della Accademia Nazionale dei Lincei: Memorie, Classe di Scienze morale, storiche e filoliche, ser. 8, vol. 12, fasc. 5; Rome: Accademia Nazionale dei Lincei, 1966), p. 400; or more conveniently, J.C.L. Gibson, *Textbook of Syrian Semitic Inscriptions*, II (Oxford: Clarendon Press, 1975), p. 137.

Ishtar

It has sometimes been supposed that Jeremiah's Queen of Heaven referred to the Mesopotamian goddess Ishtar.[71] She is not only called 'Lady of Heaven' (*nb.t p.t*) in New Kingdom Egyptian texts (like Astarte, Anat and Qudshu [Asherah]), but Akkadian texts refer to her explicitly as 'Queen of Heaven' (*šarrat šamê*).[72] Moreover, the word used for the cakes offered to the Queen of Heaven (*kawwānîm*) appears to be an Akkaddian loan word (*kamānu*), a word which is actually attested of offerings to Ishtar as well as to other deities.[73]

However, there are serious problems in supposing that the 'Queen of Heaven' is simply to be equated with the Mesopotamian goddess Ishtar. The chief problem is that the text in Jeremiah 44 makes it abundantly clear that the worship of the Queen of Heaven was deep-seated among both the ordinary people and rulers of Judah and Jerusalem and had gone back several generations. This strongly suggests that her worship was a popular folk custom, that is, she was a Canaanite goddess, and not some recently implanted cult from Assyria.

Astarte

At the present time the most popular view is that the 'Queen of Heaven' refers to Astarte,[74] and indeed the most plausible case can be made for

71. Originally suggested by E. Schrader, 'Die מרכת השמים und ihr aramäisch-assyrisches Aequivalent', *SKPAW* (1886), pp. 477-91, and followed, e.g. by W. Rudolph, *Jeremia* (HAT, 1.12; Tübingen: J.C.B. Mohr [Paul Siebeck], 1947), p. 47; A. Weiser, *Das Buch Jeremia* (ATD, 20; Göttingen: Vandenhoeck & Ruprecht, 5th edn, 1966), p. 64; M. Weinfeld, 'The Worship of Molech and of the Queen of Heaven and its Background', *UF* 4 (1972), pp. 133-54 (149-53); W.E. Rast, 'Cakes for the Queen of Heaven', in A.L. Merrill and T.W. Overholt, *Scripture in History and Theology: Essays in Honor of J. Coert Rylaarsdam* (Pittsburgh Theological Monograph Series, 17; Pittsburgh: Pickwick Press, 1977), pp. 167-80; M. Held, 'Studies in Biblical Lexicography', *Eretz-Israel* 16 (Harry M. Orlinsky volume; Jerusalem: Israel Exploration Society, 1982), pp. 76-85 (76-77) (Hebrew).

72. Ishtar is also called by similar epithets such as *šarrat šamê u kakkabāni*, 'Queen of Heaven and the Stars', *šarrat šamê u erṣeti*, 'Queen of Heaven and Earth', *etellet šamê (u) erṣetim*, 'Sovereign of Heaven and Earth', and *malkat šamāmī u qaqqari*, 'Ruler of Heaven and Earth'. Cf. K. Tallqvist, *Akkadische Götterepitheta* (StudOr, 7; Helsinki: Societas Orientalis Fennica, 1938), pp. 39, 64, 129, 239-40; cf. pp. 333-34.

73. *CAD* 8 (1971), pp. 110-11.

74. Astarte has been favoured by F.M. Cumont, 'Astarté', in G. Wissowa (ed.), *Real-Encyclopädie der classischen Altertumswissenschaft*, II (Stuttgart: J.B.

this goddess. In addition to being called 'Lady of Heaven' (*nb.t p.t*), along with Anat, Ishtar and Qudshu (Asherah) in New Kingdom Egypt, Astarte is the Canaanite goddess who is most frequently associated with the heavens in the first millennium BCE. For example, she is referred to as *'štrt šmm 'drm*, 'Astarte of the Highest Heavens' in line 16 of the Eshmunazar inscription (*KAI* 14). More particularly, there is considerable evidence for the popularity of the cult of Aphrodite Ourania, 'Heavenly Aphrodite' in the first-millennium BCE Mediterranean world; for example, two inscriptions from Delos, dedicated by Ascalonites are addressed 'to the heavenly Aphrodite, Astarte of Palestine',[75] thus identifying them. Further, Herodotus 1.105 states that the most ancient temple of Aphrodite Ourania was in Ascalon, and that the temple to this goddess in Cyprus was acknowledged by the Cypriots to derive from the one in Ascalon, thus indicating the Palestinian origin of her cult. Again, Pausanias, *Description of Greece* 1.14.7 mentions that the Assyrians and then the Phoenicians of Ascalon and the Paphians of Cyprus worshipped the Heavenly Aphrodite. (Ishtar and Astarte have here been confused or their equation is here reflected.)

Further, it is to be noted that the offering of cakes to Astarte is specifically mentioned in the fourth-century BCE Kition tariff, line 9, where we read, 'To the two bakers who baked the basket of cakes for the [Holy] Queen'[76] (though it is a different word for 'cakes' from that used in Jer. 7 and 44). Finally, Astarte (unlike Anat) is a goddess

Metzler, rev. edn, 1896), cols. 1776-78 (1778); M.H. Pope, ''Aṯtart, 'Aštart, Astarte', in H.W. Haussig (ed.), *Götter und Mythen*, pp. 250-52 (251); J. Fitzmyer, 'The Phoenician Inscription from Pyrgi', *JAOS* 86 (1966), pp. 285-97 (287-88); Bresciani and. Kamil, *Le lettere aramaiche*, p. 400; W. Herrmann, 'Aštart', *MIO* 15 (1969), pp. 6-155 (29 n. 67); R. du Mesnil du Buisson, *Etudes sur les dieux phéniciens hérités par l'empire romain* (EPROER, 14; Leiden: E.J. Brill, 1970), pp. 126-27; M. Delcor, 'Le culte de la "reine du ciel" selon Jer 7, 18; 44, 17-19, 25 et ses survivances', in W.C. Delsman *et al.* (eds.), *Von Kanaan bis Kerala* (AOAT, 211; Neukirchen–Vluyn: Neukirchener Verlag, 1982), pp. 101-22; S.M. Olyan, 'Some Observations Concerning the Identity of the Queen of Heaven', *UF* 19 (1987), pp. 161-74. Cf. also the works of S. Ackerman cited below in n. 77.

75. See P. Roussel and M. Launey, *Inscriptions de Délos* (Paris: Librairie Ancienne Honoré Champion, 1937), nos. 2305 and 1719. The text is perfectly preserved in the former, but has to be partially restored in the latter.

76. See J.C.L. Gibson, *Textbook of Syrian Semitic Inscriptions*, III (Oxford: Clarendon Press, 1982), pp. 124-25. This is *KAI* 37.10, though *KAI* did not succeed in translating it satisfactorily.

against whom the Deuteronomist elsewhere polemicizes.

Thus, although certainty is not possible, the best case can be made for the Queen of Heaven being Astarte. Over against Ishtar, she has the advantage of being a native Canaanite deity, such as the deep-seated, folk nature of the cult depicted in Jeremiah 44 suggests. Over against Asherah she has the advantage of being associated frequently with the heavens in the first millennium BCE. And over against Anat, she has the advantage of being mentioned explicitly elsewhere in the Deuteronomistic corpus (to which Jer. 7 and 44 belong) as a goddess worshipped in pre-exilic Israel.

Nevertheless, the fact remains that an Akkadian loan word is used for the 'cakes' in Jeremiah 7 and 44, so it is possible—as S. Ackerman[77] argues—that what we have is not simply Astarte, but Astarte in syncretism with her Mesopotamian equivalent Ishtar.

77. S. Ackerman, *Under Every Green Tree: Popular Religion in Sixth-Century Judah* (HSM, 46; Atlanta: Scholars Press, 1992), pp. 5-35, and more briefly in '"And the Women Knead Dough": The Worship of the Queen of Heaven in Sixth-Century Judah', in P.L. Day (ed.), *Gender and Difference in Ancient Israel* (Minneapolis: Fortress Press, 1989), pp. 109-24.

Chapter 6

YAHWEH AND THE ASTRAL DEITIES (SUN, MOON AND LUCIFER)

Yahweh and the Sun

The Canaanite Background of Israel's Sun Cult

The worship of the sun was widespread throughout the ancient Near East.[1] It is therefore not surprising to find allusions to it in the Old Testament. Many of these date from the period of the seventh to sixth centuries BCE (cf. Deut. 4.19, 17.3; 2 Kgs 23.5, 11; Jer. 8.2; Ezek. 8.16), though Job 31.26-28 is later. It has therefore sometimes been supposed that its occurrence in Judah was due to the influence of the Assyrians, for whom the astral cult had an important place.[2] However, various pieces of evidence suggest that the sun cult was Canaanite rather than Assyrian.[3]

First, all the other deities and cults that Josiah is said to have removed in 2 Kings 23 appear to have been Canaanite, not Assyrian. The Deuteronomist himself implies that Manasseh's astral cults (along with his other cults) were Canaanite (cf. 2 Kgs 21.2-3). Other deities mentioned are Baal, Asherah and Molech. Baal, of course, is the well-known Canaanite storm god, and Asherah was a prominent Canaanite goddess. (Spieckermann's view[4] that Asherah is here a code-name for the Assyrian Ishtar will not do in view of epigraphic evidence of Asherah

1. For the West Semites, see E. Lipiński, 'Le culte du soleil chez les Sémites occidentaux du 1er millénaire av. J.-C.', *OLP* 22 (1991), pp. 57-72.

2. So T. Oestreicher, *Das deuteronomische Grundgesetz* (Beitr. z. Förd. chr. Th., 27.4; Gütersloh: C. Bertelsmann, 1923); H. Gressmann, 'Josia und das Deuteronomium', *ZAW* 42 (1924), pp. 313-37; H. Spieckermann, *Juda unter Assur in der Sargonidenzeit* (FRLANT, 129; Göttingen: Vandenhoeck & Ruprecht, 1982), esp. p. 271, who all see considerable Assyrian influence on the cults propagated by Manasseh and removed by Josiah, including star worship.

3. J.W. McKay, *Religion in Judah under the Assyrians* (SBT 2nd series, 26; London: SCM Press, 1973), pp. 32-36, 48-51, 52-53.

4. Spieckermann, *Juda unter Assur*, pp. 212-21.

worship in Israel and the fact that the West Semitic equivalent of Ishtar should be Ashtoreth [Astarte], not Asherah.) Finally, as for Molech, there is no evidence of child sacrifice as a form of religious worship among the Assyrians, but this is attested in the Canaanite world. Consequently, unless there is strong evidence to the contrary, we should expect the sun and astral cults to be Canaanite as well.

Secondly, the evidence of place names is suggestive of the importance of the sun cult to the Canaanites. The most famous place is Beth-Shemesh, 'house of the sun',[5] on the northern border of Judah (Josh. 15.10), which was given to the Levites (sons of Aaron, Josh. 21.16; 1 Chron. 6.44 [ET 59]). Its location suggests that it could well be identical with Ir-Shemesh , 'city of the sun', assigned to Dan in Josh. 19.41 and Har-heres, 'mountain of the sun', in Judg. 1.35. There were two other sites in Palestine called Beth-Shemesh, in Issachar (Josh. 19.22) and Naphtali (Josh. 19.38), sometimes but probably wrongly equated, and an En-Shemesh, 'spring of the sun', in Judah (on the border with Benjamin) in Josh. 15.7; 18.17. Finally, there was a Timnath-heres, 'portion of the sun', in Ephraim in Judg. 2.9, where Joshua was buried; this is certainly the same place as Timnath-serah in Josh. 19.50 and 24.30, the word for 'sun' (*ḥeres*) having been deliberately distorted (to *seraḥ*) so as to avoid the polytheistic allusion to the sun cult. In total this makes perhaps five, but conceivably anything between four and seven sites in Canaan whose names are suggestive of the sun cult,[6] a higher number of theophoric place names than those of any deity apart from El and Baal. There is also a place named Shamash-Edom in Thutmose III's fifteenth-century BCE Karnak Palestinian town list.[7] The Israelites were therefore heirs to a flourishing Canaanite sun cult, so that caution is needed when ascribing later references to Israelite sun worship to Mesopotamian influence.

5. This is probably the Beth-Shemesh mentioned in an Egyptian execration text, which dates from the nineteenth or eighteenth century BCE, thus proving the great antiquity of the sun cult in Palestine. See *ANET*, p. 329, n. 8.

6. It has sometimes been supposed that the place name Kir-heres (Isa. 16.11; Jer. 48.31, 36) or Kir-hareseth (Isa. 16.7; 2 Kgs 3.25) in Moab also contains or conceals an allusion to the sun, but this is doubtful. (The spelling is *qîr ḥereś* or *qîr ḥ*^{a}*reśet*, not *qîr ḥeres*.) On the location of this place, see B.C. Jones, 'In Search of Kir Hareseth: A Case Study in Site Identification', *JSOT* 52 (1991), pp. 3-24.

7. *ANET*, p. 243. The name also recurs in Amenhotep II's Asiatic campaigns. See *ANET*, p. 245.

Two pieces of archaeological evidence attest the presence of the sun cult in Israel prior to any likely Mesopotamian influence.[8] The first is a tenth-century BCE cult stand from Taanach, which contains four tiers, the first representing what seems to be a horse and sun disc.[9] The second is a small horse's head from Hazor with a disc-like symbol on its forehead, dating from c. 925-905 BCE.[10] These are particularly significant, since 2 Kgs 23.11 specifically mentions horses and chariots of the sun as having been removed from the Jerusalem temple in the course of Josiah's reformation.[11] There is no reason to attribute these to Assyrian influence,[12] since the association of the horse with the sun had clearly already been a feature of Syro-Palestinian religion for several centuries. Further evidence, admittedly late, for the idea of the horses and chariots of the sun in the Syro-Palestinian world, comes in

8. If E. Puech's reconstruction of a Lachish bowl inscription is accepted (E. Puech, 'Origine de l'alphabet', *RB* 93 [1986], pp. 161-213 [180-82]), there was a temple of the sun at Lachish c. 1200 BCE or in the thirteenth century BCE. But Puech's reading is highly speculative in view of the fragmentary nature of the text.

9. See Taylor, 'Representations of Yahweh', pp. 557-66. Taylor notes (pp. 561-63) how two zoological experts independently agreed that the figure was an equine, not a calf as has sometimes been claimed.

10. See the discussion in J.G. Taylor, *Yahweh and the Sun: Biblical and Archaeological Evidence for Sun Worship in Ancient Israel* (JSOTSup, 111; Sheffield: JSOT Press, 1993), pp. 37-40. This was originally published by Y. Yadin, *et al.*, *Hazor*, II (Jerusalem: Magnes Press, 1960), plates 103.9 (drawing) and 163.12, 13 (photographs). See also, Y. Yadin, *Hazor* (Schweich Lectures, 1970; London: Oxford University Press, 1972), pl. 19c and pp. 145-46, n. 1, and *idem*, *Hazor: The Rediscovery of a Great Citadel of the Bible* (New York: Random House, 1975), pp. 186-90). On the other hand, Taylor, *Yahweh and the Sun*, pp. 58-66, rightly points out that it is unlikely that various alleged sun discs on horse figurines from certain eighth- to seventh-century BCE strata in Palestinian sites, including the Ophel in Jerusalem, actually are such. For these, see T.A. Holland, 'A Study of Palestinian Iron Age Baked Clay Figurines, with Special Reference to Jerusalem: Cave 1', *Levant* 9 (1977), pp. 121-55, especially 149-57.

11. However, G. Pettinato, 'Is. 2,7 e il culto del sole in Giuda nel sec. VIII av. Cr.', *OrAnt* 4 (1965), pp. 1-30, is surely wrong in finding a reference to horses and chariots of the sun in Isa. 2.7, 'their land is filled with horses, and there is no end to their chariots'. This more naturally refers to ordinary military horses and chariots, as in Mic. 5.9 (ET 10), 'I will cut off your horses from among you and will destroy your chariots'. A cultic understanding of horses and chariots is no more demanded by the reference to 'idols' in Isa. 2.8 than it is by the allusions to images, pillars and Asherim in Mic. 5.12-13 (ET 13-14).

12. *Contra* the scholars cited above in n. 2.

Herodian's account of Varius Avitus Bassianus (Elagabalus), High Priest of Emesa in Syria, who became Roman Emperor in 218 CE and in a festival in 219 CE conveyed the symbol of the sun god (Elagabal) in a chariot drawn by a team of horses.[13]

However, one passage which has occasionally been thought to refer to a Canaanite sun (and moon) cult must be rejected. This is the famous passage in Josh. 10.12-13, where Joshua declares, '"Sun, stand thou still at Gibeon, and thou Moon in the valley of Aijalon." And the sun stood still and the moon stayed, until the nation took vengeance on their enemies.' This, of course, is a text whose interpretation is highly controversial. One relatively new explanation that a few scholars have followed in recent decades is that the reference implies the existence of a sun cult in Gibeon (and of a moon cult in Aijalon), and the deities are being told not to intervene in the battle.[14] However, we lack any concrete evidence of a sun cult at Gibeon (or of a moon cult in Aijalon), and it seems more natural to regard the text as alluding to something affecting the sun and moon in the heavens, which are to be understood as being above Gibeon and the valley of Aijalon respectively, that is, the sun is to the east of the moon. This positioning suggests that the time is in the early morning, which also coheres with the reference to Joshua's preceding night march in Josh. 10.9. Probably we are to think of the sun and moon being blotted out by a thunderstorm.[15] This would not only cohere with the reference to hailstones in Josh. 10.11, but also with the similar imagery in Hab. 3.10-11, where we read that 'The sun raised high its hands; the moon stood still in its dwelling at the light of thine arrows as they sped, at the flash of thy glittering spear', the same verb, 'stood still' (*'āmad*) being used of the moon as in Josh. 10.13. It

13. Herodian, *History of the Empire from the Time of Marcus Aurelius* 5.6.6-9.

14. So J. Dus, 'Gibeon: Eine Kultstätte des *Šmš* und die Stadt der benjaminitischen Schicksals', *VT* 10 (1960), pp. 353-74; J. Heller, 'Die schweigende Sonne', *Communio Viatorum* 9 (1966), pp. 73-78; J. Blenkinsopp, *Gibeon and Israel: The Role of Gibeon and the Gibeonites in the Political and Religious History of Early Israel* (Cambridge: Cambridge University Press, 1972), pp. 44-52.

15. So A. Smythe Palmer, *A Misunderstood Miracle: An Essay in Favour of a New Interpretation of 'the Sun Standing Still' in Joshua X.12-14* (London: Swan Sonnerschein, Lowrey & Co., 1887); J. Reid, 'Did the Sun and Moon Stand Still?', *ExpTim* 9 (1897–98), pp. 151-54; H.H. Rowley, *The Re-discovery of the Old Testament* (London: James Clarke, 1946), pp. 68-69; B. Alfrink, 'Het "Still Staan" van Zon en Maan in Jos. 10:12-15', *Studia Catholica* 24 (1949), pp. 238-68; J. de Fraine, 'De miraculo solari Josue', *VD* 28 (1950), pp. 227-36.

is clear that in Habakkuk 3 it is Yahweh's theophany in the storm which leads to the blotting out of the sun and moon, and this is the most natural explanation in Josh. 10.12-13 too.[16]

16. Other explanations have less plausibility. A variation on the view adopted here is that of E. Walter Maunder, 'A Misunderstood Miracle', *The Expositor* 16 (1910), pp. 359-72 and R.B.Y. Scott, 'Meteorological Phenomena and Terminology in the Old Testament', *ZAW* 64 (1952), pp. 11-25 (19-20), who likewise envisage meteorological obscuration of the sun and moon, but think the time is midday, which, however, does not agree with the reference to the moon's presence. Others have thought that a total eclipse of the sun was intended, e.g. J.F.A. Sawyer, 'Joshua 10:12-14 and the Solar Eclipse of 30 September 1131 B.C.', *PEQ* 104 (1972), pp. 139-46; however, the eclipse in 1131 BCE took place at 12.40 pm, which makes the request to the moon likewise to be silent impossible to fathom, and 1131 BCE would generally be regarded as too late for Joshua. Yet other interpretations presuppose (as the prose commentator also understood in Josh. 10.13) that there was a prolongation of light rather than the opposite; e.g. W.J. Phythian-Adams, 'A Meteorite of the Fourteenth Centure B.C.', *PEQ* 78 (1946), pp. 116-24, proposes that a meteorite falling to earth (cf. the 'great stones' of Josh. 10.11) gave rise to an abnormal light. He thinks it was the same meteorite referred to in the annals of Mursilis II (1339–1306 BCE), but this date would now be regarded as too early for Joshua. Moreover, on the analogy of other known examples of this phenomenon, it seems unlikely that the effects of a meteorite in Asia Minor would be observable in Palestine. Others again would interpret the passage as saying that the sun and the moon literally did stand still, understanding this as pure legend, e.g. Gaster, *Myth, Legend, and Custom*, pp. 414-15; J.A. Soggin, *Joshua* (trans. R.A. Wilson; OTL; London: SCM Press, 1972), pp. 122-23; M. Weinfeld, 'Divine Intervention and War in Ancient Israel and in the Ancient Near East', in H. Tadmor and M. Weinfeld (eds.), *History, Historiography and Interpretation* (Jerusalem: Magnes Press; Leiden: E.J. Brill, 1983), pp. 121-47 (146-47). However, against all such views as the last two, it may be noted that *dmm* and *'md* used of the sun and moon more likely refer to their silencing or disappearance than to their standing still, shining, or appearing to shine for extra long. First, the closest parallel is in Hab. 3.10-11, 'The sun raised high its hands; the moon stood still (*'āmad*) in its dwelling', which, in the context of the storm theophany, is suggestive of their ceasing to shine rather than their shining longer. Secondly, in a comparable theophanic passage, Isa. 24.23 declares that 'The moon will be abashed (*ḥāpᵉrâ*), and the sun ashamed (*ûbôšâ*)', and the context likewise suggests that the sun and moon will be fading away rather than shining longer. Since the verbs *bwš* and *dmm* appear in parallelism in Ps. 31.18 (ET 17), 'let the wicked be put to shame (*yēbōšû*), let them go dumbfounded (*yiddᵉmû*) to Sheol', one would expect a similar meaning with reference to the sun and moon to be present in Isa. 24.23 and Josh. 10.12-13. A final view, quite different from any considered above, is that of J.S. Holladay, 'The Day(s) the Moon Stood Still', *JBL* 87 (1968), pp. 166-78, who supposes that the standing still of sun

Was Yahweh Equated with the Sun?

It is indubitable that the cult of the sun was sometimes celebrated in Yahweh's temple in Jerusalem (2 Kgs 23.5, 11; Ezek. 8.16). This is fully explicable on the understanding that the sun was part of the host of heaven (= the sons of God [Job 38.7]), who formed Yahweh's entourage.

However, a number of scholars earlier in the last century proposed that Yahweh was equated with the sun, and this has also been argued afresh by some more recent scholars, such as Morton Smith, H.-P. Stähli, H. Niehr, O. Keel and C. Uehlinger, E. Lipiński, and most thoroughly in a full-length book by J. Glen Taylor.[17] Mark Smith[18] has also argued for a marked influence of solar imagery on Yahweh without claiming that Yahweh was actually equated with the sun. Older scholars such as C.V.L. Charlier, J. Morgenstern, H.G. May, and F.J. Hollis[19]

and moon is to be understood in terms of Mesopotamian astrology, according to which the conjunction of (full) moon and sun on the fourteenth day of the month was regarded as a favourable omen. Such a view seems highly speculative: we have no evidence that Joshua refers to the fourteenth day or other data showing that the Israelites would have been familiar with this particular feature of Mesopotamian astrology.

17. Morton Smith, 'Helios in Palestine', in B.A. Levine and A. Malamat (eds.), *Eretz-Israel* 16 (Harry M. Orlinsky Volume; Jerusalem: Israel Exploration Society, 1982), pp. 199*-214*; H.-P. Stähli, *Solare Elemente im Jahweglauben des Alten Testaments* (OBO, 66; Göttingen: Vandenhoeck & Ruprecht, 1985); Niehr, *Der höchste Gott*, pp. 141-63; O. Keel and C. Uehlinger, 'Jahwe und die Sonnengottheit von Jerusalem', in W. Dietrich and M. Klopfenstein (eds.), *Ein Gott allein?* (OBO, 139; Freiburg: Universitätsverlag; Göttingen: Vandenhoeck & Ruprecht, 1994), 269-306; E. Lipiński, 'Shemesh', DDD, cols. 1445-52 (2nd edn, 764-68); Taylor, *Yahweh and the Sun*.

18. Mark S. Smith, *Psalms: The Divine Journey* (Mahwah, NJ: Paulist Press, 1987), pp. 52-62; *idem*, '"Seeing God" in the Psalms: The Background to the Beatific Vision in the Hebrew Bible', *CBQ* 50 (1988), pp. 171-83; *idem*, 'The Near Eastern Background of Solar Language for Yahweh', *JBL* 109 (1990), pp. 29-39; *idem*, *The Early History of God*, pp. 115-24.

19. C.V.L. Charlier, 'Ein astronomischer Beitrag zur Exegese des Alten Testaments', *ZDMG* 58 (1904), pp. 386-94; J. Morgenstern, 'The Gates of Righteousness', *HUCA* 6 (1929), pp. 1-37; *idem*, 'The King–God among the Western Semites and the Meaning of Epiphanes', *VT* 10 (1968), pp. 138-97; *idem*, *The Fire Upon the Altar* (Leiden: Brill, 1963); *idem*, 'The Cultic Setting of the "Enthronement Psalms"', *HUCA* 35 (1964), pp. 1-42; F.J. Hollis, 'The Sun-Cult and the Temple at Jerusalem', in S.H. Hooke (ed.), *Myth and Ritual* (London: Oxford University Press, 1933), pp. 87-110; W.C. Graham and H.G. May, *Culture and Conscience* (Chicago: Uni-

believed that Solomon's temple was designed as a sun temple and that at the equinoxes the sun rose above the Mount of Olives and shone into the Holy of Holies, and this was understood as a manifestation of Yahweh's glory. This was pure speculation for which there is not a shred of evidence, and it has been abandoned by more recent scholars who attribute solar connections to Yahweh. In fact, H. van Dyke Parunak[20] has produced astronomical calculations which demonstrate that the sun did not penetrate the Holy of Holies at the equinoxes.

Reasons given by scholars for envisaging the Solomonic temple as a sun temple include the following:

(i) The East–West orientation of the temple. However, this argument is not compelling, since non-solar temples in the ancient Near East also have this orientation.[21] Furthermore, Busink[22] has emphasized the fact that the Solomonic temple was completely covered over, which is not suggestive of a solar temple. In addition, there is the point mentioned above about the sun's light not penetrating the Holy of Holies on solarly significant days.

(ii) Older scholars tended to believe that the old poetic passage referring to the sun in 1 Kgs 8.12 (cf. LXX 8.53) at the time of Solomon's dedication of the temple supported a solar connection for Yahweh and Solomon's temple. The MT of 1 Kgs 8.12-13 reads, 'Then Solomon said, "The Lord has said that he would dwell in thick darkness. I have built you an exalted house, a place for you to dwell in forever"'. This passage is preserved in the LXX in 1 Kgs 8.53, which includes what is generally held to be the missing first line of the poetic couplet: 'Then Solomon said, "The Lord has set[23] the sun in the heavens, but he has

versity of Chicago Press, 1936), pp. 235-38; H.G. May, 'Some Aspects of Solar Worship at Jerusalem', *ZAW* 55 (1937), pp. 269-81; T.H. Gaster, *Thespis* (New York: Harper & Row, 2nd edn, 1966), pp. 66-67. Cf. A. Fr. von Gall, 'Ein neues astronomisch zu erschliessendes Datum der ältesten israelitischen Geschichte', in K. Marti (ed.), *Beiträge zur alttestamentlichen Wissenschaft: K. Budde zum siebzigsten Geburtstag* (BZAW, 34; Giessen: Alfred Töpelmann, 1920), pp. 52-60.

20. H. van Dyke Parunak, 'Was Solomon's Temple Aligned to the Sun?', *PEQ* (1978), pp. 29-33.

21. Cf. J.A. Montgomery, *A Critical and Exegetical Commentary on the Books of Kings* (ICC; Edinburgh: T. & T. Clark, 1951), pp. 141-42.

22. T.A. Busink, *Der Tempel von Jerusalem*, I (2 vols.; Leiden: E.J. Brill, 1970), pp. 651-56.

23. Following the Lucianic recension which has ἔστησεν, 'set'. Otherwise the LXX has ἐγνώρισεν, 'made known', which does not make such good sense.

said that he would dwell in thick darkness…"'. However, it is clear that Yahweh is here contrasted with the sun, not identified with it.[24] The word for 'thick darkness' (*'ᵃrāpel*) associated with Yahweh's dwelling is used elsewhere of the clouds and is suggestive of storm-god imagery rather than a solar deity. It is probable that the cherubim in the Holy of Holies, on which Yahweh was seated, symbolized the clouds. Cf. Ps. 18.10-11 (ET 9-10), where Yahweh rides on a cherub and has thick darkness (*'ᵃrāpel*) under his feet (v. 10 [ET 9]) in the context of a storm theophany.

(iii) The presence of a sun cult in the temple in 2 Kgs 23.5, 11 and Ezek. 8.16 has been supposed to be evidence of Yahweh's solar connection. However, whilst the presence of a cult of the sun in the temple certainly suggests that those who participated in it did not feel it to be incompatible with Yahwism, it by no means requires the equation of the sun with Yahweh. The moon and host of heaven were also worshipped in the temple as part of Manasseh's syncretism which Josiah removed (2 Kgs 21.3, cf. 23.5), but hardly anyone seriously believes that Yahweh was equated with them. Rather, it is clear that the host of heaven constituted Yahweh's heavenly court, equivalent to the 'sons of God'.[25] The sun most naturally belonged in the same category.

The sun would thus have been considered part of the host of heaven, subordinate to Yahweh. As such one might argue that the worship of the sun in Yahweh's temple would have been seen by those who participated in it as, so to speak, all 'part of the package', just as Catholics would regard veneration (not worship) of Mary as not being incompatible with worship of Christ.

(iv) More recently, Stähli and Niehr[26] have argued that Ps. 84.12 (ET 11) supports the equation of Yahweh and the sun, translating (as others have done) 'For the Lord is a sun (*šemeš*) and a shield'. However, although *šemeš* commonly means 'sun', this is not the likely rendering here. The parallelism with 'shield' (*māgēn*) supports the view that *šemeš* here has its other meaning, 'rampart', which is clearly attested (in the plural) in Isa. 54.12: 'I will make your ramparts of rubies, your

24. So, rightly, Clements, *God and Temple*, p. 66.

25. Cf. *KTU*² 1.10.I.3-4 and Job 38.7.

26. Stähli, *Solare Elemente*, pp. 42-43; Niehr, *Der höchste Gott*, pp. 156-57. Cf. Mark S. Smith, '"Seeing God" in the Psalms', p. 177, although, as noted above, he does not believe that Yahweh was actually equated with the sun.

gates of carbuncles, and all your walls of precious stones'.[27]

When God is described as a 'shield' (*māgēn*) elsewhere in the Psalter, we find words such as 'fortress' (*m*ᵉ*ṣûdâ*) and 'stronghold' (*miśgāb*) being used in parallel with it (see Pss. 18.3 [ET 2], 144.2), which are not so different from 'rampart'. Nothing comparable to 'sun' ever occurs. One should also note Ezek. 26.8, where a 'siege wall' (*dāyēq*) and a 'shield' (*ṣinnâ*) are mentioned in parallel. It is therefore probable that Ps. 84.12 (ET 11) refers to Yahweh as a 'rampart and shield' and offers no support to the idea of solar Yahwism. (Even if one were to render *šemeš* as 'sun', it would clearly be simply metaphorical, since it parallels 'shield', which is obviously a metaphor.[28])

(v) The appearance of the verb *zrḥ* in Yahwistic theophanies and personal names and the hiphil of *yp*ʿ in Yahwistic theophanies has sometimes been employed as an argument in favour of Yahweh's solar character.[29] However, in the Old Testament, *yp*ʿ (hiphil) is clearly used in connection with the light of the sun only in Job 3.4.[30] The hiphil of the verb *yp*ʿ 'shine' is used of Yahweh in Deut. 33.2: 'The Lord came from Sinai, and shone from Seir upon us, and *shone forth* from Mt Paran' and in Ps. 50.2: 'Out of Zion the perfection of beauty, God *shines forth*'. Verse 3 of the latter then goes on to say, 'before him a devouring fire, round him a mighty tempest'. In both cases, however, the context clearly reflects Yahweh's theophany on Mt Sinai and therefore more probably refers to the lightning, since we know from Exod. 19.16 that Yahweh appeared in the lightning and thunder at Mt Sinai, but we hear of no solar manifestation there. Habakkuk 3 likewise speaks of Yahweh's theophany, in which he comes up from Mt Sinai in brightness and light (v. 4). This passage actually speaks of the sun (and moon) standing still in the face of Yahweh's theophany (vv. 10-11), so Yahweh's theophany can hardly be thought of in solar terms.

27. Cf. the Targum on Ps. 84.12 (ET 11) , which reads, 'For the Lord is like a high wall and a strong shield', supported, e.g., by H. Gunkel, H. Schmidt, G.R. Driver, NEB, Revised Psalter, *The Psalms: A New Translation for Worship*, etc.

28. S.A. Wiggins, 'Yahweh: The God of Sun', *JSOT* 71 (1996), pp. 89-106 (99), rightly points out that 'sun' would be metaphorical, but fails to note that 'rampart' is a more probable translation.

29. Cf. Stähli, *Solare Elemente*, pp. 40-41 and Niehr, *Der höchste Gott*, pp. 151-53. See also, Taylor, *Yahweh and the Sun*, pp. 89-93, 233-38.

30. Wiggins is incorrect in saying it is never used of the sun, in 'Yahweh: The God of Sun', p. 100.

As for the verb *zrḥ* 'to shine', which is likewise used of Yahweh in the Old Testament passages (as well as in some theophoric personal names), this too can hardly be using solar language of Yahweh, in spite of the fact that *zrḥ* is frequently used of the sun. The first passage, Deut. 33.2, reads, '[The Lord] shone (*zāraḥ*) from Seir upon us'. As has just been seen, this verse is employing the language of Yahweh's Sinai theophany, in which the sun did not feature. The second passage where *zrḥ* is used of Yahweh is Isa. 60.1-2, 'Arise, shine, for your light has come, and the glory of the Lord has *risen* [or shone (*zāraḥ*)] upon you. For behold, darkness shall cover the earth, and thick darkness the peoples; but the Lord will *arise* [or shine (*yizraḥ*)] upon you, and his glory will be seen upon you.' It is impossible to suppose that Yahweh is here being seen as the sun, since Isa. 60.19-20 go on to say, 'The sun shall be no more your light by day, nor for brightness shall the moon give light to you by night; but the Lord will be your everlasting light and your God will be your glory. Your sun shall no more go down, nor your moon withdraw itself; for the Lord will be your everlasting light.' It is clear that Yahweh is not here being seen as the sun, but rather as one greater than, and transcending, the sun. It is quite likely that language has here been taken up from the sun and applied to Yahweh, but that is not the same as saying that Yahweh was equated with the sun. One may also compare Mal. 3.20 (ET 4.2), where we read that 'the sun of righteousness shall arise, with healing in its wings'—here taken up from the symbol of the winged sun disc. But this does not mean that Yahweh was actually identified with the sun. If Yahweh had been equated with the sun, it is surprising that no Hebrew theophoric names combining Yahweh and *šemeš* are attested, either in the Old Testament or epigraphically. Names such as Yehoshemesh or Shemeshiah are simply unknown, which stands in stark contrast to the compounds of Yahweh and Baal that are attested, Bealiah (1 Chron. 12.6 [ET 5]) and Yehobaal,[31] or compounds of Yahweh and El, such as Elijah and Joel.

The most detailed argument for Yahweh's equation with the sun has been put forward by J.G. Taylor, who has devoted a whole book to the subject.[32] In addition to some of the points already criticized above, Taylor also has a large number of other arguments which are very weak indeed, so that there is no point in going through them all. An idea of their weakness can be gained from the following few examples. First,

31. See Avigad, 'Hebrew Seals and Sealings', pp. 8-9.

32. Taylor, *Yahweh and the Sun*. See my review in *PEQ* 128 (1996), pp. 185-86.

Taylor[33] supposes that the command to the sun to stand still over Gibeon in Josh.10.12 implies its equation with Yahweh because the Deuteronomistic framework introduces the command with the words, 'Then Joshua spoke *to the Lord*...' But this is a very tenuous argument, since the Deuteronomists clearly did not equate Yahweh with the sun, and Joshua's address was to the moon as well as to the sun. As another example of an extremely weak argument, I cite Taylor's belief[34] that the other Old Testament sun miracle in the time of Hezekiah (2 Kgs 20.8-11) implies that the king equated Yahweh with the sun; this seems extremely unlikely considering the high esteem in which the Deuteronomists held Hezekiah. Finally, Taylor's claim[35] that the term 'Lord of hosts' implies Yahweh's equation with the chief member of the heavenly host, the sun, is by no means obvious.

Taylor also appeals to the tenth-century cult stand from Taanach referred to earlier.[36] This consists of four tiers. The second and fourth tiers (counting from the top) are generally accepted to be representations of the goddess Asherah, the former in the form of a stylized tree and the latter in the form of a goddess with lions. The top tier, as mentioned earlier, depicts the sun disc and a horse. The third tier has two winged sphinxes or cherubim, and here Taylor supposes that they depict the throne of Yahweh, who is to be understood as seated invisibly above them. Taylor suggests that the top and third tiers are parallel: on his understanding, then, they provide evidence of Yahweh's equation with the sun. If Taylor's interpretation is justified, we would have a plausible argument in favour of Yahweh's solar connection. However, his interpretation is not certain, since (i) we do not know that the top and third tiers are strictly parallel, and (ii) the third tier need not represent Yahweh's throne. Cherubim are elsewhere known as guardians, and Hestrin suggests that here their significance is that of guardians of the temple.[37]

Samson

Although certainty is not possible, it seems likely that behind the figure of the judge Samson there lies ultimately a solar hero. Various reasons

33. Taylor, *Yahweh and the Sun*, pp. 114-18.

34. Taylor, *Yahweh and the Sun*, pp. 165-68.

35. Taylor, *Yahweh and the Sun*, pp. 99-105.

36. See Taylor, 'Representations of Yahweh', pp. 557-66; *idem*, *Yahweh and the Sun*, pp. 24-37.

37. Hestrin, 'The Cult Stand from Ta'anach', p. 71.

for this have been put forward over the years, but the most compelling suggestions are the following:

(i) The name Samson (Hebrew, *šimšôn*) means 'sunny' (from Hebrew, *šemeš*). Although comparable names are occasionally found in the ancient Near East, this is the only one in Hebrew in the Old Testament (though *šimšay* occurs in Aramaic in Ezra 4.8, 9, 17, 23).

(ii) Samson's birthplace at Zorah is only 2.5 miles from Beth-Shemesh, a name indicating the presence of a sun temple and cult, and various other places in the Samson story—Eshtaol, Timnah and the valley of Sorek—are all within a six-mile radius of Beth-Shemesh.

(iii) Psalm 19 clearly reflects sun mythology. The sun is explicitly mentioned and personified in vv. 5c-6 (ET 4c-5): 'In them he has set a tent for the sun, which comes forth like a bridegroom leaving his chamber, and like a strong man runs its course with joy'. This corresponds very well with the picture of Samson. If anyone is a frolicking strong man (*gibbôr*) in the Old Testament, it is Samson, a motif which pervades the stories about him.

(iv) Samson's strength is embodied in his seven locks of hair, which he loses because of Delilah. The sound of the name Delilah (*d^{e}lîlâ*) is suggestive of the word for 'night' (Hebrew, *laylâ*), and the sun's rays are often depicted as hair. One might note that Helios is depicted with seven rays coming from his head (e.g. in the synagogue mosaics at Hammath Tiberias, Beth Alpha, etc.)

Although the view that a solar hero lies behind the figure of Samson was more commonly held in the past, the attribution of solar features to Samson is still found in more recent scholars of the book of Judges, such as J.D. Martin, J.A. Soggin and B. (F.C.) Lindars).[38] As the points made above indicate, a reasonable case for this can be made. However, it is clear that Samson is more than a solar hero and this latter aspect has been overlaid with Israelite features, such as Samson's being a judge and a Nazirite.[39]

If this interpretation is correct, there is evidence that the Canaanite

38. J.D. Martin, *The Book of Judges* (CBC; Cambridge: Cambridge University Press, 1975), p. 152; J.A. Soggin, *Judges* (trans. J.S. Bowden; OTL; London: SCM Press, 1981), p. 231; B. (F.C.) Lindars, *Interpreting Judges Today* (Ethel M. Wood Lecture, 1983; London: University of London, 1983), p. 11.

39. Cf. A. Lods, 'Quelques remarques sur l'histoire de Samson', in *Actes du Congrès International d'Histoire des Religions*, I (Paris: Librairie ancienne Honoré Champion, 1925), pp. 504-16.

sun deity could at times be masculine, in contrast to the Canaanite sun goddess, Shapash, at Ugarit, and in the El-Amarna letters, where the deity Shamash is feminine (letter 323, line 22).[40] The sun's being a masculine deity is in keeping with the fact that the Hebrew word *šemeš* is attested both as masculine and feminine and the masculine form is actually the more frequent. (One may compare Akkadian and Arabic, where the gender of the noun for 'sun' is the same as that of the deity.)

Yahweh and the Moon

There are not many references in the Old Testament to moon worship, and these are mostly Deuteronomistic (Deut. 4.19, 17.3; 2 Kgs 23.5; Jer. 8.2). In addition, there is the non-Deuteronomistic passage, Job 31.26. Moon worship is doubtless included in some other references to the host of heaven (e.g. 2 Kgs 21.3, 5; Zeph. 1.5). A couple of place names also testify to the moon cult: Beth-yerah (= Khirbet Kerak), which is known from rabbinic sources (e.g. *b. Bek.* 55a and *Gen. R.* 94.9 and 98.16) and probably Jericho.

The moon cult was also prominent in LBIII, thirteenth-century BCE Canaanite Hazor,[41] where in area C a temple contained both a statue (probably of the god, according to Yadin) with a crescent on its chest, and also a stela depicting two hands stretched upwards towards a crescent with a disc within the crescent. A cult stand with a crescent was also found in area C. But this moon deity is not to be equated with Baal-ḥamman, *contra* Yadin.[42] The Old Testament references to moon worship therefore need not be to the Assyrian cult, since Israel was heir to an old Canaanite cult.[43] The fact that the deity is never referred

40. For the Akkadian see J.A. Knudtzon, *Die El-Amarna-Tafeln*, I (Leipzig: J.C. Hinrichs, 1915), p. 932.

41. See Y. Yadin, *Hazor*, I (Jerusalem: Magnes Press, 1958), pp. 87-89 and pls. XXVII-XXXI, and *Hazor*, III (Jerusalem: Magnes Press, 1960), pp. 117-18, pl. CLXXXI. See also Y. Yadin, *Hazor* (Schweich Lectures, 1970; London: Oxford University Press, 1972), pp. 71-74, pls. XIVa and XVc, XXIa; and *idem*, *Hazor: The Rediscovery of a Great Citadel*, pp. 44-47, 55-57.

42. Y. Yadin, 'Symbols of Deities at Zinjirli, Carthage and Hazor', in J.A. Sanders (ed.), *Near Eastern Archaeology in the Twentieth Century: Essays in Honor of Nelson Glueck* (Garden City, NY: Doubleday, 1970), pp. 199-231. Baal-ḥamman is more naturally to be seen as a form of Baal.

43. *Contra* Oestreicher, *Das deuteronomische Grundgesetz*; Gressmann, 'Josia und das Deuteronomium', pp. 313-37; Spieckermann, *Juda unter Assur*, esp. p. 27,

to as Sin, but continually as *yārēaḥ* supports its being Canaanite.

Similarly, there is no necessity to suppose that the growth of moon worship in Judah in the seventh century BCE was due to Aramaean influence, as O. Keel[44] has recently claimed. Thus, the Deuteronomist himself claims that Manasseh's astral cults, along with his other cults, were Canaanite (2 Kgs 21.2-3), and since there is no doubt that this was true of his non-astral cults (Baal, Asherah, Molech/human sacrifice), the presumption is that this was the case with the astral ones too. Next, the Old Testament was in the habit of referring to deities by their correct names. If Manasseh's moon cult were Aramaean, it is surprising that the Aramaean name for the moon god, Sahar[45] (or occasionally Sin[46]) was not used, but rather *yārēaḥ* (2 Kgs 23.5), the Hebrew word for 'moon' corresponding to the name of the Canaanite moon god. Finally, as was noted earlier, Israel was heir to an old Canaanite moon cult.

Occasional attempts to find a greater role for the moon cult have not convinced many. For example, J. Lewy[47] saw the golden calves (both in Exod. 32 and 1 Kgs 12) as Sin, the god who originally revealed himself at Sinai as Sin, and the god worshipped by the patriarchs as Sin. An older, discredited attempt to find evidence of moon worship among the ancient Hebrews, including the golden calf, is to be found in F. Hommel.[48] Again, Lloyd R. Bailey[49] claimed that El-Shaddai is to be identified with Bêl Šadê and that the latter was an epithet of Sin. This, however, seems unlikely.[50] Also, as has been noted earlier, it is highly

who all see considerable Assyrian influence on the cults propagated by Manasseh and removed by Josiah, including star worship.

44. O. Keel, *Goddesses and Trees, New Moon and Yahweh: Ancient Near Eastern Art and the Hebrew Bible* (JSOTSup, 261; Sheffield: Sheffield Academic Press, 1998), pp. 60-120. This view was previously held by Cogan, *Imperialism and Religion*, pp. 82-87.

45. See *KAI* 202 B.24; 225.2, 9; 226.1, 9; 258.5; 259.4.

46. See *KAI* 222 A.9

47. Lewy, 'The Old West Semitic Sun-god Ḥammu', pp. 442-43, and 'The Late Assyro-Babylonian Cult of the Moon', pp. 441-48. A.F. Key sets out the views of Lewy posthumously in 'Traces of the Worship of the Moon God'.

48. F. Hommel, *Der Gestirndienst der alten Araber und die altisraelitische Ueberlieferung* (Munich: H. Lukaschik, 1901).

49. Bailey, 'Israelite *'Ēl Šadday*', pp. 434-38, followed by Ouellette, 'More on 'Êl Šadday', pp. 470-71, except that Ouellette thinks the meaning is 'Lord of the steppe', and not 'Lord of the mountain'.

50. See Cross, *Canaanite Myth and Hebrew Epic*, p. 57 n. 52.

speculative to suppose, as some have done, that Josh. 10.12-13 is evidence for a Canaanite moon cult at Aijalon.

Where new light recently has been shed on the moon cult and the Old Testament is in the matter of the god Sheger. The word *šeger* occurs in the following Old Testment passages: Deut. 7.13, 28.4, 18 and 51 speak of *šᵉgar 'ᵃlāpêkā wᵉ'aštᵉrôt ṣō'nekā*, 'the increase of your cattle and the young of your sheep'. Just as in the Deuteronomistic references *'aštārôt* (construct, *'aštᵉrôt*) is a demythologization of the goddess Astarte, so it is clear that *šeger* (construct, *šᵉgar*) is the demythologization of a god Sheger. This had long been suspected in view of the Punic personal name, *'bdšgr*, 'servant of Sheger'.[51] We have testimony to him at Ugarit in *KTU*² 1.148.31, where *šgr* is mentioned alongside *'iṯm* as receiving a sheep. In *KTU*² 1.5.III.16,17 *šgr* is again mentioned and in line 24 *'iṯm* is likewise referred to. It is now known that *'iṯm* is the Ugaritic equivalent of Mesopotamian Ishum, an underworld god. He also appears in the Balaam text from Tell Deir 'Allā, interestingly with Ashtar,[52] comparable to the Old Testament allusions above. More recently it has become known that *šgr* is a moon god. This is proved from the hieroglyphic Hittite correspondences to syllabically written personal names (^{d}30 = sà-ga-ra/i).[53] Also, at Emar the fifteenth day of the month, that is, the day of the full moon, was sacred to Shaggar.[54] It is probable that the connection between Sheger, the moon god, and the Old Testament's use of the name in connection with the herd, lies in the crescent moon's looking like a bull's horn.[55] There is certainly

51. Cf. F.L. Benz, *Personal Names in the Phoenician and Punic Inscriptions* (Studia Pohl, 8; Rome: Biblical Institute Press, 1972), p. 163.

52. Cf. J. Hoftijzer and G. van der Kooij, *Aramaic Texts from Deir 'Alla* (Documenta et monumenta orientis antiqui; Leiden: E.J. Brill, 1976), first combination, line 16 (p. 180) and p. 273.

53. E. Laroche, 'Les hiéroglyphes de Meskéné-Emar et le style "syro-hittite"', *Akkadica* 22 (1981), pp. 5-14 (11); H. Gonnet, 'Les légendes des empruntes hiéroglyphiques anatôliennes', in D. Arnaud, *Textes syriens de l'âge du Bronze Récent* (AulOr Sup, 1; Barcelona: Editorial Ausa, 1991), pp. 198-208 (199, 207).

54. D. Arnaud, *Recherches au pays d'Aštata: Emar* VI.3 (Paris: Recherche sur les Civilisations, 1986), pp. 350-66, text 373 = Msk 74292a + 74290d + 74304a + 74290c.

55. On this deity generally see S. Dalley and B. Teissier, 'Tablets from the Vicinity of Emar and Elsewhere', *Iraq* 54 (1992), pp. 83-111 (90-91); K. van der Toorn, 'Sheger', *DDD*, cols. 1437-40 (2nd edn, pp. 760-62).

evidence throughout the ancient Near East showing that the crescent moon was sometimes conceived of as a bull's horn.[56]

The Rise and Fall of Lucifer (Isaiah 14.12-15)

Introduction

The notion that the devil or Satan was a fallen angel, who could also be called Lucifer, was derived from the passage about the fall of the Shining One, son of the dawn (*hêlēl ben šāḥar*), Lucifer in the Vulgate, found in Isa. 14.12-15. This understanding appears to be already presupposed in Lk. 10.18, and is found later in Church Fathers such as Origen, Eusebius, Tertullian and Gregory the Great.[57] The interpretation of the verses in this way was, in effect, a remythologization of the passage, for the author of Isa. 14.12-15 had used an ancient myth simply as an illustration of the hubris of a historical ruler, 'the king of Babylon' (cf. Isa. 14.4) rather than literally, and the historical context in Isaiah was ignored by those who remythologized the verses.

In this section I shall discuss first the nature and origin of the myth employed in Isa. 14.12-15 and then the precise historical background which it presupposes. So first the nature and origin of the myth in Isa. 14.12-15. These verses read as follows in the oracle against the king of Babylon:

> 12 How you have fallen from heaven,
> O Shining One[58] son of the dawn!
> How[59] you are cut down to the ground,
> you who laid the nations low![60]

56. See Keel, *Goddesses and Trees*, pp. 117-18, whose discussion arises from the discovery of this motif on a stela recently discovered at Beth-saida (see pp. 115-20).

57. Cf. K.L. Schmidt, 'Lucifer als gefallene Engelmacht', *TZ* 7 (1951), pp. 161-79, for the relationship between Isa. 14.12-15 and the New Testament. See also, more generally, N. Forsyth, *The Old Enemy: Satan and the Combat Myth* (Princeton: Princeton University Press, 1987).

58. Retaining the MT's reading, *hêlēl*, rather than emending to *hêlāl*. Cf. P. Grelot, 'Sur la vocalisation de הילל (Is. XIV 12)', *VT* 6 (1956), pp. 303-304.

59. Inserting *'ēt* before *nigda'tā*, since the *qînâ* metre of this passage seems to require it.

60. The Hebrew here is *ḥôlēš 'al-gôyim*. The verb *ḥlš* clearly means 'defeat', 'cut off', 'mow down', 'be victorious over', as is evident from Exod. 17.13, which reads, *wayyaḥ*^{a}*lōš y*^{e}*hôšua' 'et-*$^{'a}$*mālēq w*^{e}*'et-'ammô l*^{e}*pî-ḥāreb*, 'And Joshua

13 You said in your heart,
'I shall ascend into the heavens;
above the stars of God
I will set my throne on high;
and I shall sit on the Mount of Assembly
on the heights[61] of Zaphon;
14 I shall ascend above the heights of the clouds,
I shall make myself like the Most High.'
15 But you have been brought down to Sheol,
to the bottom of the Pit.

The Shining One as Venus

The view that 'the Shining One, son of the dawn' denotes the morning star, Venus, is the most likely one.[62] This star rises before the dawn and

defeated Amalek and his people with the edge of the sword'. Such a meaning fits the military context of Isa. 14.12 and provides a good ironic contrast with the Shining One himself being cut down in this verse. Some scholars have seen a problem in that *ḥlš* is followed by the accusative, *'et*, in Exod. 17.13, but by *'al* in Isa. 14.12. But this is no problem at all, since there are other verbs that can take either the direct object or *'al* (so *šlḥ*, *qr'*) and one can compare the existence in German of both *besiegen* and *siegen über* (cf. D. Barthélemy, *Critique Textuelle de l'Ancien Testament*, II [OBO, 50.2; 3 vols.; Fribourg: Editions Universitaires; Göttingen: Vandenhoeck & Ruprecht, 1986], p. 103, who cites scholars making these points). The force of *'al* can be rendered in English by translating 'was victorious *over*'. There is therefore no necessity to emend *'al* to *kol*, 'all', on the basis of the LXX. Nor is there any need to take *ḥôlēš* intransitively with the rendering 'sprawling, helpless across the nations' (NEB) or 'prostrate among the nations' (REB). It seems more natural to see a contrast with the previous line, not synonymity, just as there is in the two lines of the first half of the verse. Neither is it necessary to posit a substantival sense for *ḥôlēš*, as in J.B. Burns's rendering, 'warrior over the nations', '*ḥôlēš 'al* in Isaiah 14:12: A New Proposal', *ZAH* 2 (1989), pp. 199-204.

61. I translate *yark^etē ṣāpôn* as 'heights of Zaphon' rather than 'recesses of Zaphon', since, as O. Eissfeldt first pointed out in *Baal Zaphon*, pp. 14-15, the expression is to be understood in a vertical rather than a horizontal sense. This is clear from the contrast with *yark^etê bôr* (Isa. 14.15) and the fact that the Shining One's goal is to ascend into the heavens to the greatest height, where God dwells. That such a meaning is feasible is suggested also by Isa. 37.24, where *yark^etê l^ebānôn* is parallel to *m^erôm hārîm*, 'the heights of the hills'.

62. Among the many scholars who equate the figure of Isa. 14.12 with the morning star, Venus, are Gunkel, *Schöpfung und Chaos*, pp. 133-34 (or Mercury); P. Grelot, 'Isaïe XIV:12-15 et son arrière-plan mythologique', *RHR* 149 (1956), pp. 18-48; J.W. McKay, 'Helel and the Dawn-goddess', *VT* 20 (1970), pp. 451-64; Clements, *Isaiah 1–39*, p. 142.

is eventually blotted out by the light of the sun. The view that the star in Isa. 14.12-15 denotes Venus finds strong support in the ancient Versions. The LXX renders the name by 'Εωσφόρος ὁ πρωὶ ἀνατέλλων, 'the Morning Star, that rose in the morning', and the Vulgate similarly translates *Lucifer, qui mane oriebaris*, 'the Morning Star, that used to rise in the morning'. Again, the Targum has *dhwyt' zywtn bgw bny 'nš' kkwkb ngh' byn kwkby'*, 'who wast resplendent among the sons of men as the bright star (Venus) among the stars'.[63] As for the notion that the dawn begets the morning star, a similar conception is found in classical literature,[64] where Eos (called Erigineia, 'Early-born', an epithet for 'Dawn') 'brought forth... the Star Eosphoros'.

Alternative identifications of the 'Shining One, son of the dawn' with other heavenly luminaries are not persuasive. For example, it has occasionally been claimed that it is Jupiter–Marduk (called *ellu* in Akkadian),[65] but against this stands the fact that Marduk was already the king of the gods and Jupiter does reach the zenith, whereas the star in Isa. 14.12-15 does not. A comparable objection may be brought against the recent view of W.R. Gallagher[66] that the Shining One, son of the dawn is the Mesopotamian god Enlil (Akkadian *ellil/illil*), who could be conceived astrally, for he was already supreme and did not strive in vain to reach this position; nor is it clear why Enlil should be called 'son of the dawn'. Both the above views are open to the objection that various aspects of the imagery in Isa. 14.12-15 strongly suggest a Canaanite, not Mesopotamian background to the myth (see below). Again, it has occasionally been supposed that the reference is to the moon. For example, H. Winckler[67] emended *hêlēl*, 'shining one', to *hêlāl*, 'new moon', and *šāḥar* (pausal form of *šaḥar*), 'dawn', to *šāhar*

63. Cf. M. Jastrow, *A Dictionary of the Targumim, the Talmud Babli and Yerushalmi, and the Midrashic Literature*, I (2 vols.; New York: Pardes, 1950), p. 619, who confirms that *kôkab nôghā'* = Venus, comparing Targum II Esther 2.7 and Yalkuṭ Esther 1053.

64. E.g. Hesiod, *Theogony* 381.

65. S.H. Langdon, 'The Star Hêlēl, Jupiter?', *ExpTim* 42 (1930-31), pp. 172-74; G.R. Driver, 'Stars', in J. Hastings (ed.), *Dictionary of the Bible* (rev. H.H. Rowley and F.C. Grant; Edinburgh: T. & T. Clark, 2nd edn, 1963), pp. 936-37.

66. W.R. Gallagher, 'On the Identity of Hêlēl Ben Šaḥar of Is. 14:12-15', *UF* 26 (1994), pp. 131-46.

67. H. Winckler, *Geschichte Israels*, II (Leipzig: E. Pfeiffer, 1900), p. 24; N.H. Snaith, *The Jewish New Year Festival* (London: SPCK, 1947), p. 97; D.W. Thomas, in *BHS*, emends *hêlēl* to *hêlāl*, 'new moon', but retains *šāḥar*.

(pausal form of *śahar*), 'moon', but these emendations are unsupported in any of the versions and, moreover, *śahar* would be a *hapax legomenon* (though cf. Isa. 3.18). Moreover, no Semitic myth is attested in which the moon attempts to usurp the heavenly throne. This last objection also holds against the view more recently put forward by K. Spronk and M.J.A Korpel[68] that *hêlēl* should be equated with the Ugaritic deity *hll*, who seems to represent the crescent moon (*KTU*^{2} 1.17.II.26-27; 1.24.6). It is also somewhat odd for the moon to be described as 'son of the dawn'. Yet another view has identified *hêlēl* with the summer sun and *šāḥar* with the winter sun,[69] but elsewhere in the Old Testament *šaḥar* clearly means 'dawn' rather than 'winter sun'. Recently, K. Spronk, having rejected his earlier equation of the Shining One with the moon, has suggested that he denotes the sun.[70] However, he does not think that Isa. 14.12-15 is an extract from an astral myth involving divine rivalry. Rather, he holds that the king's being referred to as the sun is a reflection of divine kingship ideology and that this is what brings him into conflict with Yahweh. However, against this it may be noted that Isa. 14.12-15 does read like an extract from an astral myth, as most scholars suppose. Moreover, the Mesopotamian rulers of the first millennium did not regard themselves as divine, let alone the sun.

A recent original suggestion is that the Shining One, son of the dawn,

68. K. Spronk, *Beatific Afterlife in Ancient Israel and in the Ancient Near East* (AOAT, 219; Kevelaer: Butzon & Bercker; Neukirchen–Vluyn: Neukirchener Verlag, 1986), p. 224; M.J.A. Korpel, *A Rift in the Clouds: Ugaritic and Hebrew Descriptions of the Divine* (UBL, 8; Münster: Ugarit Verlag, 1990), p. 576.

69. H.G. May, 'Some Aspects of Solar Worship', p. 273, and 'The Departure of the Glory of Yahweh', *JBL* 56 (1937), pp. 309-21 (311-12).

70. K. Spronk, 'Down with Hêlēl! The Assumed Mythological Background of Isa. 14.12', in Dietrich and Kottsieper, with Schaudig (eds.), *'Und Mose schrieb dieses Lied auf': Studien zum Alten Testament und zum Alten Orient: Festschrift für Oswald Loretz*, pp. 717-26. Spronk's case for equating the Shining One with the sun rests on a structural comparison of Isa. 13.1-22 with 14.4-23, within which he finds Isa. 14.12-15 to correspond to Isa. 13.10-11, where we read of the darkening of the heavenly luminaries on the Day of the Lord, and there Spronk thinks that the reference to the sun not rising is the most appropriate equivalent to the Shining One, son of the dawn. If we grant Spronk's parallelism, however, it still needs to be noted that Isa. 13. 10 speaks of the darkening of the stars and their constellations and the moon, as well as the sun, and the use there of the verb *yahēllû* 'give light', reminding one of *hêlēl*, is employed of the stars rather than the sun. It is by no means obvious, therefore, that Spronk's structural comparison requires the equation of the Shining One with the sun.

is Halley's comet.[71] Not surprisingly, the article in which this was suggested dates from 1986, not long after Halley's comet had been in the news. The author supposes that it was the appearance of this comet in c. 540 BCE which gave rise to the motif in Isaiah 14. However, this date for Isaiah 14 is unsatisfactory, since in Isa. 13.17 it is the Medes who are expected to bring about the downfall of Babylon, thereby presupposing a date before 550 BCE for the oracle, since the Median empire came to an end in that year.

That the verses represent an excerpt from a myth was first recognized by Herder[72] and it was Gunkel[73] who first suggested either a Babylonian or a Phoenician origin. On the basis of a number of words and phrases used it is now generally accepted that the origin of the myth must be sought specifically in Canaanite mythology, and this has especially become clear in the light of Ugaritic parallels. Thus, Zaphon (Isa. 14.13) is well known from the Ugaritic texts as the mountain which constituted Baal's throne (cf. *KTU*² 1.5.I.11; 1.6.I.57-9, etc.), and the words 'I shall ascend above the heights of the clouds' (Isa. 14.14a) again recall Baal, one of whose stock epithets was *rkb 'rpt*, 'Rider of the clouds' (*KTU*² 1.5.II.7, etc.). Again, the 'Mount of Assembly' (*har mō'ēd*) in v. 13 recalls the Mountain of divine Assembly (*pḫr m'd*, *KTU*² 1.2.I.14,20,31,[74] also called *ġr ll*, 'Mt. Ll', *KTU* 1.2.I.20) in the Ugaritic texts. Some have thought also that 'the dawn' (*šāḥar*) in v. 12 reflects the Canaanite god Shaḥar. In v. 14 God is called 'the Most High', Elyon,[75] who is attested as a Canaanite god both in Philo of Byblos (Eusebius, *Praeparatio Evangelica* I.10.15, Ἐλιοῦν καλούμενος Ὕψιστος) and in the Old Testament, where he is the Jebusite god of Jerusalem (Gen. 14.18-20, 22), although he is also equated with Yahweh, as in the passage being discussed here. As an Aramaean deity he also appears as Elyon in the Sefire treaty (*KAI* 222.A.11).[76] Although

71. D. Etz, 'Is Isaiah xiv 12-15 a Reference to Comet Halley?', *VT* 36 (1986), pp. 289-301.

72. J.G. von Herder, *Vom Geist der Ebräischen Poesie*, I (Leipzig: 3rd rev. edn, 1825), p. 168; ET, *The Spirit of Hebrew Poetry*, I (trans. J. Marsh; Burlington: E. Smith, 1833), p. 149.

73. Gunkel, *Schöpfung und Chaos*, p. 134.

74. *KTU*² 1.2.1.20 is exceptional in reading *phr*, but this is clearly a scribal error for *pḫr*.

75. For more on Elyon, see J. Day, *God's Conflict with the Dragon and Sea*, pp. 129-36.

76. Cf. *KAI*, pp. 239, 246.

he appears to have been basically an El figure (cf. the references to his (seventy) sons in Deut. 32.8,[77] his function as a creator god in Gen. 14.19, 22, and his dwelling on the Mount of Assembly like El in Isa. 14.13), he also appears to have absorbed some of Baal's functions (he is enthroned like Baal in Ps. 47.3 [ET 2] and 97.9, he dwells on Zaphon in Isa. 14.13, he thunders like Baal in Ps. 18.14 [ET 13]). The fact that Elyon has features of both El and Baal would indicate that the myth in Isa. 14.12-15 derives ultimately from the mythology of one of these gods, as do the other Canaanite mythological features noted above. The fact that no attempt by a god to usurp El's throne is known,[78] whereas Baal was in conflict with various enemies, would suggest that it is in the mythology surrounding the god Baal that one should seek the origin of the myth in Isa. 14.12-15.

Venus as Athtar

In the light of the above discussion it has emerged that Isa. 14.12-15 refers to the rise and disappearance of the morning star Venus and that this has been interpreted in terms of Canaanite mythology. Is it possible to identify the morning star Venus with a figure in Canaanite mythology? It is very probable that this role was filled by the god Athtar, even though this is nowhere explicitly stated. In South Arabia the god Athtar was certainly identified with Venus, and in Mesopotamia the cognate deity, the goddess Ishtar (sometimes represented as male) likewise represented the planet Venus.[79] Similarly, the Canaanite female equivalent

77. Reading *bᵉnê ʾᵉlôhîm* for MT *bᵉnê yiśrāʾēl*, with support of 4Q Deut., LXX and Old Latin. See discussion above in Chapter 1.

78. *Contra* Pope, Kapelrud and Oldenburg, who supposed that Baal sought to usurp El's throne. See C. L'Heureux, *Rank Among the Canaanite Gods*, pp. 3-10. Elnes and Miller, 'Elyon', col. 564 (2nd edn, p. 295), have recently suggested that Isa. 14.12-15 reflects Baal's alleged replacement of El; it is not clear, however, why Baal should be called 'Shining One, son of the dawn'. Also recently, H.R. Page, *The Myth of Cosmic Rebellion: A Study of its Reflexes in Ugaritic and Biblical Literature* (VTSup, 65; Leiden: E.J. Brill, 1996), *passim*, has sought to show that Athtar rebelled against El, but there is no concrete evidence for this.

79. Cf. G. Ryckmans, *Les religions arabes préislamiques* (Bibliothèque de Muséon, 26; Louvain: Publications Universitaires and Bureaux du Muséon, 2nd edn, 1951), p. 41; *idem*, 'Il dio stellare nell' Arabia meridionale preislamica', *Atti della Accademia nazionale dei Lincei* 3 (ser. 8, 1948), pp. 360-69. The Mesopotamian Ishtar is identified with DIL-BAT, the Sumerian name of Venus, e.g. in J. Plessis, *Etude sur les textes concernant Ištar-Astarté: Recherches sur sa nature et*

of Athtar, Astarte (Athtart), was equated with the Greek goddess Aphrodite (= Venus). It is probable that Athtar and Astarte represent Venus as the morning and evening star respectively. Interestingly, Athtar was equated in the Ugaritic pantheon list with the Hurrian war god Ashtabi,[80] which fits the warlike context of Isaiah 14.

Now, it so happens that we possess a Canaanite myth from Ugarit, part of the Baal cycle, which speaks of Athtar's abortive attempt to occupy Baal's throne on Mt Zaphon and this has most commonly been thought[81] to be the prototype of the myth in Isa. 14.12-15. It is to be found in the Ugaritic text *KTU*^{2} 1.6.I.43-67, where after Baal's descent into the underworld the god Athtar was appointed by El and Athirat to the kingship in succession to Baal on Mt Zaphon, but he proved to be too small to occupy Baal's throne and therefore had to descend to the earth and rule from there. The text reads as follows:

43	*yṣḥ 'il*	El cried out
44	*lrbt. 'aṯrt ym. šm'*	to Lady Athirat of the sea: 'Hear
45	*lrbt. 'aṯr[t] ym. tn*	O Lady Athir[at] of the sea: give
46	*'aḥd.b.bnk. 'am{.}lkn*	one of your sons that I may make him king.'
47	*wt'n.rbt. 'aṯrt ym*	And Lady Athirat of the sea answered:
48	*bl. nmlk. yd'.ylḥn*	'Indeed. Let us make king one who knows and has understanding.'
49	*wy'n. lṭpn. 'il dp'i*	And the benevolent, kindly El answered:
50	*d. dq. 'anm. lyrẓ*[82]	'Let the finest of pigments be ground;
51	*'m. b'l. ly'db. mrḥ*	Let the people of Baal prepare unguents;
52	*'m. bn. dgn. ktmsm*	Let the people of the son of Dagon

son culte dans le monde sémitique et dans la Bible (Paris: P. Geuthner, 1921), p. 77. The astral character of Athtar is also in evidence at Emar, where he is called ^{d}*Aš-tar* mul, 'Aštar of the stars'; see Arnaud, *Recherches au pays d'Aštata*, p. 373, text 378.39'. That he was an astral god may also be indicated by references to 'Athtar of heaven', a name which occurs in various Aramaic, Akkadian and Arabian texts. For references, see Mark S. Smith, 'The God Athtar', pp. 633-34.

80. See *Ugaritica* V, 137.IVb.16.

81. E.g. J. Gray, 'The Desert God 'Aṯtar in the Literature and Religion of Canaan', *JNES* 8 (1949), pp. 72-83; P. Grelot, 'Isaïe XIV:12-15 et son arrière-plan mythologique', *RHR* 149 (1956), pp. 18-48; G. Fohrer, *Jesaja*, I (Zürcher Bibelkommentare; Zürich: Zwingli, 2nd edn, 1960), p. 196; Albright, *Yahweh and the Gods of Canaan*, p. 163, n. 73; Albright, *Archaeology and the Religion of Israel*, pp. 81-82, 83-84; P.C. Craigie, 'Helel, Athtar and Phaethon (Jes 14 12-15)', *ZAW* 85 (1973), pp. 223-25; W.G.E. Watson, 'Helel', *DDD*, cols. 746-50 (747) (2nd edn, pp. 392-94 [393]).

82. *KTU*^{2} reads *lyrq* where scholars have generally read *lyrẓ*.

	prepare crushed herbs.’[83]
53 *w‘n. rbt. ’aṯrt ym*	And Lady Athirat of the sea answered:
54 *blt. nmlk. ‘ṯtr. ‘rẓ*	‘Yea, let us make Athtar the terrible[84] king,
55 *ymlk. ‘ṯtr. ‘rẓ*	the terrible Athtar shall be king.’
56 *’apnk. ‘ṯtr. ‘rẓ*	Thereupon Athtar the terrible
57 *y‘l. bṣrrt. ṣpn*	went up to the heights of Zaphon,
58 *yṯb. lkḥṯ. ’al’iyn*	he sat on the throne of the Victor
59 *b‘l.p‘nh. ltmġyn*	Baal; but his feet did not[85] reach to
60 *hdm[.] r‘išh. lymġy*	the footstool, his head did not reach
61 *’apsh. wy‘n. ‘ṯtr. ‘rẓ*	the top of it. And Athtar the terrible answered,
62 *l ’amlk. bṣrrt. ṣpn*	‘I cannot be king on the heights of Zaphon.’
63 *yrd. ‘ṯtr. ‘rẓ. yrd*	Athtar the terrible came down, came down
64 *lkḥṯ. ’al’iyn. b‘l*	from the throne of the victor Baal
65 *wymlk. b’arṣ. ’il.klh*	and ruled on earth, god of it all.
66 [.] *tš’abn. brḥbt*	[ ] they drew water from casks,
67 [.*t*]*š’abn. bkknt*	[they] drew water from barrels.

However, the differences between the Ugaritic myth of Athtar’s ascent to Zaphon and subsequent descent therefrom and the myth about the Shining One, son of the dawn, in Isa. 14.12-15 are too great for the

83. Lines 50-52 are difficult and have been translated in many different ways. The translation here follows J.A. Emerton, ‘Ugaritic Notes’, *JTS* NS 16 (1965), pp. 441-42. It involves connecting *’anm* with Egyptian *’wn*, ‘colour, pigment’ (following Albright), *yrẓ* with Hebrew *rṣṣ*, ‘to crush’, *mrḥ* with Egyptian *mrḥt*, ‘ointment’, and *ktmsm* as *kt* as a construct form from the same root as Hebrew *ktt*, ‘to beat, crush by beating’, followed by enclitic *mem* and a noun, *sm*, cognate with biblical Hebrew *sammîm*, ‘spices’, etc.

84. *‘rẓ*, ‘terrible’ (cf. Heb. *‘ārīṣ*), may seem a rather surprising epithet of the hapless Athtar, but this meaning seems assured from the parallelism between *’idm ’adr* and *’idm ‘rẓ* in *KTU*^{2} 1.12.II.29-30. As was noted above, Athtar is equated with the Hurrian war god Aštabi in the Ugaritic pantheon list.

85. The troublesome Ugaritic particle, *l*, in lines 59, 60 and 62 may be translated either positively, as ‘verily, truly, surely’, or negatively, as ‘not’. Most scholars here take *l* negatively, but Grelot, ‘Isaïe XIV:12-15’, p. 37, understands *l* positively. I take *l* negatively, since in this way the passage flows more easily: Athtar goes up to Baal’s vacant throne, is too small for it, therefore because he is not fit to rule from the heights of Zaphon he comes down and rules on the earth. The fact that Athtar immediately comes down from Zaphon is more naturally explicable on the view that he was unable to occupy the throne. It is true that Baal was called *zbl b‘l ’arṣ*, but he did not have to come down from Zaphon in order to rule the earth. That Athtar should rule on earth itself rather than from the heights of Zaphon agrees with the evidence associating him with the water used in artificial irrigation during the summer months when rain no longer falls from the sky. Cf. below, n. 87.

myths simply to be equated.[86] Thus, while the Shining One seeks the throne on Zaphon out of sheer pride and arrogance, Athtar is clearly appointed to the throne by the supreme god El and his consort Athirat. Again, because of his hubris the Shining One is abruptly cast down to the ground, to the depths of Sheol, whereas Athtar meekly accepts his inability to fill Baal's throne and descends of his own accord to the earth. Moreover, the Shining One is clearly represented as deprived of all power in Sheol following his demise, whereas Athtar 'ruled on earth, god of it all', which may be an allusion to his role as a god of artificial irrigation, upon which Syria–Palestine is dependent when Baal's rains cease during the summer months.[87] However, although the two myths manifest certain differences, they do both provide variations on the theme of Athtar's inability to ascend the divine throne on Mt Zaphon, and so there is probably some ultimate connection between them.

A few scholars have argued that the myth about the Shining One, son of the dawn, is dependent on, or at any rate connected with, a Greek myth in Hesiod's *Theogony* (984-91), about Phaethon (= Shining One) the son of Eos (= Dawn), who is sometimes thought to represent Venus.[88] No myth, however, is actually attested in Greek mythology

86. Among the scholars who reject the view that the myth about Athtar in this Baal text underlies Isa. 14.12-15 are A. Caquot, 'Le dieu Athtar et les textes de Ras Shamra', *Syria* 35 (1958), pp. 45-60, and McKay, 'Helel', pp. 451-64.

87. This view has been supported by Gaster, *Thespis*, p. 127, followed by a number of other scholars, on the basis of Arabic *'aṯṯārī*, which is held to mean soil artificially irrigated, and *'āṯūr*, denoting a canal or trench dug for purposes of irrigation. Similarly, W. Robertson Smith, *The Religion of the Semites*, p. 99, already before the discovery of the Ugaritic texts. However, as Caquot points out, in 'Le dieu Athtar', p. 59, the meaning of Arabic *'aṯṯārī* is more equivocal. Whereas Ibn ul Athir states that the expression refers to palm trees that imbibe with their roots of the rain water that collects in a part hollowed out in the ground, the Ṭağ al 'Arūs declares that *'aṯṯārī* is synonymous with *'īḏī*, 'such as is watered by the rain'. (See E.W. Lane, *An Arabic–English Lexicon*, part 5 [8 parts and supplement; London: Williams & Norgate, 1863], p. 1952.) Nevertheless, I would note that it is possible that evidence for Athtar's connection with artificial irrigation might be found in the lines at the end of the Ugaritic text cited above (66-67) referring to drawing of water.

88. Cf. O. Gruppe, review of 'Phaethon', *Hermes* 18 (1883), pp. 396-434, by U. von Wilamowitz-Möllendorff, and C. Robert, 'Die Phaethonsage bei Hesiod', *Hermes* 18 (1883), pp. 434-41, in *Philologische Wochenschrift*, III (1883), cols. 1537-47 (1539-40); and O. Gruppe, 'Aithiopenmythen, 1: Der phoinikische Urtext

about Phaethon the son of Eos (i.e. Venus) rising up above the stars and being cast down for his hubris. Rather, the actual myth about Phaethon's hubris which we possess concerns Phaethon son of *Helios*, the sun (and the name of the other parent is also different), who drives the sun's chariot so near to the earth that the latter is in danger of catching fire, with the result that Zeus finally casts him down with his thunderbolt.[89] This is quite different from Isa. 14.12-15: nothing is said of Phaethon's wishing to set up his throne above the stars or to usurp the position of the chief deity.

A further myth which many scholars[90] erroneously identify with that of Isa. 14.12-15 is the one contained in Ezek. 28.12-19. We there read:

> 12 Son of man, raise a lamentation over the king of Tyre,
> and say to him, Thus says the Lord God:
> 'You were the signet[91] of perfection,
> full of wisdom,
> and perfect in beauty.

der Kassiepeialegende. Zusammenhang derselben mit anderen Aithiopenmythen', *Philologus* 47 (1889), pp. 92-107 (98); B. Duhm, *Das Buch Jesaia* (Göttinger Handkommentar zum Alten Testament, 3.1; Göttingen: Vandenhoeck & Ruprecht, 4th edn, 1922), p. 119; Grelot, 'Isaïe XIV: 12-15', pp. 24-32; J.W. McKay, 'Helel, Athtar and Phaethon (Jes 14 12-15)', *ZAW* 85 (1973), pp. 223-25, however, points out that 'the weight of evidence indicates Near Eastern influence on early Greek literature, rather than vice versa' (p. 224). Similarly, McKay, *Religion in Judah*, p. 118 n. 110.

89. Cf. Ovid, *Metamorphoses* 1.748-49, 2.1-400. There are also allusions in Euripides, Aristotle, Diodorus Siculus, Horace, Cicero and Lucretius. On the Phaethon myth, see J. Diggle, *Euripides, Phaethon* (Cambridge: Cambridge University Press, 1970). J.C. Poirier, 'An Illuminating Parallel to Isaiah XIV 12', *VT* 49 (1999), pp. 371-89, has recently defended the dependence of Isa. 14.12 (though not 14.13-15) on the Phaethon myth. He draws attention to Callimachus' Epigram 56, part of which reads 'Hesperus, how art thou fallen?' and compares Isa. 14.12. Hesperus was the Evening Star and Poirier supposes that, along with Eosphoros, the Morning Star, it was a hypostasis of Phaethon. However, in so far as both Isa. 14.12 and Callimachus' Epigram 56 reflect a common human experience of the fading of the Evening/Morning Star, the similarity in language need not surprise us. At the same time, as noted above, it needs to be emphasized that the myth of Phaethon's hubris that we possess concerns Phaethon son of Helios, not the Morning Star Phaethon son of Eos.

90. E.g. Clements, *God and Temple*, pp. 7-8; H. Barth, *Die Jesaja-Worte in der Josiazeit* (WMANT, 48, Neukirchen–Vluyn: Neukirchener Verlag, 1977), pp. 134-35; Page, *The Myth of Cosmic Rebellion*, *passim*.

91. Reading *ḥōtam* with one MS, LXX, Peshiṭta and Vulgate for MT *ḥōtēm*.

13 You were in Eden, the garden of God;
every precious stone was your covering,
carnelian, topaz, and jasper,
chrysolite, beryl, and onyx,
sapphire, carbuncle, and emerald;
and wrought in gold were your settings
and your engravings.
On the day that you were created
they were prepared.
14 With[92] an anointed guardian cherub I placed you;[93]
You were on the holy mountain of God;
You walked in the midst of the fiery stones.
15 You were perfect in your ways
from the day of your creation
until iniquity was found in you.
16 In the abundance of your trade
you were filled[94] with violence, and you sinned;
so I cast you out as a profane thing from the mount of God,
and the guardian cherub drove you out[95]

92. Reading *'et* with LXX and Peshiṭta for MT *'att* as is commonly done. J. Barr has recently defended the MT in ' "Thou art the cherub": Ezekiel 28.14 and the post-Ezekiel understanding of Genesis 2–3', in E.C. Ulrich *et al.* (eds.), *Priests, Prophets and Scribes: Essays on the Formation and Heritage of Second Temple Judaism in Honour of Joseph Blenkinsopp* (JSOTSup, 140; Sheffield: JSOT Press, 1992), pp. 213-23. He claims that it is easier to comprehend how the rare second person singular masculine pronoun, *'att* 'you' was misunderstood as *'et* 'with' than the reverse. However, the fact that both the previous and subsequent verses address the king in the second person, combined with the fact that it is rare for a sentence to begin with *'et* 'with' allow one to see how a scribe could well have misread *'et* as *'att*. The parallels between Ezek. 28.12-19 and Gen. 2–3 are such that it is natural to suppose that they provide variants of the same myth and that therefore Ezekiel is referring to the fall of the first human: in both Ezek. 28.12-19 and Gen. 2–3 we read of the creation of an originally perfect figure in the garden of Eden who was expelled because of sin, and in both a cherub or cherubim was somehow involved. Barr holds that we should not, however, connect Gen. 2–3 with Ezek. 28.12-19. But I would note that whereas the fall of the first humans is attested in Gen. 2–3, nowhere else in the Old Testament or Jewish thought is there the expulsion of a cherub from Eden. Also it should be noted that the wisdom of the figure in Ezek. 28.12, 17 is paralleled by that of the first man in Job 15.7-8.

93. Reading *n*^{e}*tattîkā* with LXX and Arabic version for MT *ûn*^{e}*tattîkā*.

94. Reading *millē'tā* with LXX and Peshiṭta for MT *mālû*, the *t* having fallen out through haplography with the *t* of the following word, *tōk*^{e}*kā*.

95. Reading *w*^{e}*'ibbad*^{e}*kā* for MT *wā'abbed*^{e}*kā*.

from the midst of the fiery stones.
17 Your heart was proud because of your beauty;
you corrupted your wisdom for the sake of your splendour,
I cast you to the ground;
I set you before kings,
to feast their eyes on you.
18 By the multitude of your iniquities,
in the unrighteousness of your trade
you profaned your sanctuaries;
so I brought forth fire from the midst of you;
it consumed you,
and I turned you to ashes upon the earth
in the sight of all who saw you.
19 All who know you among the peoples are appalled at you;
You have come to a dreadful end
and you shall be no more for ever.'

Over against those scholars who equate the myths of Isa. 14.12-15 and Ezek. 28.12-19, it must be maintained that their similarities are counterbalanced by significant differences which indicate that we have here two distinct myths.[96] Thus, although symbolizing the king of Babylon, the leading figure of the myth in Isa. 14.12-15 is a star, whereas the one in Ezek. 28.12-19 is human. Ezekiel 28.13 presents the man as having been in Eden from the beginning, in contrast to the figure of Isa. 14.12-15, who had to ascend into heaven in order to reach Zaphon and then failed to gain control of it. The man in Ezekiel is expressly described as perfect until his expulsion, whereas the figure in Isaiah is represented as arrogant even before he has reached Zaphon. Ezekiel 28.14 represents God as being responsible for the figure's presence on the mountain, in contrast to the Shining One, who ascends to Zaphon out of his own desire. Finally, it may be noted that the equation of the 'stones of fire' (Ezek. 28.14, 16) with the stars of Isa. 14.13, which upholders of the view that we have here a common myth tend to assume, is almost certainly to be rejected in favour of the view that we have here an allusion to the lightning. It appears to have been overlooked that elsewhere when we find a cherub or cherubim associated with fire there is no doubt that lightning is intended (see Ps. 18.11, 13, 15 [ET 10, 12, 14] and Ezek. 10.2 [cf. 1.13]), with Ps. 18.13 (ET 12) and Ezek. 10.2 even referring to 'coals of fire', reminiscent of the 'stones of

96. Cf. McKenzie, 'Mythological Allusions', p. 326; similarly, Ohler, *Mythologische Elemente*, pp. 175-76.

fire' in Ezek. 28.14, 16.[97] In view of this, the flaming sword associated with the cherubim in Gen 3.24 is probably lightning too.

Rather, as a number of scholars have pointed out,[98] what we have in Ezek. 28.12-19 is a more mythological version of the story of the first man of Genesis 2–3. The points of comparison are as follows: in both there is a human figure who dwells in the garden of Eden; in both he is at first perfect, but his sin leads to his expulsion from the garden; in Ezekiel a cherub expels the figure, while in Gen. 3.24 we similarly find cherubim associated with the expulsion from the garden, although they themselves do not expel the man, but guard the way to the tree of life. There is also another point of comparison between Ezekiel 28 and what we know of the first man from elsewhere in the Old Testament, in that Job 15.7-8 alludes to the first man's wisdom, just as Ezekiel 28 emphasizes the man's wisdom. Thus, in spite of certain similarities, I reject the view that the myth in Ezek. 28.12-19 is the same as that in Isa. 14.12-15. What they have in common are the themes of hubris and nemesis associated with a sacred mountain, but they certainly derive from different myths.

Some scholars would go further and relate the myth in Isa. 14.12-15 not only to that in Ezek. 28.12-19, but also to that of the fall of the gods or angels in Psalm 82 and Gen. 6.1-4.[99] It is clear, however, that these do not pertain to the same myth as that in Isa. 14.12-15, any more than Ezek. 28.12-19 does. Psalm 82.6-7 refers to the death of the 'sons of the Most High (Elyon)' as a whole, that is, the entire seventy guardian deities of the nations. It is clear that this cannot reflect the myth present

97. Those erroneously equating Ezekiel's stones of fire with stars include H.G. May, 'The King in the Garden of Eden', in B.W. Anderson and W. Harrelson (eds.), *Israel's Prophetic Heritage* (New York: Harper & Brothers, 1962), pp. 166-76 (170) and Page, *The Myth of Cosmic Rebellion*, pp. 149 (n. 264) and 154. Those equating the stones of fire with lightning include U. (M.D.) Cassuto, *A Commentary on the Book of Genesis*. I. *From Adam to Noah* (trans. I. Abrahams; Jerusalem: Magnes Press, 1961), p. 80; F.C. Fensham, 'Thunder-stones in Ugaritic', *JNES* 18 (1959), pp. 273-74. Fensham shows that the concept of 'thunder stones', flints with which the deity made lightning, is widespread throughout the world. However, against Fensham and others, it is unlikely that Ugaritic *'abn brq* (*KTU*[2] 1.3.III.26) refers to these stones of lightning—cf. de Moor, *Seasonal Pattern*, p. 106.

98. E.g. McKenzie, 'Mythological Allusions', pp. 322, 326-27.

99. Cf. Caquot, 'Le dieu Athtar', p. 54; J. Gray, *The Legacy of Canaan* (VTSup, 5; Leiden: E.J. Brill, 2nd edn, 1965), p. 288, n. 1; Page, *The Myth of Cosmic Rebellion*, *passim*.

in Isa. 14.12-15, since the Shining One seeks to dominate the 'stars of God (El)', namely, precisely the sons of Elyon or El whose 'fall' is alluded to in Psalm 82. As for Gen. 6.1-4, this appears to be yet another myth, for there, unlike Isa. 14.12-15, the sons of God are not guilty of seeking to ascend the Mount of Assembly, where they presumably already belong, but, quite the reverse, of descending to the earth and engaging in sexual intercourse with the daughters of men.

One scholar who equates the myth of Isa. 14.12-15 with that of Ezek. 28.12-19 and Psalm 82 is M.H. Pope, but he also thinks that it ultimately reflects the attempt of El together with his cohorts, including Yam, to regain his throne on Mt Zaphon from Baal.[100] However, it is dubious whether El and Baal were in opposition to one another or that El was dethroned, so that this understanding of Isa. 14.12-15 is to be rejected.

In conclusion, it appears that Isa. 14.12-15 contains a Canaanite myth about the morning star Venus, which seeks to rise and usurp the chief god's seat on Mt Zaphon, but is cast down to the underworld by the light of the rising sun. There are good grounds for believing that the Canaanite morning star Venus was equated with the god Athtar. The Ugaritic myth contained in the Baal epic at least attests an abortive attempt by Athtar to claim the divine throne (of Baal) on Mt Zaphon: this does not correspond exactly to the myth contained in Isa. 14.12-15, but is perhaps a kind of variant on it. On the other hand, the myth in Isa. 14.12-15 seems unconnected with the Greek Phaethon myth or the myth in Ezekiel 28.

Jebusite Background

As an original suggestion I would propose that the myth contained in Isa. 14.12-15 was appropriated by the Israelites from the Jebusites. Several factors suggest this and, combined together, they make a plausible cumulative case. First, Isa. 14.14 employs the name Elyon for God, which we know from Gen. 14.19, and 22 was the distinctive name of the Jebusite god of Jerusalem. (Similarly, v. 13 speaks of 'the heights of Zaphon', which occurs also in Ps. 48.3 [ET 2] and the related Psalm 46 again speaks of Elyon in v. 5 [ET 4].) Secondly, Ps. 110.3 contains a mythical allusion to the dawn ('from the womb of [the] dawn') in close proximity to a reference (in v. 4) to the Davidic king being a priest after

100. Pope, *El in the Ugaritic Texts*, pp. 97, 102-103.

the order of Melchizedek; Melchizedek, we know from Genesis 14, was the Jebusite priest of El-Elyon, and it seems natural to hold that the royal priesthood after the order of Melchizedek reflects a fusion of the Israelite and Jebusite royal ideologies effected soon after the conquest of the city.[101] In that case the mythical sounding reference to the dawn in Ps. 110.3 could well derive from the same source. Thirdly, what further bears this out is the very name of the city of Jerusalem. It is generally accepted that in origin this denoted 'the foundation of [the god] Shalem', Shalem being the god of dusk (cf. Jeruel, 'foundation of El' in 2 Chron. 20.16). It is interesting that Shaḥar (dawn) and Shalem (dusk) are brothers in Ugaritic mythology, as they were begotten at the same time by the god El (*KTU*[2] 1.2.3). If the god Shalem ('dusk') was prominent in Jebusite Jerusalem mythology, it is only natural that his brother Shaḥar, 'dawn', would appear there too.

The Historical Background of Isaiah 14.12-15

Against what historical background are we to understand the mythological allusions in Isa. 14.12-15? The heading of the section Isa. 13.1-14.23 in 13.1, *maśśā' bābel*, indicates that we have an oracle directed against Babylon, and this is further borne out by the references to Babylon in 13.19, 14.4 and 14.22. The fact that the fall of Babylon is expected at the hands of the Medes (13.17), moreover, has led most scholars to conclude that the oracle is directed against Babylon a little before the middle of the sixth century BCE, not only before the rise of Cyrus the Persian, who in fact captured Babylon in 539 BCE, but also before the fall of the Median empire to Cyrus in 550 BCE.

S. Erlandsson[102] has argued for a date of Isaiah 13–14 around 700 BCE, and, in spite of what the title of his book, *The Burden of Babylon*, might lead one to expect, he holds that only Isa. 13.19-22 and 14.22b-23 actually relate to Babylon, the judgment pronounced in the rest of the oracle being directed against Assyria. This view, however, is forced, and its evident weaknesses have been well exposed in a review by P.-E. Dion.[103] If Isa. 13.1-14.21 really has in mind the Assyrians almost entirely throughout, it is incomprehensible that there is no

101. Cf. J.A. Emerton, 'The Riddle of Genesis XIV', *VT* 21 (1971), pp. 403-39.

102. S. Erlandsson, *The Burden of Babylon: A Study of Isaiah 13:2-14:23* (ConBOT, 4; Lund: C.W.K. Gleerup, 1970).

103. P.-E. Dion, review of *The Burden of Babylon*, by S. Erlandsson, in *Bib* 52 (1971), pp. 439-42 (439).

explicit mention of them before 14.24-27, verses which in any case do not obviously belong with 13.1-14.23. Moreover, the break which Erlandsson posits between 13.18 and 13.19 is artificial, so that the reference to the expected attack by the Medes in 13.17 must on any natural view relate to Babylon (13.19), which does not agree with his dating of the oracle to c. 700 BCE, when the Medes were Babylon's allies. Finally, the explicit references to Babylon in Isa. 13.1, 14.4 and 14.22 make Erlandsson's view untenable: the fact that the oracle as a whole is headed *maśśā' bābel*, 'oracle concerning Babylon', is irreconcilable with Erlandsson's view that Babylon is the subject of only 13.19-22 and 14.22b-23; his explanation that in 14.4 Babylon can mean Assyria, on the grounds that Tiglath-pileser III of Assyria is referred to by his Babylonian name Pul in 2 Kgs 15.19, is not only confusing and inconsistent in the light of the other references to Babylon in the oracle which Erlandsson himself accepts actually mean Babylon (13.1, 19, 14.22), but cannot even claim the support of 2 Kgs 15.19, since even there Pul is referred to as king of Assyria; and his dissociation of 14.22 from the previous verses by his translation 'and as for Babylon, I will eradicate its name...' fails in view of the fact that the Hebrew text in 14.22 has not *ûl^{e}bābel 'akrît* but *w^{e}hikrattî l^{e}bābel*, clearly suggesting the identity of the Babylonians with the enemies mentioned at the beginning of the verse and in the preceding poem. Erlandsson's view should therefore be rejected. Another odd view is that of J.H. Hayes and A. Irvine,[104] who see the king as Tiglath-pileser III, the Assyrian king who also ruled Babylon; but in that case it is not clear why he is not called king of Assyria.

More commonly it has been held that, although Isa. 13.1–14.23 in its present redaction is directed against Babylon, the taunt song in 14.14b-21 originally applied to an Assyrian king, in view of the degree of cruelty which is there imputed to the oppressive ruler. Sargon II and Sennacherib have been favourite candidates.[105] Sargon, in particular, has been favoured because he was not buried,[106] thus agreeing with Isa.

104. J.H. Hayes and A. Irvine, *Isaiah: The Eighth-Century Prophet* (Nashville: Abingdon Press, 1987), pp. 227-29.

105. Cf. H. Wildberger, *Jesaja*, II (BKAT, 10.2; Neukirchen–Vluyn: Neukirchener Verlag, 1974), p. 543 for references, and in addition to those cited there, H.L. Ginsberg, 'Reflexes of Sargon in Isaiah after 715 B.C.E', *JAOS* 88 (1968), pp. 47-53.

106. For evidence that Sargon was not buried at home, see A. Livingstone, *Court*

14.18-20. However, v. 20 suggests that the destruction of his people goes hand in hand with this, which does not fit either of these kings and we probably have here a genuine prophecy rather than a *vaticinium ex eventu*. However, even if the latter were the case, the oracle is clearly directed against a Babylonian king in its present redaction. This being the case, the Babylonian king in question is almost certainly Nebuchadrezzar, since the expectation that the Medes would destroy Babylon (Isa. 13.17-22) requires a date within the period c. 609–550 BCE (probably between 586 and 562 BCE[107]) and during this period Nebuchadrezzar was by far the most important king and the one above all others who fits the picture of the world-conquering Babylonian ruler of Isa. 14.4b-21. (Nabonidus, the last king of Babylon, who reigned from 555-539 BCE, and identified by some with the king,[108] is not really appropriate, since he was not a great conqueror.) Jeremiah 50–51, in fact, which is closely related to Isaiah 13–14, and takes up many allusions from it (including Isa. 14.12-15, cf. Jer. 51.53),[109] is specifically directed against Nebuchadrezzar (Jer. 51.34, cf. 50.17). Moreover, the discovery of the Chaldaean Chronicle (now in the British Museum) reveals Nebuchadrezzar, a Babylonian, acting very much like an Assyrian king, conducting annual campaigns to gather the tribute that would be forthcoming under the pressure of the presence of his well-equipped army. His planning was on a broad and international scale, and he punished his defeated enemies as harshly as any Assyrian king would have done.[110] Accordingly, although it is not impossible, it seems

Poetry and Literary Miscellanea (State Archives of Assyria, 3; Helsinki: Helsinki University Press, 1989), pp. 77-79.

107. The fact that it is the Medes who are expected to conquer Babylon rules out the postexilic dates for this oracle proposed by J.Vermeylen, *Du Prophète Isaïe à l'Apocalyptique* (Paris: J. Gabalda, 1977), pp. 286-92 and B. Gosse, 'Un texte pré-apocalyptique du règne de Darius: Isaïe XIII, 1–XIV, 23', *RB* 92 (1985), pp. 200-22.

108. E.g. Langdon, 'The Star Hêlēl, Jupiter?', p. 174; Etz, 'Isaiah XIV 12-15', pp. 298-99.

109. The parallels are noted in Erlandsson, *The Burden of Babylon*, pp. 154-59. From the section Isa. 14.12-15 we find v. 13, *haššāmayim 'e'ᵉleh*, reflected in Jer. 51.53, *kî ta'ᵃleh bābel haššāmayim*.

110. D.J. Wiseman, *Chronicles of Chaldaean Kings (626–556 BC) in the British Museum* (London: Trustees of the British Museum, 1956), pp. 64-75 (cf. also pp. 20-37, 46-48). For a more recent translation of these chronicles, see A.K. Grayson, *Assyrian and Babylonian Chronicles* (Texts from Cuneiform Sources, 5; Locust Valley, NY: J.J. Augustin, 1975), pp. 97-102 (cf. pp. 19-20).

unnecessary to suppose that Isa. 14.4b-21 originally referred to an Assyrian king, and there is every reason to believe that the king in view here is Nebuchadrezzar. It may further be noted that the cutting down of cedars of Lebanon attributed to the king (Isa. 14.8) is attested of Nebuchadrezzar elsewhere in the Old Testament in Hab. 2.17.[111] Interestingly, the rabbis almost unanimously saw the king in Isaiah 14 as Nebuchadrezzar.[112]

I shall now propose a view never previously discussed, so far as I am aware, that in the passage with which we are here particularly concerned, Isa. 14.12-15, the attempted usurpation of Zaphon is not simply a symbol of the king's hubris in general, as is usually supposed, but specifically reflects Nebuchadrezzar's capture of Jerusalem and destruction of the temple in 586 BCE.[113] In support of this the following points may be made. First, it may be noted that Zaphon was the name of both Yahweh's heavenly dwelling place (Isa. 14.13; Job 26.7) and his earthly dwelling place on Mt Zion (Ps. 48.3 [ET 2]), and any attempted usurpation of the earthly throne naturally had repercussions in the heavenly sphere. Since for many Jews the most flagrant act of hubris on the part of Nebuchadrezzar would have been his destruction of the temple in Jerusalem, it is attractive to suppose that Isa. 14.12-15 is a heavenly reflection of this. This seems preferable to the view of scholars such as Eissfeldt and J.J.M. Roberts[114] that it is the Syrian Mt Zaphon that is here alluded to, or the view of F.M. Cross[115] that the reference is to Mt Amanus, since Yahweh was surely not regarded as dwelling on either of these mountains, but rather in Jerusalem and in heaven. Secondly, it is interesting to note that the passage similar to Isa. 14.12-15 contained

111. It is most natural to suppose that the foreign oppressor against whom the woes in Hab. 2.6-19 are directed is to be equated with the Chaldaeans (cf. Hab. 1.6), whose violence is lamented in Hab. 1.12-17. Hab. 2.17 would then refer to Nebuchadrezzar, who, it may be noted, himself records his transportation of cedars from Lebanon. Cf. J.P. Brown, *The Lebanon and Phoenicia: Ancient Texts Illustrating their Physical Geography and Native Industries*, I (Beirut: American University of Beirut, 1969), pp. 196-99.

112. Cf. D. Halperin, *The Faces of the Chariot* (Texte und Studien zum antiken Judentum, 16; Tübingen: J.C.B. Mohr [Paul Siebeck], 1988), p. 321.

113. F. Stolz, *Strukturen und Figuren im Kult von Jerusalem* (BZAW, 118; Berlin: W. de Gruyter, 1970), p. 166 n. 73, lists Isa. 14.13 alongside Ps. 48.3 (ET 2) as alluding to Jerusalem, but does not discuss the identification.

114. Eissfeldt, *Baal Zaphon*, p. 15; Roberts, 'ṢĀPŌN', p. 556.

115. Cross, *Canaanite Myth and Hebrew Epic*, p. 38.

in Dan. 8.9-14, in which a little horn rises above the stars even up to 'the Prince of the host' (i.e. God) and is subsequently cast down, also specifically reflects an attack on the temple in Jerusalem, namely, that of Antiochus IV Epiphanes in 168 BCE. Thirdly, it is to be noted that the oracle against Babylon in Jeremiah 50–51, which has many allusions to Isaiah 13–14, has as a recurring theme that the downfall of Babylon will come about as revenge for Nebuchadrezzar's violation of Zion and its temple (cf. Jer. 50.28-29; [note v. 28: 'for she (Babylon) has proudly defied the Lord, the Holy One of Israel']; 51.11, 24, 34-37, 49-51), the last cited passage (vv. 49-51) being soon followed in Jer. 51.53 by an actual allusion to Isa. 14.12-15. Jeremiah 51.53 reads, 'Though Babylon should mount up to heaven, and though she should fortify her strong height, yet destroyers would come from me upon her, says the Lord'.[116] It is therefore entirely in keeping that Isa. 14.12-15 should similarly declare that judgment is to fall upon the king of Babylon because of his violation of the temple.

It may therefore be argued that in Isa. 14.12-15 it is to Nebuchadrezzar and his violation of the temple that mythological imagery is applied.

116. It has been suggested to me that Jer. 51.53 is dependent rather on the story of the tower of Babel in Gen. 11.1-9. However, the fact that Jer. 50–51 has so many other parallels in Isa. 13–14 suggests that Jer. 51.53 is derived from Isa. 14.12-15. For the parallels between Isa. 13–14 and Jer. 50–51, see Erlandsson, *The Burden of Babylon*, pp. 154-59.

Chapter 7

YAHWEH AND THE UNDERWORLD DEITIES (MOT, RESHEPH, MOLECH AND THE REPHAIM)

In the Old Testament Yahweh and the underworld (Sheol) stand rather remote from each other much of the time. Only gradually did a meaningful afterlife belief emerge in which Yahweh's power over Sheol was fully manifested. In Ugaritic mythology the supreme god of the underworld is called Mot (Death), and another underworld deity is called Resheph. There are grounds for believing that Molech was also associated with the netherworld, whilst the divinized spirits of the dead were called *rp'um*, a term clearly related to the Rephaim (shades) of the Old Testament. I shall consider in turn what became of these various netherworld deities in the Old Testament.

Mot

Mot is depicted in the Ugaritic texts as having a large throat which is insatiable in swallowing people up and delivering them up to the underworld. Similar language is used in the Old Testament of Sheol, the word *nepeš* (cognate to Ugaritic *npš*, which is used of Mot) being used of its throat.[1] However, although language suggestive of personification is used of Sheol, this does not mean that Sheol is actually a person in the way that Mot was. Thus, of Mot we read such things as 'even as Mot has jaws reaching to earth, lips to heaven and a tongue to the stars, Baal will enter his stomach and go down into his mouth as the olive, the produce of the earth and fruit of the trees is swallowed' (*KTU*^{2} 1.5.II.1-6); 'verily you must come down into the throat of Mot son of El, into the miry gorge of the hero beloved of El' (*KTU*^{2} 1.5.I.6-8). Similarly, in

1. On the recognition that Hebrew *nepeš* could mean 'throat', already before the discovery of the Ugaritic texts, see L. Dürr, 'Hebr. נֶפֶשׁ = akk. napištu = Gurgel, Kehle', *ZAW* 43 (1925), pp. 262-69.

the Old Testament we read of Sheol: 'Therefore Sheol has enlarged its throat and opened its mouth beyond measure; and down go her nobility, and her multitude, her throng and the strength of her heart'[2] (Isa. 5.14); 'And even though the treacherous one is presumptuous,[3] the arrogant man shall not abide. His throat is as wide as Sheol; like death he has never enough. He gathers for himself all nations, and collects as his own all peoples' (Hab. 2.5). Sheol is also referred to as swallowing people up in Prov. 1.12, and its insatiable appetite is alluded to in Prov. 27.20 and 30.15b-16. In Ps. 49.15 (ET 14) death is a shepherd and those who go to Sheol are like sheep, 'Like sheep they are appointed for Sheol; Death shall be their shepherd...' Although this is only poetic language, it recalls what is said of the god Mot in the Baal text, *KTU*^{2} 1.6.II.21-23, *ngš. 'ank. 'al'iyn b'l 'dbnn 'ank. <k>'imr. bpy kll'i. bṯbrn q<n>y. <n>ḫt'u hw*, 'I myself came upon the victor Baal, I myself made him as lamb in my mouth; he himself like a kid in my jaws was carried away'. The same word 'mouth' (*pî*) is used of Sheol in Ps. 141.7.

An interesting verse in this connection comes from the so-called Isaiah apocalypse in Isa. 25.8, where we read that God 'will swallow up death for ever'. There is an evident irony here, for, as we have seen, it is elsewhere Death or Mot that does the swallowing, but here it is the swallower that is to be swallowed up. Although imagery used of the Canaanite god Mot ultimately lies in the background, the question remains what the precise meaning is in the present context of the Isaiah apocalypse. Some hold that there is a literal hope for the abolition of death here, and this is certainly how the passage was later interpreted

2. The translation 'the strength of her heart' follows J.A. Emerton, 'The Textual Problems of Isaiah V 14', *VT* 17 (1967), pp. 135-42, reading *w^{e}'ōz libbāh* for *w^{e}'ālēz bāh*.

3. The translation 'presumptuous' presupposes the reading *hayyān* or *hawwān* in place of MT *hayyayin*, which, like IQpHab *hôn* 'wealth' is clearly wrong, since a personal reference is demanded by the context. As a personal reference *hayyān*, or *hawwān*, 'presumptuous', is to be preferred to *hayyôneh* 'the oppressor' because (i) it is closer to the MT, (ii) it has the support of LXX κατοιόμενος (mistakenly emended by Rahlfs to κατοινωμένος), (iii) although a *hapax legomenon* the verbal root occurs in Deut. 1.41, where *tāhînû* stands in place of *ya'pilû* (Num. 14.44)—compare the fact that the root *'pl* is also found in Hab. 2.4 (though there in the sense 'puffed up'). The view that we should read *hayyān* or *hawwān* was first put forward by M.T. Houtsma, 'Habakuk II, vs. 4 en 5 verbeterd', *Theologisch Tijdschrift* 19 (1885), pp. 180-83.

(cf. 1 Cor. 15.54; Rev. 7.17, 21.4). However, a case can be made that in the original understanding 'death' was a metaphor for exile. First, Isa. 25.8 goes on to speak of Yahweh's removing 'the reproach of his people', which surely refers to the situation of the Jewish exile. Secondly, the only other comparable passage in the work, Isa. 26.19, which uses the imagery of death and resurrection in connection with Israel, must, as I have argued elsewhere, refer to exile and restoration (as in Ezek. 37) rather than literal life after death (as in Dan. 12.2).[4] Isaiah 27.8 specifically refers back to the exile, taking up imagery from Hos. 13.15, just as Isa. 26.19 has appropriated imagery from the preceding verse, Hos. 13.14.[5] Accordingly, Isa. 26.19 must be read in the light of Isa. 27.8, and so very likely should the related Isa. 25.8.

One expression in the Old Testament which can claim a Ugaritic parallel involving the god Mot is Azmaweth (*'azmāwet*), which occurs both as a personal name of several people (a. 2 Sam. 23.31; 1 Chron. 11.33; b. 1 Chron. 12.3; c. 1 Chron. 27.25; d.1 Chron. 8.36, 9.42) and as part of a place name, Beth-Azmaweth (*bêt-'azmāwet*) (Ezra 2.24; Neh. 7.28, 12.29, modern El-Ḥizmeh), and with which one may also compare Cant. 8.6, *kî-'azzâ kammāwet 'ah*^{a}*bâ*, 'for love is strong as death'. This expression recalls *mt. 'z*, 'Mot was strong', which occurs several times in the Ugaritic Baal text when describing the fight between Baal and Mot (*KTU*^{2} 1.6.VI.17-22).

17 *mt. 'z.b'l. 'z.ynghn*	Mot was strong, Baal was strong, they gored
18 *kr'umm.mt.'z.b'l*	like wild oxen. Mot was strong, Baal
19 *'z.ynṯkn.kbṯnm*	was strong; they bit like serpents
20 *mt. 'z.b'l.'z.ymṣḫn*	Mot was strong, Baal was strong, they kicked (?)
21 *klsmm.mt.ql*	like chargers. Mot fell down,
22 *b'l.ql. 'ln.*	Baal fell down on top of him.

Basically, the same expression also occurs in a Ugaritic letter, *KTU*^{2} 2.10.11-13: *w.yd 'ilm. p. kmtm 'z. m'id*, 'Also, the "hand of a god" is

4. See J. Day, 'The Development of Belief in Life after Death in Ancient Israel', in J. Barton and D.J. Reimer (eds.), *After the Exile: Essays in Honour of Rex Mason* (Macon, GA; Mercer University Press, 1996), pp. 231-57 (243-44); *idem*, 'Resurrection Imagery', pp. 130-31. Also, see above, Chapter 4 (section on Baal and resurrection imagery).

5. See J. Day, 'A Case of Inner Scriptural Interpretation', pp. 309-19, reprinted with slight revisions in Broyles and Evans (eds.), *Writing and Reading the Scroll of Isaiah: Studies of an Interpretive Tradition*, pp. 357-68. Also, see above, Chapter 4 (section on Baal and resurrection imagery).

here, for Death (here) is very strong'.[6] It does seem very likely that the place (and hence the personal) name Azmaweth originally meant 'strong as Mot', not simply 'strong as death', both because divine names tend to occur in Canaanite place names and also because of the evidence from Ugarit that this was a stereotypical phrase involving Mot. (One may compare the fact that the phrase 'Baal is strong' also lived on, since it occurs in the name of a Cypriot god, Baal-Az, and a Cypriot king, Azbaal.)[7] Also in Cant. 8.6, there is evidence that the original mythological background was not out of sight, since love's arrows (*rᵉšāpîm*) are mentioned in connection with love being as strong as death, and *rešep* derives from Resheph, the underworld god in Canaanite mythology. (See section below on Resheph.)

Passage Where Echo of Mot Is Uncertain

There is one place where an allusion to the god Mot has been found by various scholars which is possible but not certain. This is Jer. 9.20 (ET 21), 'For death has come up into our windows, it has entered our palaces, cutting off the children from the streets and the young men from the squares'. Cassuto and others[8] argued that the imagery of death (or rather Death) coming through the windows is derived from the episode in the Ugaritic texts concerning the building of Baal's palace where Baal at first refuses to allow the craftsman god Kothar-and-Ḫasis to put a window in his palace, for fear, it is presumed, that Mot would come through it and kill his wives. The text is as follows:

6. On this passage, and for the Ugaritic letter as a whole, see D. Pardee, 'As Strong as Death', in Marks and Good (eds.), *Love & Death in the Ancient Near East*, pp. 65-69.

7. For a recently discovered Cypriot inscription mentioning the god Baal Az, see P. Xella, 'Le dieu B'l 'z dans une nouvelle inscription phénicienne de Kition (Chypre)', *SEL* 10 (1993), pp. 61-69. Azbaal ruled c. 449–425 BCE and was king of Idalion and Kition. See G.F. Hill, *Catalogue of the Greek Coins of Cyprus* (London: Trustees of the British Museum, 1904), pp. xxx-xxxi, xxxii-xxxiii, lii, 10-13, 16 note, plate III.1-9.

8. U. (M.D.) Cassuto, *The Goddess Anath* (trans. I. Abrahams; Jerusalem: Magnes Press, 1971), pp. 22, 33, 63; J. Bright, *Jeremiah* (AB, 21; Garden City, NY: Doubleday, 1965), p. 72, also seems to favour this view.

KTU² 1.4.V.58–VI.15

1.4.V 58 *wy‘n. kṯr. wḫss*	And Kothar-and-Ḫasis answered,
59 *šm‘. l’al’iyn. b‘l*	‘Hear, O victor Baal,
60 *bn. lrkb. ‘rpt*	understand O rider of the clouds.
61 *bl. ’ašt. ’urbt. bbh*[*tm*]	I shall surely put a lattice in the mansion,
62 *ḥln. bqrb. hklm*	a window in the midst of the palace’.
63 *wy‘n. ’al’iyn b‘l*	And the victor Baal answered,
64 *’al. tšt. ‘urbt. b*[*bhtm*]	‘Do not put a lattice in the mansion,
65 [*ḥl*]*n. bqrb. hk*[*lm*]	a window in the midst of the palace’.
...	
1.4. VI. 1 *wy‘n.k*[*ṯr. wḫ*]*ss*	And Ko[thar]-and-Ḫasis answered,
2 *ṯtb. b‘l. l*[*hwty*]	‘You will come back to my words, Baal’.
3 *ṯn. rgm. k*[*ṯr.*]*wḫss*	Ko[thar-]and-Ḫasis repeated his speech,
4 *šm‘. m‘. l’al* [*’i*]*yn b‘l*	‘Hear, I pray, victor Baal,
5 *bl. ’ašt. ’ur* [*bt.*] *bbhtm*	I shall surely put a lattice in the mansion
6 *ḥln. bqrb*[*.hk*]*lm*	a window in the midst of the palace’.
7 *w‘n. ’al’i*[*yn.*] *b‘l*	And the victor Baal answered,
8 *’al. tšt. u*[*rb*]*t. bbhtm*	‘Do not put a lattice in the mansion,
9 *ḥln. bq*[*rb.h*]*klm*	a window in the midst of the palace’.
10 *’al.td*[*d.pdr*]*y.bt ’ar*	lest [Pidri]ya daughter of dew run away
11 [?] *h/’iṯ/ḫ*[? *.ṭl*]*y.bt.rb*	[or Ṭali]ya daughter of showers...
12 [...*m*]*dd. ’il ym*	...Yam [be]loved of El
13 ...*qlṣn. wpṯm*	...abase me or spit
14 ...*wy‘n. kṯr*	...And Kothar[-and-Ḫasis] answered,
15 [*wḫss.*] *ṯtb. b‘l. lhwty*	‘You will come back to my words, Baal’.

As will be seen from the above citation of the relevant Ugaritic text, there is no mention of Mot here, a point first noted by T.H. Gaster.[9] Rather, the text indicates that it is the god Yam whom Baal fears, lest he come through the window and abduct his daughters, the dew goddesses Pidriya and Ṭaliya. There are therefore no grounds for believing that this passage lies behind the imagery in Jer. 9.20 (ET 21).

S.M. Paul[10] prefers to find the origin of the picture of death in Jer. 9.20 (ET 21) in the Mesopotamian Lamaštu demon, who preys upon infants and pregnant women; two texts actually describe him as attacking human beings by entering the windows. However, as F. Saracino[11] has noted, there are Ugaritic texts in which Mot threatens humanity in a

9. Gaster, *Thespis*, pp. 188-89.

10. S.M. Paul, ‘Cuneiform Light on Jer 9,20’, *Bib* 49 (1968), pp. 373-76.

11. Saracino, ‘Ger. 9, 20, un polmone ugaritico e la forza di Môt’, *AION* 44 (1984), pp. 539-53.

way comparable to Death in Jer. 9.20 (ET 21), for example *KTU*² 21.127.29-31 and 2.10.11-13,[12] though there is no specific mention of coming through a window. *KTU*² 1.127.30-31 is particularly interesting, as Mot is said to go up (*y'l*) against a person, the same verb as is employed in Jer. 9.21 (ET 21, *'ālâ*). Mark Smith[13] likewise finds the Mot parallels significant, and also refers to a Mesopotamian demon *mūtu* 'Death' who attacks people, though again so far no reference to its entering through a window has been found. At the moment it is probably safest to reserve judgment: Mot may lie behind the imagery in Jer. 9.20 (ET 21), but we cannot be certain.

Passages where Alleged Allusions to Mot are Dubious

Another verse where an allusion to Death or Mot has been seen is Ps. 48.15 (ET 14). The Hebrew reads, *'ᵉlōhênû 'ôlām wā'ed hû' yᵉnahᵃgēnû 'al-mût*. Some scholars, such as A.R. Johnson,[14] prefer to translate *mwt* as 'Death', reading *māwet*, that is, 'our God who abideth for ever, is our leader against "Death"'. Although he sees Mot as ultimately lying in the background, Johnson denies that 'Death' in the psalm is fully personal, but refers to the powers of the underworld that struggle against Yahweh and his people. Such a translation can claim the support of the Syriac *l'l mn mwt'* and Jerome's *in mortem*. However, there is no reference to the powers of Death elsewhere in the psalm, so their mention here at the very end is rather surprising. It is better to read with many manuscripts *'lmt* and to point the word as *'ōlāmôt* 'eternally'. This has the advantage of providing an excellent parallel to *'ôlām wā'ed* in the previous line, that is, 'our God for ever and ever, he will be our God eternally' and can also claim the support of LXX's εἶς τοὺς αἰῶνας. L. Krinetzki[15] has, moreover, pointed out that such a word *'lmt* occurs in

12. Saracino also cites *KTU*² 1.119.26-36, though it is doubtful whether 'the strong one' (*'z*) attacking the gate there is actually Mot.

13. Mark S. Smith, 'Death in Jeremiah, ix, 20', *UF* 19 (1987), pp. 289-93; *idem*, *The Early History of God*, pp. 53, 72-73.

14. S. Mowinckel, *Offersang og sangoffer* (Oslo: H. Aschehoug, 1951), p. 178; ET *The Psalms in Israel's Worship* (trans. D.R. Ap-Thomas; 2 vols.; Oxford: Basil Blackwell, 1962), I, p. 182; Johnson, *Sacral Kingship*, pp. 91-92; J.H. Eaton, *Psalms* (Torch Bible Paperbacks; London: SCM Press, 1967), p. 133; Stolz, *Strukturen und Figuren*, p. 65 n. 25 ('vielleicht'); Goulder, *The Psalms of the Sons of Korah*, pp. 167, 169-70.

15. L. Krinetzki, 'Zur Poetik und Exegese von Ps 48', *BZ* NS 4 (1960), pp. 70-97 (73 n. 14). *'lmt* occurs in *KTU*² 3.5 (*UT* 1008.15) as part of the following: (11)

Ugaritic where it is parallel to *'d 'lm*. There is no reason, therefore, to see an allusion to 'Death' or Mot in this psalm. It is also unnecessary to emend the text to *'al-'ᵃlāmôt*, a musical notation (Ps. 46.1, ET heading), and transfer it to the beginning of the next psalm, Psalm 49, as some have advocated.[16]

Another place where it has sometimes been thought there is an allusion to Mot is in Ps. 68.21 (ET 20), 'Our God is a God of salvation; and to God, the Lord, belongs escape from death'.[17] However, there seems no particular reason to believe that 'death' is personified here. Yet a further suggestion about the presence of Mot in the Psalms has been made by M. Mannati,[18] who has sought to find the name of the god Mot in Ps. 73.4. She offers no precise translation, but it is clear that she understands the first half of the verse to mean 'There are no shackles from their Mot…', that is, the god Mot makes no impositions upon the wicked. However, apart from the oddity of the expression 'their Mot', it may be noted against this view that the metre is bad. Perfect metre is restored to the verse only if we follow the view apparently first put forward by Mörl[19] in 1737 and divide *lᵉmôtām* between the two halves of the verse into *lāmô* and *tām*. The translation is then, 'For they have no pangs, their bodies are sound and fat'. *Tām* would then have a non-moral sense as in Job 21.23, where it is followed by a reference to 'fatness' (v. 24), just as here in Ps. 73.4, 'fat' (*bārî'*) and *tām* are associated. Mannati's view that there is a reference to the god Mot here should therefore be rejected. He also sees an allusion to Mot in v. 9 of

wytn.nn (12) *l.b'ln.bn* (13) *kltn.w.l* (14) *bnh. 'd*[.] *'lm* (15) *šḥr. 'lmt* (16) *bnš bnšm* (17) *l.yqḥnn.bd* (18) *b'ln.bn.kltn* (19) *w.bd.bnh. 'd* (20) *'lm. w. 'unṯ* (21) *'in. bh*, 'And he gives it to Baalin, son of Kltn and to his son for ever, till the dawn of eternities. Nobody shall take it from the hands of Baalin son of Kltn and from the hands of his son for ever. No statute labour is imposed on it.'

16. Favoured, for example, by H.-J. Kraus, *Psalmen*, I (BKAT, 15.1; 2 vols.; Neukirchen–Vluyn: Neukirchener Verlag, 5th edn, 1978), p. 515; ET, *Psalms 1–59* (trans. H.C. Oswald; Minneapolis: Augsburg, 1988), p. 476.

17. E.g. Mowinckel, *The Psalms in Israel's Worship*, I, p. 152 (not in Norwegian original); M.E. Tate, *Psalms 51–100* (WBC, 20; Dallas: Word Books, 1990), p. 181 ('perhaps').

18. M. Mannati, 'Les adorateurs de Môt dans le Psaume LXXIII', *VT* 22 (1972), pp. 420-25.

19. According to Mannati, 'Les adorateurs de Môt', pp. 423-24. The reference must be to T.S. Mörl, *Scholia philologica et critica ad selecta S. Codicis loca* (Nürnberg, 1737) (unavailable to me).

this psalm, where we read, 'they set their mouths against the heavens, and their tongue struts through the earth'. He compares the passage in the Ugaritic texts about Mot: [*špt. l'a*]*rṣ. špt. lšmm* [*wl*]*šn. lkbkbm.*, '[lips to ea]rth, lips to heaven [and a t]ongue to the stars' (*KTU*[2] 1.5.II.2-3). Although there is a similarity, it should be noted that the context of Ps. 73.9 surely implies that this is a reference to the impious and not to a god (Mot), contrary to what Mannati supposes.

According to Albright,[20] there is a reference to 'Death' (ultimately Mot) in Hab. 3.13b. The Hebrew text has *māḥaṣtā rō'š mibbêt rāšā' 'ārôt y*^{e}*sôd 'ad-ṣawwā'r*, but Albright wants to emend this to *māḥaṣtā rō'š māwet rāšā' 'ārôt y*^{e}*sôd 'ad-ṣawwā'r*, 'Thou didst smite the head of wicked Death [Mot], Destroying [him] tail-end to neck', in view of LXX's θάνατον in ἔβαλες εἰς κεφαλὰς ἀνόμων θάνατον, ἐξήγειρας δεσμοὺς ἕως τραχήλου. However, the LXX clearly understood 'death' as that with which the wicked was smitten, rather than the name of the wicked, and this is surely more likely to be correct, since death is what 'smiting' in the Old Testament normally entails and, in fact, Hab. 3.5 does speak of Yahweh's being accompanied by 'Plague and Pestilence'. Furthermore, nothing in the text previously has led one to expect that 'death' is actually the name of the enemy. How exactly the verse should be translated is uncertain. One possibility is to maintain the reading of the MT, except for emending *ṣawwā'r* 'neck' to *ṣûr* 'rock', resulting in the translation, 'You smote the top off the house of the wicked, laying bare the foundation as far as the rock'. (A similar rendering is found, for example, in the NEB.) Alternatively, one might omit *mibbêt* and render with RSV, 'Thou didst crush the head of the wicked, laying him bare from thigh to neck'. Yet other renderings have also been proposed, all of which avoid seeing a reference to 'Death' or Mot here.[21]

It is maintained by Lehmann, Soggin and Croatto, Tromp and Mulder[22] that the name of the god Mot occurs in the Hebrew word *š*^{e}*dēmôt*

20. W.F. Albright, 'The Psalm of Habakkuk', in H.H. Rowley (ed.), *Studies in Old Testament Prophecy Presented to Professor T.H. Robinson* (Edinburgh: T. & T. Clark, 1950), pp. 1-18 (11, 13 and 17 n. oo).

21. See the survey in D.T. Tsumura, 'Ugaritic Poetry and Habakkuk 3', *TynBul* 40 (1989), pp. 24-48 (40-45).

22. Cf. M.R. Lehmann, 'A New Interpretation of the Term שדמות', *VT* 3 (1953), pp. 361-71; J.S. Croatto and J.A. Soggin, 'Die Bedeutung von שׁדמות im Alten Testament', *ZAW* 74 (1962), pp. 44-50; N.J. Tromp, *Primitive Conceptions of Death and the Nether World in the Old Testament* (BibOr, 21: Rome: Pontifical

(construct *šadmôt*) and its Ugaritic equivalent *šdmt*. In Ugaritic the word occurs in *KTU*^{2} 1.23.10, part of the text dealing with the birth of the gods Shaḥar and Shalem. I here cite it in its context:

1.23 [8] *mt.wšr.yṯb.bdh.ḫṭ.ṯkl.bdh*	Mot-and-Shar sits, having in one hand the staff of bereavement[23] and in the other hand
9 *ḫṭ. ʾulmn.yẓbrnn.ẓbrm.gpn*	the staff of widowhood; the vine-pruners prune him
10 *yṣmdnn.ṣmdm.gpn.yšql.šdmth*	the vine-binders bind him. They fell him on the field
11 *km gpn*	like a vine.

There can be no doubt that *š^{e}dēmôt* is the Hebrew equivalent of Ugaritic *šdmt*. The contexts in which the Hebrew word occurs leave no doubt that it is the same word as Ugaritic *šdmt*: the meaning is clearly something like 'field' and it is even found in close association with the word for vine (*gepen*) in three instances (Deut. 32.32; Isa. 16.8; Hab. 3.17), just as is the case with Ugaritic *šdmt* in the passage cited above. The Old Testament instances of this word are as follows: 'For their vine comes from the vine of Sodom, and from the fields (*šadmôt*) of Gomorrah; their grapes are grapes of poison, their clusters are bitter' (Deut. 32.32); 'For the fields (*šadmôt*) of Heshbon languish, and the vine of Sibmah; the lords of the nations have struck down its branches, which reached to Jazer and strayed to the desert; its shoots spread abroad and passed over the sea' (Isa. 16.8); 'Though the fig trees do not blossom, nor fruit be on the vines, the produce of the olive fail and the fields (*š^{e}dēmôt*) yield no food, the flock be cut off from the fold and there be no herd in the stalls, yet will I rejoice in the Lord, I will joy in the God of my salvation (Hab. 3.17-18); 'The whole valley of the dead bodies and the ashes, and all the fields (*hašš^{e}rēmôt*[24]) as far as the wadi Kidron, to the corner of the Horse Gate toward the east, shall be sacred to the Lord. It shall not be uprooted or overthrown any more for ever' (Jer. 31.40); 'And the king commanded Hilkiah, the chief priest, and the priests of the second order, and the keepers of the threshold, to

Biblical Institute, 1969), p. 53; Mulder, *Kanaänitische Goden*, pp. 68-69.

23. D.T. Tsumura, '"A Ugaritic God, *mt-w-šr*, and his Two Weapons" (UT 52:8-11)', *UF* 6 (1974), pp. 407-13 (409), interestingly reproduces in illustration of this the depiction of an Aramaic magic bowl of the Angel of Death, bearing a sword in one hand and a spear in the other.

24. Read *hašš^{e}dēmôt* with many manuscripts, the *qere* and Aquila.

bring out of the temple of the Lord all the vessels made for Baal, for Asherah, and for all the host of heaven; he burned them outside Jerusalem in the fields (*šadmôt*) of the Kidron, and carried their ashes to Bethel' (2 Kgs 23.4). In addition, there is Isa. 37.27, where the form *š*ᵉ*dēmâ* occurs. This has been traditionally understood as the singular form of *š*ᵉ*dēmôt.* Lehmann noted that both in Isa. 16.8 and Hab. 3.17 *š*ᵉ*dēmôt* has a singular verb and so he held that this is to be regarded as the actual singular form and *š*ᵉ*dēmâ* is a corrupt form based on the misunderstanding that *š*ᵉ*dēmôt* is plural. That *š*ᵉ*dēmâ* is corrupt is supported by the fact that the parallel passage in 2 Kgs 19.26 has *š*ᵉ*dēpâ* and the Qumran Isaiah scroll (1QIsa^{a}) has *hnšdp*. However, Isa. 16.8 and Hab. 3.17 by no means prove that *š*ᵉ*dēmôt* is the singular form of the verb, since in both verses another word intervenes between *š*ᵉ*dēmôt* and the verb.

As the meaning of the word is something like 'field', and since *šd* means 'field' in Ugaritic, and Mot is mentioned in close proximity to *šdmt* in the Ugaritic passage (it is, in fact, his field), it might seem natural to understand the word as a compound, literally, 'field of Mot', with the scholars noted above. However, in view of the fact that the Hebrew equivalent of Ugaritic *šd* has *ś* and not *š* (*śādeh*), we should expect *š*ᵉ*dēmôt* to have *ś* and not *š* if the word 'field' were really contained within it. Philological considerations are therefore against the view that *š*ᵉ*dēmôt* (and likewise its Ugaritic equivalent *šdmt*) means 'field of Mot'.[25]

In *KTU*^{2} 1.6.II.26-37, Anat attacks and destroys Mot, an event which precipitates Baal's resurrection from the dead. The description of her action is as follows:

25. N. Wyatt, 'A New Look at Ugaritic *šdmt*', *JSS* 37 (1992), pp. 149-53, has an original argument, according to which the word means 'shoot' in Ugaritic and most of the Old Testament references except 'field of Mot' in Jer. 31.40 and 2 Kgs 23.4. But it is by no means obvious that the word should be divided into two in this way, and in fact the meaning 'field' fits all the contexts admirably. I have already noted above the philological difficulty in understanding the word to mean 'field of Mot', and in addition it should be pointed out with regard to 2 Kgs 23.4 and Jer. 31.40 that the Molech (not Mot) cult was associated with the valley of Hinnom, not the wadi Kidron. Furthermore, Wyatt's hypothesis that *šdmt* as 'shoot' was a *š* formation derived from *dm* 'blood'→'juice' seems fanciful, since it was only by way of occasional metaphor that *dm* 'blood' ever meant 'juice' in the expressions for wine, *dm. 'ṣm* 'blood of trees' (*KTU*^{2} 1.4.IV.38, etc.) and *dam-*ᵃ*nābîm* and *dam-'ēnāb*, 'blood of grape (s)' (Gen. 49.11; Deut. 32.14).

26 *ym.ymm.y‘tqn.lymm*	A day, days passed,
27 *lyrḫm.rḥm. ‘nt.tngṯh*	verily days, verily months, the damsel Anat sought him.
28 *klb. ’arḫ.l ‘glh.klb*	Like the heart of a heifer for her calf, like the heart
29 *ṯ’at.l’imrh.km.lb*	of a ewe for her lamb, so was the heart of
30 *‘nt. ’aṯr.b‘l.t’iḫd*	Anat after Baal. She seized
31 *bn. ’ilm.mt.bḥrb*	the son of El, Mot, with a cutting blade
32 *tbq‘nn.bḫṯr.tdry*	she split him, with a sieve she winnowed him,
33 *nn.b’išt.tšrpnn*	with fire she burnt him,
34 *brḥm.tṭḥnn.bšd*	with millstones she ground him, in a field
35 *tdr‘.nn.š’irh.lt’ikl*	she sowed him; verily the birds ate
36 *‘ṣrm . mnth.ltkly*[*y*]	the pieces of him, verily the sparrows made an end
37 *npr*[*m*]. *š’ir.lš’ir.yṣḥ*	of the parts of him piece by piece.

As the description shows, the destruction of Mot is no ordinary destruction, since it is clear that the treatment given to him corresponds to that given during the harvesting and sowing of corn. Mot therefore corresponds in some way with the corn, which strongly supports the seasonal interpretation of the Baal text at this point. This has been questioned by some, such as Loewenstamm,[26] but the arguments are unconvincing. The view of Loewenstamm is entirely unnatural in seeking to deny the meaning ‘to sow’ for *dr‘* and reducing its meaning to merely ‘to scatter’.[27] As de Moor writes,[28] ‘the piling up of so many related comparisons in the right agricultural order would hardly be unintentional’.

Loewenstamm and others[29] have held that the description of Mot’s

26. Cf. U. (M.D.) Cassuto, ‘Baal and Mot in the Ugaritic Texts’, *IEJ* 12 (1962), pp. 77-86; S.E. Loewenstamm, ‘The Ugaritic Fertility Myth: The Result of a Mistranslation’, *IEJ* 12 (1962), pp. 87-88; S.E. Loewenstamm, ‘The Ugaritic Fertility Myth: A Reply’, *IEJ* 13 (1963), pp. 130-32; S.E. Loewenstamm, ‘The Killing of Mot in Ugaritic Myth’, *Or* NS 41 (1972), pp. 378-82; P.L. Watson, ‘The Death of “Death” in the Ugaritic Texts’, *JAOS* 92 (1972), pp. 60-64.

27. Cf. A.S. Kapelrud, ‘Baal and Mot in the Ugaritic Texts’, *IEJ* 13 (1963), pp. 127-29; de Moor, *Seasonal Pattern*, pp. 209-15.

28. De Moor, *Seasonal Pattern*, p. 213.

29. Cf. Loewenstamm, ‘Mistranslation’, p. 88; S.E. Loewenstamm, ‘The Making and Destruction of the Golden Calf’, *Bib* 48 (1967), pp. 481-90; S.E. Loewenstamm, ‘The Making and Destruction of the Golden Calf: A Rejoinder’, *Bib* 56 (1975), pp. 330-43; F.C. Fensham, ‘The Burning of the Golden Calf and Ugarit’, *IEJ* 16 (1966), pp. 191-93; O. Hvidberg-Hansen, ‘Die Vernichtung des goldenen Kalbes und der ugaritische Ernteritus’, *AcOr* 33 (1971), pp. 5-46.

destruction here provided the model for the description of Moses' destruction of the golden calf in Exod. 32.20. There we read, 'And he took the calf which they had made, and burnt it with fire, and ground it to powder, and scattered it upon the water, and made the people of Israel drink it'. However, this view is to be rejected since, as others have pointed out,[30] the parallel, on examination, is not very close. Thus, three of the verbs used in the account of the destruction of Mot (*'aḫd*, *bq'* and *'akl*) have no equivalent in the description of the destruction of the golden calf, and two verbs (*dqq* and *hšqh*) used in the latter have no equivalent in the former. Furthermore, *dr'* 'to sow' and *zrh* 'to scatter' are not strictly equivalent. Rather, the description of the destruction of the golden calf has its closest analogues in references to the destruction of cultic objects in the Deuteronomistic history. For example, in 2 Kgs 23.6b we read of Josiah's treatment of the Asherah that 'he burned (*śrp*) it at the wadi Kidron, and beat it to dust (*dqq*)'. Also, the water motif is present, for in 2 Kgs 23.12 we read that the dust of the destroyed altars was cast into the wadi Kidron. It may be safely concluded, therefore, that the description of the destruction of the golden calf does not, as some have held, reflect an early literary pattern employed in the Ugaritic texts to describe the destruction of Mot.

Another Old Testament passage that has been connected with Anat's treatment of Mot is Lev. 2.14. There we read: 'If you offer a cereal offering of first fruits to the Lord, you shall offer for the cereal offering of your first fruits crushed new grain from fresh ears, parched with fire'. We have here a ritual treatment of the first sheaf, which a number of scholars[31] have compared with Anat's attack on Mot when she treated him as corn. Besides threshing, winnowing, grinding and sowing, the verb *šrp* is also used of her action towards him and a number of scholars translate this as 'to parch' and relate it to Lev. 2.14. However, it is to be noted that Anat's action relates to the last sheaf, whereas Lev. 2.14 is concerned with the first sheaf. Dussaud and Gray[32] hold that in earlier times in Israel this may have applied to the last sheaf also, but any such connection between Anat's action and Lev. 2.14 is ruled out

30. Cf. L.G. Perdue, 'The Making and Destruction of the Golden Calf: A Reply', *Bib* 54 (1973), pp. 237-46, for a detailed refutation.

31. E.g. R. Dussaud, 'La mythologie phénicienne d'après les tablettes de Ras Shamra', *RHR* 104 (1931), pp. 353-408 (388); Gray, *Legacy of Canaan*, p. 68.

32. Dussaud, 'La mythologie phénicienne', p. 388; Gray, *Legacy of Canaan*, p. 68.

on philological grounds, since whereas in Lev. 2.14 the verb *qlh* 'to parch' is used, the verb used of Anat's action, *šrp*, can only mean 'to burn' and not 'to parch'. The burning of Mot probably refers to the burning of the waste straw and chaff.[33]

Resheph

The worship of the god Resheph was remarkably widespread in the ancient world. It is found not only in Palestine and Syria, including such places as Ugarit and Ebla, but also in Egypt, North Africa, Cyprus and Cilicia. A surprisingly large literature has grown up around this god,[34] which partly reflects the widespread nature of his cult and partly

33. In these conclusions I agree with de Moor, *Seasonal Pattern*, p. 210. De Moor's view has the advantage that the burning comes in the right place in the order. As he writes (p. 210), 'Threshing and winnowing produce three things: grain for milling, grain for sowing, and waste (straw, chaff, weeds). The latter was burnt in the Orient' (he cites G. Dalman, *Arbeit und Sitte in Palästina*, II [7 vols. in 8 parts; Gütersloh: C. Bertelsmann, 1932], pp. 145-46, and III [1933], pp. 133, 137-38). However, J.F. Healey, 'Burning the Corn: New Light on the Killing of Mōtu', *Or* 52 (1983), pp. 248-51 (249), objects that the text states that 'she burnt him', but this is hardly decisive, since the chaff was clearly part of the corn (Mot). Healey suggests two alternative ways of understanding the reference to burning, based on G. Hillman's ethnographic research on traditional farming techniques in northern and eastern Turkey, and referred to in the latter's article, 'Reconstructing Crop Husbandry Practices', in R. Mercer (ed.), *Farming Practice in British Prehistory* (Edinburgh: Edinburgh University Press, 1981), pp. 123-62, neither of which involves the destruction of the corn. 'In one procedure whole sheaves would be burnt as a substitute for primary threshing and winnowing, immediately after reaping. This dries the material, gets rid of gross waste (stalks, etc.) and renders the husks brittle so that the grains can be pounded or rubbed free and then winnowed if necessary. In the alternative procedure, which is less efficient and much less common, the sheaves are threshed first, the waste is removed by winnowing and then the spikelets are burnt with straw in order to render the husks brittle' (Healey, 'Burning the Corn', p. 250). Because of the rarity of the latter, Healey prefers the former alternative, though he admits that in that case the order of Anat's actions will not be systematic. In my view this suggests an advantage for de Moor's explanation cited above.

34. Among the contributions are the following: M. Barré, '[d]LAMMA and Rešep at Ugarit: The Hittite Connection', *JAOS* 98 (1978), pp. 465-67; A. Caquot, 'Sur quelques démons de l'Ancien Testament: Reshef, Qeteb, Deber', *Sem* 6 (1956), pp. 53-68; D. Conrad, 'Der Gott Reshef', *ZAW* 83 (1971), pp. 157-83; I. Cornelius, *The Iconography of the Canaanite Gods Reshef and Ba'al* (OBO, 140; Fribourg:

the uncertainties to which it has given rise. It used to be thought that he might be a weather and fertility god,[35] but this is now seen to be a misunderstanding. It is clear rather that he was an underworld god, whose arrows brought plague and pestilence.[36] He was equated with the Mesopotamian underworld and plague god Nergal at Ugarit (*KTU*² 1.47.27; 1.118.26 = *Ugaritica* V, 18A.26) and brought pestilence on one of Keret's family (*KTU*² 1.141.1.18-19). In keeping with his being an underworld god we read that he was the sun goddess's gatekeeper (*KTU*²

University Press; Göttingen: Vandenhoeck & Ruprecht, 1994), and 'The Iconography of the Cannanite Gods Reshef and Baal: A Rejoinder', *JNSL* 24.2 (1998), pp. 167-77; M.J. Dahood and G. Pettinato, 'Ugaritic *ršp gn* and Eblaite *Rasap gunu(m)*', *Or* NS 46 (1977) pp. 230-32; J. Day, 'New Light on the Mythological Background of the Allusion to Resheph in Habakkuk iii 5', *VT* 29 (1979), pp. 353-55; G.R. Driver, 'Ugaritic Problems', in S. Segert (ed.), *Studia Semitica philologica necnon philosophica Ioanni Bakoš dicata* (Bratislava: Vydavatel'stvo Slovenskej akadémie vied, 1965), pp. 95-110 (esp. 96-98); R. Giveon, 'Reshep in Egypt', *JEA* 66 (1980), pp. 144-50; B. Grdseloff, *Les débuts du culte de Rechef en Egypte* (Cairo: Impr. de l'Institut français d'archéologie orientale, 1942); E. Lipiński, 'Resheph Amyklos', in E. Lipiński (ed.), *Phoenicia and the East Mediterranean in the First Millennium B.C.* (Studia Phoenicia, 5; Leuven: Peeters, 1987), pp. 87-99; P. Matthiae, 'Note sul dio siriano Rešef', *OrAnt* 2 (1963), pp. 27-42; J.F.A. Sawyer and F.R. Stephenson, 'Literary and Astronomical Evidence for a Total Eclipse of the Sun Observed in Ancient Ugarit on 3 May 1375 B.C.', *BSO(A)S* 33 (1970), pp. 467-89; M.K. Schretter, *Alter Orient und Hellas: Fragen der Beeinflussung griechischen Gedankengutes aus altorientalischen Quellen, dargestellt an den Göttern Nergal, Rescheph, Apollon* (Innsbrucker Beiträge zur Kulturwissenschaft, 33; Innsbruck: Institut für Sprachwissenschaft der Universität Innsbruck, 1974); W.K. Simpson, 'New Light on the God Reshef', *JAOS* 73 (1953), pp. 86-89; W.K. Simpson, 'Reshep in Egypt', *Or* 29 (1960), pp. 63-74; F. Vattioni, 'Il dio Resheph', *AION* NS 15 (1965), pp. 39-74; A. van den Branden, 'Le dieu Rešeph et ses épithètes', *Parole de l'Orient* 2 (1971), pp. 389-416; A. van den Branden, '"Rešeph" nella Bibbia', *Bibbia e Oriente* 13 (1971), pp. 211-25; Y. Yadin, 'New Gleanings on Resheph from Ugarit', in A. Kort and S. Morschauer (eds.), *Biblical and Related Studies Presented to Samuel Iwry* (Winona Lake, IN: Eisenbrauns, 1985), pp. 259-74; P. Xella, 'Le dieu Rashap à Ugarit', *Les Annales Archéologiques Arabes Syriennes* 29-30 (1979–80), pp. 145-62; P. Xella, 'D'Ugarit à la Phénicie: Sur les traces de Rashap, Horon, Eshmun', *WO* 19 (1988), pp. 45-64; P. Xella; 'Resheph', *DDD*, cols. 1324-30 (2nd edn, pp. 700-703); F. Pomponio, 'Adamma paredra di Rasap', *SEL* 10 (1993), pp. 3-7. The best overall survey hitherto is W.J. Fulco, *The Canaanite God Rešep* (AOS, 8; New Haven: American Oriental Society, 1976).

35. Most recently defended by Conrad, 'Der Gott Reschef'.

36. See most decisively, Fulco, *The Canaanite God Rešep*.

1.78.2-4), that is, he guarded the entrance to the netherworld when the sun went down into it. Various of the above-mentioned features—association with plague, underworld, arrows and plurality of Reshephs—are found in the Old Testament allusions, as will be seen below.

Passages where Resheph(s) is/are Demon(s) of Plague

Habakkuk 3.5

> 5 Before him went Pestilence (*deber*)
> and Plague (*rešep*) followed close behind.

These words occur as part of Yahweh's theophany in which he comes up from the south (vv. 2-7) prior to engaging in conflict with the chaos waters (vv. 8-15). Both *deber* and *rešep*, rendered here respectively 'Pestilence' and 'Plague', appear to be personified, and form as it were angelic or perhaps rather demonic accompaniers of Yahweh. Although in previous centuries *rešep* was sometimes rendered otherwise (cf. AV 'burning coals, RV 'fiery bolts'), the combination of the fact that Resheph was a plague god and the parallelism with *deber*, 'pestilence', leaves no doubt that *rešep* is here the personified Plague.

As I have pointed out earlier,[37] it is attractive to suppose that Resheph's presence here derives from the Canaanite mythology embodied in a Ugaritic text *KTU*^{2} 1.82 (= *PRU* II.1).

> 1 [ ] *mḫṣ.b'l* [ ]*y. tnn. wygl. wynsk. 'd*[ ]
> 2 [ ]*y. l'arṣ* [*.'i*]*dy. 'alt. l'aḥš. 'idy. 'alt. 'in ly*
> 3 []*b/dt. b'l. ḥẓ. ršp. bn.km. yr. klyth. wlbh*

> 1 Baal smote…the dragon and rejoiced and poured out…
> 2 …on the earth…throne…I have no throne
> 3 …the archer Resheph…shot his kidneys and his heart.

It will be noted that in addition to *rešep*, *deber* 'Plague' is also personified in Hab. 3. 5. Does a god lie behind this too? Possibly, since *dabí-ir* is attested as the name of the patron god at Ebla (^{d}*da-bí-ir* dingir-*eb-la*^{ki}), though there is uncertainty as to his identification.[38] The idea of

37. J. Day, 'New Light on the Mythological Background of the Allusion to Resheph in Habakkuk III 5', *VT* 29 (1979), pp. 353-55.

38. The Eblaite text is TM.75.G.1464 v.XI 12'-18'. For various views on this deity, see A. Archi, 'Diffusione del culto di ^{d}NI-da-kul', *Studi Eblaiti* 1 (1979), pp. 105-13 (105 n. 2); G. Pettinato, *The Archives of Ebla* (ET; Garden City, NY: Doubleday, 1981), pp. 245, 247, and M.J. Dahood's comments in the 'Afterword:

a leading god being accompanied by two bodyguards is attested elsewhere in the ancient Near East. Most often cited is the case of Adad in the Gilgamesh epic, tablet 11, lines 98-100:

> Inside it Adad thunders,
> While Shullat and Ḫanish go in front,
> Moving as heralds over hill and plain.[39]

Other examples of a twofold bodyguard for gods are also attested.[40]

Psalm 78.48 and 49

> 48 He gave over their cattle to the pestilence[41]
> and their flocks to the plague (*r*ᵉ*šāpîm*).
> 49 He let loose on them his fierce anger,
> wrath, indignation, and distress,
> a company of destroying angels.

With regard to v. 48 there is a division amongst scholars as to whether one should retain the MT reading *labbārād* and translate 'he

Ebla, Ugarit, and the Bible', in Pettinato, *The Archives of Ebla*, pp. 271-321 (296); F. Pomponio and P. Xella, *Les Dieux d'Ebla* (AOAT, 245; Münster: Ugarit-Verlag, 1997), pp. 123-24.

39. Cf. *ANET*, p. 94. On Shullat and Ḫanish see I.J. Gelb, 'Šullat and Ḫaniš', *ArOr* 18 (1950), pp. 189-98.

40. For examples, see T.H. Gaster, 'Demon, Demonology', *IDB*, I, pp. 817-24 (819). However, de Moor is incorrect in claiming a more direct cuneiform parallel in which Plague and Pestilence allegedly march at the side of Marduk (*The Rise of Yahwism*, p. 134 n. 154 [2nd edn, p. 203 n. 490]), citing J. Hehn, *Hymnen und Gebete an Marduk* (Beiträge zur Assyriologie, 5; Leipzig: J.C. Hinrichs, 1905), p. 314, lines 4-5. I am grateful to Professor W.G. Lambert, who has recently collated the tablet (BM 99173) and in a private communication offers the following translation (reverse, lines 3-5):

> Praiseworthy prince, the gazelles [fa]ll in your net. On your right [march…]
> on your left Erragal, the most mighty of the gods,
> in front of you the Sibitti, the valiant gods, [behind you…],
> right and left the Fire-god burns, where you are angry […].

As will be seen there is no reference to Pestilence here. Further, Lambert writes: 'Erragal is a name of Erra, who is identified with Nergal, and is a god of plague, but since the text stresses his might, that is what is to be taken from this context. This is confirmed by the Sibitti (Pleiades) being called "valiant". It fits a hymn of praise: Marduk advances escorted by minor gods.'

41. Reading *laddeber* 'to the pestilence' for MT *labbārād* 'to the hail' with one Hebrew manuscript and Symmachus. See discussion in main body of the text.

gave over their cattle to the *hail* and their flocks to the thunderbolts', or emend *labbārād* to *laddeber* and render 'He gave over their cattle to the *pestilence*, and their flocks to the plague'. In favour of the latter is not simply the fact that *rešep* and *deber* occur in parallel in Hab. 3.5; there is also the significant point, seldom noted, that Psalm 78 confines itself to the plagues listed in the J account in Exodus, but as the MT stands, we lack an equivalent to the one contained in Exod. 9.1-7, the cattle plague, whereas on the reading *laddeber* all seven J plagues are paralleled, including that in Exod. 9.1-7 (cf. *deber*, Exod. 9.3). The corruption *labbārād* could easily have taken place, especially as *babbārād* occurs in the previous verse (v. 47). Another reason for reading *laddeber* instead of *labbārād* is the parallel with v. 50: v. 50 has *laddeber hisgîr* 'he gave over to the pestilence', which would cohere better with v. 48 if we read *wayyasgēr laddeber* 'and he gave over to the pestilence'.

A further interesting point is to be found in v. 49. The end of this verse alludes to Yahweh's destroying angels. Since it is clear that Resheph in the Old Testament still retains something of its personalized mythological background, it is possible that the destroying or evil angels are another allusion to the *rešāpîm*, the Resheph demons or 'sons of Resheph' (Job 5.7) bringing pestilence.[42]

Job 5.7

> For man is born to trouble and the sons of Resheph fly upwards.

These words are part of Eliphaz's first speech, and there are three main ways in which 'the sons of Resheph' in this verse have been understood:

(i) Because of *rešep*'s fiery associations (cf. Cant. 8.6), it has been suggested that we render 'but man is born for trouble as the sparks fly upward'. This view is followed by S.R. Driver and G.B. Gray, H.H. Rowley, M.H. Pope (possibly), and R. Gordis (possibly), as well as the RSV and NRSV.[43] But whilst there is evidence that *rešep* can mean

42. Resheph appears in the plural also in Ugaritic, cf. *KTU*² 1.91.11, *t'rbn. ršpm* 'the Reshephs enter'. In addition, there is an Egyptian text referring to the chariot-warriors of Rameses III being 'as mighty as Reshephs' (W.F. Edgerton and J.A. Wilson, *Historical Records of Ramses III: The Texts in Medinet Habu* [Chicago: University of Chicago Press, 1936], p. 24), but it is debated whether this really attests a plurality of Resheph deities. Cf. Fulco, *The Canaanite God Rešep*, p. 18 n. 91.

43. Driver and Gray, *The Book of Job*, p. 52; Rowley, *Job*, pp. 53-54; Pope, *Job*,

'plague' or 'arrow' in biblical Hebrew, there is no place where 'flame' or 'spark' is the certain meaning (even though the former may be the ultimate etymological root meaning).

(ii) A second view sees here an allusion to birds. This goes back to some of the ancient versions: LXX has νεοσσοὶ δὲ γυπὸς, Aquila υἱοὶ πτηνοῦ, Symmachus τὰ τέκνα τῶν πετεινῶν, Syriac *bny 'wp'*, and Vulgate *avis*. In modern times it has been followed by the NEB, and such scholars as E.(P.) Dhorme, G. Hölscher, N. Tur-Sinai, and F. Horst.[44] However, nothing about the god Resheph can explain how *rešep* might come to mean 'bird', and it seems clear that this was a later misunderstanding encouraged by the reference to flying in this verse.[45]

(iii) A third view sees a mythological allusion here, an interpretation followed by T.H. Gaster, N.C. Habel, R. Gordis (possibly), M.H. Pope (possibly), and D.J.A. Clines.[46] It has the advantage that it conforms with the association of Resheph with pestilence or the underworld which dominates the Old Testament allusions elsewhere (cf. Hab. 3.5; Ps. 78.48; Deut. 32.24; Ps. 91.5 [implicit]; Cant. 8.6), which in turn agrees with what we know of the Canaanite god Resheph; also the reference to the flying of the sons of Resheph calls to mind the flying of Resheph's implied pestilential arrow in Ps. 91.5 and the Canaanite god Resheph, whose epithets in Phoenician *ršp ḥṣ* 'Resheph of the arrow' and Ugaritic *b'l ḥẓ. ršp* 'the archer Resheph', surely refer to his pestilential function.

Another advantage of this view is that it also coheres so well with the

p. 43; R. Gordis, *The Book of Job* (New York: Jewish Theological Seminary, 1978), p. 55.

44. E. (P.) Dhorme, *Le Livre de Job* (Etudes Bibliques; Paris. V. Lecoffre, 1926), p. 56; ET *A Commentary on the Book of Job* (trans. H. Knight; London: T. Nelson, 1967), pp. 61-62; G. Hölscher, *Das Buch Hiob* (HAT, 17; Tübingen: J.C.B. Mohr [Paul Siebeck], 2nd edn, 1952), pp. 18-19; N. Tur-Sinai, *The Book of Job* (ET; Jerusalem: Kiryath Sepher, rev. edn, 1967), pp. 97-98; F. Horst, *Hiob* (BKAT, 16; Neukirchen–Vluyn: Neukirchener Verlag, 3rd edn, 1974), pp. 81-82.

45. Although it was sometimes thought in the past that the epithet *ršp ṣprm* in the Karatepe inscription (*KAI* 26.II.10-11) indicated a connection between Resheph and birds, the corresponding hieroglyphic Hittite version of the text depicts a stag or some other antlered animal, so this view is now generally rejected.

46. Gaster, *Myth, Legend, and Custom*, p. 789; Pope, *Job*, p. 43; N.C. Habel, *The Book of Job* (CBC; Cambridge: Cambridge University Press, 1975), p. 32 and Gordis, *The Book of Job*, p. 55; D.J.A. Clines, *Job 1–20* (WBC, 17; Dallas: Word Books, 1989), p. 142.

preceding verse, especially if we phrase this in the form of a question (a proposal never previously made), since Resheph was an underworld deity (or for the book of Job, a demon), and *'āpār* in v. 6 can denote the underworld (cf. 17.16):

> For does not affliction come from the dust
> and does not trouble sprout from the ground?
> For man is born to trouble
> and the sons of Resheph fly upwards [from the underworld].

Just as 'the firstborn of death' brings pestilence in Job 18.13, 'By disease his skin is consumed, the firstborn of death consumes his limbs', so here in Job 5.7 'the sons of [the underworld demon] Resheph' bring pestilence.

Deuteronomy 32.24

> They shall be smitten[47] with hunger, and fought[48] by plague and poisonous pestilence;
> and I will send the teeth of beasts against them,
> with venom of crawling things of the dust.

From the context it is clear that here again *rešep* alludes to plague (cf. parallelism with 'poisonous pestilence', *m^{e}zê qeṭeb*). From the preceding verse it is clear that it is sent by Yahweh. The question may be raised, is it simply impersonal plague or is there a demonic reference here? Although not certain, the latter is surely possible, since there clearly seems to be an element of personification in all the other pestilential *rešep* allusions (Hab. 3.5; Ps. 78.48 [cf. 49]; Job 5.7). The use of the verb *lḥm* 'fight' in connection with *rešep*, as noted in the footnote, also seems to be an echo of the mythological archer god Resheph (cf. reference to 'arrows' in v. 23).

47. See J.C. Greenfield, 'Smitten by Famine, Battered by Plague (Deuteronomy 32:24)', in Marks and Good (eds.), *Love & Death in the Ancient Near East*, pp. 151-52, esp. p. 152.

48. *ûl^{e}ḥumê rešep* has often been translated 'and devoured (lit. 'eaten') by plague', but the other meaning of the root *lḥm*, 'to fight, battle', seems more appropriate in connection with *rešep*, given the nature of the god Resheph as a warrior archer. Cf. Caquot, 'Sur quelques démons', p. 59 nn. 1 and 2; Fulco, *The Canaanite God Rešep*, p. 56; Greenfield, 'Smitten by Famine', pp. 151-52, esp. 152 (Greenfield prefers 'battered' rather than 'battled').

Resheph Demythologized with Reference to Love's Arrows, but Retaining an Awareness of the Underlying Mythological Background

Song of Songs 8.6-7

6 Set me as a seal upon your heart,
as a seal upon your arm;
for love is strong as death,
jealousy is cruel as the grave.
Its arrows (*rᵉšāpêhā*) are arrows of (*rišpê*) fire,
a most vehement flame.
7 Many waters cannot quench love,
neither can floods drown it.
If a man offered for love
all the wealth of his house,
it would be utterly scorned.

These words are spoken by the woman to her lover, and the passage commencing 'for love is strong as death…' has been claimed to be the climax of the Song of Songs. We may accept this as true, even though we should not accept M.H. Pope's claim[49] that this verse provides any evidence for his view that the Song of Songs had its setting in a cultic *Marzēaḥ* ceremony in which allegedly mourning for the dead and sexual licentiousness were combined.

Resheph occurs in the plural in Cant. 8.6 as follows: 'Its arrows (*rᵉšāpêhā*) are arrows of (*rišpê*) fire'. The plural of *rešep* clearly does not allude *literally* to the Resheph gods or demons, nor does it refer *literally* to plague, unlike the passages considered above (Hab. 3.5; Ps. 78.48; probably Job 5.7), as the term is applied analogically to love. Modern scholars have suggested either 'arrows/darts/shafts',[50] 'flashes',[51] or 'sparks',[52] or 'Gluten' (= 'glows, fires')[53] as the

49. Pope, *Song of Songs*, p. 226.

50. O. Keel, *Das Hohelied* (Zürcher Bibelkommentare; Zürich: Theologischer Verlag, 1986), p. 245, renders 'arrows' (*Pfeile*); Pope, *Song of Songs*, p. 653 and Fox, *Song of Songs*, p. 167, translate 'darts'; R.E. Murphy, *The Song of Songs* (Hermeneia; Minneapolis, MN: Fortress Press, 1990), p. 190, understands it as 'shafts'.

51. R. Gordis, *The Song of Songs and Lamentations* (New York: Ktav, rev. edn, 1974), p. 74; M.D. Goulder, *The Song of Fourteen Songs* (JSOTSup, 36; Sheffield: Sheffield Academic Press, 1986), p. 65.

52. F. Landy, *Paradoxes of Paradise: Identity and Difference in the Song of Songs* (Bible and Literature Series, 7; Sheffield: Almond Press, 1983), p. 121.

53. W. Rudolph, *Das Buch Ruth—Das Hohe Lied—Die Klagelieder* (KAT,

best translation. However, of these, only the meaning 'arrows' is clearly attested elsewhere in the Old Testament, in Ps. 76.4 (ET 3), where we read of *rišpê-qāšet* 'arrows of the bow' literally 'Reshephs of the bow'. The underlying image derives ultimately from the fact that the god Resheph was noted for his arrows, and its reutilization in connection with love reminds one of the classical allusions to Cupid's or Eros' arrows.

Fulco is right to say that Resheph(s) is here demythologized.[54] However, unlike Ps. 76.4 (ET 3)—on which see below—this passage does still manifest an awareness of the underlying mythological background. So far as I am aware, surprisingly only N.J. Tromp[55] has hitherto pointed to the fact that a comparison of love with Resheph (or the Reshephs) is thematically appropriate in this verse, since Resheph was an underworld god, which fits the declaration 'love is strong as death' (though Tromp inconsistently also associates Resheph with lightning here). We may compare Hos. 13.14, where Sheol/death has its plagues (from *deber*) and destruction (from *qeṭeb*), words elsewhere connected with *rešep* (cf. Deut. 32.24; Hab. 3.5; Ps. 78.49). The phrase 'strong as death' also has a mythological background, for we read that 'Mot was strong' (*mt. 'z*) in the Ugaritic texts (*KTU*[2] 1.6.VI.17-18, 20), as has been noted earlier. The references to 'mighty waters' (*mayim rabbîm*) and 'floods' (*n*[e]*hārôt*) in Cant. 8.7 and their inability to quench love also have a mythical background, for elsewhere in the Old Testament it is Yahweh who overcomes the waters, and in Ugaritic mythology it is Baal. Possibly, the fact that *rešep* accompanies Yahweh in his battle against the 'mighty waters' or 'floods' in Hab. 3.5 (cf. vv. 8 and 15 for *n*[e]*hārîm* and *mayim rabbîm*) lies behind this imagery (and ultimately Resheph's accompaniment of Baal against the dragon at Ugarit, noted above).

17.1-3; Gütersloh: Gerd Mohn, 1962), p. 179; G. Gerleman, *Ruth—Das Hohelied* (BKAT, 18; Neukirchen–Vluyn: Neukirchener Verlag, 1965), p. 216; G. Krinetzki, *Kommentar zum Hohenlied* (Beiträge zur biblischen Exegese und Theologie, 16; Frankfurt am Main: Peter Lang, 1981), p. 218.

54. Fulco, *The Canaanite God Rešep*, p. 60.

55. N.J. Tromp, 'Wisdom and the Canticle. Ct., 8, 6[c]-7[b]: Text, Character, Message and Import', in M. Gilbert (ed.), *La Sagesse de l'Ancien Testament* (BETL, 51; Gembloux: J. Duculot; Leuven: Leuven University Press, 1979), pp. 88-95 (90).

Passage where Resheph is Totally Demythologized
Psalm 76.4 (ET 3)

> There he broke the arrows of (*rišpê*) the bow,
> the shield, the sword, and the weapons of war.

This is the Old Testament passage in which the god Resheph has been most clearly and totally demythologized. This verse is part of one of the Zion psalms and speaks of Yahweh's victory over the forces which attack Jerusalem. The reference must clearly be to arrows, and the fact that a series of human weapons are mentioned alongside them indicates that they must likewise be human arrows and not the plague-bringing arrows that are associated with Resheph elsewhere. Clearly the origin of the expression is in the god Resheph, whose arrows caused plague (cf. Phoenician *ršp ḥṣ* 'Resheph of the arrow'[56]), but in this Hebrew psalm the divine name in the plural has been totally demythologized so as to refer simply to human arrows of war.

Other Allusions to Resheph without Explicit Mention of the Name
Psalm 91.5-6

> 5 You will not fear the terror of the night,
> nor the arrow that flies by day,
> 6 nor the pestilence that stalks in darkness,
> nor the plague that wastes at noonday.

Although it has sometimes been supposed that 'the arrow that flies by day' alludes to the literal arrow of warfare,[57] it has rightly been held by others that this is an allusion to the arrow of a pestilence-causing demon.[58] Unlike other psalms in which the individual is confronted by enemies, the foes appear to be not human but the malignant forces that cause plague and pestilence. In support of this interpretation we may also note the reference to 'deadly pestilence' (*deber hawwôt*) in v. 3 and the 'scourge' (*nega'*) of v. 10.

56. *KAI* 32.3-4.

57. E.g. A.R. Johnson, *The Cultic Prophet and Israel's Psalmody* (Cardiff: University of Wales Press, 1979), pp. 187-88.

58. E.g. W.O.E. Oesterley, *The Psalms*, II (2 vols.; London: SPCK, 1939), pp. 409-10; Gaster, 'Demon, Demonology', p. 820; H.-J. Kraus, *Psalmen*, II (BKAT, 15.2; 2 vols.; Neukirchen–Vluyn: Neukirchener Verlag, 5th edn, 1978), p. 806; ET *Psalms 60–150* (trans. H.C. Oswald; Minneapolis: Augsburg, 1989), p. 223. In addition, those equating the demonic force more precisely with Resheph should be included here (see next footnote).

We can probably be more precise in our interpretation of v. 5. As mentioned earlier, Resheph as a god was noted for his arrows, and the terms employed for 'pestilence' and 'plague' in v. 6, *deber* and *qeṭeb*, are elsewhere used alongside *rešep* or *r*ᵉ*šāpîm* (Deut. 32.34; Ps. 78.48 [emended]; Hab. 3.5). It therefore seems very likely that the allusion in v. 5 to 'the arrow that flies by day' is to Resheph as a bringer of pestilence.[59] Probably Resheph is thought of as a plague demon, as in some Old Testament passages considered above. There is no evidence to support the view that it is sunstroke which is in mind (cf. Ps. 121.6).[60]

Interestingly, the demonic understanding of this passage was not forgotten by later Judaism. The rabbis understood the psalm as 'A song for plague spirits' (*b. Šebu.* 15b) to be used to avert demonic attacks.[61] Further, the Targum saw v. 5 as referring to 'the arrow of the death angel', and in v. 6 the LXX implies that *yāšûd* was read as *w*ᵉ*šēd* 'and a demon'. The Midrash on the Psalms states that 'there is a harmful spirit that flies like a bird, and shoots like an arrow'.

Job 18.13-14

> 13 By disease his skin is consumed,[62]
> the first-born of death consumes his limbs

59. Most confidently asserted by Fulco, *The Canaanite God Rešep*, p. 59. So far as I am aware, this was first suggested as a possibility by Dahood, *Psalms*, II, p. 331; also O. Keel, *Die Welt der altorientalischen Bildsymbolik und das Alte Testament: Am Beispiel der Psalmen* (Zürich: Benziger Verlag; Neukirchen–Vluyn: Neukirchener Verlag, 1972), pp. 73-74; ET *The Symbolism of the Biblical World* (New York: Seabury Press, 1978), pp. 84-85. Dahood, it should be noted, offers also the alternative possibility that the reference is to the hunter's arrow.

60. Suggested as a possibility by H. Gunkel, *Die Psalmen* (Göttinger Handkommentar zum Alten Testament; Göttingen: Vandenhoeck & Ruprecht, 1926), p. 404; A.A. Anderson, *Psalms*, II (NCB; 2 vols.; London: Oliphants, 1972), p. 657.

61. See P. Hugger, *Jahwe meine Zuflucht: Gestalt und Theologie des 91. Psalms* (Münsterschwarzacher Studien, 13; Münsterschwarzach: Vier-Türme-Verlag, 1971), pp. 331-33.

62. Reading *yē'ākēl bid*ᵉ*way 'ôrô* 'by disease his skin is consumed', instead of MT's *yō'kal baddê 'ôrô* 'it consumes the limbs of his skin', which is meaningless. Moreover, the repetition of 'limbs' in this verse in the MT is not good, and the emendation restores better parallelism with the second half of the verse. Also, it may be noted that the passive *yē'ākēl* is supported by the LXX and the Peshiṭta. The above emendation was first proposed by G.H.B. Wright, *The Book of Job* (London: Williams & Norgate, 1883), p. 165, and has been widely followed.

14 He is torn from the tent in which he trusted
and is brought to the king of terrors.

In these verses we have part of Bildad's second speech, in which he describes the fate of the wicked. There is disagreement about the precise mythological background of 'the first-born of death' in v. 13. Some scholars think that the reference is to Mot's first-born,[63] but nowhere in the Ugaritic texts do we hear of Mot's having children. Even more problematic is the suggestion of M.H. Pope, N.C. Habel and N. Wyatt[64] that we render instead 'the first-born Death', since although we know that Mot was the son of El, nowhere is he described as his first-born.

Others believe that the background in this instance is to be sought in Mesopotamian mythology.[65] Namtar, the god of plague, was the son and vizier of Ereshkigal, the queen of the underworld, and since we know that in Mesopotamian mythology, the first-born, if male, was generally the vizier of his parent, it follows that Namtar was very likely Ereshkigal's first-born.

This does seem the most illuminating parallel to Job 18.13. It is true that other mythological allusions in Job seem to reflect a Canaanite rather than a Mesopotamian background. Perhaps the Mesopotamian idea had already influenced the Canaanite mythology on which Job drew. It should be noted that Ereshkigal's husband was Nergal, the god of the underworld, and we know that Nergal in turn was equated with the Canaanite god Resheph. That plague should be personified as the first-born of Resheph then coheres with the fact that the book of Job elsewhere speaks of 'the sons of Resheph' as bringing disaster (Job 5.7), and since Resheph or the Reshephs is/are elsewhere connected with pestilence (e.g. Hab. 3.5; Ps. 78.48; Deut. 32.34), this may well be the case in Job 18.13.

63. N.M. Sarna, 'The Mythological Background of Job 18', *JBL* 82 (1963), pp. 315-18.

64. Pope, *Job*, pp. 132, 135; N.C. Habel, *The Book of Job* (OTL; London: SCM Press, 1985), pp. 280-81; N. Wyatt, 'The Expression *b^ekôr māwet* in Job XVIII 13 and its Mythological Background', *VT* 40 (1990), pp. 207-16.

65. First proposed by E.(P.) Dhorme, 'Le séjour des morts chez les Babyloniens et les Hébreux', *RB* NS 4 (1907), pp. 59-78 (65); *idem*, *Le Livre de Job*, p. 240; ET, *A Commentary on the Book of Job*, p. 265; defended most strongly recently by J.B. Burns, 'The Identity of Death's First-born (Job XVIII 13)', *VT* 37 (1987), pp. 362-64.

Molech

Molech a God, not a Sacrifice

Until 1935 all scholars accepted that Molech in the Old Testament (Lev. 18.21, 20.2-5; 2 Kgs 23.10; Jer. 23.35; cf. Isa. 30.33, 57.9; Jer. 7.31, 10.5; perhaps Zeph. 1.5) was the name of a god. Although there was a disagreement as to the god's identity, no one disputed that it was a divine name. In 1935, however, Otto Eissfeldt[66] wrote a short book in which he argued that Hebrew *mōlek* is not a divine name but rather the name of a sacrifice, just as *molk* occurs as a sacrificial term in Punic inscriptions, and several other scholars have followed this view.[67] Although it has occasionally been supposed that Punic *molk* is not a sacrificial term, but the word for 'king',[68] the latter is inappropriate in a number of contexts.[69]

However, whilst Punic *molk* definitely is a sacrifice, Eissfeldt's view that Hebrew *mōlek* is a sacrificial term rather than a divine name is certainly incorrect, and has been widely criticized.[70] First, Lev. 20.5 refers to those 'who follow him in playing the harlot after *mōlek*', and

66. O. Eissfeldt, *Molk als Opferberiff im Punischen und Hebräischen und das Ende des Gottes Moloch* (Beiträge zur Religionsgeschichte des Altertums, 4; Halle: Niemeyer, 1935).

67. Eissfeldt's view has been followed by such scholars as R. Dussaud, review of *Molk als Opferberiff im Punischen und Hebräischen und das Ende der Gottes Moloch*, by O. Eissfeldt, in *Syria* 16 (1935), pp. 407-409, and R. Dussaud, *Les origines cananéennes du sacrifice israélite* (Paris: E. Leroux, 2nd edn, 1941), pp. 352-54 (though in his review of Eissfeldt's book in *AfO* 11 [1936], pp. 167-68, he concedes that in *some* places the redactors have made Molech a god, e.g. Lev. 20.5); Albright, *Yahweh and the Gods of Canaan*, pp. 205-206 (though cf. his book *Archaeology and the Religion of Israel*, pp. 156-58, for a more nuanced presentation of his view); L.E. Stager and S.R. Wolff, 'Child Sacrifice at Carthage: Religious Rite or Population Control?' *BARev* 10.1 (1984), pp. 31-51 (47).

68. E.g. Weinfeld, 'Worship of Molech', pp. 135-40; Cooper, 'Divine Names', p. 446.

69. See J. Day, *Molech*, pp. 4-7 for details.

70. Cf. A. Bea, 'Kinderopfer für Moloch oder für Jahwe?', *Bib* 18 (1937), pp. 95-107; A. Jirku, 'Gab es im Alten Testament einen Gott Molek (Melek)?', *ARW* 35 (1938), pp. 178-79; W. Kornfeld, 'Der Moloch: Eine Untersuchung zur Theorie O. Eissfeldts', *WZMK* 51 (1952), pp. 287-313; K. Dronkert, *De Molochdienst in het Oude Testament* (Leiden: Drukkerij 'Luctor et Emergo', 1953); G.C. Heider, *The Cult of Molek: A Reassessment* (JSOTSup, 43; Sheffield: JSOT Press, 1985); J. Day, *Molech*, pp. 9-13.

whilst the Old Testament often speaks of the Israelites playing the harlot after pagan deities (e.g. Exod. 34.15, 16; Lev. 17.7; Deut. 31.16; Judg. 2.17, 8.33), we never hear of people playing the harlot after a sacrifice. Secondly, other verbs employed in connection with the Molech cult (hiphil of *‘br* ‘to offer up, devote’, *ntn* ‘to give’, *śrp* ‘to burn’) are well attested elsewhere with *l*^{e} + the divine name, but never occurs with *l*^{e} + a sacrificial term alone.

Another view to be rejected is the idea that *mōlek* was originally a sacrificial term but the Old Testament writers later came to misunderstand it as a divine name.[71] To suppose that this was so is unlikely, because it presupposes that not one but several different Old Testament writers misunderstood it, some of whom should certainly have been in a good position to know its true meaning. Furthermore, as we shall see below, there is evidence outside the Bible for the existence of a god named Molech (*mlk*).

Human Sacrifice or Cultic Dedication in the Fire?

There has been dispute as to whether the Molech cult involved the practice of child sacrifice or whether more harmless rites of cultic dedication to the fire were in view. Those who adopt the latter opinion fall into two groups, namely those who deny that the Old Testament itself speaks of child sacrifice[72] and others who accept that it does but claim that this is simply unreliable polemic.[73] Both of these latter positions

71. Cf. H. Cazelles, ‘Molok’, *DBSup*, V, cols. 1337-46; R. de Vaux, *Les Sacrifices de l’Ancien Testament* (Les Cahiers de la Reine Biblique, 1; Paris: J. Gabalda, 1964), pp. 79-81; ET *Studies in Old Testament Sacrifice* (trans. J. Bourke and R. Potter; Cardiff: University of Wales Press, 1964), pp. 87-90. K.A.D. Smelik, ‘Moloch, Molekh or Molk-sacrifice? A Reassessment of the Evidence concerning the Hebrew Term Molekh’, *SJOT* 9 (1995), pp. 133-42, believes that Old Testament *mōlek* was originally a sacrificial term but was later deliberately altered to a divine name by scribes through the addition of the definite article in *lammōlek* (instead of *l*^{e}*mōlek*) and by adding the words *liznôt ’aḥ*^{a}*rê hammōlek* ‘to play the harlot after Molech’ in Lev. 20.5. However, this is unconvincing. As I have pointed out above, *mōlek* in the Old Testament is associated with the verbs *‘br* (in the hiphil) ‘to offer up, devote’, *ntn* ‘to give’, and *śrp* ‘to burn’, none of which ever occurs elsewhere with *l*^{e} + sacrificial term alone, but they are all attested with *l*^{e} + divine name. The evidence for Molech in the Old Testament having been a god from the beginning is thus much more deeply ingrained in the texts than Smelik allows.

72. N.H. Snaith, ‘The Cult of Molech’, *VT* 16 (1966), pp. 123-24; D. Plataroti, ‘Zum Gebrauch der Wortes *mlk* im Alten Testament’, *VT* 28 (1978), pp. 286-300.

73. Weinfeld, ‘The Worship of Molech’, pp. 140-41.

are mistaken. Thus, with regard to what the Old Testament itself claims, it is clear that it speaks of burning (cf. Jer. 7.31, 19.5; cf. 32.35). Isaiah 30.33 is particularly significant in that it takes imagery from the Molech cult and applies it to the coming destruction of the Assyrians: 'For the oven (*topteh*) has long been prepared, yea for the king (*lammelek*) it is made ready, its pyre made deep and wide,[74] with fire and wood in abundance; the breath of the Lord, like a stream of brimstone, kindles it'. This makes sense only on the sacrificial interpretation of the Molech cult but does not agree with the dedicatory view. One factor which may have encouraged the dedicatory view is the use of the expression *he'ebîr* (*bā'ēš*) in connection with Molech (Lev. 18.21; Jer. 32.35; 2 Kgs 23.10; cf. 2 Kgs 16.3, 21.6; 2 Chron. 33.6), traditionally rendered 'he passed...[through the fire]'. However, it is clear from various Old Testament allusions that this phrase denoted actual sacrifice and not something more harmless like running through the fire. Thus, in Exod. 13.12-13 it is apparent that *h'byr* = *zbḥ* 'sacrifice' (cf. v. 15), and Ezek. 20.26 confirms that *h'byr* applied to human beings was something terrifying: 'and I defiled them through their very gifts in making them offer (*beha'abîr*) all their first-born, that I might horrify them'. A more appropriate translation of *h'byr b'š* would be 'he offered up in the fire' rather than 'he passed...through the fire'.

There is overwhelming evidence that the Old Testament itself implies that children were offered up in fiery human sacrifice to Molech. The next question to discuss is whether we should believe this or follow certain modern scholarly sceptics who claim that the Old Testament allusions are simply unreliable polemic. However, no concrete evidence has been cited to support this supposition. In fact, we have independent evidence that child sacrifice was practised in the Canaanite (Carthaginian and Phoenician) world from many classical sources, Punic inscriptions and archaeological evidence, as well as Egyptian depictions of the ritual occurring in Syria–Palestine, and from a recently discovered

74. Reading *ha'mēq harḥēb* for MT *he'mîq hirḥib*; cf. Targum.

75. For translations of the classical allusions see J. Day, *Molech*, pp. 86-91 and for the Punic texts see J. Day, *Molech*, pp. 4-9. For Egyptian depictions of the ritual of human sacrifice in Syria–Palestine see A. Spalinger, 'A Canaanite Ritual Found in Egyptian Reliefs', *Journal of the Society for the Study of Egyptian Antiquities* 8 (1978), pp. 47-60. For the Phoenician inscription from Turkey see the brief notice by H. Shanks, 'Who—or what—was Molech? New Phoenician Inscription may Hold Answer', *BARev* 22.4 (1996), p. 13. Contrary to this early report this inscrip-

Phoenician inscription from Turkey.[75] There is therefore no reason to doubt the biblical testimony to Canaanite child sacrifice.[76]

The Meaning of Topheth

On several occasions in the Old Testament the location of the Molech sacrifices is stated to be at the Topheth in the valley of Hinnom, which in relation to ancient Jerusalem was just outside the city. Although there have been various theories as to the etymology of the word Topheth (*tōpet*) in recent centuries,[77] for the last hundred years, since the time of W. Robertson Smith,[78] it has been widely supposed that Topheth (*tōpet*) is cognate with Aramaic *tapyā* 'stove, fireplace, pot', Syriac *t^e^payā* (or *t^e^pāyā*) 'bakehouse, oven, kettle, three-legged cauldron', and Arabic *'uṯfiyā* 'the stove (which is one of three) whereon the cooking-pot is placed'. (The Arabic is a loan word from the Aramaic.) This view seems entirely natural in view of the incineratory nature of the Topheth. However, where scholars have often gone wrong over the last century is in supposing that Topheth is also cognate with Hebrew *špt* 'to set', used of setting a pot on a fire in both 2 Kgs 4.38 and Ezek. 24.3. Although Hebrew *š* sometimes equals Aramaic *t*, it is clear that this cannot be the same verb as underlies Hebrew *tōpet* and Aramaic *tepayā*, since Aramaic experts agree that the root of the latter is actually *'p'* 'to bake'. In any case, *špt* is not only used of setting a pot on a fire, but can mean 'to set' more generally (cf. Ps. 22.16 [ET 15]).

Who Was Molech?

Granted that Molech in the Old Testament really is the name (or title) of a god, not a sacrificial term, the question is raised as to his identity. Here there has been no shortage of suggestions. All the Old Testament evidence indicates that a Canaanite deity is in view. Most explicit are the references in Lev. 18.21 and 20.2-5, the context of which indicates that Molech worship is part of the Canaanite abominations (cf. Lev. 18.3, 24-35, 27; 20.23). Similarly, the probable reference to Molech in

tion (which still awaits publication) does not mention a god Molech (so S.A. Kaufman in a private communication).

76. That real human sacrifice was involved in the Molech cult has been argued in recent years, e.g. by Heider, *The Cult of Molek*, *passim*, and J. Day, *Molech*, pp. 15-20.

77. See Day, *Molech*, pp. 24-28.

78. See W.Robertson Smith, *The Religion of the Semites*, p. 377 n. 2.

Isa. 57.9 is set in a context of the Canaanite fertility cult of the high places (cf. Isa. 57.5, 7, 9). Old Testament allusions to human sacrifice, presumably alluding to the Molech cult, also state it to be Canaanite (Deut. 12.31, 18.9-10; 2 Kgs 16.3 and 21.6 [cf. 23.10] against the background of 2 Kgs 16.3, 21.2).

In the light of the Canaanite background, the view that Molech is to be seen as the Ammonite god Milkom[79] may be rejected (though conceivably they may have a common origin). Likewise the idea that Molech is to be equated with Adad-Milki is to be rejected for various reasons. For example, not only would the cult in question not be Canaanite, which Molech's seems to have been, but it is now apparent that the Akkadian texts once believed to refer to human sacrifice to Adad-Milki are to be understood as relating rather to the god Sin.[80]

It has sometimes been suggested that Molech is simply an epithet of Baal[81] (cf. Jer. 19.5; 32.35), but against this stands the fact that the two are clearly distinguished in 2 Kgs 23.5, 10. It has also occasionally been supposed that Molech was the Canaanite underworld god Mot.[82] However, if this were the case, it is surprising that the Old Testament does not simply call him Mot or *māwet*; Mot was not the only god to be regarded as a king, so that there is no reason why he in particular should be denoted by the name Molech.

Since Canaanite gods are characteristically referred to by their proper names in the Old Testament, it is most natural to assume that lying behind Old Testament Molech lies a Canaanite god *mlk*. The original vocalization would presumably have been *mōlēk* 'king'. As A. Geiger[83]

79. E.g. G.C. O'Ceallaigh, 'And so David did to all the Cities of Ammon', *VT* 12 (1962), pp. 179-89 (185-89).

80. Advocates of the view that Molech was Adad-milki include, Weinfeld, 'The Worship of Molech', pp. 144-49, who presents the Akkadian texts once believed to refer to human sacrifice to this god on pp. 144-45. For the evidence that the deity is Sin rather than Adad-milki, see S.A. Kaufman, 'The Enigmatic Adad-milki', *JNES* 37 (1978), pp. 101-109 and Day, *Molech*, pp. 41-43. Adrammelech in 2 Kgs 17.31 has also sometimes been thought to be in need of emendation to Adad-melek. See, however, J. Day, *Molech*, pp. 44-46 for compelling arguments against this.

81. E.g. L. Sabottka, *Zephanja: Versuch einer Neuübersetzung mit philologischem Kommentar* (BibOr, 25; Rome: Biblical Institute Press, 1972), pp. 24-25, 36-38.

82. Lehmann, 'New Interpretation'; Mulder, *Kanaänitische Goden*, pp. 68-70.

83. A. Geiger, *Urschrift und Uebersetzungen der Bibel* (Breslau: Verlag Madda, 1857), p. 301.

long ago suggested, the name has probably been distorted with the vowels of the word *bōšet* 'shame', a term substituted for Baal in the Old Testament (e.g. 2 Sam. 2.10, 4.4; Jer. 11.13; Hos. 9.10), just as Ashtoreth is a distortion of Ashtart (= Astarte).That there was such a deity is shown by two Ugaritic serpent charms which mention him (*KTU*² 1.100.41 [*Ugaritica* V.7, RS 24.244] and *KTU*² 1.107.17 [*Ugaritica* V.8, RS 24.251]). In both places it is associated with the place name Ashtaroth (*'ṯtrt*) in Transjordan, a place elsewhere connected in the Ugaritic texts with *rp'u* (*KTU*² 1.108.1-2), indicating an underworld association. He also appears as Malik in various god lists[84] and in personal names from Ebla, Mari, and Ugarit.[85] Significantly, Malik is twice equated with Nergal, the Mesopotamian underworld god, once in an Old Babylonian god-list where we read ᵈMa-lik = ᵈNergal,[86] and again in a later god-list from Ashur,[87] which likewise has ᵈMa-lik = ᵈNergal. This clearly indicates an underworld deity.[88] Nergal is more often equated with Resheph, another god of the netherworld; it is thus interesting that a Ugaritic text was discovered a few years ago in which Mlk and Resheph are paired together: 'fifteen jars (of barley) for the

84. In addition to the references cited below in nn. 85 and 86, the following is a list of some of the other occurrences of Malik: K.F. Müller, *Das assyrische Ritual*. I. *Texte zum assyrischen Königsritual* (MVAG [E.V.], 41.3; Leipzig: J.C. Hinrichs, 1937), pp. 16-17, line 19; R. Frankena, *Tākultu, de sacrale maaltijd in het Assyrische ritueel* (Leiden: E.J. Brill, 1954), p. 5 col. 2 line 9, and p. 25 line 16; B. Menzel, *Assyrische Tempel*, II (Studia Pohl. Series maior, 10; 2 vols.; Rome: Biblical Institute Press, 1981), p. T129, text 58, line 59, p. T130, text 58 vs., line 29, and p. T148, text 64, line 32A and B.

85. See J. Day, *Molech*, pp. 47-48 n. 68.

86. Cf. S.H. Langdon (ed.), *The H. Weld-Blundell Collection in the Ashmolean Museum*. I. *Sumerian and Semitic Religious and Historical Texts* (Oxford Editions of Cuneiform Inscriptions, 1; London: Oxford University Press, 1923), p. 31 text 9 obv. col. 2 line 8.

87. Cf. O. Schroeder, *Keilschrifttexte aus Assur verschiedenen Inhalts* (Ausgrabungen der deutschen Orient-Gesellschaft in Assur. E: Inschriften, 3; Leipzig: J.C. Hinrichs, 1920), 63.II.37; Tallqvist, *Akkadische Götterepitheta*, p. 359. According to W.G. Lambert, 'Götterlisten', *RLA*, III, pp. 473-79 (474a), this text is Late Assyrian in date. However, this text is not included in Menzel, *Assyrische Tempel*, presumably on the assumption that it is Middle Assyrian.

88. In addition to J. Day, *Molech*, pp. 46-55 (cf. pp. 58-64), the view that Molech was an underworld deity has also been defended in recent years by Heider, *The Cult of Molek*, pp. 93-143.

horses of Resheph, fifteen jars (of barley) for the horses of Mlk of Ashtaroth' (RS 1986.2235.16-17).

Another piece of evidence for the underworld character of Molech comes in Isa. 57.9, where the prophet declares, 'You journeyed to Molech (MT *melek*) with oil and multiplied your perfumes; you sent your envoys far off and sent down even to Sheol'. The emendation of *melek* to (the god) *mōlek* is very likely, since the general context is that of the syncretistic Canaanitizing cult and v. 5 specifically mentions human sacrifice. Now, on any natural interpretation v. 9 locates Molech's dwelling in Sheol. Circumstantial evidence for Molech's underworld character is also provided by the Aramaic term Gehenna, literally 'valley of Hinnom', which came to be used for hell. Fiery rites associated with Molech had earlier been a feature of the valley of Hinnom, so if Molech was an underworld god it would help explain why Gehenna became a term specifically for hell.[89]

Was Molech Equated with Yahweh?

A number of scholars have felt that Molech was identified by his worshippers with Yahweh.[90] The most suggestive evidence for this is the threefold repetition in the prose of Jeremiah that Yahweh had not commanded the sacrifices to Molech. For example, Jer. 32.35 states, 'They built the high places of Baal in the valley of the son of Hinnom, to offer up their sons and daughters to Molech, though I did not command them, nor did it enter my mind, that they should do this abomination to cause Judah to sin' (cf. Jer. 7.31, 19.5). However, the phrase *'ašer lō' ṣiwwîtî*, literally, 'which I have not commanded' is found elsewhere in the Deuteronomistic corpus in Deut. 17.3, where reference is made to one who 'has gone and served other gods and worshipped them or the sun or the moon or any of the host of heaven, *which I have*

89. This understanding is much more plausible than the popular view that Gehenna became a term for hell because of an allegedly constantly burning rubbish dump in the valley of Hinnom. This view is first attested only about 1200 CE in Ḳimḥi's commentary on Ps. 27.13.

90. E.g. W. Eichrodt, *Theologie des Alten Testaments*, I (2 vols. in 3 parts; Stuttgart: Klotz, 5th edn, 1957), pp. 89-90, 123; ET *Theology of the Old Testament*, I (trans. J.A. Baker; 2 vols.; London: SCM Press, 1967), pp. 149-50, 197; M. Buber, *Königtum Gottes* (Heidelberg: L. Schneider, 3rd edn, 1956), p. 173; ET *Kingship of God* (trans. R. Scheimann; London: Allen & Unwin, 3rd edn, 1967), p. 180; H. Irsigler, *Gottesgericht und Jahwetag* (Arbeiten zu Text und Sprache im Alten Testament, 3; St Ottilien: Eos Verlag, 1977), p. 34.

not commanded'. Most translations now render this latter passage as 'which I forbade', and the same is probable in the Jeremiah passages.

Various factors, indeed, argue against Molech's equation with Yahweh. First, the Molech sacrifices did not take place in the Yahweh temple on Mt Zion, but a little distance away in the valley of Hinnom. Secondly, as we have seen, Molech was an underworld deity, but Yahweh was notably separated from the underworld through long periods of Israel's history.

Those who have seen veiled allusions to Yahweh in the Old Testament's references to Molech have tended to equate the child sacrifices offered to Molech with the first-born given to Yahweh. However, there are two indications that these are not the same. First, the law of the first-born refers only to boys (Exod. 13.12-15, 22, 28-29 [ET 29-30], 34.19-20; Num. 3.12-13, 40-51, 8.16-18; cf. Deut. 15.19-20), but girls as well as boys are mentioned as having been offered to Molech (Jer. 7.31, 32.35; 2 Kgs 23.10; cf. Deut. 12.31, 18.10; Jer. 3.24; Ezek. 16.20; 2 Kgs 17.17; Ps. 106.37-38). Secondly, it was only the first-born who are ever spoken of as being offered to Yahweh (Exod. 13.2, 12-15, 22.28-29 [ET 29-30], 34.19-20; Ezek. 20.25-26; Mic. 6.7) but children generally are sacrificed to Molech. These considerations militate against those who would equate the offerings to Molech and Yahweh.[91]

91. Smelik, 'Moloch, Molekh', pp. 140-42, claims that the attribution of child sacrifice to Molech was a postexilic attempt to cover up the fact that child sacrifice had been offered to Yahweh in the pre-exilic period. This view too faces the objections noted above that the children offered to Yahweh do not correspond with those it is claimed were given to Molech. Again, at one point in a most stimulating book entitled *The Death and Resurrection of the Beloved Son: The Transformation of Child Sacrifice in Judaism and Christianity* (New Haven: Yale University Press, 1993), p. 34, J.D. Levenson accepts my points above about the differences in those offered to Molech and Yahweh, but claims that 'The involvement of the practice of child sacrifice in the Canaanite and Punic regions with the ancient myth of El suggests that the Molech cult and the biblical law of the first-born are not to be so sharply distinguished as most scholars have thought'. Levenson has in mind the reference in Philo of Byblos to El (Kronos) offering up his only begotten son (in Eusebius, *Praeparatio Evangelica* 1.10.26). However, Levenson's conclusion from this reference is far too sweeping: the reference is late, and whilst Yahweh became equated with El, Molech was certainly not El and the Carthaginian child sacrifices were not limited to the first-born and were offered to Baal-ḥammon, who, as I have argued elsewhere (*Molech*, pp. 37-10), was not El but, as his name suggests, a form of Baal.

The Rephaim

The expression *r*^{e}*pā'îm* is employed of the shades of the dead in the Old Testament. With this meaning it occurs in Isa. 14.19, 26.14, 19; Ps. 88.11 (ET 10); Job 26.5; Prov. 2.18, 9.18, and 21.16. In addition the term Rephaim is also used of legendary giants amongst the original population of Palestine (Gen. 14.5, 15.20; Deut. 2.11, 20, 3.11; Josh. 12.4, 17.15). In spite of much scholarly discussion, there is still no general agreement on what relationship, if any, there is between these two usages of the term Rephaim, and this is one of the problems that I shall deal with and hope to solve below.

We should first note that the Rephaim occur also in Phoenician and Punic texts as a name for the shades of the dead. On the sarcophagi of the Sidonian kings Tabnit and Eshmunazar (sixth and fifth centuries BCE) *rp'm* clearly denotes the shades of the dead generally (*KAI* 13.7-8, 14.8-9). Later, a neo-Punic bilingual inscription from Al-Amruni in Libya (*KAI* 117.1) reads *l'l*[*nm*] *'r'p'm* 'to the go[ds], the Rephaim', which is equivalent to the Latin D(is) M(anibus) SAC(rum).

Although there was at first uncertainty over the precise meaning of the *rp'um* in the Ugaritic texts—whether they referred to underworld shades or living humans—it is now clear that the term refers to the deified dead, in particular the royal dead. The most explicit text is *KTU*^{2} 1.161, where 'the ancient *rp'um*' are invoked (*rp'im qdmym*, line 9), the names of the individuals concerned making it clear that we have to do with a number of dead Ugaritic kings. They are also called 'the *rp'um* of the land...the assembly of *ddn*' (lines 9-10),[92] a formulation nearly identical to which (except we have *dtn* for *ddn*) occurs in the Keret text (*KTU*^{2} 1.15.III.14-15),[93] thus making clear the underworld background of this allusion, which had previously been doubted. Again, at the end of the Baal myth, *KTU*^{2} 1.6.VI.46-48, *rp'im*/*'ilnym* 'shades/ghosts' are parallel with *'ilm*/*mtm* 'gods/the dead', further supporting the view that they are the deified dead.[94] The *rp'um* also feature prominently in *KTU*^{2} 1.20-22.

92. Also in lines 2-3, with *d*[*dn*] restored in line 3.

93. A similar phrase occurs in Prov. 21.16, where 'the assembly of the Rephaim' (*q*^{e}*hal r*^{e}*pā'îm*) is mentioned, though unlike the passage in Keret just referred to, to be included in this is not an honour.

94. My former student Brian B. Schmidt, in *Israel's Beneficent Dead* (Forschungen zum Alten Testament, 11; Tübingen: J.C.B. Mohr [Paul Siebeck], 1994), pp. 84-122 has recently challenged this consensus view. He maintains that the

In view of the fact that it has been shown that the Ugaritic *rp'um* are the deified dead, it is striking that there are traces of the belief in the divinization of the dead in the Old Testament. The verse often quoted is 1 Sam. 28.13, where the medium of Endor says of the shade of Samuel, 'I see a god (*'ᵉlōhîm*) coming up out of the earth'. But there is a further text in the Old Testament, less cited, where the dead are also treated as gods. This is in Isa. 8.19, 'Now if people say to you, 'Consult the ghosts and the familiar spirits that chirp and mutter; should not a people consult their gods, the dead on behalf of the living?''[95] Although it has sometimes been proposed to translate rather 'shall not a people consult their God', seeing this as the prophet's response to the people's words (e.g. RSV), this is not satisfactory, since the verse continues '[should not they consult] the dead on behalf of the living?' which is hardly appropriate on the lips of the prophet; the RSV had to get round this by supposing that the 'not' does not apply to the later words, thus reading 'Should they consult the dead on behalf of the living?', which is forced. In both 1 Sam. 28.13 and Isa. 8.19 the use of *'ᵉlōhîm* to describe the dead clearly reflects the divinization of the dead such as is attested in the Ugaritic texts. It may be significant that in both Old Testament instances the words are found on the lips of those deemed 'heterodox'.

rp'um are living figures and that only the *rp'um qdmym* 'ancient *rp'um*' in *KTU*² 161 are the shades of dead kings. However, as Philip Johnston has pointed out (review of *Israel's Beneficent Dead*, by B.B. Schmidt, in *JTS* NS 47 [1996], pp. 169-72 [170-71]), this view involves an unnatural alternation between invocation of the living and dead *rp'um* in lines 2-5, 9-10 and 6-8, 11-12, and the identical grammatical forms in lines 4-7 tell against it. Further, with regard to *KTU*² 1.6.VI.46-48, Schmidt sees a chiastic pattern so that the outer pair, the *rp'im* and *mtm* (understood as 'men', not 'dead') are parallel and understood as human, whilst the inner pair of *'ilnym* and *'ilm* are understood as divine. However, whilst ingenious, this is unconvincing, since as Mark S. Smith has rightly noted (review of *Israel's Beneficent Dead*, by B.B. Schmidt, in *CBQ* 58 [1996], pp. 724-25), the word *'dk* is found with both *'ilm* and *mtm*, and the word *tḥtk* occurs with both *rp'im* and *'ilnym*, suggesting that in both instances we have synonymous, not antithetic parallelism, and that therefore the *rp'um* are divine.

95. For this widely accepted translation, equating the *'ᵉlōhîm* with the dead, see e.g. H. Wildberger, *Jesaja*, I (BKAT, 10.1; Neukirchen–Vluyn: Neukirchener Verlag, 2nd edn, 1980), pp. 342, 351-52; ET *Isaiah 1–12* (trans. T.H. Trapp; Minneapolis: Fortress Press, 1991), pp. 364, 373; Clements, *Isaiah 1–39*, p. 102; T.J. Lewis, *Cults of the Dead in Ancient Israel and Ugarit* (HSM, 39; Atlanta: Scholars Press, 1989), pp. 128-32.

Alternatively, if this is not significant, we would have to say that the term *'ᵉlōhîm* had become something of a linguistic fossil, since the Old Testament no longer regarded the dead as literally divine.

Etymology

There have been three main views of the meaning of the expression *rp'um*/Rephaim.

(i) Traditionally it was supposed that the root of the Old Testament expression Rephaim was *rph* 'to be weak', which aptly seemed to describe the state of the shades; cf. Isa. 14.9.

(ii) (a) The most common view, however, especially since the discovery of the Ugaritic *rp'um*, is that the root is *rp'* 'to heal', so that *rp'um* would mean 'healers',[96] possibly alluding to their role in promoting fertility.

(b) C. L'Heureux, whilst accepting that the root is *rp'*, prefers rather to take the word as a stative, meaning 'hale ones'.[97]

(c) R.M. Good[98] has argued that the word means the 'healed ones', that is, 'embalmed ones', claiming that *rp'* means 'to embalm' in Gen. 50.2.

(iii) H.L. Ginsberg and G.R. Driver[99] have suggested that the root is *rp'*, but rather with the meaning 'join'—cf. Arabic *rafa'a* 'sewed together, united'.

That the root is *rp'* rather than *rph* is now generally recognized. This is clear because not only in Hebrew but also in Phoenician and much earlier in Ugaritic, an ' is present. Most probably this is to be taken in the sense 'healers'. Although the meaning 'join' is found in Arabic, it is not clearly attested in West Semitic for *rp'*. *Rp'* in the sense 'to heal', however, is clearly attested in West Semitic including religious contexts, for example the angel Raphael (lit. 'God has healed') mentioned in the book of Tobit, who 'was sent to heal...Tobit...and Sarah' (3.17).

96. This was already suggested long before the discovery of the Ugaritic texts by M.J. Lagrange, *Etudes sur les religions sémitiques* (Paris: V. Lecoffre, 1903), p. 273.

97. L'Heureux, *Rank among the Canaanite Gods*, pp. 215-18.

98. R.M. Good, 'Supplementary Remarks on the Ugaritic Funerary Text RS 34.126', *BASOR* 239 (1980), pp. 41-42.

99. H.L. Ginsberg, *The Legend of King Keret* (BASOR Supplementary Studies, 2–3; New Haven: American Schools of Oriental Research, 1946), p. 41; Driver, *Canaanite Myths and Legends*, pp. 10 n. 2, 155 n. 22.

Moreover, with regard to R.M. Good's view that it means 'embalmed ones', it should be pointed out that Gen. 50.2 does not prove that *rp'* can mean 'to embalm'; rather the *rōp*^{e}*'îm* there are the physicians who do the embalming, but *ḥnṭ* is the actual verb meaning 'to embalm' there. If so, the expression may have a broader connotation than what we mean by healing, and refer to the provision of fertility. *Rp'* has this meaning in the Old Testament in Gen. 20.17, 2 Kgs 2.22, and 2 Chron. 7.14. One may compare Hos. 11.2, where there could be a conscious reference back to the thought of Baal as *rp'*: 'The more I[100] called them, the more they went from me; they kept sacrificing to the Baals, and burning incense to idols. Yet it was I who taught Ephraim to walk, I took them up in my arms, but they did not know that I healed them.' This verse may be illuminated by Hos. 2.10 (ET 8), 'And she did not know that it was I who gave her the grain, the wine, and the oil, and who lavished upon her silver and gold which they used for Baal'. The connection between underworld and fertility is attested elsewhere, for example in the Egyptian god of the dead, Osiris, also responsible for fertility. However, as James Barr has emphasized,[101] the original root meaning of a word is not necessarily a good guide to its current meaning. This is certainly true of Rephaim in the Old Testament: all thought of the Rephaim as 'healers' or providers of fertility is absent there. We appear to have here a demythologization of the original Canaanite concept. In this connection is it possible that there may also have been a deliberate alteration of the vocalization from *rōp*^{e}*'îm* to *r*^{e}*pā'îm*?

Who is Rp'u?

In addition to the plural form *rp'um*, the Ugaritic texts also attest the singular form *rp'u*. *KTU*^{2} 1.108 (RS 24.252) is a text especially in honour of a deity call *rp'u*.

1 [ ]*n. yšt. rp'u. mlk. 'lm. wyšt*
2 [*'il*] *gṯr. wyqr. 'il. yṯb. b'ṯtrt*
3 *'l ṯpẓ. bhdr'y. dyšr. wyḏmr*
4 *bknr. wṯlb. btp. wmṣltm. bm*
5 *rqdm. dšn. bḥbr. kṯr. ẓbm*

100. Reading, as is generally done, 'I' with the LXX rather than MT's 'they'.

101. J. Barr, *The Semantics of Biblical Language* (Oxford: Oxford University Press, 1961), *passim*.

[1] ...May Rp'u drink, the king of eternity, and may
[2] the strong and honorable [god] drink, the god who dwells in Ashtaroth,
[3] the god who judges at Edrei,[102] who sings and makes music
[4] with the harp and flute, with the tambourine and cymbals, with the
[5] castanets of ivory, among the good companions of Kothar.

The question naturally arises, who is Rp'u? Several different views have been put forward. These are:

(i) that the god is El;[103]
(ii) that the god is Baal;[104]
(iii) that it is an independent deity Rp'u;[105]
(iv) that it is Resheph;[106]

102. The view that we have here references to the places Ashtaroth and Edrei was first proposed by B. Margalit (Margulis), 'A New Ugaritic Psalm (RŠ 24.252)', *JBL* 89 (1970), pp. 292-302, and has now become the generally accepted rendering. See e.g. M. Dietrich and O. Loretz, 'Baal *rpu* in *KTU* 1.108; 1.113 und nach 1.17 VI 25-33', *UF* 12 (1980), pp. 171-82 (172-74); J.C. de Moor, *An Anthology of Religious Texts from Ugarit* (Leiden: E.J. Brill, 1987), p. 187; D. Pardee, *Les Textes Para-Mythologique de la 24*[e] *Campagne (1961)* (Ras Shamra–Ougarit, 4; Paris: Editions Recherche sur les Civilisations, 1988), pp. 94-97. This rendering has now generally replaced the older understanding of the passage as 'the god who sits next to Astarte, the god who judges with Hadad the shepherd'. *Yṯb b* never means 'sit next to' but always 'dwell in' in Ugaritic. Ashtaroth was also the dwelling place of the underworld god Mlk (Molech) in the Ugaritic texts (*KTU*[2] 1.100.41, 1.107.14), which coheres with the underworld nature of Rp'u. See below for the illuminating parallel with Josh. 12.4, etc.

103. C. Virolleaud, 'Les nouveaux textes mythologiques et liturgiques de Ras Shamra, (XXIV[e] Campagne, 1961)', in C.F.A. Schaeffer (ed.), *Ugaritica* V (Paris: Imprimerie Nationale and P. Geuthner, 1968), pp. 545-606 (553), followed by many others, e.g. J. Blau and J.C. Greenfield, 'Ugaritic Glosses', *BASOR* 200 (1970), pp. 11-17 (12); Cross, *Canaanite Myth and Hebrew Epic*, pp. 20, 177 n. 131; C. L'Heureux, 'The Ugaritic and Biblical Rephaim', *HTR* 67 (1974), pp. 265-74.

104. J.C. de Moor, 'Studies in the New Alphabetic Texts from Ras Shamra I', *UF* 1 (1969), pp. 167-88 (176) and elsewhere, followed e.g. by A.F. Rainey, 'The Ugaritic Texts in Ugaritica 5', *JAOS* 94 (1974), pp. 184-94 (188); J.C.L. Gibson, *Canaanite Myths and Legends* (Edinburgh: T. & T. Clark, 1978), p. 7.

105. A. Jirku, 'Rapa'u, der Fürst der Rapa'uma–Rephaim', *ZAW* 77 (1965), pp. 82-83 (Jirku wrote of the Rp'u in the Ugaritic Daniel text prior to the publication of *KTU*[2] 1.108); S.B. Parker, 'The Ugaritic Deity Rāpi'u', *UF* 4 (1972), pp. 97-104.

106. A. Cooper, 'MLK 'LM: "Eternal King" or "King of Eternity"?', in Marks and Good (eds.), *Love & Death in the Ancient Near East*, pp. 1-7.

(v) that it is Molech;[107]
(vi) that it is a way of alluding to a dead king.[108]

Certainty is not possible, since the text in question does not mention any other name for the deity apart from *rp'u*. However, the name is suggestive of an underworld connection (cf. the plural *rp'um*), and the underworld god Molech is likewise associated with Ashtaroth (*KTU*² 1.100.41 and 1.107.17). The most likely possibility seems to be either that this is an independent underworld deity, that it is another name for Molech (*mlk 'lm* would then be a play on this name), or that it is an allusion to the shade of a dead king (one of the *rp'um*).[109]

107. M.H. Pope, 'Notes on the Rephaim Texts from Ugarit', in J.M. Efird (ed.), *The Use of the Old Testament in the New and other Essays* (Durham, NC: Duke University Press, 1977), pp. 163-82 (169-72, 181-82); Heider, *The Cult of Molek*, pp. 115-23; Pardee, *Les Textes para-mythologique*, pp. 84-94.

108. E.g. A. Caquot, 'La tablette RS 24.252 et la question des Rephaïm ougaritiques', *Syria* 53 (1976), pp. 295-304 (303-304) (= Ditanu?); *idem*, 'Ras Shamra: La littérature ugaritique', *DBSup*, IX, cols. 1361-1417 (1386) ('un roi d'autrefois'); *idem*, 'Rephaïm', *DBSup*, X, cols. 344-57 (353-55) ('un roi d'autan', perhaps Yaqaru'); M. Dietrich, O. Loretz and J. Sanmartín, 'Die Totengeister ugaritischen *rpu(m)* und die biblischen Rephaim', *UF* 8 (1976), pp. 45-52 (51) ('Totengeist', 'ein verstorbener König'); S. Ribichini and P. Xella, 'Mlk'aštart, *Mlk(m)* e la tradizione siropalestinese sui Refaim', *RSF* 7 (1979), pp. 145-58 (154-55) (= Yaqaru); B. Margalit [Margulis], 'The Geographical Setting of the AQHT Story and its Ramifications', in G.D. Young (ed.), *Ugarit in Retrospect* (Winona Lake, IN: Eisenbrauns, 1981), pp. 131-58 (151-56) (= Ditanu).

109. It has been claimed by M.H. Pope ('Notes on the Rephaim Texts', in M. de Jong Ellis [ed.], *Essays on the Ancient Near East in Memory of Jacob Joel Finkelstein* [Memoirs of the Connecticut Academy of Arts and Sciences, 19; Hamden, CT: Archon Books, 1977], pp. 163-82 [170]) and Mark S. Smith ('Rephaim', *ABD*, V, pp. 674-76 [676]), that the god Rp'u is mentioned in the New Testament, in Stephen's speech before the Sanhedrin in Acts 7.43 where he quotes a version of Amos 5.26, 'And you took up the tent of Moloch, and the star of the god Raiphan, the figures which you made to worship; and I will remove you beyond Babylon'. This seems most unlikely, however. First, the reference to 'the star of the god Raiphan ('Ραιφάν)' must imply an astral deity, not an underworld god like Rp'u. Secondly, since the words are adapted from the Septuagint version of Amos 5.26, where the Hebrew MT has the word *kiyyûn* 'pedestal', widely regarded as a deliberate misvocalization (with the vowels of *šiqqûṣ* 'abomination') of *kêwān* (Saturn), the name Raiphan is surely a corruption of this word.

The Rephaim as an Ethnic Group and their Relationship to the Underworld Rephaim

As we have noted earlier, the inhabitants of the gloomy underworld are frequently called the Rephaim in the Old Testament (Job 26.5; Ps. 88.11 [ET 10]; Prov. 2.18, 9.18, 21.16; Isa. 14.9, 26.14, 19). Curiously, the Old Testament also uses the same name to describe part of the pre-Israelite population of Canaan (Gen. 14.5, 15.20; Deut. 2.11, 20, 3.11, 13; Josh. 12.4, 17.15), but there is no agreement on what relation, if any, there is between the two usages. Some, for example, S. Talmon,[110] have argued that there is no relationship between them. I am convinced, however, that there is a direct relationship and that the ethnic Rephaim derive from the underworld Rephaim. First, in the Old Testament the ethnic Rephaim are most particularly associated with the place Ashtaroth or Ashteroth-Karnaim in northern Transjordan (Gen. 14.5; Josh. 12.4; 13.12); the same place is attested in the Ugaritic texts as the seat of *rp'u*, the leader of the underworld *rp'um*. Thus, in the Ugaritic text *KTU*² 1.108.1 we read of *rp'u. mlk. ʿlm*, 'Rp'u, king of eternity' and he is described in lines 2-3 as *'il. yṯb. bʿṯtrt ʿil ṯpẓ bhdrʿy*, 'the god who dwells in Ashtaroth, the god who judges at Edrei' according to the translation now accepted by most Ugaritologists, with which I now concur.[111] This too supports an ultimate connection between the underworld and ethnic Rephaim of the Bible, since on the one hand *rp'um*, of which *rp'u* is the singular, are elsewhere the spirits of the dead at Ugarit, whereas on the other hand, the reference to 'the god who dwells in Ashtaroth, the god who judges in Edrei' strikingly resembles one of the ethnic Rephaim, 'Og, king of Bashan, one of the remnant of the Rephaim, who dwelt at Ashtaroth and at Edrei' (Josh. 12.4; cf. Josh. 13.12). This therefore tells against the view of those such as J.R. Bartlett[112] who see the Old Testament's connection of the Rephaim with Transjordan as simply late and Deuteronomistic, appropriated from the southern Judahite tradition.

Secondly, the same place, Ashtaroth, was the seat of the god Mlk in the Ugaritic texts (*KTU*² 1.100.41 and 1.107.42). Mlk is the same as the god known in the Old Testament as Molech, and as I have argued else-

110. S. Talmon, 'Biblical *repāʾîm* and Ugaritic *rpu/i(m)*', *HAR* 7 (1983), pp. 235-49.

111. See above, n. 102.

112. J.R. Bartlett, 'Sihon and Og, Kings of the Amorites', *VT* 20 (1970), pp. 257-77 (268-71); A. Caquot, 'Rephaïm', *DBSup*, X, cols. 344-57 (345-46).

where (both in my book,[113] and above), he was an underworld deity. His seat was in the valley of Hinnom (2 Kgs 23.10; Jer. 32.35), where fiery human sacrifices were offered. (Hence the later name for hell, Gehenna, literally 'valley of Hinnom'.[114]) Interestingly, the valley of Hinnom joins on to a valley known as the valley of Rephaim (Josh. 18.16). All this suggests that there is indeed a relationship between the underworld Rephaim and the ethnic Rephaim. It would appear that the concept of the ethnic Rephaim is derivative from that of the underworld Rephaim, since the latter are already attested at Ugarit in the second millennium BCE (the *rp'um*), as we have seen earlier.

In keeping with the view expressed here that the divinized underworld Rephaim gave rise to the giant ethnic Rephaim, it may be pointed out that there are other analogies for this in the Old Testament.[115] Thus, the giant Nephilim (Num. 13.33) are said to be the offspring of the sons of God and daughters of men in Gen. 6.1-4. Further, as we have seen in the previous chapter, the figure of Samson (admittedly a mighty man rather than a giant) partly derives from the sun god. Again, Nimrod, another mighty man in Gen. 10.8-12, described as 'a mighty hunter before the Lord' (v. 9) may derive (at any rate in part) from Ninurta, the Mesopotamian god of hunting.

Since the evidence supports the view that the ethnic giant Rephaim developed from the originally divinized underworld Rephaim, there is no need to follow any of the alternative views that were once popular. The idea that the giant Rephaim were so called because they were dead and gone, proposed by F. Schwally,[116] is clearly fanciful.

Nor, in spite of the popularity of the view in the past, is there any particular reason why belief in the giant Rephaim should have been inspired by the existence of a number of dolmens (megalithic monuments) in Transjordan.[117] The Old Testament itself never connects the

113. J. Day, *Molech*, pp. 45-55.

114. For the evidence that the imagery of the fires of Gehenna derives from the fiery Molech sacrifices rather than an alleged burning rubbish dump in the valley of Hinnom, see J. Day, *Molech*, pp. 52-55.

115. Cf. too Homer, *Odyssey* 11.240-332, *Iliad* 12.23, and Plato, *Cratylus* 33, for the notion that giants and heroes are the offspring of marriages between gods and humans.

116. F. Schwally, *Das Leben nach dem Tode nach den Vorstellungen des alten Israels* (Giessen: J. Ricker, 1892), pp. 64-65 n. 1; *idem*, 'Ueber einige palästinische Völkernamen', *ZAW* 18 (1898), pp. 126-48 (131-34).

117. E.g. P. Karge, *Rephaim: Die vorgeschichtliche Kultur Palästinas und*

Rephaim with these structures,[118] and they are not attested at Ashteroth-Karnaim, the site particularly associated with the Rephaim in the Old Testament.[119] Dolmens are also attested at other sites in Palestine with which the Old Testament does not associate the Rephaim or other giants (e.g. Galilee).

Nor again is there any need to see the Rephaim as the name of an actually existing tribal group. Quite apart from the fact that it is never attested as such in any extra-biblical documents, the decisive point remains that a derivation of the ethnic Rephaim from the underworld Rephaim is strongly supported by the fact that the place Ashteroth-Karnaim is associated with both in ancient records.

2 Sam. 21.15-22 refers four times to 'the descendants of the Rapha' (*y*ᵉ*lîdê hārāpâ*) in connection with various Philistine mighty men in the time of David. Although *hārāpâ* is here spelled with a final *h* rather than ', this looks like a singular form of the word *r*ᵉ*pā'îm*. However, this does not prove that Rephaim was a genuine ethnic term in origin; rather, after the emergence of belief in the giant Transjordanian Rephaim from the deified Rephaim, the term is here applied analogously to certain Philistine giants.

Phöniziens (Collectanea Hierosolymitana, 1; Paderborn: F. Schöningh, 1917), p. 612; G.E. Wright, 'Troglodytes and Giants in Palestine', *JBL* 57 (1938), pp. 305-309; E.C. Broome, 'The Dolmens of Palestine and Transjordania', *JBL* 59 (1940), pp. 479-97.

118. Karge, *Rephaim*, pp. 638-39, and a number of more recent scholars have held that Og's bed in Deut. 3.11 was in reality a dolmen. However, Og's bed is said to have been made of iron, not stone. See A.R. Millard, 'King Og's Bed and other Ancient Ironmongery', in Eslinger and Taylor, *Ascribe to the Lord*, pp. 481-92, and, in more popular form, 'King Og's Iron Bed: Fact or Fancy?', *BR* 6.2 (April 1990), pp. 16-21, 44.

119. See J.L. Swauger, 'Dolmen Studies in Palestine', *BA* 29 (1966), pp. 106-14 (113), for a map showing locations of dolmen fields in Transjordan and Palestine.

Chapter 8

CONCLUSION: THE CANAANITE GODS AND GODDESSES AND THE RISE OF MONOTHEISM

I have now come to the end of my survey of the various gods and goddesses of Canaan and how they related to Yahweh in ancient Israel. There are, however, some general questions that deserve treatment by way of conclusion.

First of all, there is the question of the extent to which other deities were worshipped in ancient Israel. I am here speaking of pre-exilic Israel, since although the measures of Nehemiah and Ezra against mixed marriages indicate that there was still some danger from syncretism then, absolute monotheism seems to have been predominant in the postexilic period. If we follow the evidence of the Old Testament itself it would seem that the worship of other deities was quite frequent. One may compare, for example, the condemnations found in prophets such as Hosea, Jeremiah and Ezekiel, the cyclical pattern of apostasy and faithfulness depicted by the Deuteronomist in the book of Judges, and the fact that the books of Kings represent most of the kings as having done evil in the sight of the Lord, either by worshipping other deities or by tolerating them by not abolishing the high places. Only David, Hezekiah and Josiah receive total commendation from the Deuteronomistic historian for their religious policies, though several others are commended for doing what was right in the sight of the Lord, even though they did not abolish the high places. J.H. Tigay,[1] however, has fairly recently challenged this picture, arguing on the basis of Hebrew theophoric personal names in ancient Palestinian inscriptions that the worship of other gods and goddesses was in fact rather rare and that Israel was essentially monolatrous throughout. As a result of his survey he concludes that Yahwistic names (i.e. names incorporating

1. Tigay, *You Shall have no Other Gods*.

yhw, etc.) were sixteen times more common than pagan names, and consequently believes that only a small proportion of Israelites actually worshipped other deities. The contrary impression given by the Old Testament he ascribes to rhetorical exaggeration. Tigay's study is interesting and carefully argued. However, a number of caveats need to be made, the net effect of which is to suggest that the worship of other gods and goddesses was more frequent than he allows.

First, it may be noted that the overwhelming preponderance of Yahwistic names need not imply that Yahweh was the only deity worshipped but is equally compatible with the idea that Yahweh was rather the most important deity worshipped. Those who worshipped other gods and goddesses surely still saw Yahweh as the chief god, with the other deities being regarded as subordinate members of his pantheon. Secondly, it should be observed that Hebrew theophoric personal names do not necessarily give a fair idea of the frequency of the worship of a god and goddess, since many names could well be traditional. For example, the names of female deities hardly ever occur in Ugaritic personal names, even though we know that Asherah, Anat and Astarte were prominent goddesses at Ugarit. If this was the case of Ugarit, there is no reason why the virtual absence of Hebrew theophoric personal names including the name of a goddess should indicate the absence of goddess worship in ancient Israel if there is other evidence to the contrary. As we have seen earlier, there is indeed evidence to the contrary. For example, quite apart from the Old Testament's allusions to Asherah worship, the texts referring to 'Yahweh and his Asherah' found at Kuntillet 'Ajrud and Khirbet el-Qom, though referring to the Asherah cult object, nevertheless imply a close relationship (doubtless that of god and consort) between Yahweh and the goddess Asherah, since the cult object symbolized the goddess. Again, the presence of vast numbers of pillar figurines of the goddess Asherah, in particular from eighth- and seventh-century BCE Judah, clearly imply the popularity of her cult. Interestingly, this is the very time and place from which much of Tigay's epigraphic material derives, in which Asherah is so absent from personal names. A further point with regard to goddesses, as we have seen earlier, is the occurrence of the worship of the goddesses Anat-Yahu and Anat-Bethel alongside Yahu (Yahweh) at Elephantine, which is most naturally understood as a continuation of the worship of Anat in pre-exilic Israel. Thirdly, both the geographical and temporal limitations of the epigraphic material collected by Tigay should be noted. Thus, most of the personal names attested epigraphically come from Judah, and it is conceivable that if more material from the Northern Kingdom were available we would find more evidence of polytheism, as indeed is the case with the Samaria ostraca with their theophoric personal names incorporating Baal (in addition to Yahweh). Again, most of Tigay's material comes from the latter part of the monarchical period, and it is possible that a different picture would emerge if we had more personal names from earlier centuries, when 'the Yahweh alone party' was less in evidence. Fourthly, as Graham Davies has noted in a review of Tigay's work,[2] there is evidence that Tigay tends to overestimate the number of Yahwistic names and underestimates the number of pagan names, so that the proportion of Yahwistic to non-Yahwistic names may be nearer ten to one rather than sixteen to one. My overall conclusion is that Yahweh was very much the chief god in ancient Israel, and the other gods and goddesses would have been worshipped as part of his pantheon, but the frequency of their worship has been underestimated by Tigay.

At the opposite extreme to J.H. Tigay stands A.P. Hayman,[3] who claims that absolute monotheism among the Jews was not finally achieved until the Middle Ages. This too is an extreme position. Much of Hayman's case hangs on the prominent position given to angels in Second Temple Judaism and subsequently, but over against this it should be noted that throughout history monotheists have not felt belief in angels to be incompatible with monotheism.

Over against the above extreme views I would argue that it is clear that there was indeed a monolatrous party already in the pre-exilic period, though it was not as dominant as Tigay supposes, and absolute monotheism was first given explicit expression by the prophet Deutero-Isaiah in the exile and became fully operative in the post-exilic period. There has been a general rejection in recent decades of the view (once associated with W.F. Albright) that absolute monotheism can be traced back to the time of Moses. The tendency to trace absolute monotheism to Deutero-Isaiah goes with a general understanding, already maintained a century ago by J. Wellhausen, that the achievement of mono-

2. G.I. Davies, review of *You Shall Have no other Gods: Israelite Religion in the Light of Hebrew Inscriptions* (HSS, 31; Atlanta: Scholars Press, 1986), by J.H. Tigay, in *JTS* NS 40 (1989), pp. 143-46 (145).

3. A.P. Hayman, 'Monotheism: A Misused Word in Jewish Studies', *JJS* 42 (1991), pp. 1-15.

theism was a gradual process in the development of which the monolatrous challenge of Elijah,[4] the work of the classical prophets, the Deuteronomic reform movement and Josiah's reform replayed an important role. There has been much talk of a 'Yahweh alone movement', following the work by B. Lang,[5] who borrowed the expression from Morton Smith.[6] Unlike Lang, however, some scholars are willing to grant that this minority monolatrous movement may indeed go all the way back to earliest times,[7] perhaps to Moses.[8]

One significant factor in the decline of the Canaanite deities and the enforcement of monolatry appears to have been Josiah's reformation in 621 BCE. According to 2 Kings 23 Josiah abolished the high places, centralizing worship in Jerusalem and purifying the cult of Yahweh in the process. All this is supposed to have taken place in accordance with the law book found in the Jerusalem temple, traditionally understood as an early form of our book of Deuteronomy. In recent years, some scholars have doubted the historicity of Josiah's reform,[9] but there are

4. On this see now M. Beck, *Elia und die Monolatrie* (BZAW, 281; Berlin: W. De Gruyter, 1999).

5. B. Lang, 'Die Jahwe-allein-Bewegung', in B. Lang, *Der einzige Gott* (Munich: Kösel, 1981), pp. 47-83; ET 'The Yahweh-Alone-Movement and the Making of Jewish Monotheism', in *Monotheism and the Prophetic Minority* (Sheffield: Almond Press, 1983), pp. 13-59.

6. Morton Smith, *Palestinian Parties and Politics that Shaped the Old Testament* (New York: Columbia University Press, 1971).

7. E.g. E.W. Nicholson, 'Israelite Religion in the Pre-exilic Period', in J.D. Martin and P.R. Davies (eds.), *A Word in Season: Essays in Honour of William McKane* (JSOTSup, 42; Sheffield: JSOT Press, 1986), pp. 3-34 (28); Mettinger, 'The Elusive Essence', p. 412; R. Albertz, *Religionsgeschichte Israels in alttestamentlicher Zeit* (2 vols.; Göttingen: Vandenhoeck & Ruprecht, 1992), I, p. 98; ET *A History of Israelite Religion in the Old Testament Period* (trans. J.S. Bowden; 2 vols.; London: SCM Press, 1994), I, p. 62.

8. Other recent works on monotheism that may be noted include O. Keel (ed.), *Monotheismus im alten Israel und seiner Umwelt* (Biblische Beiträge, 14; Fribourg: Schweizerisches Katholisches Bibelwerk, 1980); W. Dietrich and M.A. Klopfenstein (eds.), *Ein Gott allein?* (OBO, 139; Göttingen: Vandenhoeck & Ruprecht, 1994); R.K. Gnuse, *No other Gods: Emergent Monotheism in Israel* (JSOTSup, 141; Sheffield: JSOT Press, 1997); H. Shanks and J. Meinhardt (eds.), *Aspects of Monotheism: How God is One* (Washington, DC: Biblical Archaeology Society, 1997).

9. E. Würthwein, 'Die josianische Reform und das Deuteronomium', *ZTK* 73 (1976), pp. 365-423 (417-21); C. Levin, 'Joschija im deuteronomistischen Geschichtswerk', *ZAW* 96 (1984), pp. 351-71.

good grounds for believing that a religious reformation did take place in his reign.[10] Thus, on the one had, the prophet Zephaniah, whose oracles date from sometime (presumably early on) in the reign of Josiah (Zeph. 1.1), condemns religious syncretism in Judah and Jerusalem of a type attested in 2 Kings 23 prior to Josiah's alleged reform (Zeph. 1.4-5; cf. Jer. 2.8, 23, 27-28). On the other hand, in a clearly non-Deuteronomistic, poetic section of Jeremiah, the prophet looks back on Josiah and hails him as a just king (Jer. 22.15-16), which he could not have done if Josiah had allowed religious syncretism to flourish after the manner of Manasseh or the later Jehoiakim. The contrast between the words of Zephaniah and Jeremiah implies that some religious reformation must have taken place in his reign. This also coheres with the fact that there is a shortage of oracles from the time of Josiah in the book of Jeremiah (apart from the early chapters 2–6), which makes sense if Josiah had undertaken a religious reform of which Jeremiah approved. A further point supporting the historicity of Josiah's reform is the fact that the account in 2 Kings 22–23 is in all likelihood contemporary with the events described: there is a growing consensus that, in addition to the final redaction of the Deuteronomistic history in the exile, there was a first edition during the reign of Josiah himself, as F.M. Cross and others have argued.[11] Amongst other arguments, only such a supposition can satisfactorily explain the tensions in the text with regard to the reign of Josiah. No one inventing the whole story in the exile would have created such tensions as that in which the prophetess Huldah, in commending Josiah's positive response to the Deuteronomic law book, predicts that he will die in peace (2 Kgs 22.20), when he actually died in battle (2 Kgs 23.29-30) or would have made up the account of Josiah's reform 'so that there was no king like him' (2 Kgs 23.25), only to have the kingdom of Judah fall shortly afterwards, so that in the very next verse the disaster has to be blamed on the wicked deeds of Manasseh, a predecessor of Josiah (2 Kgs 23.26).

10. E.g. Spieckermann, *Juda unter Assur*, pp. 53, 76, 79-130, 378-81; N. Lohfink, 'The Cult Reform of Josiah of Judah: 2 Kings 22–23 as a Source for the History of Israelite Religion', in P.D. Miller, P.D. Hanson and S.D. McBride (eds.), *Ancient Israelite Religion: Essays in Honor Frank Moore Cross* (Philadelphia: Fortress Press, 1987), pp. 459-75.

11. E.g. Cross, *Canaanite Myth and Hebrew Epic*, pp. 274-89; R.D. Nelson, *The Double Redaction of the Deuteronomistic History* (JSOTSup, 18; JSOT Press, 1981).

By the way of contrast, the account of Josiah's reform in 2 Chronicles 34–35 dates from about three centuries later. It is thus somewhat surprising that certain scholars have attributed to it a greater degree of historicity than the account of 2 Kings 22–23. According to the Chronicler, Josiah began to seek the Lord in his eighth year, while still a boy, and he began to purge Judah and Jerusalem of idolatry in his twelfth year (2 Chron. 34.3) already before the discovery of the law book in his eighteenth year. Chronicles' differences from Kings are fully explicable in terms of the Chronicler's own theology: if Josiah really was such a good king, the Chronicler doubtless thought, why did he not begin his reforming measures as soon as possible instead of waiting till his eighteenth year? Josiah's twelfth year, when he was twenty, was the time he reached the age of majority and was therefore first able to engage in independent action.[12] This makes much more sense than F.M. Cross and D.N. Freedman's attempt[13] to correlate the Chronicler's dates for Josiah's reforms with significant events pertaining to the decline of the Assyrian empire; not only are the Assyrian dates in question highly uncertain, but it is doubtful whether Josiah's reforms should be understood as being directed against specifically Assyrian cults anyway. J.W. McKay and M.D. Cogan[14] have both independently argued that the Assyrians did not impose their deities on subject peoples and that Josiah's purges were directed against Canaanite rather than Assyrian cults. H. Spieckermann,[15] however, has revived the earlier view that Josiah's reforms were anti-Assyrian. He has drawn attention to certain Assyrian texts in which subject peoples have to do obeisance to Assyrian gods, especially Ashur.[16] Over against Spieckermann, however, it needs to be pointed out that from all the Assyrian records he is able to cite only one text relating to Syria–Palestine, namely that concerning Ḫanunu of Gaza,[17] and there we read that the

12. Cf. H.G.M. Williamson, *1 and 2 Chronicles* (NCB; Grand Rapids: W.B. Eerdmans; London: Marshall, Morgan & Scott, 1982), pp. 397-98, who holds that the Chronicler did not use any source in his composition of 2 Chron. 34.1-13 apart from 2 Kgs 22–23.

13. F.M. Cross and D.N. Freedman, 'Josiah's Revolt against Assyria', *JNES* 12 (1953), pp. 56-58.

14. McKay, *Religion in Judah*; Cogan, *Imperialism and Religion.*

15. Spieckermann, *Juda unter Assur.*

16. Spieckermann, *Juda unter Assur*, pp. 322-44.

17. Spieckermann, *Juda unter Assur*, pp. 325-30.

Assyrian images were set up not in the temple, but in the palace. as A. Laato rightly states,[18] there was clearly no systematic policy by the Assyrians of enforcing their cults on subject peoples. Moreover, the explicit details of the cults removed by Josiah in 2 Kings 23 clearly indicate Canaanite deities: Baal (2 Kgs 23.4, 5) and Asherah (2 Kgs 23.4; cf. vv. 6, 7, 14) are well-known Canaanite deities, and human sacrifice, associated with the god Molech (2 Kgs 23.10), is not a native Assyrian custom but is something well attested in the Canaanite religious sphere. Since the Canaanites also worshipped the sun and other astral deities, there is every presumption that the removal of these too (2 Kgs 23.4, 5, 11) was a response to Canaanite cults, and this is further supported by the fact that the moon is denoted by the West Semitic word *yārēaḥ* (2 Kgs 23.11) rather than by the name of the Mesopotamian god Sin. Spieckermann's supposition[19] that Asherah does not denote the Canaanite goddess Asherah but is rather a code name for the Assyrian goddess Ishtar is quite forced, since the Canaanite equivalent of Ishtar was not Asherah but Astarte (Ashtoreth). In support of his view he claims that the Canaanite Asherah was unimportant in pre-exilic Israel, so Asherah must denote some other goddess, but it should be noted that Spieckermann was writing at a time when the Kuntillet 'Ajrud and Khirbet el-Qom texts referring to 'Yahweh and his Asherah' had not yet become widely known, texts which reveal the importance of Asherah in pre-exilic Israel.

Absolute monotheism having been established in postexilic Israel, what then happened to the Canaanite deities? Of course, amongst such people as the neighbouring Phoenicians they continued to be worshipped. Even amongst monotheistic Jews, though no longer worshipped, the Canaanite deities sometimes left a kind of 'afterglow'. This is perhaps most marked in the world of apocalyptic. For example, the seventy sons of God, originally denoting the gods of the pantheon under El, with whom Yahweh became identified, now became demoted to the status of angels, the seventy guardian angels of the nations attested in *1 Enoch*. Again, I have noted how the name of 'Baal the Prince' (*ẓbl b'l* in Ugaritic) became transformed into Beelzebul, the Prince of the Demons or Satan, in the gospels. The relation between Baal and El became encapsulated in the relationship of the one like son

18. A. Laato, *Josiah and David Redivivus* (ConBOT, 33; Stockholm: Almqvist & Wicksell, 1992), p. 43.

19. Spieckermann, *Juda unter Assur*, pp. 212-21.

of man and the Ancient of Days in the apocalyptic imagery of Daniel 7, as did the chaos monster, and the seven-headed Leviathan of Canaanite mythology lives on even in the New Testament, where both the seven-headed dragon of Revelation 12, symbolizing Satan, and the seven-headed beast of Revelation 13, symbolizing Rome, derive from him. I have argued too that the imagery of the resurrection of the dead, another important concept in apocalyptic, also derives ultimately from the resurrection of Baal. However, although these images lived on, everything became transformed in the light of monotheism, and it is arguably monotheism (at first monolatry), rather than God's mighty acts in history as used to be argued, that most distinguishes the Old Testament from the religions of the other nations of the ancient Near East.

BIBLIOGRAPHY

Aartun, K., 'Neue Beiträge zum ugaritischen Lexikon I', *UF* 16 (1984), pp. 1-52.

Ackerman, S., ' "And the Women Knead Dough": The Worship of the Queen of Heaven in Sixth-Century Judah', in P.L. Day (ed.), *Gender and Difference in Ancient Israel* (Minneapolis: Fortress Press, 1989), pp. 109-24.

—*Under Every Green Tree: Popular Religion in Sixth-Century Judah* (HSM, 46; Atlanta: Scholars Press, 1992).

—*Warrior, Dancer, Seductress, Queen: Women in Judges and Biblical Israel* (ABRL; New York: Doubleday, 1998).

Aharoni, Y., *The Land of the Bible: A Historical Geography* (trans. and ed. A.F. Rainey; Philadelphia: Westminster Press, 1979).

Aistleitner, J., *Wörterbuch der ugaritischen Sprache* (ed. O. Eissfeldt; Berichte über die Verhandlungen der Sächsischen Akademie der Wissenschaften zu Leipzig. Philologische-Historische Klasse, 106.3; Berlin: Akademie Verlag, 1965).

Akurgal, E., and M. Hirmer, *Die Kunst der Hethiter* (Munich: Hirmer Verlag, 1961).

Albertz, R., *Religionsgeschichte Israels in alttestamentlicher Zeit* (2 vols.; Göttingen: Vandenhoeck & Ruprecht, 1992); ET *A History of Israelite Religion in the Old Testament Period* (trans. J.S. Bowden; 2 vols.; London: SCM Press, 1994).

Albright, W.F., 'Gilgames and Engidu: Mesopotamian Genii of Fecundity', *JAOS* 40 (1920), pp. 306-35.

—'A Revision of Early Hebrew Chronology', *JPOS* 1 (1921), pp. 49-79.

—'The Location of the Garden of Eden', *AJSL* 39 (1922), pp. 15-31.

—'The Evolution of the West-Semitic Divinity 'An-'Anat-'Attâ', *AJSL* 41 (1925), pp. 73-101.

—'The North-Canaanite Epic of 'Al'êyân Ba'al and Mot', *JPOS* 12 (1932), pp. 185-208.

—'The Names Shaddai and Abram', *JBL* 54 (1935), pp. 180-87.

—'Zabûl Yam and Thâpiṭ Nahar in the Combat between Baal and the Sea', *JPOS* 16 (1936), pp. 17-20.

—'The Psalm of Habakkuk', in H.H. Rowley (ed.), *Studies in Old Testament Prophecy Presented to Professor T.H. Robinson* (Edinburgh: T. & T. Clark, 1950), pp. 1-18.

—'Baal-Zephon', in W. Baumgartner, O. Eissfeldt, K. Elliger and L. Rost (eds.), *Festschrift Alfred Bertholet* (Tübingen: J.C.B. Mohr [Paul Siebeck], 1950), pp. 1-14.

—'A Catalogue of Early Hebrew Lyric Poems (Psalm LXVIII)', *HUCA* 23 (1950–51), pp. 1-39.

—*From the Stone Age to Christianity* (Garden City, NY: Doubleday, 1957).

—'The High Place in Ancient Palestine', in *Volume du Congrès, Strasbourg 1956* (VTSup, 4; Leiden: E.J. Brill, 1957), pp. 242-58.

—'Some Remarks on the Song of Moses in Deuteronomy XXXII', *VT* 9 (1959), pp. 339-46.

—*The Archaeology of Palestine* (Harmondsworth: Penguin Books, rev. edn, 1960).

—*Yahweh and the Gods of Canaan* (London: Athlone Press, 1968).
—*Archaeology and the Religion of Israel* (Garden City, NY: Doubleday, 5th edn, 1969).
Alfrink, B., 'Der Versammlungsberg im äussersten Norden', *Bib* 14 (1933), pp. 41-67.
—'Het "Still Staan" van Zon en Maan in Jos. 10:12-15', *Studia Catholica* 24 (1949), pp. 238-68.
Allen, L.C., *The Books of Joel, Obadiah, Jonah and Micah* (NICOT; London: Hodder & Stoughton, 1976).
Alt, A., 'Institut im Jahre 1925', *PJB* 22 (1926), pp. 5-80.
—'Megiddo im Übergang vom kanaanäischen zum israelitischen Zeitalter', *ZAW* 60 (1944), pp. 67-85.
—'Das Gottesurteil auf dem Karmel', in A. Weiser (ed.), *Festschrift G. Beer zum 60. Geburtstage dargebracht* (Stuttgart: W. Kohlhammer, 1935), pp. 1-18; reprinted in A. Alt, *Kleine Schriften*, II (Munich: C.H. Beck, 1953), pp. 135-49.
Andersen, F.I., 'A Lexicographical Note on Exodus XXXII 18', *VT* 16 (1966), pp. 108-12.
Andersen, F.I., and D.N. Freedman, *Hosea* (AB, 24; Garden City, NY: Doubleday, 1980).
Anderson, A.A., *Psalms* (NCB; 2 vols.; London: Oliphants, 1972).
Anderson, H., *The Gospel of Mark* (NCB; London: Oliphants, 1976).
Angerstorfer, A., 'Ašerah als "Consort of Jahwe" oder Aširtah?', *BN* 17 (1982), pp. 7-16.
Archi, A., 'Diffusione del culto di dNI-da-kul', *Studi Eblaiti* 1 (1979), pp. 105-13.
Arnaud, D., *Recherches au pays d'Aštata: Emar* VI.3 (Paris: Recherche sur les Civilisations, 1986).
Astour, M.C., 'Yahweh in Egyptian Topographic Texts', in M. Görg and E. Pusch (eds.), *Festschrift Elmar Edel* (Ägypten und Altes Testament, 1; Bamberg: M. Görg, 1979), pp. 17-34.
Attridge, H.W., and R.A. Oden, *Philo of Bybos: The Phoenician History* (CBQMS, 9; Washington DC: Catholic Biblical Association of America, 1981).
Auld, A.G., 'A Judean Sanctuary of 'Anat (Josh. 15:59)?', *Tel Aviv* 4 (1977), pp. 85-86; reprinted in A.G. Auld, *Joshua Retold* (Old Testament Studies; Edinburgh: T. & T. Clark, 1998), pp. 61-62.
Avigad, N., 'Excavations in the Jewish Quarter of the Old City of Jerusalem, 1971', *IEJ* 22 (1972), pp. 193-200.
—'Hebrew Seals and Sealings and their Significance for Biblical Research', in J.A. Emerton (ed.), *Congress Volume, Jerusalem 1986* (VTSup, 40; Leiden: E.J. Brill, 1988), pp. 7-16.
Avishur, Y., 'The Ghost-expelling Incantation from Ugarit (Ras Ibn Hani 78/20)', *UF* 13 (1981), pp. 13-25.
Avi-Yonah, M., 'Mount Carmel and the God of Baalbek', *IEJ* 2 (1952), pp. 118-24.
Bailey, L.R., 'Israelite '*Ēl Šadday* and Amorite *Bêl Šadê*', *JBL* 87 (1968), pp. 434-38.
—'The Golden Calf', *HUCA* 42 (1971), pp. 97-115.
Ball, C.J., 'Israel and Babylon', *PSBA* 16 (1894), pp. 188-200.
Barr, J., *The Semantics of Biblical Language* (Oxford: Oxford University Press, 1961).
—'"Thou Art the Cherub": Ezekiel 28.14 and the Post-Ezekiel Understanding of Genesis 2–3', in E.C. Ulrich *et al.* (eds.), *Priests, Prophets and Scribes: Essays on the Formation and Heritage of Second Temple Judaism in Honour of Joseph Blenkinsopp* (JSOTSup, 140; Sheffield: JSOT Press, 1992), pp. 212-23.
Barré, M., 'dLAMMA and Rešep at Ugarit: The Hittite Connection', *JAOS* 98 (1978), pp. 465-67.

Barstad, H.M., *The Religious Polemics of Amos: Studies in the Preaching of Am 2, 7B-8; 4, 1-13; 5, 1-27; 6, 4-7; 8, 14* (VTSup, 34; Leiden: E.J. Brill, 1984).

Barth, H., *Die Jesaja-Worte in der Josiazeit* (WMANT, 48, Neukirchen–Vluyn: Neukirchener Verlag, 1977).

Barthélemy, D., 'Les tiqquné sopherim et la critique textuelle de l'Ancien Testament', in *Congress Volume, Bonn 1962* (VTSup, 9; Leiden: E.J. Brill, 1963), pp. 285-304.

—*Critique Textuelle de l'Ancien Testament* (3 vols.; OBO, 50.1-3; Fribourg: Editions Universitaires; Göttingen: Vandenhoeck & Ruprecht, 1982–92).

Bartlett, J.R., 'Sihon and Og, Kings of the Amorites', *VT* 20 (1970), pp. 257-77.

Barton, G.A., 'Ashtoreth and her Influence in the Old Testament', *JBL* 10 (1891), pp. 73-91.

Battenfield, J.K., 'YHWH's Refutation of the Baal Myth through the Actions of Elijah and Elisha', in A. Gileadi (ed.), *Israel's Apostasy and Restoration: Essays in Honor of Roland K. Harrison* (Grand Rapids, MI: Baker Book House, 1988), pp. 19-37.

Baudissin, W.W. von, *Studien zur semitischen Religionsgeschichte* (2 vols.; Leipzig: Georg Reimer, 1876–78).

—*Adonis und Esmun* (Leipzig: J.C. Hinrichs, 1911).

Bea, A., 'Kinderopfer für Moloch oder für Jahwe?', *Bib* 18 (1937), pp. 95-107.

Beck, M., *Elia und die Monolatrie* (BZAW, 281; Berlin: W. de Gruyter, 1999).

Beck, P., 'The Drawings from Ḥorvat Teiman (Kuntillet 'Ajrud)', *Tel Aviv* 9 (1982), pp. 3-68.

Benz, F.L., *Personal Names in the Phoenician and Punic Inscriptions* (Studia Pohl, 8; Rome: Biblical Institute Press, 1972).

Bernhardt, K., 'Aschera in Ugarit und im Alten Testament', *MIO* 13 (1967), pp. 163-74.

Bertholet, A., *Hesekiel* (HAT, 13; Tübingen: J.C.B. Mohr [Paul Siebeck], 1936).

Biale, D., 'The God of the Breasts: El Shaddai in the Bible', *HR* 21 (1981–82), pp. 240-56.

Bickerman(n), E., *Der Gott der Makkabäer* (Berlin: Schocken Verlag and Jüdischer Buchverlag, 1937); ET *The God of the Maccabees* (trans. H.R. Moehring; SJLA, 32; Leiden: E.J. Brill, 1979).

Binger, T., *Asherah: Goddesses in Ugarit, Israel and the Old Testament* (JSOTSup, 232; Sheffield: Sheffield Academic Press, 1997).

Blau, J., and J.C. Greenfield, 'Ugaritic Glosses', *BASOR* (1970), pp. 11-17.

Blenkinsopp, J., *Gibeon and Israel: The Role of Gibeon and the Gibeonites in the Political and Religious History of Early Israel* (Cambridge: Cambridge University Press, 1972).

Block, D.I., *The Gods of the Nations: Studies in Ancient Near Eastern National Mythology* (Evangelical Theological Monograph Series, 2; Jackson, MI: Evangelical Theological Society; Winona Lake, IN: Eisenbrauns, 1988).

Bochart, S., *Hierozoicon* (2 vols.; London, 1663).

Bonnet, C., 'Typhon et Baal Ṣaphon', in E. Lipiński (ed.), *Phoenicia and the East Mediterranean in the First Millennium B.C.* (Studia Phoenicia, 5; Leuven: Peeters, 1987), p. 101-43.

—*Melqart: Cultes et mythes de l'Héraclès tyrien en Méditerranée* (Studia Phoenicia, 8; Leuven: Peeters and Presses Universitaires de Namur, 1988).

—*Astarté: Dossier documentaire et perspectives historiques* (Collezione di Studi Fenici, 37; Rome: Consiglio Nazionale delle Ricerche, 1996).

Borger, R., 'Anath-Bethel', *VT* 7 (1957), pp. 102-104.

Bousset, W., *Die Religion des Judentums im späthellenistischen Zeitalter* (Tübingen: J.C.B. Mohr [Paul Siebeck], 3rd edn, 1906).
Boyce, M., *A History of Zoroastrianism* (3 vols., Leiden: E.J. Brill, 1975–91).
Branden, A. van den, 'Le dieu Rešeph et ses épithètes', *Parole de l'Orient* 2 (1971), pp. 389-416.
—'"Rešeph" nella Bibbia', *Bibbia e Oriente* 13 (1971), pp. 211-25.
Bresciani, E., and M. Kamil, *Le lettere aramaiche di Hermopoli* (Atti della Accademia Nazionale dei Lincei: Memorie, Classe di Scienze morale, storiche e filoliche, ser. 8, vol. 12, fasc. 5; Rome: Accademia Nazionale dei Lincei, 1966).
Bright, J., *Jeremiah* (AB, 21; Garden City, NY: Doubleday, 1965).
Brock, S.P., 'Νεφεληγερέτα = *rkb 'rpt*', *VT* 18 (1968), pp. 395-97.
Bronner, L., *The Stories of Elijah and Elisha as Polemics against Baal Worship* (Pretoria Oriental Studies, 6; Leiden: E.J. Brill, 1968).
Broome, E.C., 'The Dolmens of Palestine and Transjordania', *JBL* 59 (1940), pp. 479-97.
Brown, J.P., *The Lebanon and Phoenicia: Ancient Texts Illustrating their Physical Geography and Native Industries*, I (Beirut: American University of Beirut, 1969).
Brownlee, W.H., *The Meaning of the Qumrân Scrolls for the Bible with Special Attention to the Book of Isaiah* (New York: Oxford University Press, 1964).
Buber, M., *Königtum Gottes* (Heidelberg: L. Schneider, 3rd edn, 1956); ET *Kingship of God* (trans. R. Scheimann; London: Allen & Unwin, 3rd edn, 1967).
Budde, K., *Das Buch Hiob* (HAT, 2.1; Göttingen: Vandenhoeck & Ruprecht, 1896).
Bunge, J.G., 'Der "Gott der Festungen" und der "Liebling der Frauen"', *JSJ* 4 (1973), pp. 169-82.
Burns, J.B., 'The Identity of Death's First-born (Job XVIII 13)', *VT* 37 (1987), pp. 362-64.
—'*ḥôlēš 'al* in Isaiah 14:12: A New Proposal', *ZAH* 2 (1989), pp. 199-204.
Burstein, S.M., *The Babyloniaca of Berossus* (Sources and Monographs: Sources from the Ancient Near East, I.5; Malibu: Undena, 1978).
Busink, T.A., *Der Tempel von Jerusalem* (2 vols.; Leiden: E.J. Brill, 1970–80).
Cantineau, J., 'Tadmorea (*suite*)', *Syria* 19 (1938), pp. 72-82.
Caquot, A., 'Le dieu Athtar et les textes de Ras Shamra', *Syria* 35 (1958), pp. 45-60.
—'La tablette RS 24.252 et la question des Rephaïm ougaritiques', *Syria* 53 (1976), pp. 295-304.
—'Sur quelques démons de l'Ancien Testament: Reshep, Qeteb, Deber', *Sem* 6 (1956), pp. 53-68.
—'Ras Shamra: La littérature ugaritique', *DBSup*, IX, cols. 1361-1417.
—'Le dieu Athtar et les textes de Ras Shamra', *Syria* 35 (1958), pp. 45-60.
—'Rephaïm', *DBSup*, X, cols. 344-57.
Caquot, A., M. Sznycer and A. Herdner, *Textes Ougaritiques*, I (Paris: Cerf, 1974).
Caquot, A., and J. de Tarragon, *Textes Ougaritiques*, II (Paris: Cerf, 1989).
Cassuto, U. (M.D.), *A Commentary on the Book of Genesis*. I. *From Adam to Noah* (trans. I. Abrahams; Jerusalem: Magnes Press, 1961).
—'Baal and Mot in the Ugaritic Texts', *IEJ* 12 (1962), pp. 77-86.
—*The Goddess Anath* (trans. I. Abrahams; Jerusalem: Magnes Press, 1971).
Cazelles, H., 'L'hymne ugaritique à Anat', *Syria* 33 (Hommage à M. Charles Virolleaud, 1956), pp. 48-57.
—'Molok', *DBSup*, V, cols. 1337-46.
Ceresko, A., *Job 29–31 in the Light of Northwest Semitic* (BibOr, 36; Rome: Biblical Institute Press, 1980).

Charlier, C.V.L., 'Ein astronomischer Beitrag zur Exegese des Alten Testaments', *ZDMG* 58 (1904), pp. 386-94.
Charpin, D., and J-M. Durand, '"Fils de Sim'al": Les origines tribales des rois de Mari', *RA* 80 (1986), pp. 141-83.
Cheyne, T.K., 'Baalzebub', in T.K. Cheyne and J.S. Black (eds.), *Encyclopaedia Biblica* (one vol. edn; London: A. & C. Black, 1904), cols. 407-408.
Chiera, E., and E.A. Speiser, 'Selected "Kirkuk" Documents', *JAOS* 47 (1927), pp. 36-60.
Childs, B.S., *The Book of Exodus* (OTL; London: SCM Press, 1974).
Clements, R.E., *God and Temple* (Oxford: Basil Blackwell, 1965).
—'Baal-Berith of Shechem', *JSS* 13 (1968), pp. 21-32.
—*Isaiah 1–39* (NCB; Grand Rapids: Eerdmans; London: Marshall, Morgan & Scott, 1980).
Clifford, R.J., *The Cosmic Mountain in Canaan and the Old Testament* (HSM, 4; Cambridge, MA: Harvard University Press, 1972).
Clines, D.J.A., *Job 1–20* (WBC, 17; Dallas: Word Books, 1989).
Cogan, M.D., *Imperialism and Religion* (SBLMS, 19; Missoula, MT: SBL and Scholars Press, 1974).
Colenso, J.W., *The Pentateuch and Book of Joshua Critically Examined* (7 parts; London: Longmans, Green, & Co., 1879).
Conrad, D., 'Der Gott Reschef', *ZAW* 83 (1971), pp. 157-83.
Coogan, M.D., 'Of Cults and Cultures: Reflections on the Interpretation of Archaeological Evidence', *PEQ* 119 (1987), pp. 1-8.
—'Canaanite Origins and Lineage: Reflections on the Religion of Ancient Israel', in P.D. Miller, P.D. Hanson, S. Dean McBride (eds.), *Ancient Israelite Religion: Essays in Honor of Frank Moore Cross* (Philadelphia: Fortress Press, 1987), pp. 115-24.
Cooke, G., 'The Sons of (the) Gods', *ZAW* 76 (1964), pp. 22-47.
Cooper, A., 'Divine Names and Epithets in the Ugaritic Texts', in S. Rummel (ed.), *Ras Shamra Parallels*, III (Rome: Pontificial Biblical Institute, 1981), pp. 333-469.
—'MLK 'LM: "Eternal King" or "King of Eternity"?', in Marks and Good (eds.), *Love & Death in the Ancient Near East*, pp. 1-7.
—'A Note on the Vocalization of עַשְׁתֹּרֶת', *ZAW* 102 (1990), pp. 98-100.
Cornelius, I., *The Iconography of the Canaanite Gods Reshef and Ba'al* (OBO, 140; Fribourg: University Press; Göttingen: Vandenhoeck & Ruprecht, 1994).
—'The Iconography of the Canaanite Gods Reshef and Baal: A Rejoinder', *JNSL* 24.2 (1998), pp. 167-77.
Craigie, P.C., 'A Reconsideration of Shamgar ben Anath (Judg 3:31 and 5:6)', *JBL* 91 (1972), pp. 239-40.
—'Helel, Athtar and Phaethon (Jes 14 12-15)', *ZAW* 85 (1973), pp. 223-25.
—'Three Ugaritic Notes on the Song of Deborah', *JSOT* 2 (1976), pp. 33-49.
—'Deborah and Anat: A Study of Poetic Imagery (Judges 5)', *ZAW* 90 (1978), pp. 374-81.
Cranfield, C.E.B., *The Gospel according to Saint Mark* (CGTC; Cambridge: Cambridge University Press, 1963).
Crenshaw, J.L., *Joel* (AB, 24C; Garden City, NY: Doubleday, 1995).
Croatto, J.S., and J.A. Soggin, 'Die Bedeutung von שדמות im Alten Testament', *ZAW* 74 (1962), pp. 44-50.
Cross, F.M., 'Notes on a Canaanite Psalm in the Old Testament', *BASOR* 117 (1950), pp. 19-21.
—'The Council of Yahweh in Second Isaiah', *JNES* 12 (1953), pp. 274-77.
—'Yahweh and the God of the Patriarchs', *HTR* 55 (1962), pp. 225-59.

—*Canaanite Myth and Hebrew Epic* (Cambridge, MA: Harvard University Press, 1973).
—'Newly Found Inscriptions in Old Canaanite and Early Phoenician', *BASOR* 238 (1980), pp. 1-20.
—'Reuben, First-born of Jacob', *ZAW* 100 Supplement (1988), pp. 46-65.
Cross, F.M., and D.N. Freedman, 'Josiah's Revolt against Assyria', *JNES* 12 (1953), pp. 56-58.
—'The Song of Miriam', *JNES* 14 (1955), pp. 237-50.
Cumont, F.M., 'Astarté', in G. Wissowa (ed.), *Real-Encyclopädie der classischen Altertumswissenschaft*, II (Stuttgart: J.B. Metzler, rev. edn, 1896), cols. 1776-78.
Cunchillos Ylarri, J.L., 'Los b^ene ha'elohîm en Gen. 6, 1-4', *EstBíb* 28 (1969), pp. 5-31.
Curtis, A.H.W., 'Some Observations on "Bull" Terminology in the Ugaritic Texts and the Old Testament', in A.S. van der Woude (ed.), *In Quest of the Past: Studies on Israelite Religion, Literature and Prophetism* (OTS, 26; Leiden: E.J. Brill, 1990), pp. 17-31.
Dahood, M.J., 'La Regina del Cielo in Geremia', *RivB* 8 (1960), pp. 166-68.
—*Psalms* (AB, 16, 17, and 17A; 3 vols.; Garden City, NY: Doubleday, 1966–70).
—'Afterword: Ebla, Ugarit, and the Bible', in G. Pettinato, *The Archives of Ebla* (ET; Garden City, NY: Doubleday, 1981), pp. 271-321.
Dahood, M.J., and G. Pettinato, 'Ugaritic *ršp gn* and Eblaite *Rasap gunu(m)*', *Or* NS 46 (1977) pp. 230-32.
Dalglish, E.R., 'Bethel (Deity)', *ABD*, I, pp. 706-10.
Dalley, S., *Myths from Mesopotamia* (Oxford: Oxford University Press, 1989).
Dalley S., and B. Teissier, 'Tablets from the Vicinity of Emar and Elsewhere', *Iraq* 54 (1992), pp. 83-111.
Dalman, G., *Arbeit und Sitte in Palästina* (7 vols. in 8; Gütersloh: C. Bertelsmann, 1928–42).
Danelius, E., 'The Sins of Jeroboam Ben-Nabat [*sic*]' *JQR* 58 (1967), pp. 95-114, 204-23.
Davies, G.I., *Hosea* (NBC; London: Marshall Pickering; Grand Rapids: Eerdmans, 1992).
—review of *You Shall Have no other Gods: Israelite Religion in the Light of Hebrew Inscriptions* (HSS, 31; Atlanta: Scholars Press, 1986), by J.H. Tigay, in *JTS* NS 40 (1989), pp. 143-46.
Day, J., 'Echoes of Baal's Seven Thunders and Lightnings in Psalm XXIX and Habakkuk III 9 and the Identity of the Seraphim in Isaiah VI', *VT* 29 (1979), pp. 143-51.
—'New Light on the Mythological Background of the Allusion to Resheph in Habakkuk III 5', *VT* 29 (1979), pp. 353-55.
—'The Daniel of Ugarit and Ezekiel and the Hero of the Book of Daniel', *VT* 30 (1980), pp. 174-84.
—'A Case of Inner Scriptural Interpretation: The Dependence of Isaiah xxvi.13–xxvii.11 on Hosea xiii.4–xiv.10 (ET 9) and its Relevance to Some Theories of the Redaction of the "Isaiah Apocalypse"', *JTS* NS 31 (1980), pp. 309-19; reprinted (with minor revisions) in C.C. Broyles and C.A. Evans (eds.), *Writing and Reading the Scroll of Isaiah: Studies of an Interpretive Tradition*, I (VTSup, 70.1; Leiden: E.J. Brill, 1997), pp. 357-68.
—*God's Conflict with the Dragon and the Sea: Echoes of a Canaanite Myth in the Old Testament* (UCOP, 35; Cambridge: Cambridge University Press, 1985).
—'Asherah in the Hebrew Bible and Northwest Semitic Literature', *JBL* 105 (1986), pp. 385-408.

—*Molech: A God of Human Sacrifice in the Old Testament* (UCOP, 41; Cambridge: Cambridge University Press, 1989).
—*Psalms* (OTG; Sheffield: Sheffield Academic Press, 1990).
—'Ugarit and the Bible: Do they Presuppose the Same Canaanite Mythology and Religion?', in G.J. Brooke, A.H.W. Curtis and J.F. Healey (eds.), *Ugarit and the Bible: Proceedings of the International Symposium on Ugarit and the Bible, Manchester, September 1992* (UBL, 11; Münster: Ugarit–Verlag, 1994), pp. 35-52.
—'Ashtoreth', *ABD*, I, pp. 491-94.
—'Baal', *ABD*, I, pp. 545-49,
—'Foreign Semitic Influence on the Wisdom of Israel and its Appropriation in the Book of Proverbs', in Day, Gordon and Williamson (eds.), *Wisdom in Ancient Israel*, pp. 55-70.
—'The Development of Belief in Life after Death in Ancient Israel', in J. Barton and D.J. Reimer (eds.), *After the Exile: Essays in Honour of Rex Mason* (Macon, GA; Mercer University Press, 1996), pp. 231-57.
—review of *Yahweh and the Sun: Biblical and Archaeological Evidence for Sun Worship in Ancient Israel* (JSOTSup, 111; Sheffield: JSOT Press, 1993), by J. Glen Taylor, in *PEQ* 128 (1996), pp. 185-86.
—'Resurrection Imagery from Baal to the Book of Daniel', in J.A. Emerton (ed.), *Congress Volume, Cambridge 1995* (VTSup, 66; Leiden: E.J. Brill, 1997), pp. 125-33.
Day, J., R.P. Gordon and H.G.M. Williamson (eds.), *Wisdom in Ancient Israel: Essays in Honour of J.A. Emerton* (Cambridge: Cambridge University Press, 1995).
Day, P.L., *An Adversary in Heaven:* śāṭān *in the Hebrew Bible* (HSM, 43; Atlanta: Scholars Press, 1988).
—'Anat, Mistress of Animals', *JNES* 51 (1992), pp. 181-90.
—'Anat', *DDD*, cols. 62-77 (2nd edn, pp. 36-43).
Debus, J., *Die Sünde Jerobeams* (FRLANT, 95; Göttingen: Vandenhoeck & Ruprecht, 1967).
Deem, A., 'The Goddess Anath and some Biblical Cruces', *JSS* 23 (1978), pp. 25-30.
Delcor, M., 'Jahwe et Dagon ou le Jahwisme face à la religion des Philistins, d'après 1 Sam. V', *VT* 14 (1964), pp. 136-54; reprinted in M. Delcor, *Etudes bibliques et orientales de religions comparées* (Leiden: E.J. Brill, 1979), pp. 30-48.
—'Astarté et la fécondité des troupeaux en Deut. 7,13 et parallèles', *UF* 6 (1974), pp. 7-14; reprinted in M. Delcor, *Religion d'Israël et Proche Orient Ancien* (Leiden: E.J. Brill, 1976), pp. 86-93.
—'Le culte de la "reine du ciel" selon Jer 7, 18; 44, 17-19, 25 et ses survivances', in W.C. Delsman *et al.* (eds.), *Von Kanaan bis Kerala* (AOAT, 211; Neukirchen–Vluyn: Neukirchener Verlag, 1982), pp. 101-22.
—'Une allusion à 'Anath, déesse guerrière', *JJS* 32 (1982), pp. 145-60.
Dever, W.G., 'Iron Age Epigraphic Material from the Area of Khirbet el-Kôm', *HUCA* 40–41 (1969–70), pp. 139-204.
—'Asherah, Consort of Yahweh? New Evidence from Kuntillet 'Ajrud', *BASOR* 255 (1984), pp. 21-27.
Dhorme, E.(P.), 'Le séjour des morts chez les Babyloniens et les Hébreux', *RB* NS 4 (1907), pp. 59-78.
—*Les Livres de Samuel* (Paris: V. Lecoffre & J. Gabalda, 1910).

—*Le Livre de Job* (Etudes Bibliques; Paris: V. Lecoffre, 1926); ET *A Commentary on the Book of Job* (trans. H. Knight; London: T. Nelson, 1967).

Dietrich, M., and O. Loretz, 'Baal *rpu* in *KTU* 1.108; 1.113 und nach 1.17 VI 25-33', *UF* 12 (1980), pp. 171-82.

—*'Jahwe und seine Aschera'* (UBL, 9; Münster: Ugarit–Verlag, 1992).

Dietrich, M., and W. Mayer, 'Hurritische Wiehrauch-Beschwörungen in ugaritischer Alphabetschrift', *UF* 26 (1994), p. 73-112.

Dietrich, M., O. Loretz and J. Sanmartín, 'Die Totengeister ugaritischen *rpu*(*m*) und die biblischen Rephaim', *UF* 8 (1976), pp. 45-52.

Dietrich, W., and M.A. Klopfenstein (eds.), *Ein Gott allein?* (OBO, 139; Göttingen: Vandenhoeck & Ruprecht, 1994).

Diggle, J., *Euripides, Phaethon* (Cambridge: Cambridge University Press, 1970).

Dijk, H.J. Van, *Ezekiel's Prophecy on Tyre (Ez. 26,1–28,19)* (BibOr, 20; Rome: Pontifical Biblical Institute, 1968).

Dijkstra, M., 'El 'Olam in the Sinai?', *ZAW* 99 (1987), pp. 249-50.

Dion, P.-E., review of *The Burden of Babylon*, by S. Erlandsson, in *Bib* 52 (1971), pp. 439-42.

Driver, G.R., 'Some Hebrew Verbs, Nouns, and Pronouns', *JTS* 30 (1929), pp. 371-78.

—'Studies in the Vocabulary of the Old Testament, II', *JTS* 32 (1930–31), pp. 250-57.

—*Canaanite Myths and Legends* (Edinburgh: T. & T. Clark, 1956).

—'Stars', in J. Hastings (ed.), *Dictionary of the Bible* (rev. H.H. Rowley and F.C. Grant; Edinburgh: T. & T. Clark, 2nd edn, 1963), pp. 936-37.

—'Ugaritic Problems', in S. Segert (ed.), *Studia Semitica philologica necnon philosophica Ioanni Bakoš dicata* (Bratislava: Vydavatel'stvo Slovenskej akadémie vied, 1965), pp. 95-110.

Driver, S.R., *Notes on the Hebrew Text of the Books of Samuel* (Oxford: Clarendon Press, 1890).

—*A Critical and Exegetical Commentary on Deuteronomy* (ICC; Edinburgh: T. & T. Clark, 1895).

—*The Book of Exodus* (Cambridge Bible for Schools and Colleges; Cambridge: Cambridge University Press, 1911).

Driver, S.R., and G.B. Gray, *A Critical and Exegetical Commentary on the Book of Job* (ICC; Edinburgh: T. & T. Clark, 1921).

Dronkert, K., *De Molochdienst in het Oude Testament* (Leiden: Drukkerij 'Luctor et Emergo', 1953).

Duhm, B., *Das Buch Jesaia* (Göttinger Handkommentar zum Alten Testament, 3.1; Göttingen: Vandenhoeck & Ruprecht, 4th edn, 1922).

Dürr, L., 'Hebr. נֶפֶשׁ = akk. napištu = Gurgel, Kehle', *ZAW* 43 (1925), pp. 262-69.

Dus, J., 'Gibeon: Eine Kultstätte des *šmš* und die Stadt der benjaminitischen Schicksals', *VT* 10 (1960), pp. 353-74.

Dussaud, R., 'La mythologie phénicienne d'après les tablettes de Ras Shamra', *RHR* 104 (1931), pp. 353-408.

—review of *Molk als Opferberiff im Punischen und Hebräischen und das Ende des Gottes Moloch*, by O. Eissfeldt, in *Syria* 16 (1935), pp. 407-409.

—review of *Molk als Opferberiff im Punischen und Hebräischen und das Ende des Gottes Moloch*, by O. Eissfeldt, in *AfO* 11 (1936), pp. 167-68.

—*Les origines cananéennes du sacrifice israélite* (Paris: E. Leroux, 2nd edn, 1941).

Dyke Parunak, H. van, 'Was Solomon's Temple Aligned to the Sun?', *PEQ* (1978), pp. 29-33.
Eaton, J.H., *Psalms* (Torch Bible Paperbacks; London: SCM Press, 1967).
Ebeling, E, 'Ašratu', *RLA*, I, p. 169.
Edelmann, R., 'Exodus 32:18', *JTS* 1 (1950), p. 56.
—'To עַנּוֹת Exodus XXXII 18', *VT* 16 (1966), p. 355.
Edgerton, W.F., and J.A. Wilson, *Historical Records of Ramses III: The Texts in Medinet Habu* (Chicago: University of Chicago Press, 1936).
Eichrodt, W., *Theologie des Alten Testaments*, I (2 vols. in 3 parts; Stuttgart: Klotz, 5th edn, 1957–61); ET *Theology of the Old Testament* (trans. J.A. Baker; 2 vols.; London: SCM Press, 1961–67).
Eissfeldt, O., 'Der Gott Bethel', *ARW* 28 (1930), pp. 1-30; reprinted in O. Eissfeldt, *Kleine Schriften*, I, pp. 206-33.
—*Baal Zaphon, Zeus Kasios und der Durchzug der Israeliten durchs Meer* (Beiträge zur Religionsgeschichte des Altertums; Halle: Niemeyer, 1932).
—'Der Gott des Tabor und seine Verbreitung', *ARW* 31 (1934), pp. 14-41; reprinted in O. Eissfeldt, *Kleine Schriften*, II, pp. 29-54.
—*Molk als Opferberiff im Punischen und Hebräischen und das Ende des Gottes Moloch* (Beiträge zur Religionsgeschichte des Altertums, 4; Halle: Niemeyer, 1935).
—'Ba'alšamēm und Jahwe', *ZAW* 57 (1939), pp. 18-23; reprinted in O. Eissfeldt, *Kleine Schriften*, II, pp. 170-98.
—'Lade und Stierbild', *ZAW* 58 (1940–41), pp. 190-215; reprinted in O. Eissfeldt, *Kleine Schriften*, II, pp. 282-305.
—*El im ugaritischen Pantheon* (Berichte über die Verhandlungen der Sächsischen Akademie der Wissenschaften zu Leipzig. Phil. Hist. Klasse, 98.4; Berlin: Akademie Verlag, 1951).
—*Der Gott Karmel* (Sitzungsberichte der deutschen Akademie der Wissenschaften zu Berlin. Klasse für Sprachen, Literatur und Kunst, Jahrgang 1953, 1; Berlin: Akademie Verlag, 1953).
—'El and Yahweh', *JSS* (1956), pp. 25-37; reprinted in German as 'El und Jahwe', in O. Eissfeldt, *Kleine Schriften*, III, pp. 386-97.
—*Kleine Schriften*, I–VI (Tübingen: J.C.B. Mohr [Paul Siebeck], 1962–79).
—'Gottesnamen in Personennamen als Symbole menschlicher Qualitäten', in K. Rudolph, R. Heller and E. Walter (eds.), *Festschrift Walter Baetke* (Weimar: Hermann Böhlaus Nachfolger, 1966), pp. 110-17; reprinted in O. Eissfeldt, *Kleine Schriften*, IV, pp. 276-84.
—'Der kanaanäischer El als Geber der den israelitischen Erzvätern geltenden Nachkommenschaft- und Landbesitzverheissungen', in M. Fleischhammer (ed.), *Studia Orientalia in memoriam Caroli Brockelmann* (Wissenschaftliche Zeitschrift der Martin-Luther-Universität Halle–Wittenberg, Gesellschafts- und Sprachwissenschaftliche Reihe, 17; Halle (Saale), 1968), vols. 2–3, pp. 45-53; reprinted in O. Eissfeldt, *Kleine Schriften*, V (Tübingen: J.C.B. Mohr [Paul Siebeck], 1973), pp. 50-62.
Elnes E.E., and P.D. Miller, 'Elyon', *DDD*, cols. 560-71 (2nd edn, pp. 293-99).
Emerton, J.A., 'The Origin of the Son of Man Imagery', *JTS* NS 9 (1958), pp. 225-42.
—'Ugaritic Notes', *JTS* NS 16 (1965), pp. 441-42.
—'The Textual Problems of Isaiah V 14', *VT* 17 (1967), pp. 135-42.
—'The Riddle of Genesis XIV', *VT* 21 (1971), pp. 403-39.

—'Gideon and Jerubbaal', *JTS* NS 27 (1976), pp. 289-312.

—'New Light on Israelite Religion: The Implications of the Inscriptions from Kuntillet 'Ajrud', *ZAW* 94 (1982), pp. 2-20.

—'Leviathan and *ltn*: The Vocalization of the Ugaritic Word for the Dragon', *VT* 32 (1982), pp. 327-31.

—'The Translation and Interpretation of Isaiah vi. 13', in J. A. Emerton and S.C. Reif (eds.), *Interpreting the Hebrew Bible: Essays in Honour of E.I.J. Rosenthal* (UCOP, 32; Cambridge: Cambridge University Press, 1982), pp. 85-118.

—' "Yahweh and his Asherah": The Goddess or her Symbol?', *VT* 49 (1999), pp. 315-37.

Engelkern, K., 'Ba'alšamem: Eine Auseinandersetzung mit der Monographie von H. Niehr', *ZAW* 108 (1996), pp. 233-48, 391-407.

Engle, J.R., 'Pillar Figurines of Iron Age Asherah/Asherim' (PhD dissertation, University of Pittsburgh, 1979).

Erlandsson, S., *The Burden of Babylon: A Study of Isaiah 13:2–14:23* (ConBOT, 4; Lund: C.W.K. Gleerup, 1970).

Eslinger, L., and J.G. Taylor (eds.), *Ascribe to the Lord: Biblical and Other Studies in Memory of Peter C. Craigie* (JSOTSup, 67; Sheffield: JSOT Press, 1988).

Etz, D., 'Is Isaiah XIV 12-15 a Reference to Comet Halley?', *VT* 36 (1986), pp. 289-301.

Fensham, F.C., 'Thunder-stones in Ugaritic', *JNES* 18 (1959), pp. 273-74.

—'Shamgar ben 'Anat', *JNES* 20 (1961), pp. 197-98.

—'The Burning of the Golden Calf and Ugarit', *IEJ* 16 (1966), pp. 191-93.

—'A Possible Explanation of the Name Baal-zebub of Ekron', *ZAW* 79 (1967), pp. 361-64.

—'A Few Observations on the Polarisation Between Yahweh and Baal in 1 Kings 17–19', *ZAW* 92 (1980), pp. 227-36.

Fenton, J.C., *Saint Matthew* (Pelican Gospel Commentaries; Harmondsworth: Penguin Books, 1963).

Fenton, T., 'Chaos in the Bible? Tohu vabohu', in G. Abramson and T. Parfitt (eds.), *Jewish Education and Learning: Published in Honour of Dr David Patterson on the Occasion of his Seventieth Birthday* (London: Harwood Academic Publishers, 1993), pp. 203-20.

Finkelstein, I., 'Shiloh Yields some, but not all of its Secrets', *BARev* 12.1 (1986), pp. 22-41.

Fitzgerald, A., 'A Note on Psalm 29', *BASOR* 215 (1974), pp. 61-63.

Fitzmyer, J.A., 'The Phoenician Inscription from Pyrgi', *JAOS* 86 (1966), pp. 285-97.

—*The Aramaic Inscriptions of Sefîre* (BibOr, 19; Rome: Pontifical Biblical Institute, 1967).

—*The Gospel according to Luke (X-XXIV)* (AB, 28A; Garden City, NY: Doubleday, 1985).

Fohrer, G., 'Umkehr und Erlösung beim Propheten Hosea', *TZ* 11 (1955), pp. 161-85.

—*Jesaja* (Zürcher Bibelkommentare; 3 vols.; Zürich: Zwingli, 2nd edn, 1960–64).

—*Das Buch Hiob* (KAT, 16; Gütersloh: Gerd Mohn, 1963).

Fontenrose, J., 'Dagon and El', *Oriens* 10 (1957), pp. 277-79.

Forsyth, N., *The Old Enemy: Satan and the Combat Myth* (Princeton: Princeton University Press, 1987).

Fox, M.V. , *The Song of Songs and Ancient Egyptian Love Songs* (Wisconsin: University of Wisconsin Press, 1985).

Fraine, J. de, 'De miraculo solari Josue', *VD* 28 (1950), pp. 227-36.

Frankena, R., *Tākultu, de sacrale maaltijd in het Assyrische ritueel* (Leiden: E.J. Brill, 1954).

Freedman, D.N., 'Strophe and Meter in Exodus 15', in H.N. Bream, R.D. Heim and C.A. Moore (eds.), *A Light unto my Path: Old Testament Studies in Honor of Jacob M. Myers* (Philadelphia: Temple University Press, 1974), pp. 163-203; reprinted in D.N. Freedman, *Pottery, Poetry and Prophecy: Studies in Early Hebrew Poetry* (Winona Lake, IN: Eisenbrauns, 1980), pp. 187-227.
—'A Letter to the Readers', *BA* 40 (1977), pp. 46-48.
—review of *Job 29–31 in the Light of Northwest Semitic*, by A. Ceresko, in *JBL* 102 (1983), pp. 138-44.
Freedman, D.N., and F.I. Andersen, *Hosea* (AB, 24; Garden City, NY: Doubleday, 1980).
Frevel, C., 'Die Elimination der Göttin aus dem Weltbild des Chronisten', *ZAW* 103 (1991), pp. 263-71.
—*Aschera und der Ausschließlichkeitsanspruch YHWHs* (BBB, 94.1; 2 vols.; Weinheim: Beltz Athenäum Verlag, 1995).
Fulco, W.J., *The Canaanite God Rešep* (AOS, 8; New Haven: American Oriental Society, 1976).
Gall, A. Fr. von, 'Ein neues astronomisch zu erschliessendes Datum der ältesten israelitischen Geschichte', in K. Marti (ed.), *Beiträge zur alttestamentlichen Wissenschaft: K. Budde zum siebzigsten Geburtstag* (BZAW, 34; Giessen: Alfred Töpelmann, 1920), pp. 52-60.
Gallagher, W.R., 'On the Identity of Hêlēl Ben Šaḥar of Is. 14:12-15', *UF* 26 (1994), pp. 131-46.
Galling, K., 'Der Gott Karmel und die Ächtung der fremden Götter', in G. Ebeling (ed.), *Geschichte und Altes Testament: Festschrift A. Alt zum 70. Geburstag* (BHT, 16; Tübingen: J.C.B. Mohr [Paul Siebeck], 1953), pp. 105-25.
Gardiner, A.H., *Hieratic Papyri in the British Museum, Third Series*, I (London: British Museum, 1935).
Gaster, T.H., 'Psalm 29', *JQR* 37 (1946–47), pp. 55-65.
—'Baalzebub', *IDB*, I, p. 332.
—'Demon, Demonology', *IDB*, I, p. 817-24.
—*Thespis* (New York: Harper & Row, 2nd edn, 1966).
—*Myth, Legend, and Custom in the Old Testament* (London: Gerald Duckworth, 1969).
Geiger, A., *Urschrift und Uebersetzungen der Bibel* (Breslau: Verlag Madda, 1857).
—'Der Baal in den hebräischen Eigennamen', *ZDMG* 16 (1862), pp. 728-32.
Gelb, I.J., 'Šullat and Ḫaniš', *ArOr* 18 (1950), pp. 189-98.
Gerleman, G., *Ruth—Das Hohelied* (BKAT, 18; Neukirchen–Vluyn: Neukirchener Verlag, 1965).
Gese, H., M. Höfner, and K. Rudolph, *Die Religionen Altsyriens, Altarabiens und der Mandäer* (Stuttgart: W. Kohlhammer, 1970).
Gibson, J.C.L., *Textbook of Syrian Semitic Inscriptions* (3 vols.; Oxford: Clarendon Press, 1971–82).
—*Canaanite Myths and Legends* (Edinburgh: T. & T. Clark, 1978).
—'The Last Enemy', *SJT* 32 (1979), pp. 151-69.
Gilula, M., 'To Yahweh Shomron and his Asherah', *Shnaton* 3 (1978–79), pp. 129-37 (Hebrew).
Ginsberg, H.L., *Kitᵉbê 'ûgārît* (Jerusalem: Bialik Foundation, 1936).
—'The Ugaritic Texts and Textual Criticism', *JBL* 62 (1943), pp. 109-15.
—*The Legend of King Keret* (BASOR Supplementary Studies, 2–3; New Haven: American Schools of Oriental Research, 1946).

—'The Oldest Interpretation of the Suffering Servant', *VT* 3 (1953), pp. 400-404.

— 'Reflexes of Sargon in Isaiah after 715 B.C.E.', *JAOS* 88 (1968), pp. 47-53.

—'A Strand in the Cord of Hebraic Hymnody', in A. Malamat (ed.), *Eretz-Israel* 9 (W.F. Albright volume; Jerusalem: Israel Exploration Society, 1969), pp. 45-50.

Gitin, S., 'Ekron of the Philistines. II. Olive-Oil Suppliers to the World', *BARev* 16.2 (1990), pp. 33-42, 59.

—'Seventh Century B.C.E. Cultic Elements at Ekron', in J. Aviram (ed.), *Biblical Archaeology Today, 1990* (Jerusalem: Israel Exploration Society, 1993), pp. 248-58.

Giveon, R., 'Reshep in Egypt', *JEA* 66 (1980), pp. 144-50.

Gnuse, R.K., *No other Gods: Emergent Monotheism in Israel* (JSOTSup, 141; Sheffield: JSOT Press, 1997).

Goldin, J., *The Song at the Sea: Being a Commentary on a Commentary in Two Parts* (New Haven: Yale University Press, 1971).

Gonnet, H., 'Les légendes des empreintes hiéroglyphiques anatôliennes', in D. Arnaud, *Textes syriens de l'âge de Bronze Récent* (AulOr Sup, 1; Barcelona: Editorial Ausa, 1991), pp. 198-208.

Good, E.M., *In Turns of Tempest: A Reading of Job with a Translation* (Stanford, CA: Stanford University Press, 1990).

Good, R.M., 'Supplementary Remarks on the Ugaritic Funerary Text RS 34.126', *BASOR* 239 (1980), pp. 41-42.

—'Exodus 32:18', in Marks and Good (eds.), *Love & Death in the Ancient Near East*, pp. 137-42.

Gordis, R., 'The Root דגל in the Song of Songs', *JBL* 88 (1969), pp. 203-204; reprinted in R. Gordis, *The Word and the Book: Studies in Biblical Language and Literature* (New York: Ktav, 1976), pp. 311-12.

—*The Song of Songs and Lamentations* (New York: Ktav, rev. edn, 1974).

—*The Book of Job* (New York: Jewish Theological Seminary, 1978).

Gordon, C.H., *Before the Bible* (London: Collins, 1962).

—'El, Father of Šnm', *JNES* 35 (1976), pp. 261-62.

Gordon, R.P., 'Aleph Apologeticum', *JQR* 69 (1978–79), pp. 112-16.

Gosse, B., 'Un texte pré-apocalyptique du règne de Darius: Isaïe XIII, 1–XIV, 23', *RB* 92 (1985), pp. 200-22.

Gottstein, M.H., 'Eine Cambridger Syrohexaplahandschrift', *Le Muséon* 67 (1954), pp. 291-96.

Goulder, M.D., *The Psalms of the Sons of Korah* (JSOTSup, 20; Sheffield: JSOT Press, 1982).

—*The Song of Fourteen Songs* (JSOTSup, 36; Sheffield: JSOT Press, 1986).

Graham, W.C., and H.G. May, *Culture and Conscience* (Chicago: University of Chicago Press, 1936).

Grave, C., 'The Etymology of Northwest Semitic *ṣapānu*', *UF* 12 (1980), pp. 221-29.

Gray, J., 'The Wrath of God in Canaanite and Hebrew Literature', *Journal of the Manchester University Egyptian and Oriental Society* 25 (1947–53), pp. 9-19.

—'The Desert God 'Aṯtar in the Literature and Religion of Canaan', *JNES* 8 (1949), pp. 72-83.

—'Baal-Berith', *IDB*, I, p. 331.

—*The Legacy of Canaan* (VTSup, 5; Leiden: E.J. Brill, 2nd edn, 1965).

—*I and II Kings* (OTL; London: SCM Press, 3rd edn, 1977).

Grayson, A.K., *Assyrian and Babylonian Chronicles* (Texts from Cuneiform Sources, 5; Locust Valley, NY: J.J. Augustin, 1975).

Grdseloff, B., *Les débuts du culte de Rechef en Egypte* (Cairo: Impr. de l'Institut français d'archéologie orientale, 1942).

Greenberg, M., *Ezekiel 1–20* (AB, 22; Garden City, NY: Doubleday, 1983).

Greenberg, M., J.C. Greenfield, and N.M. Sarna (eds.), *The Book of Job* (Philadelphia: Jewish Publication Society of America, 1980).

Greenfield, J.C., 'Ugaritic *mdl* and its Cognates', *Bib* 45 (1964), pp. 527-34.

—'The Hebrew Bible and Canaanite Literature', in R. Alter and F. Kermode (eds.), *The Literary Guide to the Bible* (London: Collins, 1987), pp. 545-60.

—'Smitten by Famine, Battered by Plague (Deuteronomy 32:24)', in Marks and Good (eds.), *Love & Death in the Ancient Near East*, pp. 151-52.

Grelot, P., 'Isaïe XIV:12-15 et son arrière-plan mythologique', *RHR* 149 (1956), pp. 18-48.

—'Sur la vocalisation de הילל (Is. XIV 12)', *VT* 6 (1956), pp. 303-304.

Gressmann, H., 'Josia und das Deuteronomium', *ZAW* 42 (1924), pp. 313-37.

Gruppe, O., review of 'Phaethon', *Hermes* 18 (1883), pp. 364-434 by U. von Wilamowitz-Möllendorf, 'Die Phaethonsage bei Hesiod', *Hermes* 18 (1883), pp. 434-41, by C. Robert, in *Philologische Wochenschrift* (1883), cols. 1537-47.

—'Aithiopenmythen, 1: Der phoinikische Urtext der Kassiepeialegende. Zusammenhang derselben mit anderen Aithiopenmythen', *Philologus* 47 (1889), pp. 92-107.

Gunkel, H., *Schöpfung und Chaos in Urzeit und Endzeit* (Göttingen: Vandenhoeck & Ruprecht, 1895).

—*Die Psalmen* (Göttinger Handkommentar zum Alten Testament; Göttingen: Vandenhoeck & Ruprecht, 1926).

Güterbock, H.G., *Kumarbi* (Zürich and New York: Europaverlag, 1946).

—'The Song of Ullikummi: Revised Text of the Hittite Version of a Hurrian Myth', *JCS* 5 (1951), pp. 135-61, and *JCS* 6 (1952), pp. 8-42.

Guyard, S., 'Remarques sur le mot assyrien *zabal* et sur l'expression biblique *bet zeboul*', *JA* 12 (7th series, 1878), pp. 220-25.

Habel, N.C., *The Book of Job* (CBC; Cambridge: Cambridge University Press, 1975).

—*The Book of Job* (OTL; London: SCM Press, 1985).

Hackett, J.A., *The Balaam Text from Deir 'Allā* (HSM, 31; Chico, CA: Scholars Press, 1980).

Hadley, J.M., 'Yahweh and "his Asherah": Archaeological and Textual Evidence for the Cult of the Goddess', in W. Dietrich and M.A. Klopfenstein (eds.), *Ein Gott allein?* (OBO, 139; Freiburg: Unversitätsverlag, 1994), pp. 235-68.

—'Wisdom and the Goddess', in Day, Gordon and Williamson (eds.), *Wisdom in Ancient Israel*, pp. 234-43.

—'The Fertility of the Flock? The De-personalization of Astarte in the Old Testament', in B. Becking and M. Dijkstra (eds.), *On Reading Prophetic Texts: Gender-specific and Related Studies in Memory of Fokkelien van Dijk-Hemmes* (BibInt Series, 18; Leiden: E.J. Brill, 1996), pp. 115-33.

—*The Cult of Asherah in Ancient Israel and Judah: Evidence for a Hebrew Goddess* (UCOP, 57; Cambridge: Cambridge University Press, 2000).

Hahn, J., *Das 'Goldene Kalb': Die Jahwe-Verehrung bei Stierbildern in der Geschichte Israels* (Frankfurt: Peter Lang, 2nd edn, 1987).

Halperin, D., *The Faces of the Chariot* (Texte und Studien zum antiken Judentum, 16; Tübingen: J.C.B. Mohr [Paul Siebeck], 1988).

Hamilton, G.J., 'New Evidence for the Authenticity of *bšt* in Hebrew Personal Names and for its Use as a Divine Epithet in Biblical Texts', *CBQ* 60 (1998), pp. 228-50.

Hanson, P.D., 'Zechariah 9 and the Recapitulation of an Ancient Ritual Pattern', *JBL* 92 (1973), pp. 37-59.

Haran, M., 'The Graded Numerical Sequence and the Phenomenon of "Automatism" in Biblical Poetry', *Congress Volume, Uppsala 1971* (VTSup, 22; Leiden: E.J. Brill, 1972), pp. 238-67.

Hartley, J.E., *The Book of Job* (NICOT; Grand Rapids: Eerdmans, 1988).

Hasel, G.F., 'Resurrection in the Theology of Old Testament Apocalyptic', *ZAW* 92 (1980), pp. 267-84.

Haussig, H.W. (ed.), *Götter und Mythen im vorderen Orient* (Worterbuch der Mythologie, 1.1; Stuttgart: E. Klett, 1965).

Hayes, J.H., and A. Irvine, *Isaiah: The Eighth-Century Prophet* (Nashville: Abingdon Press, 1987).

Hayman, A.P., 'Monotheism: A Misused Word in Jewish Studies', *JJS* 42 (1991), pp. 1-15.

Healey, J.F., 'The Underworld Character of the God Dagan', *JNSL* 5 (1977), pp. 43-51.

—'Burning the Corn: New Light on the Killing of Mōtu', *Or* 52 (1983), pp. 248-51.

—'The Kindly and Merciful God: On Some Semitic Divine Epithets', in M. Dietrich and I. Kottsieper, with H. Schaudig (eds.), *'Und Mose schrieb dieses Lied auf': Studien zum Alten Testament und zum Alten Orient. Festschrift für Oswald Loretz* (AOAT, 250; Münster: Ugarit–Verlag, 1998), pp. 349-56.

Hehn, J., *Hymnen und Gebete an Marduk* (Beiträge zur Assyriologie, 5; Leipzig: J.C. Hinrichs, 1905).

Heider, G.C., *The Cult of Molek: A Reassessment* (JSOTSup, 43; Sheffield: JSOT Press, 1985).

Held, M., 'Studies in Biblical Lexicography', in B.A. Levine and A. Malamat (eds.), *Eretz-Israel* 16 (Harry M. Orlinsky volume; Jerusalem: Israel Exploration Society, 1982), pp. 76-85 (Hebrew).

Heller, J., 'Die schweigende Sonne', *Communio Viatorum* 9 (1966), pp. 73-78.

Hempel, J., 'Zu IVQ Deut 32 8', *ZAW* 74 (1962), p. 70.

Hengel, M., *Judentum und Hellenismus* (WUNT, 10; 2 vols.; Tübingen: J.C.B. Mohr [Paul Siebeck], 2nd edn, 1973); ET *Judaism and Hellenism* (trans. J.S. Bowden; 2 vols.; London: SCM Press, 1974).

Herder, J.G. von, *Vom Geist der Ebräischen Poesie* (Leipzig: 3rd rev. edn, 1825); ET *The Spirit of Hebrew Poetry* (trans. J. Marsh; 2 vols.; Burlington: E. Smith, 1833).

Herrmann, W., 'Aštart', *MIO* 15 (1969), pp. 6-155.

—'Baal Zebub', *DDD*, cols. 293-96 (2nd edn, pp. 154-56).

Hess, R.S., 'Yahweh and his Asherah? Epigraphic Evidence for Religious Pluralism in Old Testament Times', in A.D. Clarke and B.W. Winter (eds.), *One God, One Lord in a World of Religious Pluralism* (Cambridge: Tyndale House, 1991), pp. 5-33.

Hestrin, R., 'The Cult Stand from Ta'anach and its Religious Background', in E. Lipiński (ed.), *Phoenica and the East Mediterranean in the First Millennium B.C.* (Studia Phoenicia, 5; Leuven: Peeters, 1987), pp. 61-77.

—'The Lachish Ewer and the 'Asherah', *IEJ* 37 (1987), pp. 212-23.

Hill, G.F., *Catalogue of the Greek Coins of Cyprus* (London: Trustees of the British Museum, 1904).

Hillman, G., 'Reconstructing Crop Husbandry Practices', in R. Mercer (ed.), *Farming Practice in British Prehistory* (Edinburgh: Edinburgh University Press, 1981), pp. 123-62.

Hoffner, H.A., 'The Elkunirsa Myth Reconsidered', *Revue Hittite et Asianique* 23 (1965), pp. 5-16.

—*Hittite Myths* (SBL Writings from the Ancient World, 2; Atlanta: Scholars Press, 1990).

Hoftijzer, J., and G. van der Kooij, *Aramaic Texts from Deir 'Alla* (Documenta et monumenta orientis antiqui; Leiden: E.J. Brill, 1976).

Holladay, J.S., 'The Day(s) the Moon Stood Still', *JBL* 87 (1968), pp. 166-78.

Holland, T.A., 'A Study of Palestinian Iron Age Baked Clay Figurines, with Special Reference to Jerusalem: Cave 1', *Levant* 9 (1977), pp. 121-55.

Hollis, F.J., 'The Sun-Cult and the Temple at Jerusalem', in S.H. Hooke (ed.), *Myth and Ritual* (London: Oxford University Press, 1933), pp. 87-110.

Hölscher, G., *Das Buch Hiob* (HAT, 17; Tübingen: J.C.B. Mohr [Paul Siebeck], 2nd edn, 1952).

Holter, K., 'Was Philistine Dagon a Fish-God? Some New Questions and Old Answers', *SJOT* 1 (1989), pp. 142-47.

Hommel, F., *Der Gestirndienst der alten Araber und die altisraelitische Ueberlieferung* (Munich: H. Lukaschik, 1901).

Hooker, M.D., *The Gospel according to St Mark* (BNTC; London: A. & C. Black, 1991).

Horst, F., *Hiob* (BKAT, 16: Neukirchen–Vluyn: Neukirchener Verlag, 3rd edn, 1974).

Houtman, C., *Exodus*, II (HCOT; Kampen: Kok, 1996).

Houtsma, M.T., 'Habakuk II, vs. 4 en 5 verbeterd', *Theologisch Tijdschrift* 19 (1885), pp. 180-83.

Hugger, P., *Jahwe meine Zuflucht: Gestalt und Theologie des 91. Psalms* (Münsterschwarzacher Studien, 13; Münsterschwarzach: Vier-Türme-Verlag, 1971).

Hvidberg, F.F., *Graad og Latter: Det gamle Testamente* (Copenhagen: G.E.C. Gad, 1938); ET *Weeping and Laughter in the Old Testament* (trans. N. Haislund; Leiden: E.J. Brill; Copenhagen: Nyt Nordisk Forlag, 1962).

Hvidberg-Hansen, F.O., 'Die Vernichtung des goldenen Kalbes und der ugaritische Ernteritus', *AcOr* 33 (1971), pp. 5-46.

—*La déesse TNT: Une étude sur la religion canaanéo-punique* (2 vols.; Copenhagen: G.E.C. Gad, 1979).

Hyatt, J.P., 'The Deity Bethel in the Old Testament', *JAOS* 59 (1939), pp. 81-98.

Irsigler, H., *Gottesgericht und Jahwetag* (Arbeiten zu Text und Sprache im Alten Testament, 3; St Ottilien: Eos Verlag, 1977).

Iwry, S., '*Maṣṣēbāh* and *bāmāh* in IQ Isaiah^{A} 6 13', *JBL* 76 (1957), pp. 225-32.

Jacob, E., C.-A. Keller, and S. Amsler, *Osée, Joël, Abdias, Amos* (CAT, 11a; Neuchâtel: Delachaux & Niestlé, 1965).

Jaroš, K., *Die Stellung der Elohisten zur kanaanäischen Religion* (OBO, 4; Freiburg: Unversitätsverlag; Göttingen: Vandenhoeck & Ruprecht, 1982).

Jastrow, M., *A Dictionary of the Targumim, the Talmud Babli and Yerushalmi, and the Midrashic Literature* (2 vols.; New York: Pardes, 1950).

Jeppesen, K., 'Myth in the Prophetic Literature', in B. Otzen, H. Gottlieb and K. Jeppesen, *Myths in the Old Testament* (trans. F.H. Cryer; London: SCM Press, 1980), pp. 94-123, 134-38.

Jeremias, Jörg, *Das Königtum Gottes in den Psalmen: Israels Begegnung mit dem kanaanäischen Mythos in den Jahwe-König-Psalmen* (FRLANT, 141; Göttingen: Vandenhoeck & Ruprecht, 1987).

Jeshurun, G., 'A Note on Job XXX [*sic*]: 1', *Journal of the Society of Oriental Research* 12 (1928), pp. 153-54.

Jirku, A., 'Gab es im Alten Testament einen Gott Molek (Melek)?', *ARW* 35 (1938), pp. 178-79.

—'Rapa'u, der Fürst der Rapa'uma–Rephaim', *ZAW* 77 (1965), pp. 82-83.

—'Šnm (Schunama), der Sohn des Gottes 'Il', *ZAW* 82 (1970), pp. 278-79.

Johnson, A.R., *Sacral Kingship in Ancient Israel* (Cardiff: University of Wales Press, 2nd edn, 1967).

—*The Cultic Prophet and Israel's Psalmody* (Cardiff: University of Wales Press, 1979).

Johnston, P., review of *Israel's Beneficent Dead* (Forschungen zum Alten Testament, 11; Tübingen: J.C.B. Mohr [Paul Siebeck], 1994), by B.B. Schmidt, in *JTS* NS 47 [1996], pp. 169-72).

Jones, B.C., 'In Search of Kir Hareseth: A Case Study in Site Identification', *JSOT* 52 (1991), pp. 3-24.

Jones, G.H., *1 and 2 Kings* (NCB; London: Marshall, Morgan & Scott; Grand Rapids: Eerdmans, 1984).

Jüngling, H.-W., *Der Tod der Götter: Eine Untersuchung zu Psalm 82* (SBS, 38; Stuttgart: Katholisches Bibelwerk, 1969).

Kapelrud, A.S., *Joel Studies* (UUÅ, 4; Uppsala: Lundeqvist, 1948).

—'Baal and Mot in the Ugaritic Texts', *IEJ* 13 (1963), pp. 127-29.

Karge, P., *Rephaim: Die vorgeschichtliche Kultur Palästinas und Phöniziens* (Collectanea Hierosolymitana, 1; Paderborn: F. Schöningh, 1917).

Kaufman, S.A., 'The Enigmatic Adad-milki', *JNES* 37 (1978), pp. 101-109.

Keel, O., *Die Welt der altorientalischen Bildsymbolik und das Alte Testament: Am Beispiel der Psalmen* (Zürich: Benziger Verlag; Neukirchen–Vluyn: Neukirchen Verlag, 1972); ET *The Symbolism of the Biblical World* (New York: Seabury Press, 1978).

—*Das Hohelied* (Zürcher Bibelkommentare; Zürich: Theologischer Verlag, 1986).

—*Goddesses and Trees, New Moon and Yahweh: Ancient Near Eastern Art and the Hebrew Bible* (JSOTSup, 261; Sheffield: Sheffield Academic Press, 1998).

—'Kie kultischen Massnahmen Antiochus' IV. in Jerusalem: Religionsverfolgung und/oder Reformversuch? Eine Skizze', in J. Krašovec (ed.), *The Interpretation of the Bible: The International Symposium in Slovenia* (JSOTSup, 289; Sheffield: Sheffield Academic Press, 1999), pp. 217-42.

Keel, O. (ed.), *Monotheismus im alten Israel und seiner Umwelt* (Biblische Beiträge, 14; Fribourg: Schweizerisches Katholisches Bibelwerk, 1980).

Keel, O., and C. Uehlinger, 'Jahwe und die Sonnengottheit von Jerusalem', in W. Dietrich and M. Klopfenstein (eds.), *Ein Gott allein?* (OBO, 139; Freiburg/Göttingen: Universitätsverlag/Vandenhoeck & Ruprecht, 1994), pp. 269-306.

—*Göttinnen, Götter und Gottessymbole* (Freiburg: Herder, 1992); ET *Gods, Goddesses and Images of God* (trans. T.H. Trapp; Minneapolis: Fortress Press, 1998).

Key, A.F., 'Traces of the Worship of the Moon God Sîn among the Early Israelites', *JBL* 84 (1965), pp. 20-26.

Kissane, E.J., *The Book of Job* (Dublin: Browne and Nolan, the Richview Press, 1939).

Kittel, R., 'Das Buch der Richter', in E. Kautzsch and A. Bertholet (eds.), *Die heilige Schrift des Alten Testaments* (Tübingen: J.C.B. Mohr [Paul Siebeck], 4th edn, 1922), pp. 367-407.

Kletter, R., *The Judean Pillar-Figurines and the Archaeology of Asherah* (British Archaeological Reports, International Series, 636; Oxford: Tempus Reparatum, 1996).

Kloos, C., *Yhwh's Combat with the Sea: A Canaanite Tradition in the Religion of Ancient Israel* (Leiden: E.J. Brill, 1986).

Knudtzon, J.A., *Die El-Amarna-Tafeln* (2 vols.; Leipzig: J.C. Hinrichs, 1915).
Koch, K., 'Aschera als Himmelskönigin in Jerusalem', *UF* 20 (1988), pp. 97-120.
Kornfeld, W., 'Der Moloch: Eine Untersuchung zur Theorie O. Eissfeldts', *WZKM* 51 (1952), pp. 287-313.
Korpel, M.J.A., *A Rift in the Clouds: Ugaritic and Hebrew Descriptions of the Divine* (UBL, 8; Münster: Ugarit Verlag, 1990).
Kramer S.N. (ed.), *Mythologies of the Ancient World* (Garden City, NY: Doubleday, 1961).
Kraus, H.-J., *Psalmen*, I–II (BKAT, 15.1-2; 2 vols.; Neukirchen–Vluyn: Neukirchener Verlag, 5th edn, 1978); ET *Psalms 1–59* and *Psalms 60–150* (trans. H.C. Oswald; Minneapolis: Augsburg Publishing House, 1988–89).
Krinetzki, G., *Kommentar zum Hohenlied* (Beiträge zur biblischen Exegese und Theologie, 16; Frankfurt am Main: Peter Lang, 1981).
Krinetzki, L., 'Zur Poetik und Exegese von Psalm 48', *BZ* NS 4 (1960), pp. 70-97.
Kuenen, A., *The Religion of Israel* (trans. A.H. May; 3 vols.; London: Williams & Norgate, 1874–75).
Laato, A. *Josiah and David Redivivus* (ConBOT, 33; Stockholm: Almqvist & Wicksell, 1992).
Lack, R., 'Les origines de *Elyon*, le très-haut, dans la tradition cultuelle d'Israël', *CBQ* 24 (1962), pp. 44-64.
Lagrange, M.J., *Etudes sur les religions sémitiques* (Paris: V. Lecoffre, 1903).
Lambert, W.G., 'Götterlisten', *RLA*, III, pp. 473-79.
—'Niṣir or Nimush?', *RA* 80 (1986), pp. 185-86.
Landy, F., *Paradoxes of Paradise: Identity and Difference in the Song of Songs* (Bible and Literature Series, 7; Sheffield: Almond Press, 1983).
Lane, E.W., *An Arabic–English Lexicon* (8 parts and supplement; London: Williams & Norgate, 1863–93).
Lang, B., 'Die Jahwe-allein-Bewegung', in B. Lang, *Der einzige Gott* (Munich: Kösel, 1981), pp. 47-83; ET 'The Yahweh-Alone-Movement and the Making of Jewish Monotheism', in *Monotheism and the Prophetic Minority* (Sheffield: Almond Press, 1983), pp. 13-59.
—'Street Theater, Raising the Dead, and the Zoroastrian Connection in Ezekiel's Preaching', in J. Lust (ed.), *Ezekiel and his Book* (BETL, 74; Leuven: Leuven University Press and Peeters, 1986), pp. 297-316.
Langdon, S.H., 'The Star Hêlēl, Jupiter?', *ExpTim* 42 (1930–31), pp. 172-74.
Langdon S.H. (ed.), *The H. Weld-Blundell Collection in the Ashmolean Museum*. I. *Sumerian and Semitic Religious and Historical Texts* (Oxford Editions of Cuneiform Inscriptions, 1; London: Oxford University Press, 1923).
Langhe, R. de, *Les Textes de Ras Shamra–Ugarit et leurs Rapports avec le Milieu Biblique de l'Ancien Testament* (2 vols.; Gembloux: Duculot, 1945).
Laroche, E., 'Les hiéroglyphes de Meskéné-Emar et le style "syro-hittite"', *Akkadica* 22 (1981), pp. 5-14.
Lauha, A., *Zaphon: Der Norden und die Nordvölker im Alten Testament* (Annales Academiae scientiarum Fennicae, 49.2; Helsinki: Druckerei-A.G. der finnischen Literaturgesellschaft, 1943).
Leclant, J., 'Astarté à cheval', *Syria* 37 (1960), pp. 1-67.
Lehmann, M.R., 'A New Interpretation of the Term שדמות', *VT* 3 (1953), pp. 361-71.
Lemaire, A., 'Les inscriptions de Khirbet el-Qôm et l'Ashérah de Yhwh', *RB* 84 (1977), pp. 595-608 .

Lemche, N.P., 'The Development of Israelite Religion in the Light of Recent Studies on the Early History of Israel', in J.A. Emerton (ed.), *Congress Volume, Leuven 1989* (VTSup, 43; Leiden: E.J. Brill, 1991), pp. 97-115.

Levenson, J.D., *Creation and the Persistence of Evil: The Jewish Drama of Divine Omnipotence* (San Francisco: Harper & Row, 1988).

—*The Death and Resurrection of the Beloved Son: The Transformation of Child Sacrifice in Judaism and Christianity* (New Haven: Yale University Press, 1993).

Levi della Vida, G., 'El 'Elyon in Genesis 14 18-20', *JBL* 63 (1944), pp. 1-9.

Levin, C., 'Joschija im deuteronomistischen Geschichtswerk', *ZAW* 96 (1984), pp. 351-71.

Lewis, T.J., *Cults of the Dead in Ancient Israel and Ugarit* (HSM, 39; Atlanta: Scholars Press, 1989).

Lewy, J., 'The Old West Semitic Sun-god Ḥammu', *HUCA* 18 (1943–44), pp. 429-81.

—'The Late Assyro-Babylonian Cult of the Moon and its Culmination at the Time of Nabonidus', *HUCA* 19 (1945–46), pp. 405-89.

L'Heureux, C., 'The Ugaritic and Biblical Rephaim', *HTR* 67 (1974), pp. 265-74.

—*Rank among the Canaanite Gods: El, Ba'al, and the Repha'im* (HSM, 21; Missoula, MT: Scholars Press, 1979).

Lightfoot, J.B., *Horae Hebraicae et Talmudicae* (new edn by R. Gandell; 4 vols.; repr.; Oxford: Oxford University Press, 1859).

—*The Apostolic Fathers, Part I. St Clement of Rome*, II (London: Macmillan, 2nd edn, 1890).

Lindars, B. (F.C.), *New Testament Apologetic* (London: SCM Press, 1961).

—*Interpreting Judges Today* (Ethel M. Wood Lecture, 1983; London: University of London, 1983).

Lipiński, E., 'El's Abode: Mythological Traditions Related to Mount Hermon and to the Mountains of Armenia', *OLP* 2 (1971), pp. 13-69.

—'The Goddess Aṯirat in Ancient Arabia, in Babylon, and in Ugarit', *OLP* 3 (1972), pp. 101-19.

—'Resheph Amyklos', in E. Lipiński (ed.), *Phoenicia and the East Mediterranean in the First Millenium B.C.* (Studia Phoenicia, 5; Leuven: Peeters, 1987), pp. 87-99.

—'צְפוֹנִי צָפוֹן', *ThWAT*, VI, cols. 1093-1102.

—'Le culte du soleil chez les Sémites occidentaux du 1er millénaire av. J.-C.', *OLP* 22 (1991), pp. 57-72.

—'Shemesh', DDD, cols. 1445-52 (2nd edn, pp. 764-68).

Livingstone, A., *Court Poetry and Literary Miscellanea* (State Archives of Assyria, 3; Helsinki: Helsinki University Press, 1989).

Lods, A., 'Quelques remarques sur l'histoire de Samson', in *Actes du Congrès International d'Histoire des Religions*, I (Paris: Librairie ancienne Honoré Champion, 1925), pp. 504-16.

Loewenstamm, S.E., 'The Ugaritic Fertility Myth: A The Result of a Mistranslation', *IEJ* 12 (1962), pp. 87-88.

—'The Ugaritic Fertility Myth: A Reply', *IEJ* 13 (1963), pp. 130-32.

—'The Making and Destruction of the Golden Calf', *Bib* 48 (1967), pp. 481-90.

—'The Killing of Mot in Ugaritic Myth', *Or* NS 41 (1972), pp. 378-82;

—'The Making and Destruction of the Golden Calf: A Rejoinder', *Bib* 56 (1975), pp. 330-43.

Lohfink, N. 'The Cult Reform of Josiah of Judah: 2 Kings 22–23 as a Source for the History of Israelite Religion', in P.D. Miller, P.D. Hanson and S.D. McBride (eds.),

Ancient Israelite Religion: Essays in Honor of Frank Moore Cross (Philadelphia: Fortress Press, 1987), pp. 459-75.
Løkkegaard, F., 'A Plea for El, the Bull, and other Ugaritic Miscellanies', in F.F. Hvidberg (ed.), *Studia Orientalia Ioanni Pedersen septuagenario dicata* (Copenhagen: E. Munskgaard, 1953), pp. 219-35.
—'Some Comments on the Sanchuniathon Tradition', *ST* 8 (1954), pp. 68-73.
Loretz, O., 'Der Sturz des Fürsten von Tyrus (Ez 28, 1-19)', *UF* 8 (1976), pp 455-58.
—'Der kanaanäische Ursprung des biblischen Gottesnamens *El šaddaj*', *UF* 12 (1980), pp. 420-21.
—*Psalm 29: Kanaanäische El- und Baal Traditionen in jüdischer Sicht* (UBL, 2; Altenberge: CIS–Verlag, 1984).
Lutzky, H.C., 'On the "Image of Jealousy" (Ezekiel VIII 3, 5)', *VT* 46 (1996), pp. 121-25.
Macalister, R.A.S., *The Philistines: Their History and Civilization* (Schweich Lectures; London: Oxford University Press, 1913).
Mackrodt, R., 'Olympos', in W. Roscher (ed.), *Ausführliches Lexikon der griechischen und römischen Mythologie*, III (6 vols.; Leipzig: B.G. Teubner, 1897–1909, cols. 847-58.
Maier, W.A., *'Ašerah: Extrabiblical Evidence* (HSM, 37; Atlanta: Scholars Press, 1986).
Mannati, M., 'Les adorateurs de Môt dans le Psaume LXXIII', *VT* 22 (1972), pp. 420-25.
Margalit, B. (Margulis), 'A New Ugaritic Psalm (RŠ 24.252)', *JBL* 89 (1970), pp. 292-302.
—'The Geographical Setting of the AQHT Story and its Ramifications', in G.D. Young (ed.), *Ugarit in Retrospect* (Winona Lake, IN: Eisenbrauns, 1981), pp. 131-58.
—'The Meaning and Significance of Asherah', *VT* 40 (1990), pp. 264-97.
Marks, J.H., and R.M. Good (eds.), *Love & Death in the Ancient Near East: Essays in Honor of Marvin H. Pope* (Guilford, CN: Four Quarters, 1987).
Martin, J.D., *The Book of Judges* (CBC; Cambridge: Cambridge University Press, 1975).
Martin-Achard, R., *From Death to Life* (trans. John Penney Smith; Edinburgh: Oliver & Boyd, 1960).
Matthiae, P., 'Note sul dio siriano Rešef', *OrAnt* 2 (1963), pp. 27-42.
Mauchline, J., *1 and 2 Samuel* (NCB; London: Oliphants, 1971).
Maunder, E. Walter, 'A Misunderstood Miracle', *The Expositor* 16 (1910), pp. 359-72.
May, H.G., 'The Fertility Cult in Hosea', *AJSL* 48 (1932), pp. 74-98.
—'Some Aspects of Solar Worship at Jerusalem', *ZAW* 55 (1937), pp. 269-81.
—'The Departure of the Glory of Yahweh', *JBL* 56 (1937), pp. 311-12.
—'The King in the Garden of Eden', in B.W. Anderson and W. Harrelson (eds.), *Israel's Prophetic Heritage* (New York: Harper & Brothers, 1962), pp. 166-76.
Mays, J.L., *Hosea* (OTL; London: SCM Press, 1969).
Mazar, A., 'The "Bull Site": An Iron Age I Open Cult Place', *BASOR* 247 (1982), pp. 27-42.
—'Bronze Bull Found in Israelite "High Place" from the Time of the Judges', *BARev* 9.5 (1983), pp. 34-40.
—'On Cult Places and Early Israelites: A Response to Michael Coogan', *BARev* 15.4 (1988), p. 45.
—*Biblical Israel: State and People* (Jerusalem: Magnes Press and Israel Exploration Society, 1992).
Mazar, B. [Maisler], 'Shamgar ben 'Anat', *PEQ* 66 (1934), pp. 192-94.
McKay, J.W., 'Helel and the Dawn-goddess', *VT* 20 (1970), pp. 451-64.
—*Religion in Judah under the Assyrians* (SBT 2nd series, 26; London: SCM Press, 1973).
—'Helel, Athtar and Phaethon (Jes 14 12-15)', *ZAW* 85 (1973), pp. 223-25.

McKenzie, J.L., 'Mythological Allusions in Ezek 28 12-18', *JBL* 75 (1956), pp. 322-27.
Meek, T.J., 'Aaronites and Zadokites', *AJSL* 45 (1929), pp. 149-66.
Menzel, B., *Assyrische Tempel* (Studia Pohl. Series maior, 10; 2 vols.; Rome: Biblical Institute Press, 1981).
Meshel, Z. *Kuntillet 'Ajrud: A Religious Centre from the Time of the Judaean Monarchy on the Border of Sinai* (Catalogue no. 175; Jerusalem: Israel Museum, 1978).
Mesnil du Buisson, R. du, *Etudes sur les dieux phéniciens hérités par l'empire romain* (EPROER, 14; Leiden: E.J. Brill, 1970).
Mettinger, T.N.D., *The Dethronement of Sabaoth: Studies in the Shem and Kabod Theologies* (ConBOT, 18; Lund: C.W.K. Gleerup, 1982).
—*In Search of God: The Meaning and Message of the Everlasting Names* (trans. F.H. Cryer; Philadelphia: Fortress Press, 1987).
—'The Elusive Essence: YHWH, El and Baal and the Distinctiveness of Israelite Faith', in E. Blum, C. Macholz and E.W. Stegemann (eds.), *Die Hebräische Bibel und ihre zweifache Nachgeschichte: Festschrift für Rolf Rendtorff zum 65. Geburtstag* (Neukirchen–Vluyn: Neukirchener Verlag, 1990), pp. 393-417.
—'The "Dying and Rising God": A Survey of Research from Frazer to the Present Day', *SEÅ* 63 (1998), pp. 111-23.
Michel, W.L., 'BTWLH, "Virgin" or "Virgin (Anat)" in Job 31:1?', *Hebrew Studies* 23 (1982), pp 59-66.
Milik, J.T., 'An Unpublished Arrowhead with Phoenician Inscription of the 11th–10th Century B.C.', *BASOR* 143 (1956), pp. 3-6.
—'Note sur une Pointe de Flèche inscrite provenant de la Beqaa (Liban)', *RB* 65 (1958), pp. 585-89.
—'Les papyrus araméens d'Hermoupolis et les cultes syro-phéniciens en Egypte perse', *Bib* 48 (1967), pp. 546-622.
Millar, F.G.B., 'The Background to the Maccabean Revolution: Reflections on Martin Hengel's *Judaism and Hellenism'*, *JJS* 29 (1978), pp. 1-21.
Millard, A.R., 'King Og's Bed and other Ancient Ironmongery', in Eslinger and Taylor (eds.), *Ascribe to the Lord*, pp. 481-92.
—'King Og's Iron Bed: Fact or Fancy?', *BR* 6.2 (April, 1990), pp. 16-21, 44.
Miller, P.D., 'El the Warrior', *HTR* 60 (1967), pp. 411-31.
—'Psalms and Inscriptions', in J.A. Emerton (ed.), *Congress Volume, Vienna 1980* (VTSup, 32; Leiden: E.J. Brill, 1981), pp. 311-32.
Miller, P.D., and J.J.M. Roberts, *The Hand of the Lord: A Reassessment of the 'Ark Narrative' of 1 Samuel* (Baltimore: The Johns Hopkins University Press, 1977).
Mittmann, S., 'Komposition und Redaktion von Psalm XXIX', *VT* 28 (1978), pp. 172-94.
—'Die Grabinschrift des Sängers Uriahu', *ZDPV* 97 (1981), pp. 139-52.
Montalbano, F.J., 'Canaanite Dagon: Origin, Nature', *CBQ* 13 (1951), pp. 381-97.
Montgomery, J.A., *A Critical and Exegetical Commentary on the Books of Kings* (ICC; Edinburgh: T. & T. Clark, 1951).
Moor, J.C. de, 'Der *mdl* Baals im Ugaritischen', *ZAW* 78 (1966), pp. 69-71.
—'Studies in the New Alphabetic Texts from Ras Shamra I', *UF* 1 (1969), pp. 167-88.
—*The Seasonal Pattern in the Ugaritic Myth of Ba'lu* (AOAT, 16; Neukirchen–Vluyn: Neukirchener Verlag, 1971).
—'Cloud', *IDBSup*, pp. 168-69.
—*An Anthology of Religious Texts from Ugarit* (Leiden: E.J. Brill, 1987).

—*The Rise of Yahwism* (BETL, 91; Leuven: Leuven University Press and Peeters, 2nd edn, 1997 [1990]).
—'אֲשֵׁרָה', *ThWAT*, I, pp. 473-74 (ET *TDOT*, I, p. 438).
Morgenstern, J., 'The Gates of Righteousness', *HUCA* 6 (1929), pp. 1-37.
—'Psalm 48', *HUCA* 16 (1941), pp. 47-87.
—*The Fire Upon the Altar* (Leiden: E.J. Brill, 1963).
—'The Cultic Setting of the "Enthronement Psalms"', *HUCA* 35 (1964), pp. 1-42.
—'The King–God among the Western Semites and the Meaning of Epiphanes', *VT* 10 (1968), pp. 138-97.
Mörl, T.S., *Scholia philologica et critica ad selecta S. Codicis loca* (Nürnberg, 1737).
Motzki, H., 'Ein Beitrag zum Problem des Stierkultes in der Religionsgeschichte Israels', *VT* 25 (1975), pp. 470-85.
Movers, F.K., *Die Phönizier* (2 vols. in 4; Bonn: E. Weber, 1841–56).
Mowan, O., 'Quatuor Montes Sacri in Ps. 89, 13?', *VD* 41 (1963), pp. 11-20.
Mowinckel, S., *Psalmenstudien* (6 vols.; Kristiania: J. Dybwad, 1921–24).
—*Det Gamle Testamentes Salmebok. Første del: Salmene i oversettelse* (Kristiania: H. Aschehoug, 1923).
—*Offersang og sangoffer* (Oslo: H. Aschehoug, 1951); ET *The Psalms in Israel's Worship* (trans. D.R. Ap-Thomas; 2 vols.; Oxford: Basil Blackwell, 1962).
—*Der achtundsechzigste Psalm* (Avhandlinger utg. av det Norske videnskaps-akademi i Oslo. II. Historisk-filosofisk klasse, 1953, 1; Oslo: J. Dybwad, 1953).
Mulder, M.J., *Kanaänitische Goden in het Oude Testament* (Exegetica, fourth series, 4 and 5; The Hague: N.V. Van Keulen Periodieken, 1965).
—*De naam van de afwezige god op de Karmel: Onderzoek naar de naam van de Baäl van de Karmel in 1 Koningen 18* (Leiden: Universitaire Pers, 1979).
—'Baal-Berith', *DDD*, cols. 226-72 (2nd edn, 141-44).
Mullen, E.T., *The Assembly of the Gods: The Divine Council in Canaanite and Early Hebrew Literature* (HSM, 24; Chico, CA; Scholars Press, 1980).
Müller, K.F., *Das assyrische Ritual*. I. *Texte zum assyrischen Königsritual* (MVAG [E.V.], 41.3; Leipzig: J.C. Hinrichs, 1937).
Murphy, R.E., *The Song of Songs* (Hermeneia; Minneapolis: Fortress Press, 1980).
Naccache, A., 'El's Abode in his Land', in N. Wyatt, G.E. Watson and J.B. Lloyd (eds.), *Ugarit, Religion and Culture: Proceedings of the International Colloquium on Ugarit, Religion and Culture, Edinburgh, July 1994; Essays Presented in Honour of Professor John C.L. Gibson* (UBL, 12; Münster: Ugarit-Verlag, 1996), pp. 249-72.
Nelson, R.D., *The Double Redaction of the Deuteronomistic History* (JSOTSup, 18; Sheffield: JSOT Press, 1981).
Nestle, E., 'Zu Daniel. 2. Der Greuel der Verwüstung', *ZAW* 4 (1884), p. 248.
Neuberg, F., 'An Unrecognized Meaning of Hebrew *dôr*', *JNES* 9 (1950), pp. 215-17.
Nicholson, E.W., 'Israelite Religion in the Pre-exilic Period', in J.D. Martin and P.R. Davies (eds.), *A Word in Season: Essays in Honour of William McKane* (JSOTSup, 42; Sheffield: JSOT Press, 1986), pp. 3-34.
Niehr, H., *Der höchste Gott* (BZAW, 190; Berlin: W. de Gruyter, 1990).
Nielsen, E., 'The Righteous and the Wicked in Habaqquq', *ST* 6 (1952), pp. 54-78.
Nims, C.F., and R.C. Steiner, 'A Paganized Version of Psalm 20:2-6 from the Aramaic Text in Demotic Script', *JAOS* 103 (1983), pp. 261-74.
Nineham, D.E., *Saint Mark* (Pelican Gospel Commentaries; Harmondsworth: Penguin Books, 1963).

Nöldeke, T., review of *Grammatik des Biblisch-Aramäischen*, by E. Kautzsch, in *Göttingische gelehrte Anzeigen* (1884), p. 1022.
Norin, S., *Er spaltete das Meer: Die Auszugsüberlieferungen in Psalmen und Kult des alten Israels* (ConBOT, 9; Lund: C.W.K. Gleerup, 1977).
Noth, M., *Die israelitischen Personennamen im Rahmen der gemeinsemitischen Namengebung* (BWANT, 3.10; Stuttgart: W. Kohlhammer, 1928).
—*Das zweite Buch Mose, Exodus* (ATD, 5; Göttingen: Vandhoeck & Ruprecht, 1959); ET *Exodus* (trans. J.S. Bowden; OTL; London: SCM Press, 1962).
Obbink, H.T., 'Jahwebilder', *ZAW* 47 (1929), pp. 264-74.
O'Ceallaigh, G.C., 'And so David did to all the Cities of Ammon', *VT* 12 (1962), pp. 179-89.
Oden, R.A., *Studies in Lucian's* De Syria Dea (HSM, 15; Missoula, MT: Scholars Press, 1977).
—'Ba'al Šāmēm and 'Ēl', *CBQ* 39 (1977), pp. 457-73.
—*The Bible without Theology* (San Francisco: Harper & Row, 1987).
Oesterley, W.O.E., *The Psalms* (2 vols.; London: SPCK, 1939).
Oestreicher, T., *Das deuteronomische Grundgesetz* (Beitr. z. Förd. chr. Th., 27.4; Gütersloh: C. Bertelsmann, 1923).
Ohler, A., *Mythologische Elemente im Alten Testament* (Düsseldorf: Patmos, 1969).
Oldenburg, U., *The Conflict between El and Ba'al in Canaanite Religion* (Leiden: E.J. Brill, 1969).
Olyan, S.M., 'Some Observations Concerning the Identity of the Queen of Heaven', *UF* 19 (1987), pp. 161-74.
—'The Cultic Confession of Jer 2, 27a', *ZAW* 99 (1987), pp. 254-59.
—*Asherah and the Cult of Yahweh in Israel* (SBLMS, 34; Atlanta: Scholars Press, 1988).
Oswalt, J., 'The Golden Calves and the Egyptian Concept of Deity', *EvQ 45* (1973), pp. 13-20.
Otten, H., 'Ein kanaanäischer Mythus aus Boğazköy', *MIO* 1 (1953), pp. 125-50.
Ouellette, J., 'More on 'Êl Šadday and Bêl Šadê', *JBL* 88 (1969), pp. 470-71.
Page, H.R., *The Myth of Cosmic Rebellion: A Study of its Reflexes in Ugaritic and Biblical Literature* (VTSup, 65; Leiden: E.J. Brill, 1996).
Palmer, A. Smythe, *A Misunderstood Miracle: An Essay in Favour of a New Interpretation of 'the Sun Standing Still' in Joshua X.12-14* (London: Swan Sonnerschein, Lowrey & Co., 1887).
Pardee, D., *Les Textes Para-Mythologiques de la 24ᵉ Campagne (1961)* (Ras Shamra–Ougarit, 4; Paris: Editions Recherche sur les Civilisations, 1988).
—'As Strong as Death', in Marks and Good (eds.), *Love & Death in the Ancient Near East*, pp. 65-69.
Parker, S.B., 'The Ugaritic Deity Rāpi'u', *UF* 4 (1972), pp. 97-104.
Patai, R., *The Hebrew Goddess* (Detroit: Wayne State University Press, 3rd edn, 1990).
Paul, S.M., 'Cuneiform Light on Jer 9,20', *Bib* 49 (1968), pp. 373-76.
Peake, A.S., *Job* (Century Bible; Edinburgh: T.C. & E.C. Jack, 1905).
Perdue, L.G., 'The Making and Destruction of the Golden Calf: A Reply', *Bib* 54 (1973), pp. 237-46.
Petersen, A.R., *The Royal God: Enthronement Festivals in Ancient Israel and Ugarit?* (JSOTSup, 259; Sheffield: Sheffield Academic Press, 1998).
Pettinato, G., 'Is. 2,7 e il culto del sole in Giuda nel sec. VIII av. Cr.', *OrAnt* 4 (1965), pp. 1-30.

—*The Archives of Ebla* (ET; Garden City, NY: Doubleday, 1981).
Pfeiffer, R.H., 'Images of Yahweh', *JBL* 45 (1926), pp. 211-22.
—*Religion in the Old Testament* (London: A. & C. Black, 1961).
Phythian-Adams, W.J., 'A Meteorite of the Fourteenth Century B.C.', *PEQ* 78 (1946), pp. 116-24.
Plataroti, D., 'Zum Gebrauch des Wortes *mlk* im Alten Testament', *VT* 28 (1978), pp. 286-300.
Plessis, J., *Etude sur les textes concernant Ištar-Astarté: Recherches sur sa nature et son culte dans le monde sémitique et dans la Bible* (Paris: P. Geuthner, 1921).
Poirier, J., 'An Illuminating Parallel to Isaiah XIV 12', *VT* 49 (1999), pp. 371-89.
Pomponio, F., 'Adamma paredra di Rasap', *SEL* 10 (1993), pp. 3-7.
Pomponio, F., and P. Xella, *Les Dieux d'Ebla* (AOAT, 245; Münster: Ugarit-Verlag, 1997).
Pope, M.H., *El in the Ugaritic Texts* (VTSup, 2; Leiden: E.J. Brill, 1955).
—'Athirat', in Haussig (ed.), *Götter und Mythen*, pp. 246-49.
—''Aṯtart, 'Aštart, Astarte', in Haussig (ed.), *Götter und Mythen*, pp. 250-52.
—'Baal-Hadad', in Haussig (ed.), *Götter und Mythen*, pp. 253-64.
—*Job* (AB, 15; Garden City, NY: Doubleday, 3rd edn, 1973).
—*Song of Songs* (AB, 7C; Garden City, NY: Doubleday, 1977).
—'Notes on the Rephaim Texts', in M. de Jong Ellis (ed.), *Essays on the Ancient Near East in Memory of Jacob Joel Finkelstein* (Memoirs of the Connecticut Academy of Arts and Sciences, 19; Hamden, CT: Archon Books, 1977), pp. 163-82.
—'Notes on the Rephaim Texts from Ugarit', in J.M. Efird (ed.), *The Use of the Old Testament in the New and other Essays* (Durham, NC: Duke University Press, 1977), pp. 163-82.
Porten, B., *Archives from Elephantine* (Berkeley: University of California Press, 1968).
Potts, T.F., S.M. Colledge, and P.C. Edwards, 'Preliminary Report on a Sixth Season of Excavations by the University of Sidney at Pella in Jordan (1983/84)', *Annual of the Department of Antiquities of Jordan* 29 (1985), pp. 181-210, with pls. XLI-XLII on pp. 339-40.
Pritchard, J.B., *Palestinian Figurines in Relation to Certain Goddesses Known through Literature* (New Haven: American Oriental Society, 1943).
Pryce, B.C., 'The Resurrection Motif in Hosea 5:8–6:6: An Exegetical Study' (PhD dissertation, Andrews University, Ann Arbor, 1989).
Puech, E., 'Origine de l'alphabet', *RB* 93 (1986), pp. 161-213.
—*La Croyance des Esséniens en la Vie Future: Immortalité, Résurrection, Vie Éternelle?* (2 vols.; Paris: J. Gabalda, 1993).
Rainey, A.F., 'The Ugaritic Texts in Ugaritica 5', *JAOS* 94 (1974), pp. 184-94.
Rast, W.E., 'Cakes for the Queen of Heaven', in A.L. Merrill and T.W. Overholt, *Scripture in History and Theology: Essays in Honor of J. Coert Rylaarsdam* (Pittsburgh Theological Monograph Series, 17; Pittsburgh: Pickwick Press, 1977), pp. 167-80.
Reed, W.L., *The Asherah in the Old Testament* (Fort Worth: Texas Christian University Press, 1949).
Reid, J., 'Did the Sun and Moon Stand Still?', *ExpTim* 9 (1897–98), pp. 151-54.
Reiterer, F.V., 'Das Verhältnis Ijobs und Ben Siras', in W. Beuken (ed.), *The Book of Job* (BETL, 114; Leuven: Leuven University Press and Peeters, 1994), pp. 405-29.
Rendtorff, R., 'El, Ba'al und Jahwe', *ZAW* 78 (1966), pp. 277-92.

—'Some Observations on the Use of אל in the Hebrew Bible', in S. Aḥituv and B. Levine (eds.), *Eretz-Israel 24* (Abraham Malamat Volume; Jerusalem: Israel Exploration Society, 1993), pp. 192*-96*.

Ribichini, S., and P. Xella, 'Mlk'aštart, *Mlk(m)* e la tradizione siropalestinese sui Refaim', *RSF* 7 (1979), pp. 145-58.

Riemschneider, M., 'Die Herkunft der Philister', *Acta Antiqua Academiae Scientiarum Hungaricae* 4 (1956), pp. 17-29.

Rin, S. and S., '*alîlôt hā'ēlîm* (Jerusalem: Israel Society for Biblical Research and 'Inbal, 1968).

Roberts, J.J.M., *The Earliest Semitic Pantheon: A Study of the Semitic Deities Attested in Mesopotamia before Ur III* (Baltimore: The John Hopkins University Press, 1972).

—'ṢĀPÔN in Job 26, 7', *Bib* 56 (1975), pp. 554-57.

Robinson, A., 'Zion and Ṣāphôn in Psalm XLVIII 3', *VT* 24 (1974), pp. 118-23.

Robinson, H.W., 'The Council of Yahweh', *JTS* 45 (1944), pp. 151-57.

Röllig, W., 'Bethel', *DDD*, cols. 331-34 (2nd edn, pp. 173-75).

Rosen, B., 'Early Israelite Cultic Centres in the Hill Country', *VT* 38 (1988), pp. 114-17.

Roussel, P., and M. Launey, *Inscriptions de Délos* (Paris: Librairie Ancienne Honoré Champion, 1937).

Rowe, A., *The Four Canaanite Temples of Beth-Shan* (Philadelphia: University of Pennsylvania Press, 1940).

Rowley, H.H., 'The Meaning of "the Shulammite"', *AJSL* 56 (1939), pp. 84-91.

—*The Re-discovery of the Old Testament* (London: James Clarke, 1946).

—'Menelaus and the Abomination of Desolation', in F.F. Hvidberg (ed.), *Studia Orientalia Ioanni Pedersen septuagenario dicata* (Copenhagen: E. Munksgaard, 1953), pp. 303-15.

—*Job* (NCB; London: Oliphants, 1976).

Rudolph, W., *Jeremia* (HAT, 1.12; Tübingen: J.C.B. Mohr [Paul Siebeck], 1947).

—*Das Buch Ruth—Das Hohe Lied—Die Klagelieder* (KAT, 17.1-3; Gütersloh: Gerd Mohn, 1962).

—*Hosea* (KAT, 13.1; Gütersloh: Gerd Mohn, 1966).

Ryckmans, G., *Les religions arabes préislamiques* (Bibliothèque de Muséon, 26; Louvain: Publications Universitaires and Bureaux du Muséon, 2nd edn, 1951).

—'Il dio stellare nell' Arabia meridionale preislamica', *Atti della Accademia dei Lincei* 3 (ser. 8, 1948), pp. 360-69.

Sabottka, L., *Zephanja: Versuch einer Neuübersetzung mit philologischem Kommentar* (BibOr, 25; Rome: Biblical Institute Press, !972).

Saracino, F., 'Ras Ibn Hani 78/20 and Some Old Testament Connections', *VT* 32 (1982), pp. 338-43.

—'Ger. 9, 20, un polmone ugaritico e la forza di Môt', *AION* 44 (1984), pp. 539-53.

Sarna, N.M., 'The Mythological Background of Job 18', *JBL* 82 (1963), pp. 315-18.

Sasson, J., 'The Worship of the Golden Calf', in H.A. Hoffner (ed.), *Orient and Occident: Essays Presented to Cyrus H. Gordon on the Occasion of his Sixty-fifth Birthday* (AOAT, 22; Kevelaer: Butzon & Bercker; Neukirchen–Vluyn: Neukirchener Verlag, 1973), pp. 151-59.

Sawyer, J.F.A., 'Joshua 10:12-14 and the Solar Eclipse of 30 September 1131 B.C.', *PEQ* 104 (1972), pp. 139-46.

Sawyer, J.F.A., and F.R. Stephenson, 'Literary and Astronomical Evidence for a Total Eclipse of the Sun Observed in Ancient Ugarit on 3 May 1375 B.C.', *BSO(A)S* 33 (1970), pp. 467-89.

Schlatter, A., *Der Evangelist Matthäus* (Stuttgart: Calwer Verlag, 1929).

Schlisske, W., *Gottessöhne und Gottessohn im Alten Testament: Phasen der Entmythisierung im Alten Testament* (BWANT, 97; Stuttgart: W. Kohlhammer, 1973).

Schmidt, B.B., *Israel's Beneficent Dead* (Forschungem zum Alten Testament, 11; Tübingen: J.C.B. Mohr [Paul Siebeck], 1994).

Schmidt, K.L., 'Lucifer als gefallene Engelmacht', *TZ* 7 (1951), pp. 161-79.

Schmidt, W.H., 'צָפוֹן ṣāfōn Norden', *THAT*, II, cols. 575-82.

Schmitt, J.J., 'Yahweh's Divorce in Hosea 2: Who is that Woman?' *SJOT* 9 (1995), pp. 119-32.

Schmitz, P.C., 'Queen of Heaven', *ABD*, I, pp. 586-88.

Schmökel, H., 'Dagan', *RLA*, II, pp. 99-101.

Schrader, E., 'Die מלכת השמים und ihr aramäisch-assyrisches Aequivalent', *SKPAW* (1886), pp. 477-91.

Schretter, M.K., *Alter Orient und Hellas: Fragen der Beeinflussung griechischen Gedankengutes aus altorientalischen Quellen, dargestellt an den Göttern Nergal, Rescheph, Apollon* (Innsbrucker Beiträge zur Kulturwissenschaft, 33; Innsbruck: Institut für Sprachwissenschaft der Universität Innsbruck, 1974).

Schroeder, O., *Keilschrifttexte aus Assur verschiedenen Inhalts* (Ausgrabungen der deutschen Orient-Gesellschaft in Assur. E: Inschriften, 3; Leipzig: J.C. Hinrichs, 1920).

Schwally, F., *Das Leben nach dem Tode nach den Vorstellungen des alten Israels* (Giessen: J. Ricker, 1892).

—'Ueber einige palästinische Völkernamen', *ZAW* 18 (1898), pp. 126-48.

Scott, R.B.Y., 'Meteorological Phenomena and Terminology in the Old Testament', *ZAW* 64 (1952), pp. 11-25.

Sellin, E., *Das Zwölfprophetenbuch.* I. *Hosea–Micha* (KAT, 12; Leipzig: A. Deichertsche Verlagsbuchhandlung, 3rd edn, 1929).

Shanks, H., 'Who—or what—was Molech? New Phoenician Inscription may Hold Answer', *BARev* 22.4 (1996), p. 13.

Shanks, H. and J. Meinhardt (eds.), *Aspects of Monotheism: How God is One* (Washington, DC: Biblical Archaeology Society, 1997).

Shupak, N., 'New Light on Shamgar ben 'Anath', *Bib* 70 (1989), pp. 517-25.

Simpson, W.K., 'New Light on the God Reshef', *JAOS* 73 (1953), pp. 86-89.

—'Reshep in Egypt', *Or* 29 (1960), pp. 63-74.

Smelik, K.A.D., 'Moloch, Molekh or Molk-sacrifice? A Reassessment of the Evidence concerning the Hebrew Term Molekh', *SJOT* 9 (1995), pp. 133-42.

Smith, H.P., *A Critical and Exegetical Commentary on the Books of Samuel* (ICC; Edinburgh: T. & T. Clark, 1899).

Smith, Mark S., *Psalms: The Divine Journey* (Mahwah, NJ: Paulist Press, 1987).

—'Death in Jeremiah, ix, 20', *UF* 19 (1987), pp. 289-93.

—'"Seeing God" in the Psalms: The Background to the Beatific Vision in the Hebrew Bible', *CBQ* 50 (1988), pp. 171-83.

—*The Early History of God* (San Francisco: Harper & Row, 1990).

—'The Near Eastern Background of Solar Language for Yahweh', *JBL* 109 (1990), pp. 29-39.

—'Rephaim', *ABD*, V, pp. 674-76.

—review of *Israel's Beneficent Dead* (Forschungen zum Alten Testament, 11; Tübingen: J.C.B. Mohr [Paul Siebeck], 1994), by B.B. Schmidt, in *CBQ* 58 (1996), pp. 724-25.

—*The Ugaritic Baal Cycle*. I. *Introduction with Text, Translation and Commentary of KTU 1.1–1.2* (VTSup, 55; Leiden: E.J. Brill, 1994).

—'The God Athtar in the Ancient Near East and his Place in KTU 1.6 I', in Z. Zevit, S. Gitin and M. Sokoloff (eds.), *Solving Riddles and Untying Knots: Biblical, Epigraphic, and Semitic Studies in Honor of Jonas C. Greenfield* (Winona Lake, IN: Eisenbrauns, 1995), pp. 627-40.

—*The Pilgrimage Pattern in Exodus* (JSOTSup, 239; Sheffield: Sheffield Academic Press, 1997).

Smith, Morton, *Palestinian Parties and Politics that Shaped the Old Testament* (New York: Columbia University Press, 1971).

—'Helios in Palestine', in B.A. Levine and A. Malamat (eds.), *Eretz-Israel* 16 (Harry M. Orlinsky volume; Jerusalem: Israel Exploration Society, 1982), pp. 199-214.

Smith, R.H., and T.F. Potts, 'The Iron Age', in A.W. McNicoll *et al.*, *Pella in Jordan*, II (Mediterranean Archaeology Supplement, 2; Sydney: Meditarch, 1992), pp. 83-101.

Smith, W. Robertson, *Lectures on the Religion of the Semites* (1st series; London: A. & C. Black, 2nd edn, 1894).

Snaith, N.H., *The Jewish New Year Festival* (London: SPCK, 1947).

—'The Cult of Molech', *VT* 16 (1966), pp. 123-24.

Soggin, J.A., *Joshua* (trans. R.A. Wilson; OTL; London: SCM Press, 1972).

—*Judges* (trans. J.S. Bowden; OTL; London: SCM Press, 1981).

Spalinger, A., 'A Canaanite Ritual Found in Egyptian Reliefs', *Journal of the Society for the Study of Egyptian Antiquities* 8 (1978), pp. 47-60.

Speiser, E.A., 'The Rivers of Paradise', in R. von Kienle, A. Moortgat, H. Otten, E. von Schuler and W. Zaumseil (eds.), *Festschrift Johannes Friedrich* (Heidelberg: Carl Winter, 1959), pp. 473-85; reprinted in E.A. Speiser, *Oriental and Biblical Studies* (eds. J.J. Finkelstein and M. Greenberg; Philadelphia: University of Pennsylvania Press, 1967), pp. 23-34.

Spieckermann, H., *Juda unter Assur in der Sargonidenzeit* (FRLANT, 129; Göttingen: Vandenhoeck & Ruprecht, 1982).

—'"Barmherzig und gnädig ist der Herr..."', *ZAW* 102 (1990), pp. 1-18.

Spronk, K., *Beatific Afterlife in Ancient Israel and in the Ancient Near East* (AOAT, 219; Kevelaer: Butzon & Bercker; Neukirchen–Vluyn: Neukirchener Verlag, 1986).

—'Down with Hêlēl! The Assumed Mythological Background of Isa. 14.12', in M. Dietrich and I. Kottsieper, with H. Schaudig (eds.), *'Und Mose schrieb dieses Lied auf': Studien zum Alten Testament und zum Alten Orient. Festschrift für Oswald Loretz* (AOAT, 250; Münster: Ugarit–Verlag, 1998).

Stager, L.E., 'When Canaanites and Philistines Ruled Ashkelon', *BARev* 17.2 (1991), pp. 25-29.

Stager, L.E., and S.R. Wolff, 'Child Sacrifice at Carthage: Religious Rite or Population Control?' *BARev* 10.1 (1984), pp. 31-51.

Stähli, H.-P., *Solare Elemente im Jahweglauben des Alten Testaments* (OBO, 66; Göttingen: Vandenhoeck & Ruprecht, 1985).

Stamm, J.J., *Beiträge zur hebräischen und altorientalischen Namenskunde* (ed. E. Jenni and M.A. Klopfenstein; OBO, 30; Freiburg/Göttingen: Universitätsverlag/Vandenhoeck & Ruprecht, 1980).

Stemberger, G., 'Zur Auferstehungslehre in der rabbinischen Literatur', *Kairos* NS 15 (1973), pp. 239-47.

Stolz, F., *Strukturen und Figuren im Kult von Jerusalem* (BZAW, 118; Berlin: W. de Gruyter, 1970).

Strack, H.L., and P. Billerbeck, *Kommentar zum Neuen Testament aus Talmud und Midrasch* (4 vols.; Munich: Beck, 1922–28).

Stuart, D., *Hosea–Joel* (WBC, 31; Waco, TX: Word Books, 1987).

Swauger, J.L., 'Dolmen Studies in Palestine', *BA* 29 (1966), pp. 106-14.

Tallqvist, K., *Akkadische Götterepitheta* (StudOr, 7; Helsinki: Societas Orientalis Fennica, 1938).

Talmon, S., 'Biblical *rep̱ā'îm* and Ugaritic *rpu/i(m)*', *HAR* 7 (1983), pp. 235-49.

Tångberg, A., 'A Note on Ba'al Zĕbūb in 2 Kgs 1,2.3.6.16', *SJOT* 6 (1992), pp. 293-96.

Tate, M.E., *Psalms 51–100* (WBC, 20; Dallas: Word Books, 1990).

Taylor, J.E., 'The Asherah, the Menorah and the Sacred Tree', *JSOT* 66 (1995), pp. 29-54.

Taylor, J.G., 'The Two Earliest Known Representations of Yahweh', in Eslinger and Taylor (eds.), *Ascribe to the Lord*, pp. 557-66.

—*Yahweh and the Sun: Biblical and Archaeological Evidence for Sun Worship in Ancient Israel* (JSOTSup, 111; Sheffield: JSOT Press, 1993).

Thenius, O., *Die Bücher Samuels* (Kurzgefasstes exegetisches Handbuch zum Alten Testament; Leipzig: Weidmann'sche Buchhandlung, 1842).

Thomas, D.W., 'Some Observations on the Hebrew Word רַעֲנָן', in B. Hartmann *et al.* (eds.), *Hebräische Wortforschung: Festschrift zum 80. Geburtstag von Walter Baumgartner* (VTSup, 16; Leiden: E.J. Brill, 1967), pp. 387-97.

Thompson, J.A., *The Book of Jeremiah* (NICOT; Grand Rapids: Eerdmans, 1980).

Tigay, J.H., *You Shall Have no other Gods: Israelite Religion in the Light of Hebrew Inscriptions* (HSS, 31; Atlanta: Scholars Press, 1986).

Toews, W.I., *Monarchy and Religious Institution in Israel under Jeroboam I* (SBLMS, 47; Atlanta: Scholars Press, 1993).

Toorn, K. van der, ''Anat-Yahu, some other Deities, and the Jews of Elephantine', *Numen* 39 (1992), pp. 80-101.

—'Sheger', *DDD*, cols. 1437-40 (2nd edn, pp. 760-62).

Torge, P., *Aschera und Astarte: Ein Beitrag zur semitschen Religonsgeschichte* (Leipzig: J.C. Hinrichs, 1902).

Torrey, C.C., *The Second Isaiah* (Edinburgh: T. & T. Clark, 1928).

Tournay, R., 'Les Psaumes complexes (*Suite*)', *RB* 56 (1949), pp. 37-60.

Tromp, N.J., *Primitive Conceptions of Death and the Nether World in the Old Testament* (BibOr, 21: Rome: Pontifical Biblical Institute, 1969).

—'Wisdom and the Canticle. Ct., 8, 6^{c}-7^{b}: Text, Character, Message and Import', in M. Gilbert (ed.), *La Sagesse de l'Ancien Testament* (BETL, 51; Gembloux: J. Duculot; Leuven: Leuven University Press, 1979), pp. 88-95.

Tsevat, M., 'Ishbosheth and Congeners: The Names and their Study', *HUCA* 46 (1975), pp. 71-87.

Tsumura, D.T., '"A Ugaritic God, *mt-w-šr*, and his Two Weapons" (UT 52:8-11)', *UF* 6 (1974), pp. 407-13.

—'Ugaritic Poetry and Habakkuk 3', *TynBul* 40 (1989), pp. 24-48.

—*The Earth and the Waters in Genesis 1 and 2: A Linguistic Investigation* (JSOTSup, 83; Sheffield: JSOT Press, 1989).

Tur-Sinai, N.H., 'אֲבִיר, אַבִּיר', *Encyclopaedia Biblica*, I (Hebrew; Jerusalem: Bialik, 1965), cols. 31-33.
—*The Book of Job* (ET; Jerusalem: Kiryath Sepher, rev. edn, 1967).
Ullendorff, E., 'Ugaritic Studies within their Semitic and Eastern Mediterranean Setting', *BJRL* 46 (1963–1964), pp. 236-49.
Ulrich, E., F.M. Cross, S.W. Crawford, J.A. Duncan, P.W. Skehan, E. Tov, J. Trebolle Barrera, *Qumran Cave 4*. IX. *Deuteronomy, Joshua, Judges, Kings* (DJD, 14; Oxford: Clarendon Press, 1995).
Van Selms, A., 'Judge Shamgar', *VT* 14 (1964), pp. 294-309.
Vattioni, F., 'Il dio Resheph', *AION* NS 15 (1965), pp. 39-74.
Vaux, R. de, 'Les Prophètes de Baal sur le Mont Carmel', *Bulletin du Musée de Beyrouth* 5 (1941), pp. 7-20; reprinted in R. de Vaux, *Bible et Orient* (Paris: Cerf, 1967), pp. 485-97; ET 'The Prophets of Baal on Mount Carmel', in R. de Vaux, *The Bible and the Ancient Near East* (trans. D.McHugh; London: Darton, Longman & Todd, 1972), pp. 238-51.
—*Les Sacrifices de l'Ancien Testament* (Les Cahiers de la Reine Biblique, 1; Paris: J. Gabalda, 1964); ET *Studies in Old Testament Sacrifice* (trans. J. Bourke and R. Potter; Cardiff: University of Wales Press, 1964).
—'Jérusalem et les prophètes', *RB* 73 (1966), pp. 481-509.
Velde, H. Te, *Seth: God of Confusion* (Leiden: E.J. Brill, 2nd edn, 1977).
Vermeylen, J., *Du Prophète Isaïe à l'Apocalyptique* (2 vols.; Paris: J. Gabalda, 1977).
Vida, G. Levi della, 'El 'Elyon in Genesis 14 18-20', *JBL* 63 (1944), pp. 1-9.
Vincent, A., *La Religion des Judéo-Araméens d'Eléphantine* (Paris: P. Geuthner, 1937).
Virolleaud, C., 'Les nouveaux textes mythologiques et liturgiques de Ras Shamra (XXIVe Campagne, 1961)', in C.F.A. Schaeffer (ed.), *Ugaritica* V (Paris: Imprimerie Nationale and P. Geuthner, 1968), pp. 545-606.
Wallace, H.N., *The Eden Narrative* (HSM, 32; Atlanta: Scholars Press, 1985).
Walls, N., *The Goddess Anat in Ugaritic Myth* (SBLDS, 135; Atlanta: Scholars Press, 1992).
Waterston, A., 'Death and Resurrection in the A.B. Cycle', *UF* 21 (1989), pp. 425-34.
Watson, P.L., 'The Death of "Death" in the Ugaritic Texts', *JAOS* 92 (1972), pp. 60-64.
Watson, W.G.E., 'Helel', *DDD*, cols. 746-50 (2nd edn, pp. 392-94).
Weinfeld, M., 'The Worship of Molech and of the Queen of Heaven and its Background', *UF* 4 (1972), pp. 133-54.
—'"Rider of the Clouds" and "Gatherer of the Clouds"', *JANESCU* 5 (Gaster Festschrift, 1973), pp. 421-26.
—'Discussion of Z. Meshel's two Publications of 1978 and 1979', *Shnaton* 4 (1980), pp. 280-84 (Hebrew).
—'Divine Intervention in War in Ancient Israel and in the Ancient Near East', in H. Tadmor and M. Weinfeld (eds.), *History, Historiography and Interpretation* (Jerusalem: Magnes Press; Leiden: E.J. Brill, 1983), pp. 121-47.
Weippert, M., 'Gott und Stier', *ZDPV* 77 (1961), pp. 93-117.
—'Erwägung zur Etymologie des Gottesnamens 'Ēl Šaddaj', *ZDMG* 111 (1961), pp. 42-62.
Weiser, A., *Die Psalmen* (ATD, 14/15; Göttingen: Vandenhoeck & Ruprecht, 5th edn, 1959); ET *The Psalms* (OTL; London: SCM Press, 1962).
—*Das Buch Jeremia* (ATD, 20; Göttingen: Vandenhoeck & Ruprecht, 5th edn, 1966).
Wellhausen, J., *Der Text der Bücher Samuelis* (Göttingen: Vandenhoeck & Ruprecht, 1871).

—*Prolegomena to the History of Israel* (trans. J.S. Black and A. Menzies; Edinburgh: A. & C. Black, 1885).

—*Die kleinen Propheten übersetzt und erklärt* (Berlin: Georg Reimer, 3rd edn, 1898).

Westermann, C., *Genesis 1–11* (BKAT, 1.1; Neukirchen–Vluyn: Neukirchener Verlag, 1974); ET *Genesis 1–11: A Commentary* (trans. J.J. Scullion; London: SPCK, 1984).

—*Die Verheissungen an die Väter* (FRLANT, 116; Göttingen: Vandenhoeck & Ruprecht, 1976); ET *The Promises to the Fathers* (trans. D. Green; Philadelphia: Fortress Press, 1980).

White, J.B., *A Study of the Language of Love in the Song of Songs and Ancient Egyptian Poetry* (SBLDS, 36; Missoula, MT: Scholars Press, 1978).

Whiting, J.D., 'Jerusalem's Locust Plague', *National Geographic Magazine* 28 (1915), pp. 511-50.

Whitt, W.D., 'The Divorce of Yahweh and Asherah in Hos 2, 4-7. 12ff', *SJOT* 6 (1992), pp. 31-67.

Whybray, R.N., ''*annôt* in Exodus XXXII 18', *VT* 17 (1967), p. 122.

—*Thanksgiving for a Liberated Prophet* (JSOTSup, 4; Sheffield: JSOT Press, 1978).

—review of *God's Conflict with the Dragon and the Sea*, by John Day, in *JTS* NS 36 (1985), pp. 402-407.

Wifall, W., 'El Shaddai or El of the Fields', *ZAW* 92 (1980), pp. 24-34.

Wiggins, S.A., *A Reassessment of 'Asherah'* (AOAT, 235; Kevelaer: Verlag Butzon & Bercker; Neukirchen–Vluyn: Neukirchener Verlag, 1993).

—'Yahweh: The God of Sun', *JSOT* 71 (1996), pp. 89-106.

Wildberger H., *Jesaja 1–39* (BKAT, 10.1-3; 3 vols.; Neukirchen–Vluyn: Neukirchener Verlag, 1972–82); ET *Isaiah 1–12* (trans. T.H. Trapp; Minneapolis: Fortress Press, 1991) and *Isaiah 13–27* (trans. T.H. Trapp; Minneapolis: Fortress Press, 1997).

Williams, A.J., 'The Mythological Background of Ezekiel 28:12-19?', *BTB* 6 (1976), pp. 49-61.

Williamson, H.G.M., *1 and 2 Chronicles* (NCB; Grand Rapids: W.B. Eerdmans; London: Marshall, Morgan & Scott, 1982).

Wilson, R.R., 'The Death of the King of Tyre: The Editorial History of Ezekiel 28', in Marks and Good (eds.), *Love & Death in the Ancient Near East*, pp. 211-18.

Winckler, H., *Geschichte Israels* (2 vols.; Leipzig: E. Pfeiffer, 1895–1900).

Wiseman, D.J., *Chronicles of Chaldaean Kings (626–556 B.C.) in the British Museum* (London: Trustees of the British Museum, 1956).

Wolfers, D., *Deep Things out of Darkness* (Grand Rapids: Eerdmans; Kampen: Kok, 1995).

Wolff, H.W., *Dodekapropheton*. I. *Hosea* (BKAT, 144.1; Neukirchen–Vluyn: Neukirchener Verlag, 2nd edn, 1965 [1961]); ET *Hosea* (trans. G. Stansell; Hermeneia; Philiadelphia: Fortress Press, 1974).

Woods, F.E., *Water and Storm Polemics against Baalism in the Deuteronomistic History* (American University Studies, Series 7, Theology and Religion, 150; New York: Peter Lang, 1994).

Wright, G.E., 'Troglodytes and Giants in Palestine', *JBL* 57 (1938), pp. 305-309.

Wright, G.H.B., *The Book of Job* (London: Williams & Norgate, 1883).

Würthwein, E., 'Die josianische Reform und das Deuteronomium', *ZTK* 73 (1976), pp. 365-423.

—*Das erste Buch der Könige* (ATD, 11.1; Göttingen: Vandenhoeck & Ruprecht, 1977).

Wutz, F.X., *Die Psalmen, textkritisch untersucht* (Munich: Kösel & Pustet, 1925).

Wyatt, N., 'The Relationship of the Deities Dagan and Hadad', *UF* 12 (1980), pp. 375-79.
—'Who Killed the Dragon?', *AulOr* 5 (1987), pp. 185-98.
—'The Expression *bᵉkôr māwet* in Job XVIII 13 and its Mythological Background', *VT* 40 (1990), pp. 207-16.
—'A New Look at Ugaritic *šdmt*', *JSS* 37 (1992), pp. 149-53.
—'Astarte', *DDD*, cols. 203-13 (2nd edn, pp. 109-14).
—'Calf', *DDD*, cols. 344-48 (2nd edn, pp. 180-82).
Xella, P., 'Le dieu Rashap à Ugarit', *Les Annales Archéologiques Arabes Syriennes* 29-30 (1979–80), pp. 145-62.
—'D'Ugarit à la Phénicie: Sur les traces de Rashap, Horon, Eshmun', *WO* 19 (1988), pp. 45-64.
—'Le dieu B'l 'z dans une nouvelle inscription phénicienne de Kition (Chypre)', *SEL* 10 (1993), pp. 61-69.
—'Le dieu et "sa" déesse: L'utilisation des suffixes pronominaux avec des théonymes d'Ebla à Ugarit et à Kuntillet 'Ajrud', *UF* 27 (1995), pp. 599-610.
—'Resheph', *DDD*, cols. 1324-30 (2nd edn, pp. 700-703).
Yadin, Y., *Hazor*, I (Jerusalem: Magnes Press, 1958).
—*Hazor*, III (Jerusalem: Magnes Press, 1960).
—'Symbols of Deities at Zinjirli, Carthage and Hazor', in J.A. Sanders (ed.), *Near Eastern Archaeology in the Twentieth Century: Essays in Honor of Nelson Glueck* (Garden City, NY: Doubleday, 1970), pp. 199-231.
—*Hazor* (Schweich Lectures, 1970; London: Oxford University Press, 1972).
—*Hazor: The Rediscovery of a Great Citadel of the Bible* (New York: Random House, 1975).
—'New Gleanings on Resheph from Ugarit', in A. Kort and S. Morschauer (eds.), *Biblical and Related Studies Presented to Samuel Iwry* (Winona Lake, IN: Eisenbrauns, 1985), pp. 259-74.
Yadin, Y., *et al.*, *Hazor*, II (Jerusalem: Magnes Press, 1960).
Yarbro Collins, A., *The Combat Myth in the Book of Revelation* (HDR, 9; Missoula, MT: Scholars Press, 1976).
Zevit, Z., 'The Khirbet el-Qôm Inscription Mentioning a Goddess', *BASOR* 255 (1984), pp. 35-47.
Zimmerli, W., *Ezechiel* (BKAT, 13.1 and 2; 2 vols.; Neukirchen–Vluyn: Neukirchener Verlag, 1969); ET *Ezekiel* (trans. R.E. Clements and J.D. Martin; Hermeneia; 2 vols.; Philadelphia: Fortress Press, 1979–83).

INDEXES

INDEX OF REFERENCES

OLD TESTAMENT

Genesis
1 98
1.2 98, 100, 101
1.6-10 100, 101
1.24 101
1.26 22, 101
2–3 28, 29, 176, 178
2.10-14 28, 29
2.13 30
3.5 19
3.6 19, 32
3.22 19, 22, 32
3.24 178
4.26 13
6.1-4 178, 179, 224
6.2 22
6.4 22
8.4 30
10 24
10.8-12 224
10.9 224
11.1-9 184
11.7 22
14 21, 180
14.5 217, 223
14.18-20 170
14.19 20, 21, 171
14.22 20, 21, 170, 171, 223
15.20 217
17.1 32
20.17 220
21.33 19
28.3 32
30.13 63
31.13 37
33.20 37
35.7 37
35.11 32
49.11 194
49.24 38, 41
49.25 32
50.2 219

Exodus
3.14 14, 20
6.3 13, 32
9.1-7 201
9.3 201
13.2 216
13.12-15 216
13.12-13 211
13.15 211
14.1 108
14.2 69
14.9 69
15 114
15.1-18 103
15.14-16 115
15.17 114, 115
15.18 104
17.13 166, 167
17.15 37
19.16-19 97
19.16 159
22.28-29 (ET 29-30) 216
32 35, 164
32.4 36
32.5 36, 40, 136
32.17 136
32.18 136, 137
32.19 136
32.20 196
34.6 26
34.13 42
34.15 210
34.16 210
34.19-20 216

Leviticus
2.14 196, 197
17.7 210
18.3 212
18.21 209, 211, 212
18.24-35 212
18.27 212
20.2-5 209, 212

20.5 209, 210
20.23 212

Numbers
3.12-13 216
3.40-51 216
8.16-18 216
13.33 224
14.44 186
21.14 37
23.22 38, 39
23.24 39
24.4 32, 34
24.8 38, 39
24.9 39
24.16 21, 32, 36
25.1-9 79
25.1-5 69
31.16 69
32.24 69
33.7 69

Deuteronomy
1.41 186
2.11 217, 223
2.20 217, 223
3.11 217, 223
3.13 223
4.3 69, 70
4.19 151, 163
4.28 65
4.31 26
7.5 42, 54
7.13 131, 165
12.3 54
12.31 213, 216
15.19-20 216
16.21 54, 60
17.3 151, 163, 215
18.9-10 213
18.10 216
28.4 131, 165
28.18 131, 165
28.51 131, 165
31.16 210
32.6 20
32.8 20-25, 171
32.14 194
32.17 80
32.23 203
32.24 202, 203, 205
32.32 193
32.34 207, 208
33.2 15, 97, 159, 160
33.17 39
33.26 92

Joshua
10.9 154
10.11 154, 155
10.12-14 155
10.12-13 154, 155
10.12 161
10.13 154, 155
11.17 68
12.4 217, 221, 223
12.7 68
13.5 68
13.12 223
13.17 69
15.7 152
15.9 68
15.10 152
15.11 69
15.24 69
15.29 69
15.41 85
15.59 133
15.60 68
17.15 217, 223
18.14 68
18.16 224
18.17 152
19.8 69
19.22 152
19.27 85
19.38 133, 152
19.41 152
19.44 69
19.50 152
21.16 152
21.18 133
22.17 69
24.30 152

Judges
1.33 133
1.39 152
2.9 152
2.11 68, 70
2.13 45, 68, 70, 130
2.17 210
3.3 68
3.7 42, 43, 45, 68, 70, 131
3.31 133, 135
5 137, 139
5.4-5 14, 15, 93, 97
5.6 133, 135
5.20 137
5.21 137
5.30 137
6.24 37
6.25-32 70
6.35 60
6.28 60
6.30 60
6.32 71, 72, 82
7.1 71
8.33 68-70, 210
9 139
9.4 69
9.27 70
9.46 69, 70
10.6 45, 68, 70, 130
10.10 68
16.23 78, 85
20.22 69

1 Samuel
1.1 20
5.1-7 86

1 Samuel (cont.)
5.2-57 78
5.7 86
7.3 45, 130
7.4 45, 68, 70, 130
12.10 45, 68, 70, 130
21.8 105
28.13 218
31.10 78, 85, 86, 130, 135

2 Samuel
2.10 72, 82, 128, 214
2.12 128
4.4 72, 82, 214
5.16 72
5.20 69
6.2 68
8.3 134
8.12 134
9.6 72, 82
11.1 145
11.21 82
13.23 68
19.25 72, 82
21.8 72, 82
21.15-22 225
22.11 92
23.27 133
23.31 187

1 Kings
2.26 133
8.12-13 157
8.12 157
8.13 114
8.53 (LXX) 157
11 129
11.5 84, 129
11.7 84
11.33 129
12 164
12.26-30 34, 35
12.26-27 36
12.28 35, 40
12.32 36, 53
12.33 35
14.1 36
14.13 42
14.15 42, 53
14.23 42, 54
15.13 42-44
16.31-33 70
16.33 42, 53
17–19 77
17 77
18 73-76
18.18 68
18.19 42-44, 60, 73
18.27 74
18.41-45 76
22.19-22 22
22.53 71

2 Kings
1 77, 80
1.2-16 71
1.2 69, 78, 79, 85
1.3 69, 78, 85
1.6 68, 78, 85
1.10 79
1.12 79
1.14 79
1.16 78, 85
2.22 220
3.2-3 71
3.2 71
3.25 152
4.38 212
4.42 69
10.18-27 71
10.28 36
10.29 36
13.6 42
15.19 181
16.3 211, 213
17.10 42, 53, 54
17.16 42, 47, 53, 71
17.17 216
17.24-28 144
18.4 42, 54
19.26 194
20.8-11 161
21 146
21.2-3 151, 164
21.2 213
21.3 42, 53, 60, 71, 158, 163
21.5 163
21.6 211, 213
21.7 42-44, 46, 47, 53, 55
21.31 47
22–23 230, 231
22.20 230
23 146, 151, 229, 230, 232
23.4-5 71
23.4 42, 43, 46, 47, 60, 194, 232
23.5 43, 151, 156, 158, 163, 164, 213, 232
23.6-7 47
23.6 42, 43, 232
23.5 232
23.6b 196
23.7 42, 47, 232
23.10 209, 211, 213, 216, 224, 232
23.11 151, 153, 156, 158, 232

23.12 196
23.13 129
23.14 42, 54, 232
23.15 42, 54
23.17 37
23.26 230
23.29-30 230

1 Chronicles
3.8 72
5.8 69
5.23 68
6.44 (ET 59) 152
6.45 133
8.33 72, 82, 128
8.34 72, 82
8.36 187
9.39 72, 82, 129
9.40 72, 82
9.42 187
10.10 78, 86, 130
11.28 133
11.33 187
12.3 133, 187
12.6 (ET 5) 160
13.6 68
14.6 72
14.11 69
27.12 133
27.25 187

2 Chronicles
7.14 220
12.6 (ET 5) 72
13.8 40
14.2 (ET 3) 42, 46
15.16 42, 44, 46
17.3 68
17.6 42, 46
19.3 42
20.16 180
24.7 68
24.18 42, 46
28.2 68
31.1 42, 46
33.3 42, 46, 47, 53, 68
33.6 211
33.7 47, 54, 62
33.15 47, 55, 62
33.19 42, 46, 54
34–35 231
34.3 42, 46, 54, 231
34.4 42, 46, 54, 68
34.7 42, 46, 54

Ezra
2.23 133
2.24 187
4.8 162
4.9 162
4.17 162
4.23 162

Nehemiah
7.27 133
7.28 187
9.31 26
12.29 187

Job
1.6 22
2.2 22
3.4 159
3.8 100, 102
5.6 203
5.7 201, 203, 204, 208
7.12 100
8.3 34
8.5 34
9.8 100, 110
9.13-14 100, 103
9.13 100
10.2 18
10.5 18
13.3 34
14.12 119
14.14 119
15.7-8 19, 22, 32, 176, 178
15.8 32
15.25 34
17.16 203
18.13-14 207, 208
18.13 203, 208
21.23 191
21.24 191
22.17 34
23.16 34
24.22 105
26.5 217, 223
26.7 107, 183
26.11 112
26.12-13 100
27.2 34
27.13 34
30 139
31.1 139, 140
31.9-12 139
31.26-28 151
32.26 163
33.4 34
34.10 34
34.12 34
34.20 105
35.13 34
36.26 18, 25, 27
37.22 111
38.7 22, 25, 47, 156, 158
38.8-11 100
40.9-14 102
40.10-13 (ET 1-21) 102
40.15–41.26 (ET 34) 100, 102
40.19 102
40.23 103

Nehemiah (cont.)
40.24 102
42.1-6 103

Psalms
18.3 (ET 2) 159
18.10-11 (ET 9-10) 158
18.10 (ET 9) 158
18.11 (ET 10) 92, 94, 177
18.13 (ET 12) 177
18.14 (ET 13) 21, 171
18.15 (ET 14) 177
19 26, 162
19.5c-6 (ET 4c-5) 162
19.2 (ET 1) 20, 26
20.3 (ET 2) 109
22.16 (ET 15) 212
26.12-13 99
27.13 215
29 91, 95, 97, 98
29.1-2 98
29.1 22, 96, 98
29.1bc (ET 1) 97
29.2 97
29.3-9b 98
29.3 96, 97, 100
29.4 97
29.4b 96
29.5-6 96
29.5 96, 97
29.7 96, 97
29.8 96, 97
29.9 96
29.9bc 97
29.9c 98
29.10-11 98
29.10 96, 97, 100
29.11 97
29.31 96
29.41 96
31.18 (ET 17) 155
33.7-8 100
44.3 (ET 2) 54
46 105, 179
46.1 (ET heading) 191
46.3 (ET 2) 105
46.5 (ET 4) 21, 32, 116, 179
46.7 (ET 6) 105
47.3 (ET 2) 171
48 105, 107, 190
48.3 (ET 2) 105, 108, 113, 115, 116, 179, 183
48.8 (ET 7) 105
48.15 (ET 14) 190
49 191
49.15 (ET 14) 186
50.2 159
50.3 159
65.7-8 (ET 6-7) 99
68 93
68.5 (ET 4) 92, 93
68.7 (ET 6) 93
68.8-9 (ET 7-8) 93, 97
68.15 (ET 14) 32
68.16-17 (ET 15-16) 104
68.21 (ET 20) 191
68.22-23 (ET 21-22) 142
68.23 (ET 22) 104, 105
68.24 (ET 23) 142
68.30 (ET 29) 104
68.34 (ET 33) 92, 93
73.4 191
73.9 191, 192
74 99
74.12-17 99
74.14 99, 103
76 105
76.4 (ET 3) 205, 206
77.17-21 (ET 16-20) 103
78 201
78.17 21
78.35 21
78.36 21
78.47 201
78.48 201-204, 207, 208
78.49 200, 201, 203, 205
78.50 201
78.56 21
78.69 115
82 178, 179
82.1 22, 25, 27
82.6-7 178
82.6 21, 22, 25
82.8 25
84.12 (ET 11) 158, 159
87.4 103
87.5 21
88.11 (ET 10) 217, 223
89 99, 112
89.6-8 (ET 5-7) 22
89.7 (ET 6) 22
89.10-15 (ET 9-14) 99
89.11 (ET 10) 99
89.13 (ET 12) 111, 112
91.3 206
91.5-6 206
91.5 202, 207
91.6 207
91.10 206
93.3-4 99
95.5 (LXX) 80
97.9 171
102.2 (ET 1) 18
102.13 (ET 12) 18
102.16 (ET 15) 18
102.17 (ET 16) 18
102.19 (ET 18) 18

102.20 (ET 19)	18
102.22 (ET 21)	18
102.23 (ET 22)	18
102.25-28 (ET 24-27)	27
102.25 (ET 24)	18, 20, 25
102.26-27 (ET 25-26)	20, 25
102.28 (ET 27)	20, 25
103.8	26
104	101
104.2	110
104.3	91, 92, 93
104.6-9	99, 101
104.6	101
104.11	101
104.20	101
104.26	101
105.37	80
106.28	69, 70
107.3	112
110.3	179, 180
110.4	179
116.10	137
121.4	15
121.6	207
127.5	67
128.1	67
141.7	186
144.2	159
Proverbs	
1.12	186
2.18	217, 223
3.13	67
3.18	67
8.22	67
8.24	100
8.27-29	100
8.32	67
8.34	67
9.18	217, 223
11.30	67
13.21	67
15.4	67
16.20	67
20.7	67
21.16	217, 223
27.20	186
28.14	67
29.18	67
30.15b-16	186
Ecclesiastes	
12.11	54
Song of Songs (Canticles)	
4.4	141
6.4	140, 141
6.10	140, 141
7.1 (ET 6.13)	140
8.6-7	204
8.6c-7b	205
8.6	140, 187, 188, 201, 202, 204
8.7	205
8.9-10	141
8.11	68
Isaiah	
2.7	153
2.13	96
3.18	169
5.14	186
6.13	64
8.5-8	104
8.19	218
10.30	133
13–14	180, 182, 184
13.1–14.23	180, 181
13.1–14.21	180
13.1-22	169
13.1	180, 181
13.6	32
13.9	180
13.10-11	169
13.10	169
13.17-22	182
13.17	170, 180, 181
13.18	181
13.19-22	180, 181
13.19	181
14	170
14.4-23	169
14.4	166, 180, 181
14.4b-21	181-83
14.8	183
14.9	219, 223
14.12-15	109, 110, 166, 168, 169, 171-75, 177-84
14.12	167, 175
14.13-14	21, 116
14.13	22, 25, 110, 113, 170, 171, 177, 182, 183
14.14	21, 110, 179
14.14a	170
14.15	167
14.18-20	181, 182
14.19	217
14.20	182
14.22	180, 181
14.22b-23	180
14.24-27	181
16.7	152
16.8	193, 194
16.11	152
17.8	42
17.12-14	104, 105
19.9	87
19.11	92
24.21	22
24.23	155
25.8	186, 187
26–27	59, 122
26.13-27.11	59

Isaiah (cont.)
26.13 (LXX) 59, 122
26.14 119, 123, 217, 223
26.17-18 59, 122, 123
26.19 59, 74, 116, 119, 122-24, 126, 187, 217, 223
27.1 99, 105, 106, 115
27.2-6 59, 122
27.8 59, 122, 124, 187
27.9 42, 59, 122
27.11 59, 122
29.1-8 105
30.7 103
30.33 209, 211
31.1-9 105
31.4 137
34.6-10 142
37.19 65
37.24 110, 167
37.27 194
40.3 22, 93
40.6 22
40.22 110
44.24 110
45.12 110
51.9 103
51.10 103
51.13 110
52.13–53.12 125
52.13 125
53 125
53.11 125
54.12 158
57.5 213, 215
57.7 213
57.9 209, 213, 215
60.1-2 160
60.19-20 160
63.1-6 142
66.16 92
66.24 124

Jeremiah
1.1 133
1.13-15 113
2–6 230
2.8 71, 230
2.18 (LXX) 30
2.23 68, 230
2.27-28 230
2.27 64, 65
2.30 119
3.24 82, 216
4.6 113
5.22 100
6.1 113
6.22 113
7 147, 149, 150
7.18 131, 144, 145, 149, 211
7.31 209, 215, 216
8.2 151, 163
9.13 (ET 14) 68
9.20 (ET 21) 188-90
10.5 209
10.12 110
11.13 82, 128, 214
11.21 133
11.23 133
17.2 42
19.5 211, 213, 215
22.15-16 230
23.13 71
23.18 22
23.22 22
23.35 209
24.6 54
29.27 133
31.35 100
31.40 193, 194
32.7 133
32.8 133
32.9 133
32.31 54
32.35 211, 213, 215, 216, 224
44 145, 147-50
44.17-19 131, 144, 145, 149
44.17 145
44.18 145
44.19 145
44.25 131, 144, 149
48.13 37, 38, 144, 147
48.31 152
48.36 152
50–51 182, 184
50.17 182
50.28-29 184
50.28 184
51.11 184
51.15 110
51.24 184
51.34-37 184
51.34 104, 182
51.49-51 184
51.53 182, 184

Lamentations
1.5 105

Ezekiel
1.1 111
1.4 111
1.13 177
8.3 62, 63
8.5 62, 63
8.14 43, 71
8.16 151, 156
10.2 177
10.5 25
16.20 216
16.23 66
17 104
19 104
20.25-26 216

20.26	211
20.32	65
24.3	212
26.8	159
27.4	27
27.32	27
28	19, 27, 28, 111, 178, 179
28.1-19	27
28.1-10	28
28.2-10	26-28
28.2-6	25
28.2	19, 25, 27, 29
28.3	19, 27
28.4	19
28.5	19
28.6	27
28.9	25, 27
28.11-19	28
28.12-19	28, 29, 175-79
28.12-14	29
28.12	19, 32, 176
28.13	30, 177
28.14	28, 30, 177
28.16	28, 30, 177
28.17-20	28
28.17	176
29.3-5	103
29.3	103
29.17	19, 32
32.2-8	103
32.2	103
32.30	113
37	123, 124, 187
38.6	113
38.15	113
39.2	113
39.10-13	28
39.17-20	142
48.35	37

Daniel

4.14 (ET 17)	22
7	15, 106, 107, 233
7.9	18
7.10	22
7.13-14	19
7.21	22
7.22	21
7.25	21, 22
7.27	21, 22
8.9-14	184
8.10-13	22
8.13	83
8.15	106
9.27	71, 83
10.13	22
10.16	106
10.18	106
10.20	22
11.31	71, 83
11.35	125
11.38	85
11.45	54
12	124, 125
12.1	22, 106
12.2	74, 116, 124, 187
12.3	125
12.4	125
12.11	71, 83

Hosea

1.4	71
2	58, 65, 72
2.4-7 (ET 2-5)	65, 66
2.4	66
2.7 (ET 5)	73
2.10 (ET 8)	73, 220
2.12-14 (ET 10-12)	65, 66
2.15 (ET 13)	65, 68, 73
2.16-17 (ET 14-15)	65
2.18-19 (ET 16-17)	65
2.18 (ET 16)	14, 72
2.19 (ET 17)	68, 71
2.21-22 (ET 19-20)	65
4.12-14	63
4.12	63
4.15	38
5–6	117, 119-21
5.8–6.6	119
5.14	119, 121
6.1-3	123
6.1	120
6.2-3	123, 126
6.2	119, 121
6.3	120, 123
6.5	119
6.13-14	126
8.5	136
8.6	39, 40
9.10	69, 70, 81, 82, 128, 214
10.15	38
11.2	68, 220
13–14	58, 117, 119, 120, 122
13	124
13.1	71, 119, 120
13.4–14.10	59
13.4	59, 122
13.7-8	119, 121
13.7	119
13.9	119
13.13	59, 122, 123
13.14-15	120
13.14	59, 117, 119, 120, 122-24, 187, 205
13.15	122, 124, 187
14	121
14.2 (ET 1)	120

Hosea (cont.)
14.5 (ET 4) 120
14.6-8 (ET 5-7) 59, 122
14.6 (ET 5) 59, 120, 122
14.9 (ET 8) 57-59, 122, 135, 144
14.10 (ET 9) 59, 122

Joel
1.15 32, 115
2.1-11 113
2.1 113
2.11 113
2.20 113
4 (ET 3) 105
4.19 (ET 3.19) 105

Amos
3.7 22
3.14 38
5.4 38
5.5 38
5.26 222
8.14 66

Jonah
4.2 26

Micah
5.7 (ET 8) 119
5.9 (ET 10) 153
5.12-13 (ET 13-14) 54, 153
5.13 (ET 14) 42
6.7 216

Habakkuk
1.6 183
1.12-17 183
2.4 186
2.5 186
2.6-19 183
2.17 183
2.19 65

3 155, 159
3.2-7 199
3.3 15, 49
3.4 159
3.5 192, 198, 199, 203-205, 207, 208
3.7 15
3.8-15 199
3.8-10 104
3.8 94, 205
3.9 97
3.10-11 154, 155, 159
3.13b 192
3.15 104, 205
3.17-18 193
3.17 193, 194

Zephaniah
1.1 230
1.4-5 230
1.5 163, 209
1.7-18 142

Zechariah
1.10-11 22
3.7 22
9 142
9.15 142
11.1-2 96
12 105
12.1 110
12.11 71, 118
14 105
14.5 22
14.18-19 106

Malachi
3.20 (ET 4.2) 160

Apocrypha
Tobit
1.5 36
3.17 219

Ecclesiasticus (*Sirach*)
9.5 140
17.17 22
24.2 22
24.27 30

Baruch
4.7 80

1 Maccabees
1.54 83, 84
1.59 83, 84
10.83-84 86
11.4 86

2 Maccabees
6.2 84
6.7 85
7.37-38 125
14.33 85

New Testament
Matthew
10.25 80, 81
12.24 80
12.27 80
23.16-22 52

Mark
3.22 80
3.25 81
3.27 81
8.31 122
9.31 122
10.34 122

Luke
10.18 166
11.15 80
11.18-19 80
13.32 121
13.33 121

John
12.24 127

Acts
7.43 222

1 Corinthians
10.20 80
15.36-37 127
15.54 187
15.55 123

Revelation
7.17 187
9.20 80
12 107, 233
13 233
13.1-10 107
13.11-18 107
21.4 187

Pseudepigrapha
1 Enoch
6.6 31
89.59-77 22
90.22-27 22

4 Maccabees
6.27-29 125
17.22 125
18.4 125

4 Ezra
7.32 126

Jubilees
15.31-32 22

Qumran
1QIsaa 194
1QpHab 186
4QDeut 23, 171

Targums
Pseudo-Jonathan
Deut. 32.8 24

Rabbinic References
b. Bek.
55a 163

b. Qidd.
71A 52

b. Šebu.
15b 207

m. 'Abod. Zar.
3.7 53
3.9 53
3.10 53

m. Ker.
1.7 52

m. Ket
2.9 52

m. Me'il
3.8 53

m. Ned
1.3 52

m. 'Or.
1.7 53

m. Suk.
3.1-3 53

m. Ta'an.
4.6 83

Gen. R.
94.9 163
98.16 163

Ugaritic Texts
KTU[2]
1.1-6 91
1.2.I.14 170
1.2.I.18-19 89
1.2.I.20 170
1.2.I.31 170
1.2.III.21 34
1.2.III.29-30 114
1.2.IV.8 91
1.2.IV.29 91
1.3.II.3-41 140
1.3.II.3-30 140
1.3.III.37-
1.3.IV.1 94
1.3.III.40-44 103
1.3.III.40-42 99
1.3.III.40 106
1.3.III.45-46 79
1.3.III.47–IV.1 105, 108, 113
1.3.V.2 18
1.3.V.24-25 18
1.3.V.35 89
1.3.V.38 27
1.3.VI.15-16 114
1.4.I.12 27
1.4.III.31 34
1.4.IV.9 95
1.4.IV.24 18, 106
1.4.IV.38 194
1.4.IV.47 89
1.4.IV.52 27
1.4.V.3 27
1.4.V.4 106
1.4.V.58–
VI.15 189
1.4.V.65 19
1.4.VI.44-59 98
1.4.VI.46 22
1.4.VII.29-31 96
1.4.VIII–
1.6.VI 117
1.5.I.1-3 99
1.5.I.1-2 106
1.5.I.1 104
1.5.I.6-8 185
1.5.I.11 107, 170
1.5.I.14 121
1.5.II.1-6 185
1.5.II.2-3 192
1.5.II.7 170
1.5.II.17 165
1.5.III.16 165
1.5.III.24 165
1.5.V.6b-11 94-95
1.5.V.18-22 142
1.5.VI.23-24 89
1.6.I.34 31
1.6.I.43-67 172
1.6.I.57-59 107, 170
1.6.I.59 173
1.6.I.60 173

KTU^2 (cont.)
1.6.I.62 173
1.6.II.21-23 186
1.6.II.26-37 194, 195
1.6.IV.34-35 90
1.6.V.8-9 97
1.6.VI.17-22 187
1.6.VI.17-18 205
1.6.VI.20 205
1.6.VI.46-48 217, 218
1.6.VI.51-53 103
1.10.I.3-4 25, 47, 158
1.10.II.26–III.25 142
1.10.III.34 90
1.11.1 142
1.12.II.29-30 173
1.13 142
1.13.13 138
1.15.II.7 25
1.15.II.11 25
1.15.III.14-15 217
1.16.I.11 48, 62
1.16.I.22 48, 62
1.16.III.13-14 87
1.17.I.30-31 18
1.17.II.5-6 18
1.17.II.26-27 169
1.17.II.19-20 18
1.19.I.42-44 97
1.19.II.3 95
1.19.II.8 95
1.19.III.45 126
1.20-22 217
1.23.10 193
1.23.19 27
1.23.54 146
1.24.14 89
1.46.3 89
1.47.4 89
1.47.5-11 68
1.47.27 198
1.48.5 89
1.53.5 27
1.78.2-4 198, 199
1.82 199
1.91.11 201
1.100.15 89
1.100.41 214, 221-23
1.101.1-3a 97
1.101.3b-4 96
1.107.14 221
1.107.17 214, 222
1.107.42 223
1.108 220, 221
1.108.1-2 214
1.108.1 223
1.108.2-3 223
1.108.6-7 137
1.108.7 147
1.114.15-19 18
1.118.26 198
1.119.26-36 190
1.123.4 89
1.127.30-31 190
1.128 69, 70
1.141.1.18-19 198
1.148.18 132
1.148.31 132, 165
1.161 217
1.161.2-5 218
1.161.2-3 217
1.161.9-10 217, 218
1.161.9 217
1.161.11-12 218
1.169.1 78
2.10.11-13 187, 190
3.5 190
4.307.6 134
4.320.4 134
6.13.2 89
6.14.2 89
21.127.29-31 190

Ugaritica V
137.IVb.16 172

Other Ancient Near Eastern Texts
Aramaic (AP)
7.7 38
22.124 38
22.125 38
44.3 52, 142, 143

CT
22.120 88

Deir ʿAll Inscription
I.2 33
I.5-6 33
I.16 132
II.6 33

Eblaite Texts
TM.75.G.1464 v.XI 12'-18' 199

El-Amarna Letters
Letter 323, line 22 163

Gilgamesh Epic
Old Babylonian version
Reverse
Line 13 31
Line 20 31

Tablet 11
Lines 98-100 200
Lines 194-97 30

KAI
12.3-4 52
13.7-8 217
14 149
14.8-9 217
14.19 87
26.A.III.18 20
31.1 69
31.2 69
32.3-4 206
37.10 149
47.1 75
67.1-2 80
86 31
87 31
94 31

117.1 217
129.1 20
222.A.11 21, 170

Kition Tariff
Line 9 149

Kuntillet ʻAjrud Pithoi
Pithos A 49

Moabite Stone
Line 9 69
Line 30 69

Papyrus Amherst Egyptian
63 lines 11-19 109
63 lines 13-14 109

Proto-Sinaitic Texts
358 19

Samaria Ostraca
41 36

Wisdom of Ahiqar
Lines 94b-95 67

Classical and Patristic Texts
Aeneas of Gaza
De Animali Immortalitate
77 126

Apollodorus
The Library
1.6.3 94

Arrian
Anabasis Alexandria
6.I.2-6 30

Athenaeus
9.392 74

Callimachus
Epigrams
56 175

Chronicon Pascale
43 74

Diogenes Laertius
Proemium
9 126

Eusebius
Praeparatio Evangelica
1.9.29 55
1.10.10 55
1.10.15 21, 170
1.10.16 38, 87
1.10.25 87
1.10.26 216
1.10.31 131

Herodian
History of the Empire from the Time of Marcus Aurelius
5.5.6-9

Herodotus
1.105 149
3.5 94

Hesiod
Theogony
381 168
984-91 174

Homer
Odyssey
11.240-332 224

Iliad
12.23 224

Jerome
Commentary on Daniel
11.31 83

Josephus
Antiquities
1.3.6 30
8.5.3 74, 126

Lucian
De Syria Dea
6 121

Ovid
Metamorphoses
1.748-49 175
2.1-400 175

Pausanias
Description of Greece
1.14.7 149
2.5.3 30

Plato
Cratylus
33 224

Plutarch
De Iside et Osiride
13.356C 121

19.366F 121
46 126

Pseudo-Scylax
Periplus
104 76

Strabo
Geography
15.1.25 30
16.2.7 94

INDEX OF AUTHORS

Aartun, K. 78
Ackerman, S. 138, 141, 149, 150
Aharoni, Y. 76
Aistleitner, J. 17, 95
Akurgal, E. 39
Albertz, R. 229
Albright, W.F. 23, 29, 32, 40, 43, 61, 64, 72, 80, 88, 93, 107, 108, 114, 133, 142, 143, 172, 192, 209, 228
Alfrink, B. 107, 154
Allen, L.C. 114
Alt, A. 76, 133
Amsler, S. 58
Andersen, F.I. 63, 118, 119, 137
Anderson, A.A. 207
Anderson, H. 81
Angerstorfer, A. 52
Archi, A. 199
Arnaud, D. 165
Astour, M.C. 16
Attridge, H.W. 87
Auld, A.G. 133
Avigad, N. 20, 72, 160
Avishur, Y. 78
Avi-Yonah, M. 76

Bailey, L.R. 33, 35, 164
Ball, C.J. 63
Barr, J. 176, 220
Barré, M. 197
Barstad, H.M. 36, 117
Barth, H. 175
Barthélemy, D. 23, 167
Bartlett, J.R. 223
Barton, G.A. 132
Battenfield, J.K. 77
Baudissin, W.W. von 42, 118, 119, 121
Bea, A. 209
Beck, M. 229
Beck, P. 51
Benz, F.L. 165
Bernhardt, K. 48
Bertholet, A. 111
Biale, D. 32
Bickerman(n), E. 84
Billerbeck, P. 81
Binger, T. 48, 64
Blau, J. 221
Blenkinsopp, J. 154
Block, D.I. 24
Bochart, S. 102
Böhl, F.M.T. 40
Bonnet, C. 74, 111, 116, 129
Borger, R. 143
Bousset, W. 125
Boyce, M. 125
Bresciani, E. 147, 149
Bright, J. 188
Brock, S.P. 91
Bronner, L. 77
Broome, E.C. 225
Brown, J.P. 183
Brownlee, W.H. 64
Buber, M. 215
Budde, K. 110
Bunge, J.G. 85
Burns, J.B. 167, 208
Burstein, S.M. 30
Busink, T.A. 157

Cantineau, J. 20
Caquot, A. 17, 48, 78, 174, 178, 197, 203, 222, 223
Caspari, W. 40

Cassuto, U. (M.D.) 17, 178, 188, 195
Cazelles, H. 138, 210
Ceresko, A. 139
Charlier, C.V.L. 156
Charpin, D. 99
Cheyne, T.K. 79
Chiera, E. 133
Childs, B.S. 114
Clements, R.E. 70, 107, 114, 123, 158, 167, 175, 218
Clifford, R.J. 27, 107, 111
Clines, D.J.A. 202
Cogan, M.D. 146, 164, 231
Colenso, J.W. 92
Colledge, S.M. 57
Collins, A.Y. 107
Conrad, D. 197, 198
Coogan, M.D. 34, 51
Cooke, G. 22
Cooper, A. 66, 128, 129, 209, 221
Cornelius, I. 197, 198
Craigie, P.C. 135, 137, 138, 172
Cranfield, C.E.B. 81
Crawford, S.W. 23
Crenshaw, J.L. 113
Croatto, J.S. 192
Cross, F.M. 13-15, 17, 19, 22, 23, 31-33, 37, 61, 69, 87, 97, 104, 111, 114, 115, 134, 135, 164, 183, 221, 230, 231
Cumont, F.M. 148
Cunchillos Ylarri, J.L. 22
Curtis, A.H.W. 36, 37, 40

Dahood, M.J. 110, 112, 145, 146, 198, 199, 207
Dalglish, E.R. 37
Dalley, S. 30, 165
Dalman, G. 197
Danelius, E. 35
Davies, G.I. 118, 119, 121, 228
Day, J. 18, 22, 24, 27, 31, 51, 58, 59, 61, 67, 73, 82, 83, 94, 96, 98, 100, 106, 109, 116, 120, 122, 130, 170, 186, 198, 199, 209, 211-14, 216, 224
Day, P.L. 81, 135, 142, 144
Debus, J. 39
Deem, A. 137
Delcor, M. 86, 131, 136, 137, 149
Dever, W.G. 49, 51
Dhorme, E.(P.) 130, 202, 208
Dietrich, M. 23, 51, 70, 221, 222
Dietrich, W. 229
Diggle, J. 175
Dijk, H.J. Van 27
Dijkstra, M. 19
Dion, P.-E. 180
Driver, G.R. 93, 95, 96, 124, 159, 168, 198, 219
Driver, S.R. 35, 110, 111, 130, 132, 201
Dronkert, K. 209
Duhm, B. 175
Duncan, J.A., 23
Durand, J.-M. 99
Dürr, L. 185
Dus, J. 154
Dussaud, R. 196, 209
Dyke Parunak, H. van 157

Ebeling, E. 61
Edelmann, R. 136
Edgerton, W.F. 201
Edwards, P.C. 57
Eichrodt, W. 215
Eissfeldt, O. 14, 16, 17, 37, 39, 74, 76, 107-13, 135, 183, 209
Elnes E.E. 21, 171
Emerton, J.A. 14, 17, 18, 49, 51, 64, 71, 73, 99, 106, 173, 180, 186
Engelkern, K. 15
Engle, J.R. 55
Erlandsson, S. 180-82, 184
Etz, D. 170

Fensham, F.C. 77, 79, 134, 178, 195
Fenton, T. 81, 101
Finkelstein, I. 34
Fitzgerald, A. 97
Fitzmyer, J.A. 21, 149
Fohrer, G. 58, 111, 172
Fontenrose, J. 89
Forsyth, N. 166
Fox, M.V. 141, 204
Fraine, J. de 154
Frankena, R. 214

Freedman, D.N. 63, 114, 115, 118, 119, 139, 231
Frevel, C. 46, 59, 65
Fulco, W.J. 198, 201, 203, 205, 207

Gall, A. Fr. von 157
Gallagher, W.R. 168
Galling, K. 76
Gardiner, A.H. 143
Gaster, T.H. 78, 97, 155, 157, 174, 189, 200, 202, 206
Geiger, A. 82, 213
Gelb, I.J. 200
Gerleman, G. 205
Gese, H. 61
Gibson, J.C.L. 36, 118, 147, 149, 221
Gilula, M. 49, 50
Ginsberg, H.L. 23, 93, 97, 125, 181, 219
Gitin, S. 47
Giveon, R. 198
Gnuse, R.K. 229
Goetze, A. 61, 94
Goldin, J. 115
Gonnet, H. 165
Good, E.M. 139
Good, R.M. 136, 219, 220
Gordis, R. 141, 201, 202, 204
Gordon, R.P. 18, 135, 145
Gosse, B. 182
Gottlieb, H. 64
Gottstein, M.H. 23
Goulder, M.D. 109, 190, 204
Graham, W.C. 156
Grave, C. 108
Gray, G.B. 40, 110, 111, 201
Gray, J. 70, 128, 141, 172, 178, 196
Grayson, A.K. 182
Grdseloff, B. 198
Greenberg, M. 62
Greenfield, J.C. 18, 95, 203, 221
Grelot, P. 166, 167, 172, 173, 175
Gressmann, H. 151
Gruppe, O. 174
Gunkel, H. 98, 159, 167, 170, 207
Güterbock, H.G. 94
Guyard, S. 79

Habel, N.C. 202, 208
Hackett, J.A. 33
Hadley, J.M. 43, 46, 47, 50, 52, 55-58, 67, 132
Hahn, J. 35-37, 40
Halperin, D. 183
Hamilton, G.J. 82
Hanson, P.D. 142
Haran, M. 97
Hartley, J.E. 111
Hasel, G.F. 123
Hayes, J.H. 181
Hayman, A.P. 228
Healey, J.F. 26, 88, 197
Hehn, J. 200
Heider, G.C. 209, 212, 214, 222
Held, M. 148
Heller, J. 154
Hempel, J. 23
Hengel, M. 84, 85
Herder, J.G. von 170
Herdner, A. 48
Herrmann, W. 79, 149
Hess, R.S. 52
Hestrin, R. 55, 56, 161
Hill, G.F. 188
Hillman, G. 197
Hirmer, M. 39
Hoffner, H.A. 31, 117
Höfner, M. 61
Hoftijzer, J. 165
Holladay, J.S. 155
Holland, T.A. 153
Hollis, F.J. 156
Hölscher, G. 202
Holter, K. 86
Hommel, F. 164
Hooker, M.D. 81
Horst, F. 202
Houtman, C. 114
Houtsma, M.T. 186
Hugger, P. 207
Hvidberg, F.F. 17, 118
Hvidberg-Hansen, F.O. 147, 195
Hyatt, J.P. 37

Irsigler, H. 215
Irvine, A. 181
Iwry, S. 64

Jacob, E. 58
Jaroš, K. 39
Jastrow, M. 168
Jeppesen, K. 64
Jeshurun, G. 139
Jirku, A. 18, 209, 221
Johnson, A.R. 93, 190, 206
Johnston, P. 218
Jones, B.C. 152
Jones, G.H. 129
Jüngling, H.-W. 22

Kamil, M. 147, 149
Kapelrud, A.S. 113, 171, 195
Karge, P. 224, 225
Kaufman, S.A. 212, 213
Kautzsch, E. 128
Keel, O. 52, 84, 146, 156, 164, 166, 204, 207, 229
Keller, C.-A. 58
Key, A.F. 35, 164
Kissane, E.J. 139
Kittel, R. 135
Kletter, R. 55
Kloos, C. 104
Klopfenstein, M.A. 229
Knudtzon, J.A. 163
Koch, K. 146
Kooij, G. van der 165
Kornfeld, W. 209
Korpel, M.J.A. 169
Kramer, S.N. 94
Kraus, H.-J. 191, 206
Krinetzki, G. 190, 205
Kuenen, A. 43

Laato, A. 232
Lack, R. 21
Lagrange, M.J. 219
Lambert, W.G. 30, 200, 214
Landy, F. 204
Lane, E.W. 174
Lang, B. 126, 229
Langdon, S.H. 168, 182, 214
Langhe, R. de 107
Laroche, E. 165
Lauha, A. 107
Launey, M. 149
Leclant, J. 130
Lehmann, M.R. 192, 194, 213
Lemaire, A. 49, 50, 53
Lemche, N.P. 15
Levenson, J.D. 102, 216
Levi della Vida, G. 21
Levin, C. 229
Lewis, T.J. 218
Lewy, J. 35, 164
L'Heureux, C. 15, 28, 171, 219, 221
Lightfoot, J.B. 23, 81
Lindars, B. (F.C.) 122, 162
Lipiński, E. 31, 44, 54, 108, 112, 116, 151, 156, 198
Livingstone, A. 181
Lods, A. 162
Løkkegaard, F. 13, 26, 90
Loewenstamm, S.E. 195
Lohfink, N. 230
Loretz, O. 23, 27, 33, 51, 97, 98, 221, 222
Lutzky, H.C. 62

Macalister, R.A.S. 77
Mackrodt, R. 84
Maier, W.A. 61
Mannati, M. 191, 192
Margalit, B. (Margulis) 62, 221, 222
Martin, J.D. 162
Martin-Achard, R. 118, 119, 121
Matthiae, P. 198
Mauchline, J. 130
Maunder, E.W. 155
May, H.G. 118, 156, 157, 169, 178
Mayer, W. 70
Mays, J.L. 63, 118
Mazar, A. 34, 133
Mazar, B. [Maisler] 74
McKay, J.W. 151, 167, 174, 175, 231
McKenzie, J.L. 177, 178
McNicoll, A.W. 57
Meek, T.J. 36
Menzel, B. 214
Meinhardt, J. 229
Meshel, Z. 49
Mesnil du Buisson, R. du 149
Mettinger, T.N.D. 13, 14, 17, 32, 114, 117, 229

Michel, W.L. 139
Milik, J.T. 37, 135
Millar, F.G.B. 85
Millard, A.R. 225
Miller, P.D. 13, 21, 50, 86, 171
Mittmann, S. 50, 97
Montalbano, F.J. 88
Montgomery, J.A. 157
Moor, J.C. de 13, 33, 92-94, 118, 195, 197, 200, 221
Morgenstern, J. 107, 156
Mörl, T.S. 191
Motzki, H. 38, 39
Movers, F.K. 14, 79
Mowan, O. 111, 112
Mowinckel, S. 92, 100, 190, 191
Mulder, M.J. 69, 74, 76, 79, 192, 193
Mullen, E.T. 22
Müller, K.F. 214
Murphy, R.E. 204

Naccache, A. 31
Nelson, R.D. 230
Nestle, E. 83, 84
Neuberg, F. 66
Nicholson, E.W. 229
Niehr, H. 15, 111, 158
Nielsen, E. 64
Nims, C.F. 109
Nineham, D.E. 81
Nöldeke, T. 128
Norin, S. 115
Noth, M. 16, 72, 115

Obbink, H.T. 40
O'Ceallaigh, G.C. 213
Oden, R.A. 75, 87, 129
Oesterley, W.O.E. 206
Oestreicher, T. 151, 163
Ohler, A. 22, 93, 177
Oldenburg, U. 17, 171
Olyan, S.M. 51, 58, 59, 61, 64, 149
Oswalt, J. 35
Otten, H. 31, 61
Otzen, B. 64
Ouellette, J. 33, 164

Page, H.R. 171, 175, 178
Palmer, A.S. 154
Pardee, D. 90, 188, 221, 222
Parker, S.B. 221
Patai, R. 44
Paul, S.M. 189
Peake, A.S. 139
Perdue, L.G. 196
Petersen, A.R. 100
Pettinato, G. 153, 198-200
Pfeiffer, R.H. 35
Phythian-Adams, W.J. 155
Plataroti, D. 210
Plessis, J. 171
Poirier, J.C. 175
Pomponio, F. 198, 200
Pope, M.H. 17, 28, 31, 60, 61, 110, 111, 116, 140, 141, 149, 171, 179, 201, 202, 204, 208, 222
Porten, B. 38, 146
Potts, T.F. 57
Pritchard, J.B. 48
Pryce, B.C. 119
Puech, E. 123, 153

Rainey, A.F. 221
Rast, W.E. 148
Reed, W.L. 54, 63
Reid, J. 154
Reiterer, F.V. 140
Rendtorff, R. 21, 25, 26
Ribichini, S. 222
Riemschneider, M. 78
Rin, S. and S. 17
Roberts, J.J.M. 86, 88, 107, 110, 183
Robinson, A. 107
Robinson, H.W. 22
Röllig, W. 37
Rosen, B. 69
Roussel, P. 149
Rowe, A. 135
Rowley, H.H. 83, 111, 140, 154, 201
Rudolph, K. 61
Rudolph, W. 63, 118, 148, 204
Ryckmans, G. 171

Sabottka, L. 213
Sanmartín, J. 222
Saracino, F. 78, 189, 190

Sarna, N.M. 208
Sasson, J.M. 137
Sawyer, J.F.A. 155, 198
Schlatter, A. 81
Schlisske, W. 22
Schmidt, B.B. 217, 218
Schmidt, K.L. 166
Schmidt, W.H. 111
Schmitt, J.J. 65, 66
Schmitz, P.C. 147
Schmöckel, H. 88
Schrader, E. 148
Schretter, M.K. 198
Schroeder, O. 214
Schwally, F. 224
Scott, R.B.Y. 155
Sellin, E. 115
Shanks, H. 211, 229
Shupak, N. 135
Skehan, P.W. 23, 87
Simpson, W.K. 198
Smelik, K.A.D. 210, 216
Smith, H.P. 130
Smith, M.S. 43-46, 52, 66, 72, 74, 115, 117, 142-44, 156, 158, 172, 190, 218, 222
Smith, M. 156, 229
Smith, R.H. 57
Smith, W.R. 42, 55, 63, 68, 132, 174, 212
Snaith, N.H. 210
Soggin, J.A. 155, 162, 192
Spalinger, A. 211
Speiser, E.A. 29, 133
Spieckermann, H. 26, 151, 163, 230-32
Spronk, K. 169
Stager, L.E. 34, 209
Stähli, H.-P. 156, 158, 159
Stamm, J.J. 72
Steiner, R.C. 109
Stemberger, G. 126
Stephenson, F.R. 198
Stolz, F. 183, 190
Strack, H.L. 81
Stuart, D. 113
Swauger, J.L. 225
Sznycer, M. 48

Tallqvist, K. 148, 214
Talmon, S. 223
Tångberg, A. 78
Tarragon, J. de 78
Tate, M.E. 191
Taylor, J.E. 53
Taylor, J.G. 56, 153, 156, 159-61
Teissier, B. 165
Thenius, O. 81
Thomas, D.W. 53, 168
Thompson, J.A. 64
Tigay, J.H. 51, 226-28
Toews, W.I. 34, 38
Toorn, K. van der 144, 165
Torge, P. 42
Torrey, C.C. 125
Tournay, R. 23
Tov, E. 23
Trebolle Barrera, J. 23
Tromp, N.J. 192, 205
Tsevat, M. 82, 83
Tsumura, D.T. 101, 192, 193
Tur-Sinai, N.H. 39, 202

Uehlinger, C. 52, 146, 156
Ullendorff, E. 91
Ulrich, E. 23

Van den Branden, A. 198
Van Selms, A. 133-135
Vattioni, F. 198
Vaux, R. de 73, 111, 210
Velde, H. Te 143
Vermeylen, J. 182
Vincent, A. 146
Virolleaud, C. 16, 221

Wallace, H.N. 27
Walls, N. 142, 143
Waterston, A. 118
Watson, P.L. 195
Watson, W.G.E. 172
Weinfeld, M. 49, 91, 148, 155, 209, 210, 213
Weippert, M. 33, 40
Weiser, A. 96, 148
Wellhausen, J. 13, 58, 86, 87, 228
Westermann, C. 16, 29

White, J.B. 141
Whiting, J.D. 114
Whitt, W.D. 65
Whybray, R.N. 24, 124, 125, 136
Wifall, W. 33
Wiggins, S.A. 45, 50, 52, 62, 159
Wildberger, H. 123, 181, 218
Williams, A.J. 28
Williamson, H.G.M. 231
Wilson, J.A. 201
Wilson, R.R. 28
Winckler, H. 168
Wiseman, D.J. 182
Wolfers, D. 139
Wolff, H.W. 57, 63, 118
Wolff, S.R. 209
Woods, F.E. 77
Wright, G.E. 225
Wright, G.H.B. 207
Würthwein, E. 40, 229
Wutz, F.X. 93
Wyatt, N. 37, 61, 88-90, 128, 130, 194, 208

Xella, P. 51, 188, 198, 200, 222

Yadin, Y. 153, 163, 198

Zevit, Z., 50, 52
Zimmerli, W. 27, 111

JOURNAL FOR THE STUDY OF THE OLD TESTAMENT
SUPPLEMENT SERIES

155 Jeffrey A. Fager, *Land Tenure and the Biblical Jubilee: Uncovering Hebrew Ethics through the Sociology of Knowledge*
156 John W. Kleinig, *The Lord's Song: The Basis, Function and Significance of Choral Music in Chronicles*
157 Gordon R. Clark, *The Word Ḥesed in the Hebrew Bible*
158 Mary Douglas, *In the Wilderness: The Doctrine of Defilement in the Book of Numbers*
159 J. Clinton McCann, Jr (ed.), *The Shape and Shaping of the Psalter*
160 William Riley, *King and Cultus in Chronicles: Worship and the Reinterpretation of History*
161 George W. Coats, *The Moses Tradition*
162 Heather A. McKay and David J.A. Clines (eds.), *Of Prophets' Visions and the Wisdom of Sages: Essays in Honour of R. Norman Whybray on his Seventieth Birthday*
163 J. Cheryl Exum, *Fragmented Women: Feminist (Sub)versions of Biblical Narratives*
164 Lyle Eslinger, *House of God or House of David: The Rhetoric of 2 Samuel 7*
165 Martin McNamara, *The Psalms in the Early Irish Church*
166 D.R.G. Beattie and M.J. McNamara (eds.), *The Aramaic Bible: Targums in their Historical Context*
167 Raymond F. Person, Jr, *Second Zechariah and the Deuteronomic School*
168 R.N. Whybray, *The Composition of the Book of Proverbs*
169 Bert Dicou, *Edom, Israel's Brother and Antagonist: The Role of Edom in Biblical Prophecy and Story*
170 Wilfred G.E. Watson, *Traditional Techniques in Classical Hebrew Verse*
171 Henning Graf Reventlow, Yair Hoffman and Benjamin Uffenheimer (eds.), *Politics and Theopolitics in the Bible and Postbiblical Literature*
172 Volkmar Fritz, *An Introduction to Biblical Archaeology*
173 M. Patrick Graham, William P. Brown and Jeffrey K. Kuan (eds.), *History and Interpretation: Essays in Honour of John H. Hayes*
174 Joe M. Sprinkle, *'The Book of the Covenant': A Literary Approach*
175 Tamara C. Eskenazi and Kent H. Richards (eds.), *Second Temple Studies: 2 Temple and Community in the Persian Period*
176 Gershon Brin, *Studies in Biblical Law: From the Hebrew Bible to the Dead Sea Scrolls*
177 David Allan Dawson, *Text-Linguistics and Biblical Hebrew*
178 Martin Ravndal Hauge, *Between Sheol and Temple: Motif Structure and Function in the I-Psalms*
179 J.G. McConville and J.G. Millar, *Time and Place in Deuteronomy*
180 Richard L. Schultz, *The Search for Quotation: Verbal Parallels in the Prophets*

181 Bernard M. Levinson (ed.), *Theory and Method in Biblical and Cuneiform Law: Revision, Interpolation and Development*
182 Steven L. McKenzie and M. Patrick Graham (eds.), *The History of Israel's Traditions: The Heritage of Martin Noth*
183 William Robertson Smith, *Lectures on the Religion of the Semites (Second and Third Series)*
184 John C. Reeves and John Kampen (eds.), *Pursuing the Text: Studies in Honor of Ben Zion Wacholder on the Occasion of his Seventieth Birthday*
185 Seth Daniel Kunin, *The Logic of Incest: A Structuralist Analysis of Hebrew Mythology*
186 Linda Day, *Three Faces of a Queen: Characterization in the Books of Esther*
187 Charles V. Dorothy, *The Books of Esther: Structure, Genre and Textual Integrity*
188 Robert H. O'Connell, *Concentricity and Continuity: The Literary Structure of Isaiah*
189 William Johnstone (ed.), *William Robertson Smith: Essays in Reassessment*
190 Steven W. Holloway and Lowell K. Handy (eds.), *The Pitcher is Broken: Memorial Essays for Gösta W. Ahlström*
191 Magne Sæbø, *On the Way to Canon: Creative Tradition History in the Old Testament*
192 Henning Graf Reventlow and William Farmer (eds.), *Biblical Studies and the Shifting of Paradigms, 1850–1914*
193 Brooks Schramm, *The Opponents of Third Isaiah: Reconstructing the Cultic History of the Restoration*
194 Else Kragelund Holt, *Prophesying the Past: The Use of Israel's History in the Book of Hosea*
195 Jon Davies, Graham Harvey and Wilfred G.E. Watson (eds.), *Words Remembered, Texts Renewed: Essays in Honour of John F.A. Sawyer*
196 Joel S. Kaminsky, *Corporate Responsibility in the Hebrew Bible*
197 William M. Schniedewind, *The Word of God in Transition: From Prophet to Exegete in the Second Temple Period*
198 T.J. Meadowcroft, *Aramaic Daniel and Greek Daniel: A Literary Comparison*
199 J.H. Eaton, *Psalms of the Way and the Kingdom: A Conference with the Commentators*
200 M. Daniel Carroll R., David J.A. Clines and Philip R. Davies (eds.), *The Bible in Human Society: Essays in Honour of John Rogerson*
201 John W. Rogerson, *The Bible and Criticism in Victorian Britain: Profiles of F.D. Maurice and William Robertson Smith*
202 Nanette Stahl, *Law and Liminality in the Bible*
203 Jill M. Munro, *Spikenard and Saffron: The Imagery of the Song of Songs*
204 Philip R. Davies, *Whose Bible Is It Anyway?*
205 David J.A. Clines, *Interested Parties: The Ideology of Writers and Readers of the Hebrew Bible*
206 Møgens Müller, *The First Bible of the Church: A Plea for the Septuagint*

207 John W. Rogerson, Margaret Davies and M. Daniel Carroll R. (eds.), *The Bible in Ethics: The Second Sheffield Colloquium*
208 Beverly J. Stratton, *Out of Eden: Reading, Rhetoric, and Ideology in Genesis 2–3*
209 Patricia Dutcher-Walls, *Narrative Art, Political Rhetoric: The Case of Athaliah and Joash*
210 Jacques Berlinerblau, *The Vow and the 'Popular Religious Groups' of Ancient Israel: A Philological and Sociological Inquiry*
211 Brian E. Kelly, *Retribution and Eschatology in Chronicles*
212 Yvonne Sherwood, *The Prostitute and the Prophet: Hosea's Marriage in Literary-Theoretical Perspective*
213 Yair Hoffman, *A Blemished Perfection: The Book of Job in Context*
214 Roy F. Melugin and Marvin A. Sweeney (eds.), *New Visions of Isaiah*
215 J. Cheryl Exum, *Plotted, Shot and Painted: Cultural Representations of Biblical Women*
216 Judith E. McKinlay, *Gendering Wisdom the Host: Biblical Invitations to Eat and Drink*
217 Jerome F.D. Creach, *Yahweh as Refuge and the Editing of the Hebrew Psalter*
218 Harry P. Nasuti, *Defining the Sacred Songs: Genre, Tradition, and the Post-Critical Interpretation of the Psalms*
219 Gerald Morris, *Prophecy, Poetry and Hosea*
220 Raymond F. Person, Jr, *In Conversation with Jonah: Conversation Analysis, Literary Criticism, and the Book of Jonah*
221 Gillian Keys, *The Wages of Sin: A Reappraisal of the 'Succession Narrative'*
222 R.N. Whybray, *Reading the Psalms as a Book*
223 Scott B. Noegel, *Janus Parallelism in the Book of Job*
224 Paul J. Kissling, *Reliable Characters in the Primary History: Profiles of Moses, Joshua, Elijah and Elisha*
225 Richard D. Weis and David M. Carr (eds.), *A Gift of God in Due Season: Essays on Scripture and Community in Honor of James A. Sanders*
226 Lori L. Rowlett, *Joshua and the Rhetoric of Violence: A New Historicist Analysis*
227 John F.A. Sawyer (ed.), *Reading Leviticus: Responses to Mary Douglas*
228 Volkmar Fritz and Philip R. Davies (eds.), *The Origins of the Ancient Israelite States*
229 Stephen Breck Reid (ed.), *Prophets and Paradigms: Essays in Honor of Gene M. Tucker*
230 Kevin J. Cathcart and Michael Maher (eds.), *Targumic and Cognate Studies: Essays in Honour of Martin McNamara*
231 Weston W. Fields, *Sodom and Gomorrah: History and Motif in Biblical Narrative*
232 Tilde Binger, *Asherah: Goddesses in Ugarit, Israel and the Old Testament*
233 Michael D. Goulder, *The Psalms of Asaph and the Pentateuch: Studies in the Psalter, III*
234 Ken Stone, *Sex, Honor, and Power in the Deuteronomistic History*

235 James W. Watts and Paul House (eds.), *Forming Prophetic Literature: Essays on Isaiah and the Twelve in Honor of John D.W. Watts*

236 Thomas M. Bolin, *Freedom beyond Forgiveness: The Book of Jonah Re-examined*

237 Neil Asher Silberman and David B. Small (eds.), *The Archaeology of Israel: Constructing the Past, Interpreting the Present*

238 M. Patrick Graham, Kenneth G. Hoglund and Steven L. McKenzie (eds.), *The Chronicler as Historian*

239 Mark S. Smith, *The Pilgrimage Pattern in Exodus*

240 Eugene E. Carpenter (ed.), *A Biblical Itinerary: In Search of Method, Form and Content. Essays in Honor of George W. Coats*

241 Robert Karl Gnuse, *No Other Gods: Emergent Monotheism in Israel*

242 K.L. Noll, *The Faces of David*

243 Henning Graf Reventlow (ed.), *Eschatology in the Bible and in Jewish and Christian Tradition*

244 Walter E. Aufrecht, Neil A. Mirau and Steven W. Gauley (eds.), *Urbanism in Antiquity: From Mesopotamia to Crete*

245 Lester L. Grabbe (ed.), *Can a 'History of Israel' Be Written?*

246 Gillian M. Bediako, *Primal Religion and the Bible: William Robertson Smith and his Heritage*

247 Nathan Klaus, *Pivot Patterns in the Former Prophets*

248 Etienne Nodet, *A Search for the Origins of Judaism: From Joshua to the Mishnah*

249 William Paul Griffin, *The God of the Prophets: An Analysis of Divine Action*

250 Josette Elayi and Jean Sapin, *Beyond the River: New Perspectives on Transeuphratene*

251 Flemming A.J. Nielsen, *The Tragedy in History: Herodotus and the Deuteronomistic History*

252 David C. Mitchell, *The Message of the Psalter: An Eschatological Programme in the Book of Psalms*

253 William Johnstone, *1 and 2 Chronicles, Volume 1: 1 Chronicles 1–2 Chronicles 9: Israel's Place among the Nations*

254 William Johnstone, *1 and 2 Chronicles, Volume 2: 2 Chronicles 10–36: Guilt and Atonement*

255 Larry L. Lyke, *King David with the Wise Woman of Tekoa: The Resonance of Tradition in Parabolic Narrative*

256 Roland Meynet, *Rhetorical Analysis: An Introduction to Biblical Rhetoric*

257 Philip R. Davies and David J.A. Clines (eds.), *The World of Genesis: Persons, Places, Perspectives*

258 Michael D. Goulder, *The Psalms of the Return (Book V, Psalms 107–150): Studies in the Psalter, IV*

259 Allen Rosengren Petersen, *The Royal God: Enthronement Festivals in Ancient Israel and Ugarit?*

260 A.R. Pete Diamond, Kathleen M. O'Connor and Louis Stulman (eds.), *Troubling Jeremiah*

261 Othmar Keel, *Goddesses and Trees, New Moon and Yahweh: Ancient Near Eastern Art and the Hebrew Bible*
262 Victor H. Matthews, Bernard M. Levinson and Tikva Frymer-Kensky (eds.), *Gender and Law in the Hebrew Bible and the Ancient Near East*
263 M. Patrick Graham and Steven L. McKenzie, *The Chronicler as Author: Studies in Text and Texture*
264 Donald F. Murray, *Divine Prerogative and Royal Pretension: Pragmatics, Poetics, and Polemics in a Narrative Sequence about David (2 Samuel 5.17–7.29)*
265 John Day, *Yahweh and the Gods and Goddesses of Canaan*
266 J. Cheryl Exum and Stephen D. Moore (eds.), *Biblical Studies/Cultural Studies: The Third Sheffield Colloquium*
267 Patrick D. Miller, Jr, *Israelite Religion and Biblical Theology: Collected Essays*
268 Linda S. Schearing and Steven L. McKenzie (eds.), *Those Elusive Deuteronomists: 'Pandeuteronomism' and Scholarship in the Nineties*
269 David J.A. Clines and Stephen D. Moore (eds.), *Auguries: The Jubilee Volume of the Sheffield Department of Biblical Studies*
270 John Day (ed.), *King and Messiah in Israel and the Ancient Near East: Proceedings of the Oxford Old Testament Seminar*
271 Wonsuk Ma, *Until the Spirit Comes: The Spirit of God in the Book of Isaiah*
272 James Richard Linville, *Israel in the Book of Kings: The Past as a Project of Social Identity*
273 Meir Lubetski, Claire Gottlieb and Sharon Keller (eds.), *Boundaries of the Ancient Near Eastern World: A Tribute to Cyrus H. Gordon*
274 Martin J. Buss, *Biblical Form Criticism in its Context*
275 William Johnstone, *Chronicles and Exodus: An Analogy and its Application*
276 Raz Kletter, *Economic Keystones: The Weight System of the Kingdom of Judah*
277 Augustine Pagolu, *The Religion of the Patriarchs*
278 Lester L. Grabbe (ed.), *Leading Captivity Captive: 'The Exile' as History and Ideology*
279 Kari Latvus, *God, Anger and Ideology: The Anger of God in Joshua and Judges in Relation to Deuteronomy and the Priestly Writings*
280 Eric S. Christianson, *A Time to Tell: Narrative Strategies in Ecclesiastes*
281 Peter D. Miscall, *Isaiah 34–35: A Nightmare/A Dream*
282 Joan E. Cook, *Hannah's Desire, God's Design: Early Interpretations in the Story of Hannah*
283 Kelvin Friebel, *Jeremiah's and Ezekiel's Sign-Acts: Rhetorical Nonverbal Communication*
284 M. Patrick Graham, Rick R. Marrs and Steven L. McKenzie (eds.), *Worship and the Hebrew Bible: Essays in Honor of John T. Willis*
285 Paolo Sacchi, *History of the Second Temple*
286 Wesley J. Bergen, *Elisha and the End of Prophetism*
287 Anne Fitzpatrick-McKinley, *The Transformation of Torah from Scribal Advice to Law*

288 Diana Lipton, *Revisions of the Night: Politics and Promises in the Patriarchal Dreams of Genesis*
289 Jože Krašovec (ed.), *The Interpretation of the Bible: The International Symposium in Slovenia*
290 Frederick H. Cryer and Thomas L. Thompson (eds.), *Qumran between the Old and New Testaments*
291 Christine Schams, *Jewish Scribes in the Second-Temple Period*
292 David J.A. Clines, *On the Way to the Postmodern: Old Testament Essays, 1967–1998 Volume 1*
293 David J.A. Clines, *On the Way to the Postmodern: Old Testament Essays, 1967–1998 Volume 2*
294 Charles E. Carter, *The Emergence of Yehud in the Persian Period: A Social and Demographic Study*
295 Jean-Marc Heimerdinger, *Topic, Focus and Foreground in Ancient Hebrew Narratives*
296 Mark Cameron Love, *The Evasive Text: Zechariah 1–8 and the Frustrated Reader*
297 Paul S. Ash, *David, Solomon and Egypt: A Reassessment*
298 John D. Baildam, *Paradisal Love: Johann Gottfried Herder and the Song of Songs*
299 M. Daniel Carroll R., *Rethinking Contexts, Rereading Texts: Contributions from the Social Sciences to Biblical Interpretation*
300 Edward Ball (ed.), *In Search of True Wisdom: Essays in Old Testament Interpretation in Honour of Ronald E. Clements*
301 Carolyn S. Leeb, *Away from the Father's House: The Social Location of na'ar and na'arah in Ancient Israel*
302 Xuan Huong Thi Pham, *Mourning in the Ancient Near East and the Hebrew Bible*
303 Ingrid Hjelm, *The Samaritans and Early Judaism: A Literary Analysis*
304 Wolter H. Rose, *Zemah and Zerubabbel: Messianic Expectations in the Early Postexilic Period*
305 Jo Bailey Wells, *God's Holy People: A Theme in Biblical Theology*
306 Albert de Pury, Thomas Römer and Jean-Daniel Macchi (eds.), *Israel Constructs its History: Deuteronomistic Historiography in Recent Research*
307 Robert L. Cole, *The Shape and Message of Book III (Psalms 73–89)*
308 Yiu-Wing Fung, *Victim and Victimizer: Joseph's Interpretation of his Destiny*
309 George Aichele (ed.), *Culture, Entertainment and the Bible*
310 Esther Fuchs, *Sexual Politics in the Biblical Narrative: Reading the Hebrew Bible as a Woman*
314 Bernard S. Jackson, *Studies in the Semiotics of Biblical Law*
315 Paul R. Williamson, *Abraham, Israel and the Nations: The Patriarchal Promise and its Covenantal Development in Genesis*
320 Claudia V. Camp, *Wise, Strange and Holy: The Strange Woman and the Making of the Bible*